Personality Dynamics

AN INTEGRATIVE PSYCHOLOGY OF ADJUSTMENT

Personality Dynamics

AN INTEGRATIVE PSYCHOLOGY OF ADJUSTMENT

BY *Bert R. Sappenfield*

PROFESSOR OF PSYCHOLOGY, MONTANA STATE UNIVERSITY

NEW YORK *Alfred A. Knopf* 1954

L. C. *catalog card number:* 53-11055

THIS IS A BORZOI BOOK,
PUBLISHED BY ALFRED A. KNOPF, INC.

FIRST EDITION

TO *Anne* AND *Mary Jean*

Preface

*T*HIS BOOK is intended to answer the need for a systematic treatment of personality dynamics. It is perhaps the first serious attempt to develop, in textbook form, a thoroughly systematic presentation of psychoanalytic principles.

In his presidential address at the Denver convention of the American Psychological Association in 1949, Dr. Ernest R. Hilgard emphasized the lack of success with which previous authors had attacked the problem of the relation of defense mechanisms to motivation. Since, prior to hearing this address, I had been teaching psychoanalytic dynamics for several years, and since I felt that in my own teaching I had been presenting a more unified treatment than any available textbook provided, it seemed to me that an attempt to formulate a systematic psychology of adjustment would be an eminently worthwhile project.

In this treatment, I have attempted to integrate psychoanalytic dynamics with an organismic conception of behavior—a conception that has been emphasized in Gestalt interpretations of behavior, and has been supported by the thinking of Alfred Korzybski, who, although working outside the field of psychology, has none the less provided a theoretical framework within which psychology can develop advantageously.

Such an integration seems highly desirable, especially in view of the fact that Sigmund Freud, whose contributions to psychology can hardly be overestimated, met with some of his most difficult problems at precisely those points where his dualistic conception of "the mental" and "the physical" interfered with clarity of thinking.

Though Freud's work was not well received by American psychologists during the first three or four decades of this century, there seems to be a growing tendency to recognize the significance of his contributions, some of which are so fundamental to an understanding of human behavior that they can hardly any longer be ignored.

I have tried to state Freud's concepts in a manner that will make them clear to the student who is not yet familiar with Freud's original works. By choice, I have retained much of Freud's terminology, in view of the fact that clinical psychologists especially will require these terms in order to communicate effectively with psychoanalytically oriented psychiatrists. I have, however, defined Freud's terminology in such a manner that it can be integrated with the current concepts of American psychology.

This book provides, I think, some important contributions to conceptual clarity. Among these may be mentioned the following:

1. Freud's tripartite division of personality functions—involving his concepts of id, ego, and superego—has been described, in somewhat modified form, in terms of definitions stating that id functions involve biogenic need-tensions (anxiety), that ego functions involve the cognitive (intellectual) and voluntary processes, and that superego functions involve all aspects of psychogenic motivation.

2. Extensive emphasis has been given to the analysis of "need integrates" or motives into the three components: need, instrumental act, and object. Such analysis aids in clarifying the concept of anxiety and in defining what occurs to motives when they undergo "defensive" modification.

3. The concept of anxiety has been defined more rigorously than previous treatments have permitted. In the present treatment, the concept of anxiety becomes equivalent to that of id functions: it implies the occurrence in consciousness of biogenic need-tensions without conscious representation of instrumental acts or objects in relation to which gratification or relief may be anticipated.

4. Two concepts of identification, which Freud often referred to indiscriminately by a single term, are separately described and distinctively named. The term *perceptual identification* is used to refer to identical (or nearly identical) interpretations of different stimuli; the term *developmental identification* is used to refer to the development of characteristics that are similar to those of respected or admired models.

I am personally indebted to Mr. Walter M. Mitchell for his active encouragement of my first work upon this book. During the early months, he spent many hours responding critically to my initial efforts to verbalize the concepts and principles of personality dynamics. This book would have been completed and published in collaboration with Mr. Mitchell had not his plans for further graduate training required his separation from the project.

I also owe a debt of gratitude to Dr. Frederick R. Fosmire, who read my manuscript in its semifinal revision and offered many helpful suggestions for its improvement.

Finally, I wish to acknowledge with gratitude the courtesy of authors and publishers who have granted permission to quote from copyrighted sources. Specific acknowledgment is given in a footnote to the page containing the first quotation from any particular source.

BERT R. SAPPENFIELD

Missoula, Montana
January 1954

Contents

Personality Dynamics

AN INTEGRATIVE PSYCHOLOGY OF ADJUSTMENT

CHAPTER One

General Introduction

Living is a process of adjustment, and . . . man does not have to understand it in order that it may function smoothly; yet the process of adjustment may be subjected to human inquiry, and a better understanding of it can lead to improved methods of controlling it.[1]

*T*HE PSYCHOLOGY of adjustment is concerned with the everyday behavior of "normal" individuals. It is concerned with the motives that underlie their continued search for satisfaction and happiness, with the frustrations and conflicts that complicate their activities, with the surges of anger and anxiety that they experience, and with the variety of techniques that they adopt for the relief of anxiety and for overcoming obstacles to peaceful living.

The processes of human adjustment cannot be understood as isolated segments of the individual's total behavior. Each thing the individual does is related to everything else he does. The individual is continually influenced by motivational distresses, which he tries to relieve; he continually perceives his environment in terms of its potentialities for gratifying his motives; he continually learns new responses to pre-existing motives, new ways to perceive his environment, new motives to arouse further actions; he is continually thinking, making judgments,

[1] Percival M. Symonds, *The Dynamics of Human Adjustment* (New York, 1946), p. 1. Reprinted by permission of Appleton-Century-Crofts, Inc. Copyright, 1946, by Appleton-Century-Crofts, Inc.

employing a combination of all of his functions to avoid distress and to achieve pleasurable experiences. He acts as a whole person, continually developing, continually changing.

If we are to achieve a practical understanding of the whole person as he interacts with his environment, it seems necessary that we adopt, at the outset, certain general principles regarding behavior. Among such general principles, the following should be included:

1. That behavior must be understood from an organismic point of view.
2. That the individual's behavior is determined by his unique perceptions.
3. That behavior must be treated in terms of molar, rather than molecular, units.
4. That human adjustment consists of activities that tend to reduce anxiety and other forms of motivational excitation.

These general principles will be given detailed consideration in the following sections of the present chapter.

ORGANISMIC CONCEPTION OF BEHAVIOR

AN ADEQUATE understanding of the psychology of human adjustment requires an organismic conception of behavior. In this section we shall first consider what is meant by an organism and then proceed to a discussion of behavior as a dynamic system of interrelated events.

Organisms as Dynamic Systems

An organism may be thought of as a dynamic system of interrelated events. When a change is introduced in any part of such a system compensatory changes will occur throughout the system; that is to say, when the equilibrium of such a system has been disturbed, processes will occur that tend toward the re-establishment of equilibrium.

Biologists regard living animals and plants as organisms; but in a broader sense every natural system of events—the atom, the molecule, the solar system, the smoke ring, the candle flame—may be regarded as an organism.

Nature is not machine-like.[2] There are no strings or wires connect-

[2] Wolfgang Kohler (*Gestalt Psychology: an Introduction to New Concepts in Modern Psychology* [New York, 1947], pp. 100–35) distinguishes between dy-

ing the sun with the planets. The parts are free to interact, so that the equilibrium achieved in the system occurs as a function of freely interacting "forces." The planets revolve around the sun according to a pattern of dynamic interrelations. The pattern of gravitational and centrifugal forces accounts for the pattern of movements occurring within the system. If it were possible to change the course of any one planet, this change would be accompanied by other changes in the system.

The discovery of the planet Neptune clearly demonstrated the occurrence of such dynamic interrelations. Before this planet was discovered, the courses of the known planets were understood sufficiently to permit mathematical predictions to be made of the position of any planet in the system at any given time. The orbit of the planet Uranus, however, manifested disturbances of unknown origin. The French astronomer, Leverrier, investigated these disturbances and concluded that they could be accounted for by the existence in the system of an unknown planet. He was able to predict the location of the unknown planet within one degree of accuracy. The planet was readily located and given the name Neptune. This was, in effect, a natural experiment that illustrated the dynamic interrelatedness—that is, the organic character—of the system.

Some organisms, such as the solar system and the atom, are highly stable systems; extraordinary forces must be introduced into such systems before a perceptible change occurs in their organizations. Other systems, like candle flames, smoke rings, explosive compounds, and living organisms, are highly unstable; slight forces, when introduced into these systems, will bring about extraordinary disturbances that require a re-establishment of equilibrium. A candle flame or a smoke ring may be destroyed by a puff of air; nitroglycerine will explode into more stable by-products if it is given a mechanical jolt; and living organisms will manifest complicated sequences of behavior in response to relatively weak stimuli.

Living organisms hardly ever—perhaps never—achieve equilibrium; they are *continually in the process of approaching a re-establish-*

---

namic conceptions and machine-like theories. He points out, for instance, that if a quantity of steam were free to distribute itself it would tend to expand in all directions; but the restraining arrangements of a piston in the cylinder of a steam engine allow the steam to expand in only one direction. Dynamic principles apply in the case of the steam in the first instance, whereas machine-like principles apply in the second instance. When processes are free to operate without restraints— that is, when they function dynamically—they will establish an equilibrium that depends upon the interactions of the processes themselves.

ment of equilibrium. The candle flame goes out; the smoke ring is dissipated; but the living organism continues to function until its final disintegration into more stable chemical compounds.

Behavior Dynamics

The emphasis on motivation is a central characteristic of dynamic psychologies. Murray, for example, states that ". . . 'dynamic' has come to be used in a special sense: to designate a psychology which accepts as prevailingly fundamental the goal-directed (adaptive) character of behavior and attempts to discover and formulate the internal as well as the external factors which determine it." [3]

This motivational emphasis is especially appropriate to a psychology that regards behavior as a dynamic system of interrelated functions.[4] Motivational stimuli operate as disturbances in the organism's equilibrium, and motivated behavior operates in the interest of re-establishing equilibrium.[5] According to Freud, "the dominating tendency of mental life, and perhaps of nervous life in general, is the effort to reduce, to keep constant or to remove internal tension due to stimuli." [6] This tendency to restore equilibrium may be regarded as a general characteristic of behavior.

Different functions of the human organism are complexly interrelated. Even the knee-jerk reflex is facilitated when muscular tensions are increased in remote regions of the body, as for example when the individual clenches his fists. When a strong emotion, such as fear, is operative, extensive physiological changes occur: the pulse quickens; the liver speeds the release of sugar into the bloodstream; the pupils become dilated; digestive fluids are decreased; and the bronchioles of the respiratory system become dilated.

PSYCHOSOMATIC INTERRELATIONS.   It has been customary to refer to certain processes of the organism as "physical" and to other processes as "mental." Such a distinction is really arbitrary; it is a distinction that does not occur clearly among different functions. The assumption

[3] Henry A. Murray, *Explorations in Personality* (New York, 1938), p. 36. Reprinted by permission of Oxford University Press, Inc. Copyright, 1938, by Oxford University Press, Inc.

[4] The term behavior is employed here as a general term to imply all of the functions of the organism. The term embodies voluntary and involuntary motor functions, sensory functions, and integrative functions of the nervous system.

[5] Probably *all* behavior should be regarded as motivated behavior.

[6] Sigmund Freud, *Beyond the Pleasure Principle* (London, 1950), p. 76. Reprinted by permission of The Hogarth Press, Ltd., and Liveright Publishing Corporation.

that mental processes occur that are distinctly separable from physical processes leads to unanswerable questions. Thus, the problem of how headaches, heart ailments, stomach ulcers, diarrhea, and other such disorders can be based on mental processes becomes difficult for those who believe that mental and physical processes are fundamentally different. Such a problem does not arise when it is accepted that behavior involves a system of interrelated functions—that behavior involves *psychosomatic* interrelations.

The combination of "psycho-" (referring to mind) and "somatic" (referring to body) in the term psychosomatic implies unity, rather than disunity, among the different functions of the organism. At any given moment, behavior involves interrelations among so-called mental and physiological processes. An emotional process, for example, is neither mental nor physical; it involves characteristic conscious experiences *in combination with* characteristic physiological events; the emotional process cannot be described in either mental or physiological terms.

MOTIVATION AS RELATED TO OTHER FUNCTIONS   All human behavior is motivated. What the individual does at any given moment is a function of his motivational pattern.

Emotions.   Emotional processes are intimately related to the gratification or the frustration of motives. The pleasurable emotions, like joy or elation, occur as a function of gratification; the unpleasant emotions, like fear or anger, occur as a function of frustration.[7]

Attention and Perception.   What the individual attends to and fails to attend to among the numerous stimulational features of the external environment depends on the motivational features of his internal environment. The hungry man is attentive to food; the lonely man is attentive to people; the music lover is attentive to the kind of music he enjoys hearing; the man about to be engaged is attentive to jewelry-store windows.

But these illustrations oversimplify the relations between an individual's attention and his complicated motivational pattern. It would be more nearly descriptive of a man's behavior to say that the hungry, lonely, music-loving man about to be engaged invites his intended financée to dine where he can listen to good music, and that on the way he observes engagement rings in jewelry-store windows. Even this, of course, is an oversimplification.

[7] Motives must be understood to include values, ideals, interests, standards, ambitions, etc., as well as biological needs.

Any perception involves the organization of external and internal stimuli into a meaningful pattern. The external situation will be perceived (interpreted) in terms of its value in gratifying the individual's needs. The hungry man will perceive situations in terms of their promise for satisfying his hunger; the sick man will perceive situations in terms of their promise for relieving his pain; the lonely person will perceive situations in terms of their promise of sociable relations with other people.

Perception, of course, is seldom so simple in its operation as these examples would imply. A person usually has a combination of needs that function simultaneously, so that it is this combination of needs, rather than a single need at a time, that will function in the perception of a situation. Frequently, too, a person will not "know" what it is that he wants, so that relatively unconscious motives will enter into the structure of the total perception.

Thinking. Thinking is said to occur when the individual is in a problem situation. But a problem situation cannot be defined except in terms of motivation. When a problem arises, the individual is in the process of trying to achieve satisfaction for some need or pattern of needs. The problem situation is a situation in which the individual's fluent activity toward a satisfying goal is momentarily disrupted by the perception of frustrating features in the environment. Solution of the problem is characteristically followed by the resumption of fluent, goal-oriented activity.

Learning. What is learned, as well as how efficiently the learning is accomplished, depends on the individual's motivation. Learning is dependent not only on the strength of motivation but also on the *kind* of motivation that is operative. Individuals learn most readily those activities which satisfy their important motives; two persons who are equally "intelligent" will learn different activities, depending on differences between their unique motivational patterns. When an individual's motives happen to be contradictory, the individual will learn contradictory activities, contradictory perceptions, contradictory generalizations, etc.

Intelligence. An individual's behavior in a given situation may be regarded as intelligent to the degree that he is able to achieve gratification of his total pattern of motives—to the degree that he can employ procedures consistent with *all* of his important motives. It requires high intelligence to behave in such a manner that the more fundamental needs can be satisfied without the simultaneous frustration of values and ethical ideals, or in such a manner that conflicting values may be satisfied by a single course of action. In other words, the concept of "intelligence" must be defined in terms of motivation.

EMOTIONS AS RELATED TO OTHER FUNCTIONS. Emotions motivate behavior; that is to say, emotions function in the organization and direction of behavior. The pleasurable emotions, especially when they are of mild intensity, organize the individual's activity in the direction of continuing a gratifying course of behavior. When pleasurable emotions are intense, they prepare the individual for celebrative or triumphant activities. Rage prepares the individual for aggression against frustrating features of the situation. Fear prepares the individual for escape from a frustrating situation. Depression and grief generally organize the behavior functions in the direction of the cessation of activity.

It is probably an incorrect emphasis to imply, as many psychological writers have implied, that emotions are *disorganizing*. It seems more appropriate to conclude that intellectual and highly skilled activities, which are disturbed during strong emotions, are extremely inappropriate activities for the relief of the emotions.[8]

Attention and Perception. During emotional activity, the individual is distracted from features of the environment which are irrelevant, and attracted to features that are relevant, to his emotional set. Thus in a "fit of anger" the individual will overlook the gratifying behavior of another person while perceiving mainly the frustrating features of his behavior.

The emotion that is operative at any given time is also related to the particular meaning with which a situation is perceived. The fearful person, as he walks through the forest at night, may see tree stumps as robbers or wild beasts; the triumphant person will fail to realize a situation of tragedy until sufficient time has elapsed to permit a change in his emotional set.

Thinking and Learning. Emotional processes, like motives, are related to thinking and learning. Emotions do not, as is frequently implied, disrupt thinking or learning unless the thinking or learning is irrelevant to the emotional set. The emotional set usually facilitates direct problem solutions, which although they are consistent with the individual's temporary emotional state are frequently inconsistent with his more permanent values, so that ultimately such solutions may func-

[8] Robert W. Leeper, "A Motivational Theory of Emotion to Replace Emotion as Disorganized Response,'" *Psychological Review,* 55 (1948), 5–21.

tion maladaptively. Thus, in a state of anger, the individual may solve his immediate problem by aggressive behavior; but his aggressive actions may eventuate in the destruction of human relations that in his calmer states he regards as highly worth maintaining.

Intelligence. Anxiety and other emotional processes are notable for their interference with maximum performance on intelligence tests. This, in turn, is related to the fact that the individual is emotionally prepared to function in a way that is inconsistent with the demands of an intelligence test. It would be incorrect to conclude from this that a person's behavior is really less intelligent in such a situation; our previous discussion of intelligence would imply that the individual who is able to perform such irrelevant tasks as well during emotional stress as he does under "normal" conditions will be displaying relatively unintelligent behavior.

INTERRELATIONS AMONG COGNITIVE FUNCTIONS. Perception, thinking, and learning have frequently been treated as distinct and readily separable functions. These processes, however, are by no means so clearly separable as they may seem. The individual in action, at any given moment, is difficult to describe in terms of a single cognitive function. It is often impossible to determine when the individual is perceiving, when he is learning, and when he is thinking. Normally these processes occur as a function of one another; they are inextricably interrelated. Perceptions and problem solutions are *retained;* that is to say, learning has occurred. Perception and thinking occur on the basis of previous *learning.* And the processes of learning and thinking are dependent on concurrent *perceptual* activities.

Easy problems are ordinarily solved by *perception.* If the psychologist were to construct a problem box with glass walls, most individuals would be able to open it after a brief inspection of the internal structure. Problem boxes with opaque walls, however, usually require for their solution a procedure that is describable as *thinking.*

Rats are usually said to *learn* difficult mazes; but Krechevsky has described the behavior of rats in mazes in terms of the adoption and testing of hypotheses.[9] It remains a controversial question, in other words, whether rats learn their way through mazes or think their way through mazes. Certainly their behavior in mazes cannot be described as a simple process of perceptual reorganization or insight.

[9] I. Krechevsky, " 'Hypotheses' versus 'Chance' in the Pre-solution Period in Sensory Discrimination-Learning," *University of California Publications in Psychology,* 6 (1932), 27–44; "The Genesis of 'Hypotheses' in Rats," *University of California Publications in Psychology,* 6 (1932), 45–64.

Human subjects, on the other hand, are forced by blindfolding to learn rather than perceive the routes through mazes; they are handicapped in order to make an easy problem more difficult. Many of our human problems, which are solved by painfully slow processes of thinking and learning, might conceivably be solved by the instantaneous perception (insight) of some transcendentally intelligent being, if such a being were to appear on the scene.

INTEGRATIVE SUMMARY. Since psychology books are usually divided into separate chapters on perception, sensory processes, motor functions, learning, thinking, emotions, motivation, etc., the student is likely to develop the conception that these processes are distinct and separable functions of human personality.

No one of these processes, however, can be understood outside the context of its complex interactions with all the others. The fact that specific names have been given to particular aspects of the functioning organism communicates the incorrect impression that these different aspects occur in isolation from one another.

Human behavior is organismic: different functions are interrelated in complex ways. Perception, motivation, learning, thinking, and emotional processes never occur alone; all these functions, and many more, occur in relation to one another. When the psychologist speaks of any one process without reference to other processes, he is momentarily directing attention to certain aspects of the organism's total organization of behavior. Since it is impossible to observe or to speak about all aspects of behavior at once, the impression is frequently given that perception, for example, occurs in isolation. This difficulty is analogous to that encountered by the six blind men of Indostan, each of whom tried to describe an elephant on the basis of the limited evidence available to him.[10] Anybody who sees a whole elephant at once will give a very different description from that given by any one, or all, of the six blind men. Although the psychologist is usually aware of the organismic character of behavior events, he cannot observe or describe all of the interrelated events that occur in even a short interval; he must limit himself to the observation or description of only one aspect at a time.

Whenever a statement of relationship between two variables is

[10] J. G. Saxe, "The Blind Men and the Elephant," in *Best Loved Poems*, R. C. MacKenzie, ed. (New York, 1948), pp. 209–10. This familiar poem tells how each of the six blind men perceived the elephant differently in terms of the particular anatomical feature he was able to investigate. The first perceived the elephant as a wall, the second as a spear, the third as a snake, the fourth as a tree, the fifth as a fan, and the sixth as a rope. They investigated, respectively, the elephant's side, tusk, trunk, leg, ear, and tail.

made, it implies that all other variables have been held constant, as in the experimental method. In the freely functioning organism, however, other variables are *not held constant;* they are in continuous interaction with the two variables that have been selected for discussion. Such a statement of relationship between two variables is, strictly speaking, never correct, since it oversimplifies the interrelations that occur among the many behavior events.

BEHAVIOR AS A FUNCTION OF PERCEPTION

Every man is in certain respects
  a. like all other men,
  b. like some other men,
  c. like no other man.[11]

        SOME of the determinants of behavior are similar for all members of the species; some are similar for members of the particular group to which the individual belongs; and some are unique to the in-dividual, since they have developed out of unique experiences. What-ever their source may be—whether they derive from the biological structure of the organism, from the common experiences of all men, from the common experiences of men in the same culture or subcul-ture, or from the unique experiences of each individual—behavior de-terminants can function as such *only to the extent that they occur as components of the individual's perception.* This, perhaps, would be regarded as self-evident were it not that some psychologists, notably, the early behaviorists, have held a contradictory point of view.

Stimulus-Response Conception

    Behaviorists once held the belief that behavior is determined by the objective nature of the external stimulating situation. The behavior formula would be S ⟶ R, in which S represents the external stimulating situation and R represents the objectively observable be-havior of the individual. This would imply that if the psychologist could give an adequate description of the situation he could predict what *anybody's* behavior would be in that situation.

    Modern psychologists, however, rarely maintain that such a simple

[11] Clyde Kluckhohn and Henry A. Murray, eds., *Personality in Nature, So-ciety, and Culture* (New York, 1948), p. 35. Reprinted by permission of Alfred A. Knopf, Inc. Copyright, 1948, by Alfred A. Knopf, Inc.

correlation can occur between the stimulus and the human response. Only in the simplest instances of reflex behavior can this close association between response and stimulus be observed. Even the reflexes, as we have seen, are facilitated when tensions occur in distant regions of the body.

It is true, perhaps, that any individual's behavior will vary consistently with changes in the stimulating conditions.[12] But the fact that prediction in terms of the stimulus situation is possible in the case of any particular individual, although not for individuals in general, argues for the need to include the individual's uniqueness in the behavior formula.

Meaning as the Behavior Determinant

The individual's unique characteristics are included in the behavior formula P ———→ R, in which P represents the individual's perception and R represents his behavior. According to this formulation, *the individual's behavior is determined at any given moment by what the situation means to him.* The meaning of any situation is dependent on his pattern of motives, as well as on the nature of his past experiences in similar situations.

This pattern of motives is dynamic: the pattern changes with the gratification and frustration of motives within the pattern. Moreover, as new experiences occur, new motives may be developed and older motives may lose significance for the individual; the new situations will provide new experiences relative to the frustration or gratification of motives that were previously operative. The personality, therefore, is in a continual process of reorganization, and successive organizations will provide the basis for different interpretations and so for different behavior.

The psychologist who maintains this point of view is not surprised that different persons behave differently in the same objective situation, or that the same person behaves differently in much the same situation on different occasions. On the basis of the P ———→ R formulation, all of these apparently inconsistent observations are understood to be consistent. A given objective situation will have different meanings for different persons, and different meanings for the same individual at different times.

[12] Even this would be true only if the time interval were sufficiently short and the individual's experiences during the interval sufficiently uniform to permit no significant changes to occur in the individual's interpretation of the stimulating conditions.

PERCEPTION. The moment the individual is aware of any kind of stimulation, he is aware of its meaning for him, even though this meaning may be merely that the situation is puzzling or ambiguous.

Perception *need not involve awareness* on the part of the individual; the fact that the situation has meaning, however, follows from the fact that the individual behaves in one way rather than in some other way. Meanings, in other words, function in the determination of behavior, regardless of the degree to which the individual is conscious of them. A person, for example, continues to walk on the sidewalk—i.e., the sidewalk has meaning for him—even though he does not become aware of it for several minutes during which his consciousness is occupied with other matters.

What is perceived in a given situation and with what meaning it is perceived depend on the nature of the stimulus itself in combination with the personality functions of the individual. In other words, *perception is a function of both the observer and the observed.*

Some stimuli are relatively unambiguous, so that most individuals will perceive them similarly; other stimuli are so ambiguous that the functions of each individual will be highly significant in determining their meaning. In fact, the degree of ambiguity in a stimulating situation can be defined only in terms of the degree to which individual differences among personalities affect the nature of the perception.

It is this fact that underlies the usefulness of projective tests of personality. Such tests make use of ambiguous stimulating situations (ink blots, cloud pictures, etc.), whose interpretations form the basis for personality diagnosis.

Often the organization or structure of a perception is of greater significance than the nature of the parts or the contents which make up the structure. Thus the individual tones of a melody are of little consequence for the perception of the melody itself, since even though the melody is played in a wide range of keys it is recognizable and distinguishable from other melodies. Similarly, the rhythmic pattern of a waltz is recognizable as distinct from other rhythms, even though the melodic and harmonic features of any particular waltz differ from those of any other.

A fundamental principle of perception is that the specific components of a larger organization are seen *in terms of* this larger organization; the parts are perceived in relation to the whole—that is to say, their meaning is determined by the meaning of the whole. A bear, for instance, will have very different meanings when seen from behind a protective enclosure in a zoo and when seen as a freely roaming wild animal in the forest. In other words, perception involves the combining of stimuli into patterns that have meanings in terms of the *structure of the total pattern* rather than in terms of the summation of specific meanings attributed to each of the separate components of the pattern.

ENVIRONMENT. The concept of environment is frequently misunderstood to imply merely "the external surroundings of an organism." [13] Such a definition implies that the environment is objectively describable by an external observer. To the extent that this conception of environment is employed in psychology, it should be termed the *objective environment*, as distinguished from the *perceptual environment* of any particular individual.

The perceptual environment is never co-extensive with the objective environment; on the one hand it is impossible to perceive all the events that occur in the objective environment; and on the other hand the perceptual environment includes events (internal processes) that are not a part of the objective environment. When not otherwise stated, we shall use the term environment to imply the perceptual environment.

The environment of an individual may be regarded as a larger organic structure of interrelations within which the individual functions as a subsystem. Environmental processes include both external and internal functions: the organism is sensitive to external stimulation by means of receptors for vision, hearing, smell, taste, pressure, pain, cold, and warmth; it is sensitive to internal processes by means of receptors for thirst, hunger, bodily orientation, the movement of muscles, etc. The perceptual environment is continually changing; it never remains the same from one moment to another.

An individual's environment cannot be described adequately by an outside observer, since any outside observer will himself be sensitive to *different* aspects of the objective situation and will therefore have a different environment.

This conception of environment is consistent with our understanding that two persons who live and work in a common setting—the same home, the same school, the same place of employment—may have

[13] Floyd L. Ruch, *Psychology and Life* (3d ed., New York, 1948), p. 8. Reprinted by permission of Scott, Foresman and Company. Copyright, 1948, by Scott, Foresman and Company.

radically different environments. Even identical twins who are together almost continually will have different environments. If, for example, one of the pair falls down the stairway and the other laughs, each of them will have had quite a different experience. Such unique experiences of the individual will be cumulative, moreover, in the sense that each experience will prepare the individual to interpret future experiences in a unique way.

SYNTHESIS: PERCEPTION AND ENVIRONMENT. It should be obvious from the preceding discussions that the concept of perceptual environment is equivalent to the concept of meaning or perception. Other authors have employed the terms *psychological field* or *psychological environment* with a similar meaning.[14] Whichever term is used, it implies a dynamic organization of external and internal components into a meaningful whole. This meaningful organization becomes the determinant of behavior at any given moment. In other words, behavior is regarded as a function of the perceptual environment, of the psychological field, or of perception. In subsequent discussions, these terms may be used interchangeably, although the term perception is preferable.

Integrative Summary

The personality processes of the individual are not merely passive recipients of stimulation. Personality processes, such as generalized habits, attitudes, beliefs, interests, and motives, have a significant function in the determination of behavior. Each individual has a unique pattern of relatively consistent behavior tendencies. What the individual believes to be true or significant or beautiful; what the individual hates or loves or respects; what the individual strives to do or wants or aims at becoming—all these, and many more relatively consistent and permanent tendencies of the individual, function as determinants of his behavior.

We may say, loosely, that the individual adjusts in the ways he does because he is the kind of person that he is. His own unique experiences have developed unique expectations, attitudes, mental sets, interests, motives. He therefore sees what others fail to see and what he sees he sees with a different meaning. Other persons, who see different aspects of the world with different meanings, will adjust in different manners.

[14] For example, Kurt Lewin, *A Dynamic Theory of Personality: Selected Papers* (New York, 1935), pp. 74–9; David Krech and Richard S. Crutchfield, *Theory and Problems of Social Psychology* (New York, 1948), pp. 33–4, 37–9.

No trait or attitude or motive can function in isolation. *The particular way in which the individual behaves in any situation depends on the combined operation of all these tendencies.* The sociable person who is hungry prefers to dine with other people; the ambitious person proceeds toward success by means that are consistent with his ethical values; the dominant person controls others in ways that are consistent with his other motives. In other words, a person's behavior in any given situation is a function of the integrated combination of behavior tendencies which constitutes his personality.[15]

The individual's perception at any given moment—the meaning that a situation has for him—combines elements from the objective environment with elements from the internal environment (including relatively permanent personality tendencies). His behavior at any given moment will be determined by the structure of this perception. In a sense, perception itself may be regarded as an unstable organism, as a dynamic system in unstable equilibrium. When perception is so regarded, it becomes reasonable to speak of behavior as functioning in the direction of establishing greater stability of perception.[16]

For example, when seated at a food-laden table, one's perception of the food-in-relation-to-one's-hunger involves a disequilibrium of perception; eating the food will eventuate in the establishment of equilibrium, for during the process of eating the perception will involve eating-food-in-relation-to-the-relief-of-hunger. Later, the perception of food-in-relation-to-gratified-hunger will again involve a disequilibrium of perception; other behavior, such as getting up from the table, will ensue, in the interest of developing a more stable perception.

---

[15] This determinism which characterizes personality is, paradoxically, the basis for the impression of "free will," which everybody experiences and which many persons regard as contradictory to the doctrine of determinism in science. The individual exercises his free will by making choices that are consistent with his unique motivation; this is really what he means when he speaks of free will. For instance, the person who is firmly guided by religious beliefs cannot do otherwise than live up to these beliefs, since they function as major determinants of his behavior.

[16] Hilgard, for example, states: "The organism seeks a perceptually stable environment in somewhat parallel fashion to the way in which it seeks an internally stable environment. There is a kind of environmental homeostasis parallel to physiological homeostasis. In both cases the stability is one of dynamic equilibrium, not of static equilibrium. . . . In normal perception, the goal of stability accounts for many of our perceptual achievements." (Ernest R. Hilgard, "The Role of Learning in Perception," in *Perception: an Approach to Personality*, Robert R. Blake and Glenn V. Ramsey, eds., [New York, 1951], p. 103. Reprinted by permission of The Ronald Press Company. Copyright, 1951, by The Ronald Press Company.)

MOLAR BEHAVIOR-UNITS

THE KIND of understanding we seek or the kind of problem we wish to solve determines the point of view we must adopt when we examine nature in our quest for knowledge. If we wish to understand the general structure of a city, we cannot hope to achieve our purpose by examining a single house; if we wish to understand a forest, we must not devote our attention to the individual trees. The city or the forest must be considered as a unit, in which the individual houses or the individual trees are of secondary interest, merely to be recognized as elements that enter into the whole.

Appropriate units may be defined only in relation to the problem that initiates investigation. From the point of view of a particular problem, the unit must be sufficiently large to involve the relationships that the investigator wishes to understand.

Units Employed in Different Sciences

The physicist of today is primarily interested in the discovery of the processes that occur within atoms; for such a physicist, the atom may be regarded as an appropriate unit, since it contains all of the interrelationships that he wishes to understand. The chemist, on the other hand, since his primary interest lies in the structure of molecules, would find individual atoms inadequate for his purpose.

The biologist, whose problems are concerned with interrelations that occur in living organisms, could discover little of significance if he were to occupy himself with the study of individual atoms or individual molecules. He must take the total living organism as his unit of investigation, for the processes that interest him will not be manifested in atoms or molecules.

Each of these units—the atom, the molecule, the living organism— is an appropriate unit from the point of view of the particular scientist —the physicist, the chemist, the biologist—who employs it. But what functions as an appropriate unit for the physicist can be of little value for answering the biologist's questions. The biologist cannot understand the phenomena of living organisms in terms of atomic units any more readily than the chemist can understand the properties of sodium chloride in terms of the distinctive properties of sodium and chlorine. This point becomes even more obvious when we consider the problems of the astronomer: how impossible it would be for him to solve his problems if he were to take molecules or living organisms as his units of study!

Similarly, in psychology, the nature of the behavior phenomena that we aim at understanding will determine the size of the behavior unit that we must investigate. If, for instance, we are interested in *what* particular individuals learn, rather than in *how efficiently* they learn, we must think in terms of larger behavior units, units that are sufficiently large to include the determinants of individual differences in what is learned.

General laws of learning leave out numerous details of value for understanding the results of learning by a particular individual. When the psychologist is interested in understanding human adjustment, he must employ behavior units that are much more inclusive than are those of the physiological psychologist.

The psychology of adjustment is concerned mainly with *what* the individual learns, *what* he is attentive to, *what* meaning he perceives in a given type of situation, *what kinds* of problems he encounters, *what* his solutions are. This being the case, the psychology of adjustment must be understood in terms of larger units than those appropriate for the understanding of principles concerning the *efficiency* of learning, thinking, perception, etc.

Since different behavior units are employed, the psychology of human adjustment involves principles that differ from principles in other fields of psychology. Nevertheless, although such principles differ in important respects from the principles, say, of physiological psychology, they are not to be regarded as contradictory to these other principles, any more than the principles of astronomy are to be regarded as contradictory to the principles of biology.

Molar Units Appropriate for the Psychology of Adjustment

The *molar* behavior-unit, which is appropriate for understanding human adjustment, is a relatively large unit, a unit more inclusive than that required for the discovery of general principles of sensation, perception, learning, thinking, etc. It includes *the entire sequence of behavior from the moment the organism begins to be reactive to a particular pattern of needs until the moment the organism is satisfied or becomes reconciled to frustration.* The "terrified" individual escapes, or reinterprets the environment as nonterrifying; the hungry individual takes whatever actions he must in order to gratify his hunger; the lonely individual finds sociable companionship or reconciles himself to loneliness.

The individual, through previous learning, has associated gratification of his needs with certain goal objects or satisfiers. The molar unit, then, involves a goal-oriented sequence of activities. It includes all of the behavior of the individual from the moment when he begins to seek a certain goal until the moment when the goal is attained or some other goal is substituted for it.

Molar units, of course, are variable in duration and complexity. Some goals can be attained quickly by means of a simple behavior sequence. The sociable person who has many friends within easy reach can quickly and easily satisfy his need for companionship; the hungry child can quickly and easily satisfy his hunger, provided that his family life is well regulated and dependable.

Other goals may require days, weeks, months, or years of complex activity before the individual can reach them to his ultimate satisfaction. Lifetime ambitions require long-enduring behavior units for their attainment. Ordinarily, however, such long-time units may be broken down into subunits, each of which will provide data for understanding adjustive behavior; yet the *sequence* of subunits cannot be understood without reference to their relation to the more inclusive lifetime ambition or long-enduring molar unit.

It should be obvious that no two molar behavior-units can be identical; there will, however, be uniformities among molar units in the behavior of the same individual from time to time, or in the behavior of different individuals. On the basis of discoverable uniformities, it becomes possible to develop general principles of adjustive behavior.

OUTLINE OF ADJUSTMENT PROCESSES

ADJUSTMENT involves a continual interaction of the individual and his environment. This is a continual process, since the environment, as it is perceived by the individual, is continually changing. It may be regarded as the function of adjustment to bring about a stable equilibrium among the various components of external and internal stimulation. As we have seen, however, the adjustment processes merely *tend toward* the achievement of such a stable equilibrium—never reaching it, presumably, until death occurs.

Motivation

The most significant components of internal and external stimulation are referred to as *motivating stimuli*. Motivating stimuli are perceived as uncomfortable or distressing. The behavior of the individual normally eventuates in the reduction or elimination of such distressing stimuli. Activities that reduce the distress of motivating stimuli are experienced as pleasurable or gratifying.

Frustration and Conflict

The individual's behavior is complicated by the fact that external and internal realities, as perceived by the individual, are often inconsistent with gratification. He perceives factors in the external environment or within himself that interfere with gratification of various motives. In other words, the individual experiences *frustration*. When he perceives that the demands of his different motives are incompatible, he is said to experience a *conflict*.

Fear and Hostility

Whenever the individual perceives a particular feature of his environment as the source of his frustration, he will feel fear or hostility in relation to it. Fear motivates (is relieved by) escape reactions; hostility motivates (is relieved by) reactions that aim at the destruction of a frustrating agent. If, for some reason, the individual can neither escape from the frustrating agent nor destroy it, fear and hostility are said to undergo frustration. Thus a vicious circle may occur: frustrated fear or hostility leads to further fear or hostility and, in turn, fear or hostility of mounting intensity is further frustrated.

When the individual cannot relieve his fear or hostility—by escaping from or destroying the source of frustration—he will likely repress awareness of the nature of the frustrating agent; but the motivation will continue, and will be experienced as anxiety.[17]

Anxiety

Anxiety is the focal point of attention in the psychology of adjustment. Anxiety is similar to other motives in that it involves unpleasant or painful experience. It differs from other motives, however, in that it is not goal-oriented; that is, no particular class of activities may be

[17] Of necessity, the relationships discussed in this section are oversimplified. Later chapters will deal with these relationships in greater detail.

regarded as especially appropriate for the relief of anxiety. Eating reduces hunger; drinking reduces thirst; sexual expression reduces sexual tension; being with other people reduces loneliness. But when anxiety is operative, the individual is aware only of his intolerable anxiety, without being aware of its source. Since he is unaware of the source, he is helpless to reduce his anxiety by the direct method of eliminating its basis. Whatever action *happens* to reduce anxiety on one occasion is likely to be employed on future occasions when anxiety is experienced. Thus any kind of behavior may become a method for gratifying (reducing or relieving) anxiety.

Defenses against Anxiety

Although any form of behavior may function as a method of relieving anxiety, there are a number of anxiety-reducing activities employed so commonly that they have been given special names. The general term embracing these common behavior forms is *defenses against anxiety*.[18]

The psychology of adjustment, with its description of various defenses against anxiety, may be compared with the science of dietetics, which is concerned with various "defenses against hunger." Foods are classified as carbohydrates, proteins, fats, minerals, vitamins, etc. From the dietitian's point of view, almost any food containing a carbohydrate will satisfy the body's need for carbohydrates, provided that the body gets enough of it. In other words, differences among different foods containing carbohydrates are overlooked when the dietitian speaks of carbohydrates. Similarly, when the psychologist speaks of rationalization, he is emphasizing the similarities among many unique behavior manifestations and, momentarily at least, is overlooking the differences among them.

The fact that names are available to emphasize the similarities among defensive activities should not obscure the fact that the activities do exhibit differences. Each rationalization is different from every other rationalization. Moreover, a specific activity may be considered an instance of one defense at one time and of another defense at another time, just as bread may be considered a source of carbohydrates at one time and of proteins at another time.

It is usually impossible to say whether a given defensive activity

[18] Other terms for defenses against anxiety are: defense mechanisms, adjustment mechanisms, defensive techniques, defensive activities, mechanisms of defense, and defense dynamisms.

should be termed rationalization or projection, for example, unless a thorough investigation has been made of the function performed by the given activity for the individual.[19] In fact, it is often evident that a given case of defensive activity involves several of these "mechanisms" in combination. For example, a person may justify his behavior (rationalize) in terms of his belief that he is being victimized by somebody else (projection).

The following terms have been used to denote commonly employed defensive methods: repression, fixation, regression, identification, displacement, projection, sublimation, reaction formation, rationalization, isolation, undoing, psychosomatic defenses, withdrawal, and compensation.[20]

Although this list is not an exhaustive enumeration of the defenses described in the literature of adjustive behavior, it should provide sufficient illustration of the fact that there are numerous ways whereby the individual can obtain relief from anxiety.

Evaluation of Defenses

Much has been written relative to the value of particular defenses for the personal adjustment of the individual. Defenses have been described as "healthy" or "unhealthy," "wholesome" or "unwholesome," "adaptive" or "maladaptive," "mentally hygienic" or "mentally unhygienic," etc. The issues can be made clear by a consideration of the following generalizations, which appear to be applicable to all defensive activities.

CRITERION FOR EVALUATING DEFENSES.   All defensive activities are useful to the persons who manifest them, in the sense that the anxiety which occurred prior to their use is relieved or reduced to a tolerable degree. In other words, any given defense may be efficient *for reducing pre-existing anxiety*. Thus, from the point of view of their anxiety-reducing effectiveness, all of the common defenses are about equal.

The different defensive activities can be differentiated, however, in terms of *the extent to which they function as a basis of further frustration,* and consequently of further anxiety. Whenever the individual becomes hypersensitive to the operation of "unworthy" motives in others—that is, when he projects—he will become involved in social

---

[19] Lewin, *op. cit.,* p. 11, has stressed a similar point of view in his distinction between phenotypes and genotypes. Cf. Gordon W. Allport, *Personality: a Psychological Interpretation* (New York, 1937), p. 16.

[20] These terms are defined in the Glossary. Many of these defenses are described in detail in subsequent chapters.

difficulties. For this reason, projection is generally regarded as a relatively maladaptive defense. Sublimation, on the other hand, is regarded as a relatively adaptive defense, since it usually involves activities that are highly valued by other people.

Defensive activities, then, are to be regarded as relatively adaptive or relatively maladaptive, not in terms of the extent to which they are adequate for relieving pre-existing anxiety but in terms of the extent to which the defensive activities themselves involve frustration for the individual.

Since many defensive activities are relatively maladaptive in the above sense—that is, since they "generate" anxiety—it becomes necessary for the individual to employ "secondary" defenses to reduce the anxiety "generated" by his "primary" defenses. The personality of the individual is thought by some writers to be describable in terms of the structure of defensive activities which he characteristically manifests.

OBJECTIONS TO EVALUATING INDIVIDUALS. Just as defensive activities have been evaluated as "adjustive" or "maladjustive," individuals themselves are frequently characterized as "adjusted" or "maladjusted." This either-or characterization, however, is detrimental to understanding. Adjustment involves a continuous variable, and therefore the evaluation of individuals in terms of this variable should not be limited to the two extremes. This, however, is only one of the objections to evaluating individuals. When a person is categorized as maladjusted, it is frequently—in fact, usually—implied that he is inferior to other people. This implication is often associated with a deficiency of tolerance toward the individual, which often functions to increase his difficulties.

It may reasonably be stated, in contrast to the usual attitude toward maladjusted individuals, that *each person is as well adjusted as he possibly can be*. In terms of his unique life experiences, his unique pattern of motives, his unique perceptions of reality, his unique environmental stresses, his unique "physical" make-up, etc., it would be impossible to conceive of his adjusting in any other manner than that which he has actually adopted.

It can further be stated that there are no "abnormal" people; *there are only normal people who have responded normally to their uniquely abnormal experiences*. The term abnormal, as applied to a given person, implies that different principles account for his behavior than account for the behavior of the so-called normal person. Thus it can be concluded that the classification of people into adjusted and maladjusted or into normal and abnormal categories involves not only a scientific inaccuracy but also a damaging offense against the persons who are detrimentally classified.[21]

SUMMARY

THIS chapter has aimed at providing an orientation within the general field of adjustive behavior. The chapter has provided a context or frame of reference within which to organize the details of adjustive behavior, which are to be considered in subsequent chapters.

A understanding of human adjustive behavior should be based on (1) an organismic conception of behavior, (2) the conception that behavior is a function of perception, (3) the treatment of behavior in terms of molar units, and (4) the conception that human adjustment involves activities that tend to reduce anxiety and other forms of motivational excitation.

An organism comprises a dynamic system of interrelated events in which a disturbance of equilibrium will operate to bring about compensatory changes throughout the system. Dynamic systems include, in addition to living organisms, such organizations as the atom, the molecule, the solar system, a smoke ring, a candle flame.

Some organisms, such as atoms and the solar system, are highly stable systems; others, such as smoke rings, candle flames, and living organisms, are highly unstable. Living organisms are continually reactive to stimuli, continually in the process of approaching a re-establishment of equilibrium.

Motivational stimuli operate as disturbances in the organism's equilibrium, and motivated behavior operates in the interest of re-establishing equilibrium.

Different functions of the human organism are complexly interrelated. Behavior involves interrelations between the so-called mental and physiological processes; behavior processes are to be regarded as psychosomatic in character; i.e., behavior must be described in terms of

[21] Many persons who could profit from psychotherapy avoid doing so for fear that it will involve frustration of their need for self-esteem. The person who has been depreciated as a maladjusted or abnormal person by laymen who use such terms loosely may fear that therapists will display a similar attitude toward him. Possibly one of the most eminent contributions of the client-centered therapy, which is emphasized by Rogers and his associates, is the explicit insistence that the client be respected and accepted as a worthy individual with high potentialities.

the combined operation of mental and physiological processes, which are not fundamentally separable except from an arbitrary point of view.

The organismic conception of behavior implies that such processes as perception, motivation, learning, thinking, and emotions never occur in isolation; these divisions of the functioning organism are separated merely for convenience of discussion and must be regarded as occurring in continual interaction with one another.

Behavior can most adequately be understood as a function not of the objective nature of the environment but of the unique perceptions of the individual. The individual's behavior at any given moment is determined by what the situation means to him; this is equivalent to saying that behavior is a function of perception, of the psychological field, or of the perceptual environment.

The individual's perception at any given moment combines elements from the external environment with elements from the internal environment (including relatively permanent personality tendencies). Perception itself may be regarded as a dynamic system in unstable equilibrium; and behavior may be regarded as functioning in the interest of developing greater stability of perception.

The kind of understanding we seek determines how large a unit of natural phenomena must be investigated. The unit must be sufficiently large to include the relationships that the investigator wishes to understand.

Different sciences may be differentiated in terms of the unit employed in each. The physicist is concerned with processes occurring within the atom, the chemist with processes occurring within the molecule, the biologist with processes occurring within the living organism, the astronomer with processes occurring within the solar system or within still larger systems.

The *molar* behavior-unit is appropriate for the understanding of human adjustment processes. The molar unit includes all of the behavior of the individual from the moment he begins to seek a certain goal to the moment he attains the goal or substitutes some other goal in its place.

Molar units differ in duration and complexity: some molar units involve simple activities that occupy only a few seconds; others involve hours, days, weeks, months, or years of complex activity.

Adjustment involves a continual interaction of the individual and his environment. Adjustive behavior manifests a continual trend toward the establishment of equilibrium among the various components of external and internal stimulation.

When motivating stimuli arise, they are perceived as uncomfortable or distressing, and the ensuing behavior normally will function to reduce the intensity of such stimuli. But behavior is complicated by the fact that features of internal and external reality are incompatible with the ready gratification or reduction of motives; therefore frustration and conflicts occur.

Frustrating agents become the objects of fear or hostility, which demand escape from, or destruction of, the frustrating agents. When fear or hostility is frustrated, the individual will frequently repress awareness of the frustrating agent; but the motivation will continue, to be experienced as anxiety.

Since anxiety is "objectless"—since there are no specifically appropriate ways to relieve anxiety—any one or more of a number of common defense mechanisms may develop, on the basis of their having once functioned successfully for the relief of anxiety. Such common defenses against anxiety include repression, fixation, regression, identification, displacement, projection, sublimation, reaction formation, rationalization, isolation, undoing, psychosomatic defenses, withdrawal, and compensation.

Perhaps all of the defenses are efficient in reducing pre-existing anxiety. But particular defenses may be regarded as relatively adaptive or relatively maladaptive in terms of the extent to which they function as sources of subsequent anxiety.

Individuals should not be referred to as "maladjusted" or "abnormal," since adjustment involves a continuous variable (either-or classifications being inapplicable), and since each person, at any given moment, is as well adjusted as he possibly can be. The term abnormal, as applied to any given person, implies that different principles account for his behavior than account for the behavior of "normal" individuals.

The following chapter will be devoted to a discussion of motivation, the concepts concerning which are of central importance in the psychology of adjustment.

► **Suggested Readings**

ORGANISMIC CONCEPTION OF BEHAVIOR
Alexander, F. *Psychosomatic Medicine: Its Principles and Applications.*
   New York, 1950.

Bruner, J. S. and Goodman, Cecile C. "Value and Need as Organizing Factors in Perception," *Journal of Abnormal and Social Psychology*, 42 (1947), 33–44.

Bruner, J. S. and Postman, L. "Tension and Tension Release as Organizing Factors in Perception," *Journal of Personality*, 15 (1947), 300–8.

Eriksen, C. W. "Perceptual Defense as a Function of Unacceptable Needs," *Journal of Abnormal and Social Psychology*, 46 (1951), 557–64.

Levine, J. M. and Murphy, G. "The Learning and Forgetting of Controversial Material," *Journal of Abnormal and Social Psychology*, 38 (1943), 507–17.

McGinnies, E. "Emotionality and Perceptual Defense," *Psychological Review*, 56 (1949), 244–51.

Martin, W. W. "Some Basic Implications of a Concept of Organism for Psychology," *Psychological Review*, 52 (1945), 333–43.

Murphy, G. *Personality: a Biosocial Approach to Origins and Structure.* New York, 1947. Chap. ii, pp. 29–44.

Postman, L., Bruner, J. S., and McGinnies, E. "Personal Values as Selective Factors in Perception," *Journal of Abnormal and Social Psychology*, 43 (1948), 142–54.

Ryan, T. A. "Interrelations of the Sensory Systems in Perception," *Psychological Bulletin*, 37 (1940), 659–98.

Saul, L. J. "Physiological Effects of Emotional Tension," in *Personality and the Behavior Disorders*, J. McV. Hunt, ed. New York, 1944. I, 269–305.

Weber, C. O. "Homeostasis and Servo-mechanisms for What?" *Psychological Review*, 56 (1949), 234–9.

Wolff, H. G. "Life Situations, Emotions, and Bodily Disease," in *Feelings and Emotions*, M. L. Reymert, ed. New York, 1950. Chap. xxiv, pp. 284–324.

BEHAVIOR AS A FUNCTION OF PERCEPTION

Combs, A. W. "A Phenomenological Approach to Adjustment Theory," *Journal of Abnormal and Social Psychology*, 44 (1949), 29–35.

Ittelson, W. H. "The Constancies in Perceptual Theory," *Psychological Review*, 58 (1951), 285–94.

Krech, D. and Crutchfield, R. S. *Theory and Problems of Social Psychology.* New York, 1948. Pp. 33–40, 76–109.

Luchins, A. S. "An Evaluation of Some Current Criticisms of Gestalt Psychological Work on Perception," *Psychological Review*, 58 (1951), 69–95.

Murphy, G. and Hochberg, J. "Perceptual Development: Some Tentative Hypotheses," *Psychological Review*, 58 (1951), 332–49.

Rogers, C. R. "Some Observations on the Organization of Personality," *American Psychologist*, 2 (1947), 358–68.

Snygg, D. and Combs, A. W. *Individual Behavior: a New Frame of Reference for Psychology.* New York, 1949. Chap. ii, pp. 10–33.

Tolman, E. C. "Cognitive Maps in Rats and Men," *Psychological Review,* 55 (1948), 189–208.

MOLAR BEHAVIOR-UNITS

Krech, D. and Crutchfield, R. S. *Theory and Problems of Social Psychology.* New York, 1948. Pp. 30–2.

Littman, R. A. and Rosen, E. "Molar and Molecular," *Psychological Review,* 57 (1950), 58–65.

Murchison, C., *A History of Psychology in Autobiography.* Worcester, Mass., 1932. II, 376–80.

Tolman, E. C. *Purposive Behavior in Animals and Men.* New York, 1932. Chap. i, pp. 3–23.

OUTLINE OF ADJUSTMENT PROCESSES

Hilgard, E. R. "Human Motives and the Concept of the Self," *American Psychologist,* 4 (1949), 374–82.

Rogers, C. R. "Significant Aspects of Client-centered Therapy," *American Psychologist,* 1 (1946), 415–22.

Rogers, C. R. *Client-centered Therapy: Its Current Practice, Implications, and Theory.* Boston, 1951. Chap. xi, pp. 481–533.

Sargent, S. S. "Reaction to Frustration—a Critique and Hypothesis," *Psychological Review,* 55 (1948), 108–14.

Symonds, P. M. *The Dynamics of Human Adjustment.* New York, 1946. Chap. i, pp. 1–11.

CHAPTER Two

Motivation

Through all animal life . . . an outstanding characteristic runs—
from clipped polyp to blood-clotting, to hungry foraging, to social
evasions—the tendency of the organism to maintain its normality
against internal or external disrupting agencies.[1]

MOTIVATION is a central concept in the psychology of adjustment. The term *motive* probably had its origin in the search for "causes" of behavior; it implied, in its original sense, a "power" or a "force." The student should, however, avoid interpreting motives as powers, forces, or causes of behavior, since motives comprise but one aspect of the complex interrelations that are involved in behavior.

The term motive, according to Sherif, is used as "a generic term to cover all the different cases and kinds of goal-directed (motivated) behavior."[2] Dashiell also uses the term in a generic sense: "The word *motive* we shall employ throughout our treatment in its widest sense, to cover every form of impulse, from the simplest physiological drive to the most elaborated, sophisticated, and intellectualized ideal."[3] Many

---

[1] John F. Dashiell, *Fundamentals of General Psychology* (Boston, 1937), p. 37. Reprinted by permission of John F. Dashiell and Houghton Mifflin Company. Copyright, 1937, by John Frederick Dashiell.

[2] Muzafer Sherif, *An Outline of Social Psychology* (New York, 1948), p. 11. Reprinted by permission of Harper & Brothers. Copyright, 1948, by Harper & Brothers.

[3] Dashiell, *op. cit.*, p. 102 n.

specific terms are implied by the term motive; the list of such terms would include, among others, needs, drives, desires, wishes, wants, urges, impulses, instincts, purposes, ideals, and values. In this book we shall follow the practice of using the term motive in this inclusive (general) sense.

If the living organism were self-sustaining—that is, if it could maintain its functions continuously without establishing relations with the external environment—there would be no need for the concept of motivation; nor would there be any need for a psychology of adjustment. But the organism is *not* self-sustaining. It must receive certain materials from the external environment, and it must rid itself of other materials. In this sense, the organism resembles a candle flame, which can maintain itself only through the continual intake of oxygen and fuel and the continual output of the products of combustion. A candle flame will die if its supply of oxygen or fuel is cut off or if the continual dissipation of carbon dioxide and water vapor is interfered with.

The organism, like the candle flame, can maintain its functional integrity only through the maintenance of relationships with the external environment. The organism is composed of cells. The cells and the organization of cells maintain their equilibrium, their integrity as living processes, by means of a complicated series of biochemical changes (metabolism). Metabolic activity involves the transformation of various chemical compounds into bodily tissues, energy, and by-products that must be eliminated from the organism.

To maintain its equilibrium, the organism must take in from the external environment the raw materials that are involved in this metabolic transformation. Moreover, the organism must rid itself of the transformed materials that are not utilized in the cell structure and that interfere with the continuation of metabolic functions. The organism must take in oxygen, water, and the various foods that are necessary for metabolism; it must eliminate waste products through urination, defecation, perspiration, respiration, etc.; and it must have periods of rest (the slowing down of metabolic processes) in order that depleting tissues may be rebuilt and that the by-products of metabolism may be eliminated more rapidly than they are being produced. The conditions underlying these processes are referred to as *tissue needs*.

The tendency of the organism to maintain dynamic equilibrium or stability has been referred to by Cannon as *homeostasis*.[4] Guthrie, in describing this conception, writes:

[4] Walter B. Cannon, *The Wisdom of the Body* (New York, 1939), p. 24.

Among the homeostatic or constant states described by Cannon in his recent book, *The Wisdom of the Body*, many reflect the primitive environment of living forms, the ocean, and are concerned with the condition of the blood which offers the cells of the human body an environment approximating the sea water to which the early forms of life were adjusted. We do not think of ourselves as marine animals, but we are. By means of an outer sac of skin we manage to get about on dry land with our "innards" still enjoying the saline water bath in which our remote ancestors swam or floated. The pressure of this blood, the quantity of the blood, its supply of sugar, of water, of salt, of protein, fat, calcium, oxygen, carbon dioxide, its acid-alkaline balance, all are constant states which are protected by a multitude of reactions.[5]

Among the multitude of reactions that protect the constant states are, of course, the "physiological" reactions. But reactions in the form of overt behavior are also involved. It is at this point that behavior becomes understandable in terms of motivation. Depletion of substances necessary for the maintenance of homeostasis, and accumulation of metabolic products interfering with homeostasis, are conditions that require behavioral relations with the external environment. The concept of homeostasis is therefore regarded as a central concept in the psychology of motivation.

MOTIVATIONAL ANALYSIS

AS FREUD,[6] Murray,[7] and Sears[8] have separately pointed out, any given motive may be analyzed into three distinct aspects: (1) the source of the motivational stimulus or the kind of disturbance occurring in the organism's equilibrium; (2) the quality of the behavior tendency aroused in the organism; and (3) the object in relation to which motivated behavior is aroused. The term *need integrate* or *motive* may be applied to the combination or synthesis of these three aspects of motivation.

[5] Edwin R. Guthrie, *The Psychology of Human Conflict* (New York, 1938), p. 8. Reprinted by permission of Harper & Brothers. Copyright, 1938, by Harper & Brothers.

[6] Sigmund Freud, *New Introductory Lectures on Psycho-Analysis* (New York, 1933), pp. 132-3.

[7] Henry A. Murray, *Explorations in Personality* (New York, 1938), pp. 109-10.

[8] Robert R. Sears, "Survey of Objective Studies of Psychoanalytic Concepts," *Social Science Research Council Bulletin*, No. 51 (1943), pp. 76-104.

Murray's terms for the distinguishable aspects of a need integrate are, respectively, *need, mode,* and *object;* [9] Freud's terms are *source, aim,* and *object;* [10] Sears's terms are *drive, instrumental act,* and *object.* [11] The terms may be presented in tabular form, as follows:

	MOTIVATING STIMULUS	QUALITY OF AROUSED BEHAVIOR	GOAL TOWARD WHICH BEHAVIOR IS AIMED
Murray	*Need*	*Mode*	*Object*
Freud	*Source*	*Aim*	*Object*
Sears	*Drive*	*Instrumental act*	*Object*

NEED, SOURCE, OR DRIVE. The terms need, source, and drive, as used respectively by Murray, Freud, and Sears, imply the character of the motivational stimulus, the kind of disturbance in the organism's equilibrium, or the part of the body in which painful or unpleasant excitation is experienced. In the case of biogenic motives, the unpleasant excitation—the hunger pang, thirst, sexual tension, etc.—may be experienced in an identifiable region of the body; but in the case of many psychogenic motives, no such localization occurs.

MODE, AIM, OR INSTRUMENTAL ACT. The terms mode, aim, and instrumental act refer, as we have seen, to the kind of behavior tendency that is associated with a given need. Such a behavior tendency may be expressed overtly, so that it can be perceived by an external observer; it may be expressed implicitly, so that it cannot be perceived by an external observer; or it may be inhibited, restrained, or otherwise modified. Thus, a gnawing hunger may be relieved by eating; it may be partially relieved through fantasies concerned with eating; or it may be endured temporarily in order that some other need—such as the need to accomplish a piece of work—may first be satisfied.

Woodworth has distinguished between *preparatory* and *consummatory* reactions.[12] Preparatory reactions consist of behavior that brings the organism into the presence of a goal object (if it is positively cathected); consummatory reactions involve activities in direct relation to the goal object itself. For example, going home for lunch would be termed preparatory behavior, but the actual process of eating would be termed consummatory behavior.

[9] Murray, *op. cit.,* pp. 109–10.
[10] Freud, *New Introductory Lectures . . . ,* pp. 132–3.
[11] Sears, *op. cit.,* pp. 76–104.
[12] Robert S. Woodworth, *Dynamic Psychology* (New York, 1918), pp. 40–2.

OBJECT. The term *object* implies anything in relation to which behavior may be directed for the satisfaction (relief) of a need. In infants and in some of the lowest animal forms, motivated behavior is characterized by increased vigor and increased variability.[13] Such behavior has adaptive significance in the sense that it *accidentally* eventuates in the reduction of motivational distress. In higher organisms, including man, the individual associates particular goal objects with the gratification of particular needs.

The mature individual anticipates (experiences images of) certain goal objects whenever a need becomes operative. Thus the hungry individual anticipates a thick steak; the lonely individual anticipates meeting certain persons; the lover anticipates seeing the object of his affection. The anticipation of goal objects functions to guide behavior, so that instead of an increase in the variability of behavior there occurs an increase in the directedness of behavior, within limits, as the strength of a particular need increases.

The nature of the object will depend on the nature of the need and on the individual's prior experience in satisfying this need. The object may be another person, an inanimate object or process, a part of the body, an internal process. In brief, anything that may become the object of perception may come to function as an object in relation to which a particular need may be gratified.

CLASSIFICATION OF MOTIVES

MOTIVES may be classified in terms of two different principles; namely, in terms of their origin and in terms of the character of their relationship with cathected goal objects. Such classifications should never be applied rigidly, on an "either-or" basis, to a particular motive as it functions in the mature individual. It would be more nearly correct, in any given instance, to refer to a motive as belonging *more* or *less* to one or another of the classifications.

Biogenic and Psychogenic Motives

The terms *biogenic* and *psychogenic* have been applied to motives to distinguish them in terms of their origin. *Biogenic motives* are said to have their origin in the biological nature of the organism. Such motives arise as a function of hereditary and maturational processes rather

[13] Dashiell, *op. cit.*, p. 109.

than on the basis of learning. They are expected to occur in every normal human individual regardless of the nature of his unique experiences. *Psychogenic motives*, on the other hand, are said to have their origin in the unique experiences of the individual. They occur as a function of learning and may be expected to exhibit differences from individual to individual.

Other terms that are approximately synonymous with *biogenic* and *psychogenic*, respectively, are listed as follows:

BIOGENIC	PSYCHOGENIC
basic	*derived*
physiological	*social*
viscerogenic	*sociogenic*
primary	*secondary*
unlearned	*learned*
organic	*functional*

The terms listed opposite each other above are frequently employed together to represent contrasting categories of motivation.

The earliest motives to become operative in the organism are, of course, the biogenic motives. During early infancy, behavior is related only to the satisfaction or frustration of such needs as hunger, thirst, or pain. Psychogenic motives are learned through the association of persons, objects, and activities with the satisfaction or frustration of the biogenic needs. Still later, further psychogenic motives may develop through association of persons, objects, and activities with the satisfaction or frustration of pre-existing psychogenic motives.

Positive and Negative Motives

Behavior in relation to goal objects may take any one of three fundamental forms or a combination of these:

1. It may seek to establish and maintain gratifying (integrative) relations with the goal object.
2. It may seek to separate the organism from the vicinity of the goal object.
3. It may seek to destroy the goal object.

Behavior of the first form is integrative and expansive; it establishes and maintains *positive* relations with objects in the environment. Behavior of the second and third forms is disintegrative; it prevents the development of relations, or breaks down existing relations, between the organism and objects in the environment. Motives underlying behavior of the first form may be termed *positive motives;* motives underlying behavior of the second and third forms may be termed *negative motives.*

The terms *cathexis* and *valence* have been employed to express the relation between a need and an object that is associated with the gratification of the need.[14] In relation to a given need an object may have a *negative* or a *positive* cathexis or valence. An object that is liked and approached is said to have positive cathexis or valence, or to be positively *cathected* (by the person or the need); an object that is disliked or feared is said to have negative cathexis or valence, or to be negatively *cathected*. Some objects may have both positive and negative cathexis for a given person; toward such objects the person is said to have an *ambivalent* attitude.

Positive motives are frequently associated with *deficits;* that is, they originate in bodily needs, such as the need for oxygen, water, or various food elements. Negative motives are frequently associated with protective behavior, which prevents injury to the organism.

Positive motives involve seeking behavior; whereas negative motives involve avoiding or destructive behavior.

The term *appetite* is sometimes used to imply positive motivation; the term *aversion* is used to imply negative motivation.

The goal object is positively cathected in the case of positive motives, and reaching such a goal is referred to as achieving satisfaction or gratification. The goal object is negatively cathected in the case of negative motives, and escape from, or destruction of, the goal object is referred to as achieving safety or security.

The individual develops a self-concept of adequacy or self-confidence when he has had frequent successes in regard to positive motives; he develops a self-concept of security when he has had frequent successes with respect to negative motives.

Love is referred to as a positive attitude, and fear and hostility are referred to as negative attitudes.

Difficulties in Classification

Any catalogue of human motives must involve an oversimplification of the unique processes of living organisms. Motives to which names have been applied are, in actual operation, unique processes, ex-

[14] Murray, *op. cit.,* p. 106; Kurt Lewin, *A Dynamic Theory of Personality* (New York, 1935), pp. 81 f.

hibiting manifold individual differences, as well as differences from time to time in the same individual.

When a particular name is applied to a motive, this name merely stresses important similarities among unique processes. For example, the word *hunger* applies to numerous specific discomforts arising from specific biochemical needs of the organism; moreover, each individual differs from every other individual in his likes and dislikes for various kinds of foods, and his likes and dislikes at one time may differ from his likes and dislikes at another time. Again, the term *dominance* embodies numerous unique methods of dominating others, numerous unique objects of domination, and numerous unique degrees of dominance over others.

Motives do not admit of classification into rigid categories. It is difficult, for instance, to determine whether a motive should be referred to as biogenic or as psychogenic. How a biogenic motive is actually expressed by the individual may have a multitude of psychogenic determinants; and the peculiar qualities of behavior that is based primarily on psychogenic motivation may have some degree of biogenic determination.

Hunger is classified as a biogenic motive, as having its basic origin in the biological nature of the organism. But *what* the individual prefers to eat depends not only on the particular society in which he has developed but also on the more particular experiences of the individual in his family setting. Moreover, the particular manner of obtaining food, the manner in which it is prepared, and the manner in which it is eaten depend on psychogenic determinants.

On the other hand, many characteristics of physique, general health, physical appearance, etc., are influential in determining which psychogenic motives will be developed and to what degree they will become manifest in the overt behavior of the individual. Whether the individual becomes highly sociable or solitary, loquacious or taciturn, altruistic or misanthropic—these and many other psychogenic aspects of his motivation will be determined in part by his physical appearance, his energy level, and his other biological assets or limitations.[15]

The problem of drug addiction as a motivational process demonstrates another difficulty frequently encountered in classification. On the one hand, one cannot be born an addict, and yet something more

[15] Strictly speaking, perhaps, only the *need* aspect of the need integrate can be biogenic; instrumental acts and objects, on the other hand, may be and usually are psychogenic.

than learning may be involved. There is, for instance, some physiological evidence that the craving for alcohol or morphine may be based, at least in part, on biochemical changes that have been induced by previous use of these drugs.

Such complex determination should be kept in mind when considering the following lists of biogenic and psychogenic motives.

List of Biogenic Motives

Murray has listed the following thirteen motives as probably biogenic.[16]

1. n Inspiration (oxygen)
2. n Water
3. n Food
4. n Sentience
5. n Sex
6. n Lactation
7. n Expiration (carbon dioxide)
8. n Urination
9. n Defecation
10. n Noxavoidance
11. n Heatavoidance
12. n Coldavoidance
13. n Harmavoidance

The first six motives in the above list are positive motives; the last seven are negative motives. The *need for sentience* involves motivation to obtain sensuous gratification, especially through stimulation of the so-called erogenous zones. The last four needs have to do with the protection of the organism against harmful stimuli: against noxious stimuli, excessive heat, excessive cold, and injurious or painful stimuli. The first four needs arise from lacks or deficits and are gratified by the intake of substances (or of stimulation) from the external environment; the next five arise from visceral distensions and are gratified by the secretion or the excretion of various products of metabolism.

Murray has also listed a fourteenth biogenic motive, the need for rest and sleep, although this need is not included in the schematic arrangement from which the above list was adapted.[17]

[16] Murray, *op. cit.*, p. 79. (The lower-case n is Murray's symbol for *need.*)
[17] Murray, *op. cit.*, p. 77.

Other writers—e.g., Tolman [18] and Young [19]—have included in the list of biogenic motives the *activity drive*, which involves the need of the organism to be active, to exercise the muscles, etc. Tolman and others have also listed the *esthetic drive*, which involves positive response to color and tone, to tactual stimulation, etc., and which has been regarded as the basis of adult enjoyment of the esthetic features of the environment. This motive is included, at least partially, in Murray's *need for sentience*.

Since the basic emotions operate as motivational processes, the emotions of fear, rage, disgust, and "startle," according to Sherif, should be included among the biogenic motives.[20] Although such emotional motives as anxiety (fear), guilt, the aggressive motive (anger, hostility), and self-assertiveness (feelings of inferiority) seem not to have a *direct* biogenic origin, they may be regarded as unlearned emotional responses to frustration of pre-existing motives of either biogenic or psychogenic origin.

Murray's List of Psychogenic Motives

The biogenic motives are undoubtedly limited in number, but there is probably no limit to the number and variety of psychogenic motives, since these derive from the unique experiences of each individual. Murray has listed and defined a number of common psychogenic motives, which operate in the behavior of individuals in present-day American society with sufficient frequency to be useful in describing different personalities.[21] The list might be different if the common motives of some other society were being listed. Murray's list follows:

1. n Acquisition: to gain possessions and property.
2. n Conservance: to collect, repair, clean, and preserve things.
3. n Order: to arrange, organize, put away objects; to be tidy and clean; to be scrupulously precise.
4. n Retention: to retain possession of things.
5. n Construction: to organize and build.
6. n Superiority:

[18] Edward C. Tolman, "Motivation, Learning, and Adjustment," *Proceedings of the American Philosophical Society, 84* (1941), 543–63.
[19] Paul T. Young, *Emotion in Man and Animal: Its Nature and Relation to Attitude and Motive* (New York, 1943), p. 95.
[20] Sherif, *op. cit.,* p. 32.
[21] Murray, *op. cit.,* pp. 80–3.

a) n Achievement: to overcome obstacles, to exercise power, to strive to do something difficult as well and as quickly as possible.

b) n Recognition: to excite praise and commendation.

c) n Exhibition: to attract attention.

7. n Inviolacy: to prevent depreciation of self-respect, to maintain psychological distance.

   a) n Infavoidance: to avoid failure, shame, humiliation, ridicule.

   b) n Defendence: to defend against blame, belittlement; to justify one's actions.

   c) n Counteraction: to overcome defeat by restriving or retaliation.

8. n Dominance: to influence or control others.

9. n Deference: to admire and willingly follow a leader.

10. n Similance: to empathize, imitate, agree, and believe; to identify with others.

11. n Autonomy: to strive for independence.

12. n Contrarience: to be unique; to act unconventionally or take opposite sides.

13. n Aggression: to assault or injure another; to belittle, harm, blame, accuse, ridicule, or punish.

14. n Abasement: to surrender, comply, accept punishment, apologize, atone, etc.

15. n Blamavoidance: to avoid blame by being well-behaved and obedient.

16. n Affiliation: to form friendships and associations; to greet, join, and live with others.

17. n Rejection: to snub, ignore, or exclude another; to be aloof and indifferent.

18. n Nurturance: to nourish, aid, or protect a helpless person; to express sympathy.

19. n Succorance: to seek aid, protection, or sympathy.

20. n Play: to relax, amuse oneself; to seek diversion and entertainment.

21. n Cognizance: to satisfy curiosity.

22. n Exposition: to give information; to explain, interpret, lecture, etc.[22]

[22] In the interest of saving space, the defining terms have been edited and condensed.

Although Murray's list of motives will provide the student with a conception of the wide variety of psychogenic motives that occur, it should not be regarded as an exhaustive list. Many relatively unique motives—in addition to the more common ones which can be named and listed—are developed in any given individual.

MOTIVATIONAL PRINCIPLES

A NUMBER of different motivational principles have been formulated. Some of these will be discussed in this section.

Unpleasant Stimulation

The individual is probably never aware of tissue needs as such. But tissue needs are accompanied by unpleasant stimuli of various kinds. The need for food is associated with stimuli arising from the rhythmic contractions of the stomach—stimuli that are perceived as hunger. The need for water is associated with stimuli that arise from dryness in the mucous membranes of the throat—stimuli that are perceived as thirst. Fatigue is associated with the need for rest; tensions in the colon are perceived when there is need to defecate; tensions in the bladder are perceived when there is a need to urinate.

All of these stimuli, which are associated with tissue needs, are experienced as unpleasant or distressing. There are various unpleasant "cravings" that are associated with such specific chemical needs as the need for phosphorus or the need for calcium. Moreover, the individual may at times be aware of a generalized discomfort or craving without being aware of the kind of goal object that will relieve his distress.

Even in the case of psychogenic motives, the individual is aware of unpleasant tensions, which may or may not be perceived in relation to an anticipated goal object.

Muscular Tensions

When either biogenic or psychogenic motives are operative, tensions occur in various muscles. The individual becomes aware of tension in the striped (voluntary) muscles through kinesthetic sensory receptors; he becomes aware of tension in the smooth (involuntary) muscles through various "organic" sensory receptors. When tensions are extreme in degree, the pain receptors may also be involved. Parturition (labor) pains and many headaches, for example, have their source in stimulation of pain receptors that are associated with intense muscular tensions.

Increased Activity

When motives are operative, the general activity of the organism increases in vigor. All animals—from one-celled paramecia to albino rats to human infants and adults—become more active when motivated. In the case of the lower organisms, which depend on "accidental" gratification, and human infants, who have not yet associated specific goal objects with gratification, there is an increase in the variability, as well as in the vigor, of activity. This increased variability has survival value, since variability of behavior increases the probability of achieving "accidental" gratification. Similar increases in variability may occur when the individual is motivated by free-floating anxiety.

When goal objects have become associated with particular motives—that is, when objects have been cathected by certain needs—behavior will not be disorganized and variable but will be organized in terms of such goal objects. Yet even in goal-oriented behavior, when goals are perceived as temporarily or permanently unobtainable, variable behavior may be resumed. Of course, such variability occurs only when the strength of the perceived frustration is limited in degree; under extremely severe frustration, the individual's behavior may become rigid rather than variable.

"Emotional Motivation"

Once an emotional process has been aroused, this process will have an organizing and directive influence on behavior. The somewhat redundant term "emotional motivation" has been used to imply such an influence on the organization of behavior.

> . . . fundamental biogenic emotions (*e.g.*, fear and anger) have the same general properties as the biogenic needs; hence the necessity of including them under the topic of motivation. To be specific: (1) They tend to persist at least until the stimulus situation that arouses them is perceived to be removed (anger) or escaped (fear). (2) The emotional state grips the entire organism, especially through the involvement of autonomic functions. (3) Yet, "there are also specific forms of behavior called out by emotional stimuli.". . . (4) These emotional states also mobilize and prime the organism for certain *ends* in relation to the situation.[23]

[23] Sherif, *op. cit.*, p. 32.

Leeper, in his theoretical discussion of emotional processes, has expressed agreement with this point of view; he has stated that "emotional processes operate primarily as motives . . . they are processes which arouse, sustain, and direct activity." [24]

Need Reduction

The processes that are involved in need reduction or motive gratification are generally accompanied by pleasurable experience rather than by discomfort or distress, by muscular relaxation rather than by tension, by decreased vigor and variability rather than by energetic and restless activity. In other words, *consummatory activities have characteristics that are approximately the opposite of the characteristics of preparatory activities.*

It should be noted that individuals gain greatest pleasure from *activities that are gratifying* rather than from the state of gratification itself. Murray and Kluckhohn have stated in this connection that "it is not a tensionless state . . . which is . . . most satisfying to a healthy organism, but the *process* of reducing tension, and, other factors being equal, the degree of satisfaction is roughly proportional to the amount of tension that is reduced per unit of time." [25] Freud has stated, along similar lines, that the "raising of . . . tensions is in general felt as *unpleasure* and their lowering as *pleasure*. It is probable, however, that what is felt as pleasure or unpleasure is not the *absolute* degree of the tensions but something in the rhythm of their changes." [26]

Unconscious Motivation

Motives frequently function in the determination of the individual's behavior even when the individual has no conscious awareness of their functioning. The individual is *sometimes* aware of his motives and *sometimes* can account for his behavior in terms of them, but most frequently he will have only a vague conception of the "real reasons" for his behavior. When asked to give an account of his motives, his response is likely to involve rationalization: although he may think that he is giving an "honest" account, he will be giving only a partial

[24] Robert W. Leeper, "A Motivational Theory of Emotion to Replace 'Emotion as Disorganized Response,'" *Psychological Review, 55* (1948), 5–21. Reprinted by permission of American Psychological Association, Inc.

[25] Clyde Kluckhohn and Henry A. Murray, eds., *Personality in Nature, Society, and Culture* (New York, 1948), p. 15.

[26] Sigmund Freud, *An Outline of Psychoanalysis* (New York, 1949), p. 16. Reprinted by permission of W. W. Norton & Company, Inc. Copyright, 1949, by W. W. Norton & Company, Inc.

and distorted description of his motives. If some other person tries to explain his behavior in terms of certain unacceptable motives, he may be insulted or shocked, even though the other person's explanation may be essentially correct.

Motivational Selectivity

The term *motivational selectivity* refers to the fact that patterns of motivation operate selectively in relation to the individual's behavior. What the individual does at any given moment will be consistent with the motivational pattern that is operative at that moment. This applies to all behavior functions—to perception, to learning, to the selection of goals, to thinking, to judgment, etc. What the individual perceives and how he perceives it, what he learns in different situations, what goals he seeks and how he seeks them, on what occasions he thinks and what his conclusions are, what judgments he makes—all of these are related in a consistent way to the wants, needs, urges, impulses, hopes, ideals, and values that happen to be operative at a given time.

PERCEPTION. It was pointed out in the preceding chapter that motivation is involved in perceptual selectivity; what is perceived and how it is perceived is dependent on the motivation that happens to be operative. Some further illustrations of this relationship will be given here. A number of experimental studies bear on this problem.

Sanford presented school children with pictures to be completed and with words to which the children were to respond with the first word occurring to them. He found that the children gave many more food-responses immediately before meals (when hungry) than immediately after meals.[27]

Levine, Chein, and Murphy presented ambiguous pictures to hungry and to non-hungry college students and found that the drawings were more frequently seen as food objects by the hungry students than by the non-hungry students.[28]

An experimental study by Schafer and Murphy involved pairs of pictures which when put together as in a jigsaw puzzle became perceptually reversible in their figure-ground relations. Either half could be seen as a face while the other half functioned as background. Sub-

[27] R. N. Sanford, "The Effects of Abstinence from Food upon Imaginal Processes: a Preliminary Experiment," *Journal of Psychology*, 2 (1936), 129–36.

[28] R. Levine, I. Chein, and G. Murphy, "The Relation of the Intensity of a Need to the Amount of Perceptual Distortion," *Journal of Psychology*, *13* (1942), 283–93.

jects were trained with the pictures separately and given a money reward when one of the pair was seen as a face and a punishment (money
taken away) when the other of the pair was seen as a face. After this
training period, the pictures were combined and shown to the subjects.
The subjects perceived the "rewarded" faces much more frequently
than the "punished" faces; that is to say, the "rewarded" faces were
more frequently perceived as figures against backgrounds consisting
of the "punished" faces.[29]

These and a number of similar experiments have demonstrated that
motivation is functionally related to perception. Such findings are consistent with the organismic conception of behavior. When a particular
need or motive is operative, the adjustment of the organism—i.e., its
"mental" set—is such that objects cathected by this need are, among
the many objects available for perception, the ones most likely to be
perceived.

Perception involves the organization of motivational stimuli into
a pattern of relations with external stimuli, so that external stimuli are
interpreted in terms of the motivational elements. The meaning of
such external stimuli is a function of the relative degree of gratification
or frustration anticipated by the individual.

LEARNING. What the individual learns in a given situation is dependent on his motivation. Since different persons have different motives, and hence different perceptions, no two persons should be expected to learn the same thing in a given situation.

The psychological literature is so replete with demonstrations of
the relations between motivational processes and learning that little
evidence need be presented here. It is of interest, however, to note that
the vocabulary of the young child is primarily concerned with biogenic needs. Gesell and Thompson, for example, have reported that at
52 weeks the most frequent words in the child's vocabulary are concerned with things to eat.[30]

THINKING. Whether a particular situation becomes a problem
situation for an individual will depend partly on the nature of his motivation. For instance, the individual who is not interested in politics
will see few problems in the political area; the individual who plans to
stay at home will see no problem in the stormy weather; the individual
who has no children may see no problems in relation to child behavior.

[29] R. Schafer and G. Murphy, "The Role of Autism in a Visual Figure-
Ground Relationship," *Journal of Experimental Psychology, 32* (1943), 335–43.

[30] A. Gesell and H. Thompson, *Infant Behavior: Its Genesis and Growth*
(New York, 1943), p. 255.

A problem situation arises for the individual only when his goal-oriented activity is frustrated. A situation that is irrelevant to the individual's motivation will involve no problems for him.

Moreover, the kind of solution an individual arrives at when in a problem situation will depend on the total pattern of his motivation. For example, the hungry but penniless individual will solve his food-getting problem in a manner that is consistent with his attitudes toward stealing, begging, menial work, etc.; in order to solve this problem, one individual might prefer to steal, another to beg, and another to take any kind of "honest work" that is available.

JUDGMENT.   Judgment is an evaluational activity that involves making a choice between two or more alternatives—a choice between two possible actions, a choice between possible goal objects, a choice between different values that are in conflict with one another, etc. This procedure is dependent not only on temporary motivational patterns but also on the enduring social motives (e.g., values, ideals, beliefs, attitudes) of the individual. *Judgment is never completely objective, never completely just.* The person who makes a judgment may have the conscious impression of objectivity, but he will nevertheless make this judgment in terms of his particular beliefs, ideals, values, etc.

Many of the enduring values function at an unconscious level, so that the basis of the individual's judgment will seldom be explicitly known by himself or by others. The insistence of the democracies upon the importance of the jury system and representative government is consistent with this principle; the vote of the many is more likely than the decision of a single individual to represent balanced objectivity of judgment, since it will involve many different patterns of motivation rather than only one such pattern.

Development of Psychogenic Motives

It has been noted that psychogenic motives develop through social learning. Very early in the life of the individual, particular persons, particular objects, and particular activities become associated with the gratification or the frustration of pre-existing biogenic motives. In other words, certain persons, objects, or activities serve in this early period as *means* of gratifying or frustrating biogenic needs.

If such means are associated with gratification they acquire positive value for the individual; if they are associated with frustration they acquire negative value for the individual; that is to say, *means* become positively or negatively cathected, and begin to function as positive and negative motives. Later, psychogenic motives themselves may serve as the basis for the development of further psychogenic motives. Thus an increasingly complex superstructure of motivation develops.

Allport has stressed the development of psychogenic motives in his treatment of the *functional autonomy of motives*.[31] The concept of functional autonomy emphasizes that although new motives develop through association with pre-existing ones these newly developed motives will continue to function in the absence of the antecedent ones from which they developed. For example, although the original beginnings of a motive of social approval may have developed during the feeding of the infant, the motive of social approval will subsequently function when the individual is not hungry.

> The pursuit of literature, the development of good taste in clothes, the use of cosmetics, the acquiring of an automobile, strolls in the public park, or a winter in Miami, may first serve, let us say, the interests of sex. But every one of these instrumental activities may become an interest in itself, held for a lifetime, long after the erotic motive has been laid away in lavender. People often find that they have lost allegiance to their original aims because of their deliberate preference for the many ways of achieving them.[32]

Woodworth expressed a similar understanding of the development of psychogenic motives in his principle that *mechanisms* may become *drives*.[33] By *mechanisms* Woodworth referred to activities that eventuate in gratification or frustration.

Dynamics of Motivational Patterns

The term *motivational pattern* refers to the organization of all of the motives that are operative in a given individual at a given time. Probably at no time does a single motive function alone. Many motives combine to determine the quality and direction of the individual's be-

[31] Gordon W. Allport, *Personality: a Psychological Interpretation* (New York, 1937), pp. 191–207. (The concept of functional autonomy is seriously at variance with the concept of sublimation and, in fact, with the general conception that defense mechanisms can operate as methods of relieving anxiety. It seems probable that the concept of functional autonomy should be discarded. For further discussion of this issue, see Chap. XIV.)

[32] Gordon W. Allport, *Personality: a Psychological Interpretation* (New York, 1937), p. 197. Reprinted by permission of Henry Holt and Company, Inc. Copyright, 1937, by Henry Holt and Company, Inc.

[33] Woodworth, *op. cit.*

havior at any particular moment. The hungry man not only eats or seeks food; he eats or seeks food in a manner consistent with other motives that are active at the time.

At any given time, the behavior of the individual is organized primarily in terms of the strongest motive in the total pattern. Such a strong motive is termed a *prepotent* motive. If the prepotent motive is sufficiently intense, the remaining motives in the pattern may become relatively insignificant—although perhaps never entirely uninfluential—in the determination of behavior.

Motivational patterns are in the process of continual change. Certain motives are increasing while others are decreasing in relative strength. Motives that are in the process of being gratified are decreasing, while others, through prolonged frustration, are increasing in strength. Some motives are in the process of being developed, while others are being "unlearned" as a function of experience. New goal objects are continually becoming endowed with varying degrees of positive or negative cathexis. All of these changes are reflected in moment-to-moment reorganizations of the motivational pattern.

PERIODICITY OF MOTIVES. The biogenic motives manifest periodic cycles of intensity. The hunger cycle, for instance, is fundamentally determined by the diminishing supply of "raw materials" for metabolism; hunger increases until it reaches an intensity sufficient to require activity that will gratify the need. The cycle recurs as a function of the rate of metabolic activity and of the amount of food intake on any one occasion. The rhythm may be influenced, however, by social regulations and conventions, as well as by numerous other factors. That is to say, individual differences in the hunger cycle may be the outcome of both biological and social factors.

Other biogenic motives (e.g., thirst, need for oxygen, need for sleep or rest, the sex drive) recur according to a similar principle of periodicity. It is also probable that many psychogenic motives manifest cycles of intensity, although the regularity of such cycles may be much less evident than it is in the case of biogenic motives.

REGRESSION TO BIOGENIC MOTIVATION. Biogenic motives, which are intimately related to the survival of the organism, are more fundamental than psychogenic motives, not only in terms of their origin but also in terms of prepotence. Psychogenic motives can be deprived of gratification over relatively long periods of time without incurring damage to the organism as such or to the personality integration of the individual. Moreover, they are much more amenable to substitute gratification than are the biogenic needs, and indeed may cease to function as motives unless they are occasionally gratified.

Accordingly, when the individual is confronted with the necessity of gratifying either a biogenic motive or a psychogenic motive (the one being incompatible with the other), the individual's choice is usually to gratify the biogenic motive. When biogenic needs have suffered intense frustration, the individual will forego his principles (values, morals, self-respect, etc.) in order to gain biogenic gratification.

It is authentically reported that during the fascist occupation of Greece 14- or 15-year-old . . . girls yielded themselves to the hated enemy soldiers merely to secure a little bread for themselves and their families. In Italy and elsewhere, mothers and sisters went to the extent of sending little boys or girls to solicit the sexually deprived men who had food, as one means of just obtaining some food.[34]

The gratification of biological needs by means of procedures that contradict the individual's "higher" social motives may be termed *regression to biogenic motivation*.

MASLOW'S THEORY OF MOTIVATION. The essential emphasis of the concept of regression to biogenic motivation is elaborated in Maslow's theory of motivation. According to this theory, motives may be related to a hierarchy in terms of the degree of their prepotence. Motives that are "lower" in the hierarchy are said to take precedence over motives occupying "higher" or less fundamental positions in the hierarchy.

Maslow has classified motives into five categories, which may be listed as follows, from the most basic (lowest in the hierarchy) to the least basic (highest in the hierarchy).

1. Physiological needs (hunger, thirst, etc.).
2. Safety needs (protection from harm or injury).
3. Love needs (affection, warmth, belongingness).
4. Esteem needs (self-respect, social approval, etc.).
5. Self-actualization (achieving maximum development of one's potentialities).

Until physiological needs have been gratified or reduced to a reasonable minimum, the individual's behavior will be organized primarily in terms of these needs. The individual will sacrifice safety, love, esteem, or self-actualization in order to satisfy these needs. Once

[34] Sherif, *op. cit.*, pp. 88-9.

these needs have been gratified, the individual's behavior will be organized in terms of the need for safety. Once the safety need has been gratified, the individual will be motivated in terms of the need for love, affection, and belongingness. When these needs have been gratified, the individual will be motivated by the esteem needs, that is, by the needs for "a stable, firmly based, (usually) high evaluation of themselves, for self-respect, or self-esteem, and for the esteem of others." [35] If the esteem needs should be gratified—a rare occurrence in modern society—the individual will be motivated by the need for self-actualization. "A musician must make music, an artist must paint, a poet must write, if he is to be ultimately happy. What a man *can* be, he *must* be." [36]

In terms of Maslow's theory, "gratification becomes as important a concept as deprivation in motivation theory, for it releases the organism from the domination of a relatively more physiological need, permitting thereby the emergence of other more social goals." [37]

Maslow's theory is consistent with the concept of regression to biogenic motivation. It renders understandable the so-called bestial nature of man when man is deprived of his most basic needs. As Maslow has admitted, however, there are exceptions to the operation of the hierarchical prepotence of motives: the "poet in the garret," the saint who foregoes "creature comforts" in order to carry out his mission, the hero in battle who sacrifices his own safety in order to remain loyal to his comrades. These and other examples can be mentioned as exceptions to the general principle, but the principle seems to apply, in many cases, to the routine living of "normal" individuals.

BEHAVIORAL SIGNIFICANCE OF SEXUAL AND AGGRESSIVE MOTIVES

IN ORDINARY circumstances, some of man's strongest motives—motives that are highly necessary to the organism's survival—are satisfied gratuitously.[38] This is especially true of the needs for air

[35] Abraham H. Maslow, "A Theory of Human Motivation," *Psychological Review*, 50 (1943), p. 381. Reprinted by permission of American Psychological Association, Inc.

[36] *Ibid.*, p. 382.

[37] *Ibid.*, p. 375.

[38] Sherif, *op. cit.*, p. 30.

and for water, which, under ordinary circumstances, are so readily gratified, with so little cost in effort, that most individuals have little awareness of the strength of these needs in the life economy of the organism. Because they are so readily gratified, these needs are minimally significant for human adjustment.

Other motives, although they are relatively less necessary for the maintenance of life, assume an important position in the psychology of human adjustment. They acquire a behavioral significance that is highly disproportionate to their importance for biological survival. Among such motives may be mentioned the sexual motive and the aggressive motive.

The Sexual Motive

The unusual behavioral significance of the sexual motive is probably attributable to the fact that it is subjected to social regulation and restrictions of a moral nature. In early life the individual is punished for sexual behavior and for the expression of sexual interests; on the basis of such punishment, the individual represses his sexual motivation. He is expected to maintain this repression throughout childhood and during the adolescent period. But at the time of marriage he is expected to engage readily in sexual expression, as if no repression had ever occurred.

Moreover, the culture is replete with stimuli that constantly remind the individual of sexual motivation during the periods when he is expected to maintain a strict repression of his impulses. Such stimuli occur in the forms of art, romantic literature, movies, plays, etc.

The individual may encounter difficulties of adjustment at either extreme of the repression continuum: he may have difficulty in *controlling* his impulses when he is expected to do so, or he may have difficulty in *expressing* his impulses after marriage if he has developed repression of too exacting a degree.

If similar restrictions were imposed on the need for oxygen, the deprivation of which would quickly result in death, the behavioral significance of this motive would far outweigh that of the sexual motive. There is experimental and descriptive evidence that under conditions of severe food deprivation hunger assumes a behavioral significance greater than that of sex under similar conditions of deprivation. For instance, in a Minnesota experiment dealing with the effects of semi-starvation, subjects became preoccupied with food and lost interest in sexual topics.[39] When men or women are hungry, their psychogenic motives break down to a degree seldom reported in the case of sex deprivations; although the ordinary man in our society would stop short of committing rape, hungry men are reported to steal and commit murder in order to obtain food.

The Aggressive Motive

The aggressive motive, which occurs as a response to the frustration of other motives, has high behavioral significance, since, like the sexual motive, it is subjected to much social regulation. Direct aggression by children against their parents, or by any subordinate against a superior, is more or less regularly punished. There are, moreover, legal sanctions against many forms of aggression; e.g., murder or assault.

The permissible forms of aggression differ from one society to another and from one time to another in the same society. Thus it is regarded as appropriate in our society to commit aggression indirectly through commercial competition and through various forms of friendly rivalry; but it is regarded as immoral and childish to strike another person or to commit physical injury. It is "all right" to humiliate another person verbally, so long as one does not employ hands, feet, or physical weapons against him. In some societies, where beliefs in magic and witchcraft prevail, verbal and symbolic aggressions are probably regarded as more dangerous than physical violence.

In our society there are moral and legal restrictions against killing another person, but in time of war it is regarded as the citizen's duty to kill other human beings and to wreak destruction upon their property.

Hatred or hostility may be directed against certain classes of human beings but not against others. At one time it is appropriate to hate the people of a particular nation, but at other times these people are expected to be loved so that hatred can be directed against the people of some other nation.

Children in our society are taught that it is wrong to express hostility against parents or other authorities, but at the same time they are expected to live in fear lest their behavior bring upon themselves the aggression of such parents or authorities.

Since the aggressive motive is subjected to such complicated social regulations, this motive has acquired great significance for human adjustment.

[39] Sherif, *op. cit.*, pp. 78–82.

SUMMARY

MOTIVATION is a central concept in behavior dynamics. The term *motive* is a generic term; it implies such specific concepts as need, drive, desire, wish, urge, instinct, impulse, etc. Motivation is a useful concept for understanding the functional relationships that occur between processes of the organism and external stimuli to which the organism adjusts.

The organism maintains equilibrium or dynamic stability in its functional relations with the internal and external environments. At the physiological level, this maintenance of equilibrium is termed *homeostasis*. At the behavioral level, this maintenance of equilibrium is termed *adjustment*.

A *need integrate* involves (1) the source or character of the motivational stimulus, (2) the quality of behavior tendency that is aroused in the organism, and (3) the object in relation to which such a behavior tendency is aroused. The terms *need, source,* and *drive* refer to the character of the motivational stimulus. The terms *mode, aim,* and *instrumental act* refer to the quality of the behavior tendency. The term *object* refers to anything in relation to which behavior may be directed for the satisfaction of a need.

The terms *cathexis* and *valence* refer to the relation between a need and an object, or between a person and an object. Cathexis or valence is *positive* if the object is liked or approached, *negative* if the object is disliked or feared. The term *motivational pattern* refers to the organization of all of the motives that are operative in a given individual at a given time.

Motives may be classified in terms of their origin and in terms of the character of activities in relation to goal objects. Biogenic motives originate in the biological nature of the organism; psychogenic motives originate through learning. Positive motives are associated with activity that establishes and maintains relations with goal objects; negative motives are associated with activity that destroys relations with goal objects.

Any catalog of human motives will involve an oversimplification of the unique processes of living organisms. How a biogenic motive is actually expressed may have a multitude of psychogenic determinants; and the peculiar qualities of behavior that is based primarily on psychogenic motivation may have some degree of biogenic determination. Such complex determination must be kept in mind when lists of motives are made on the basis of any principle of classification.

Certain principles of motivation are relatively well established. Biogenic motives arise on the basis of tissue needs. Motives are experienced, if at all, as discomforting stimuli. Muscular tensions, in both the striped and smooth muscles, regularly occur when motives are operative. There is also an increase in the activity of motivated organisms. If goal objects have been cathected and if no frustration is involved, such activity is relatively well organized; otherwise, such activity is characterized by high variability.

Emotions, which arise as a function of the frustration or the gratification of motives, have an organizing and directive influence on behavior; that is to say, emotions function as motives. Need reduction (gratification) is associated with pleasurable experience, with muscular relaxation, and with a decrease in activity. Many motives function unconsciously; they operate to arouse, sustain, and direct activity even though the individual is not aware of their operation.

Many behavior processes are related to motives. What the individual perceives and how he perceives it; what the individual learns or whether he learns anything; whether the individual thinks and what conclusions he reaches; what choices the individual makes when judgment is necessary—all of these outcomes are dependent on the pattern of motivation which functions at the time.

Psychogenic motives develop through the association of activities, persons, or objects with the gratification or the frustration of pre-existing motives. Means to previous ends, in other words, become ends in themselves.

Motivational patterns are in the process of continual change. Biogenic motives, particularly, and psychogenic motives, in some degree, manifest periodicity: they wax and wane in intensity as they undergo periods of deprivation and as they achieve gratification.

When the organism is severely deprived of biogenic gratification, psychogenic motives (such as values or standards) lose their accustomed influence in the determination of behavior. This may be referred to as *regression to biogenic motivation*. Maslow's theory of motivation extends this principle by the conception of a hierarchy of motivational prepotency. The more basic motives are said to determine behavior so long as they remain ungratified; the "higher" human motives are said to influence behavior significantly only after more fundamental motives have been gratified.

The survival value to the organism is not a satisfactory criterion of the behavioral significance of different motives. In our society, in which there is relatively widespread gratification of many basic biogenic motives, the sexual motive and the aggressive motive assume particularly high behavioral significance, since these motives are subjected to strict, and often inconsistent, social regulation.

The following chapter will be devoted to the discussion of some aspects of personality, the understanding of which will be helpful as a basis for considering the material of subsequent chapters.

▶ **Suggested Readings**

Allport, G. W. *Personality: a Psychological Interpretation.* New York, 1937. Chap. vii, pp. 190–212.

Cameron, N. and Magaret, Ann. *Behavior Pathology.* Boston, 1951. Pp. 32–44.

Child, I. L. and Whiting, J. W. M. "Effects of Goal Attainment: Relaxation versus Renewed Striving," *Journal of Abnormal and Social Psychology,* 45 (1950), 667–81.

Duffy, Elizabeth. "Leeper's 'Motivational Theory of Emotion,'" *Psychological Review,* 55 (1948), 324–8.

Freud, S. "Instincts and Their Vicissitudes," *Collected Papers.* London, 1950. IV, 60–83.

Hastorf, A. H. and Knutson, A. L. "Motivation, Perception and Attitude Change," *Psychological Review,* 56 (1949), 88–94.

Kilby, R. W. "Psychoneurosis in Times of Trouble: Evidence for a Hierarchy of Motives," *Journal of Abnormal and Social Psychology,* 43 (1948), 544–5.

Klineberg, O. *Social Psychology.* New York, 1940. Chaps. v and vi, pp. 66–165.

Koch, S. "The Current Status of Motivational Psychology," *Psychological Review,* 58 (1951), 147–54.

Lee, Dorothy. "Are Basic Needs Ultimate?" *Journal of Abnormal and Social Psychology,* 43 (1948), 391–5.

Leeper, R. W. "A Motivational Theory of Emotion to Replace 'Emotion as Disorganized Response,'" *Psychological Review,* 55 (1948), 5–21.

McClelland, D. C. *Personality.* New York, 1951. Chaps. xi–xiii, pp. 383–525.

Maslow, A. H. "A Theory of Human Motivation," *Psychological Review,* 50 (1943), 370–96.

Murphy, G. "The Freeing of Intelligence," *Psychological Bulletin,* 42 (1945), 1–19.

Murphy, G. *Personality: a Biosocial Approach to Origins and Structure.* New York, 1947. Chaps. v–vi, pp. 86–129.

Murray, H. A. *Explorations in Personality.* New York, 1938. Chaps. ii–iii, pp. 36–242.

Rethlingshafer, Dorothy. "Experimental Evidence for Functional Autonomy of Motives," *Psychological Review, 50* (1943), 397–407.

Sherif, M. *An Outline of Social Psychology.* New York, 1948. Chaps. ii–iv, pp. 9–90.

Snygg, D. and Combs, A. W. *Individual Behavior.* New York, 1949. Chap. iv, pp. 52–77.

Stagner, R. "Homeostasis as a Unifying Concept in Personality Theory," *Psychological Review, 58* (1951), 5–17.

Tolman, E. C. *Purposive Behavior in Animals and Men.* New York, 1932. Chaps. xviii–xx, pp. 271–317.

Tolman, E. C. "A Drive-Conversion Diagram," *Psychological Review, 50* (1943), 503–13.

Tolman, E. C. "The Nature and Functioning of Wants," *Psychological Review, 56* (1949), 357–69.

Waters, R. H. and Blackwood, D. F. "The Applicability of Motivational Criteria to Emotions," *Psychological Review, 56,* (1949), 351–6.

Webb, W. B. "A Motivational Theory of Emotions . . . ," *Psychological Review, 55* (1948), 329–35.

Young, P. T. *Emotion in Man and Animal.* New York, 1943. Pp. 87–155.

Young, P. T. "Appetite, Palatability, and Feeding Habit: a Critical Review," *Psychological Bulletin, 45* (1948), 289–320.

Young, P. T. "Food-seeking Drive, Affective Process, and Learning," *Psychological Review, 56* (1949), 98–121.

Young, P. T. "Emotion as Disorganized Response—a Reply to Professor Leeper," *Psychological Review, 56* (1949), 184–91.

CHAPTER Three

Aspects of Personality

Iₙ ᴀ previous chapter (Chap. I) we have noted that the personality processes of the individual are not merely passive recipients of stimulation. Each individual has his own unique pattern of relatively consistent behavior tendencies (motives in particular), which influence his perception of the environment, and which therefore enter into the determination of his behavior.

DEFINITION OF PERSONALITY

Aʟʟᴘᴏʀᴛ has formulated a definition of personality which is consistent with an organismic conception of behavior.

Personality is the dynamic organization within the individual of

[1] Schopenhauer, in *The Story of Philosophy*, Will Durant (New York, 1926), p. 339.
[2] Sigmund Freud, *New Introductory Lectures on Psycho-Analysis* (New York, 1933), p. 108. Reprinted by permission of W. W. Norton & Company, Inc. Copyright, 1933, by Sigmund Freud.

those psychophysical systems that determine his unique adjustments to his environment.[3]

This definition embodies a number of points that are worthy of emphasis:

1. That the determinants of behavior are centered in the individual, rather than in the external environment;
2. That behavior is organismic, rather than consisting of isolated processes;
3. That the "mental" and the "physical" are inseparably interrelated, as emphasized by the use of the term *psychophysical;*
4. That each person's environment and his adjustments to it are unique—depending, as we have seen, on his ever changing perceptual patterns;
5. That the personality processes—motives, generalized habits, traits, etc.—are continually changing, continually organizing and reorganizing in the interest of maintaining equilibrium.

Since all of these points have previously been discussed, they need not be given detailed treatment here. It is sufficient for our purposes to note that personality cannot be observed directly; it can only be *inferred* on the basis of the observable adjustments of the individual. "The systems that constitute personality" function as "*determining tendencies,* and when aroused by suitable stimuli provoke those adjustive and expressive acts by which the personality comes to be known." [4]

The remainder of the present chapter will be devoted to a discussion of two major aspects of personality which are of fundamental significance in psychoanalytic dynamics.

LEVELS OF CONSCIOUSNESS

OF THE total pattern of personality functions, only a minor portion is consciously perceived at any given moment. Through attentive efforts, many more aspects of the pattern may become conscious. But there are some aspects of the pattern which continue to function unconsciously, in spite of efforts to direct attention upon

[3] Gordon W. Allport, *Personality: a Psychological Interpretation* (New York, 1937), p. 48.
[4] *Ibid.,* pp. 48-9.

them; only by using specialized techniques, such as psychoanalytic free-association, can they be reinstated in consciousness, if at all. Freud distinguished among three different levels of consciousness—namely, the *conscious* level, the *preconscious* level, and the *unconscious* level.

Conscious Functions

As Freud has stated, our "consciousness is in general a very highly fugitive condition. What is conscious is conscious only for a moment." [5] When attention is directed onto some particular aspect of the environment (external or internal), there will be a momentary "illumination" of the features that are in the focus of attention. "It is," according to Murray, "as if . . . a spotlight of varying dimensions moved about the brain, revealing first one and then another sector of successive, functionally-related mental events." [6] In the periphery of attention—that is, outside the point of its sharpest focus—aspects of the environment will be only vaguely perceived, though such peripheral events may at the next moment enter the focus of attention, and therefore become the clearest contents of consciousness.

Attentive adjustments of the organism, then, are important determinants of what aspects of external and internal reality will occupy the "arena of consciousness" at any given moment. Such attentive adjustments are, as we have seen (Chap. II), a function of the motivation that happens to be operative. Any object in the external surroundings, any memory of previous perceptions which can be recalled, any ache or pain or muscular strain, may become momentarily, or for a prolonged period, the major content of an individual's awareness.

Preconscious Functions

Memories of previous perceptions, or stimuli arising from internal functions that are operative at any given moment, are said to be *preconscious* if they can become conscious through normal attentive adjustments, or through a normal "effort of the will." Preconscious functions are, in other words, readily accessible to consciousness; they can be recalled to consciousness, or reinstated in consciousness, whenever it suits the individual's purpose to become attentive to them.

. . . the greater part of what we call conscious knowledge must in any case exist for very considerable periods of time in a condition of latency, that is to say, of unconsciousness, of not being ap-

---

[5] Sigmund Freud, *An Outline of Psychoanalysis* (New York, 1949), p. 37.
[6] Henry A. Murray, *Explorations in Personality* (New York, 1938), p. 51.

prehended by the mind. . . . On the other hand, we know for certain that they have abundant points of contact with conscious mental processes; on being submitted to a certain method of operation they may be transformed into or replaced by conscious processes, and all the categories which we employ to describe conscious mental acts, such as ideas, purposes, resolutions and so forth, can be applied to them. Indeed, of many of these latent states we have to assert that the only point in which they differ from states which are conscious is just in the lack of consciousness of them.[7]

Some processes become conscious easily; they may then cease to be conscious, but can become conscious once more without any trouble: as people say, they can be reproduced or remembered. . . . Everything unconscious that behaves in this way, that can easily exchange the unconscious condition for the conscious one, is . . . described as "capable of entering consciousness," or as *preconscious.*[8]

These quotations make clear Freud's conception of the preconscious functions as comprising those functions which are readily accessible to consciousness, or which are ready to become conscious functions whenever attention is focused upon them.

Unconcious Functions

Unconscious functions are functions that cannot under ordinary circumstances become the contents of conscious perception. Some unconscious functions consist of the "unthinkable" perceptions of a previous time which have been repressed; other unconscious functions may never have been conscious during the lifetime of the individual. (There are many "physiological" functions, for example, of which the individual never becomes aware so long as these functions continue to operate normally.)

. . . we call a process "unconscious" when we have to assume that it was active *at a certain time,* although *at that time* we knew nothing about it.[9]

There are . . . mental processes or mental material which have no . . . easy access to consciousness, but which must be inferred,

[7] Sigmund Freud, *Collected Papers,* translated by Joan Riviere (London, 1950), IV, 99–101. Reprinted by permission of The Hogarth Press, Ltd.
[8] Freud, *An Outline of Psychoanalysis,* pp. 37–8.
[9] Freud, *New Introductory Lectures . . . ,* p. 100.

discovered, and translated into conscious form in the manner that has been described. It is for such material that we reserve the name of the unconscious proper. . . . What . . . is unconscious can, as a result of our efforts, be made conscious, though in the process we may have an impression that we are overcoming what are often very strong resistances. . . . The amount of effort needed, by which we estimate the resistance against the material becoming conscious, varies in magnitude in each individual case.[10]

Unconscious functions, then, are functions that require specialized techniques (e.g., psychoanalytic free-association) for their reinstatement in consciousness. They cannot become objects of conscious perception through the normal attentive adjustments of the individual.

Levels of Consciousness: a Continuum

Rather than considering levels of consciousness in terms of three distinguishable categories—conscious, preconscious, and unconscious—it seems appropriate to represent them as an infinite number of points along a continuum. This continuum may be considered to extend from the least readily accessible of the unconscious functions to the most readily accessible (already conscious) functions. According to this point of view, the terms *conscious, preconscious,* and *unconscious* may be regarded as applying to *zones* along the continuum.

The student is already familiar with the fact that there are degrees of accessibility within the preconscious range. Some ideas "come" quite easily; others may "come" only after extended concentration of attention. A "forgotten" name may escape conscious efforts to recall it, only to be recognized the moment somebody else mentions it. What is known regarding methods of "measuring" retention of learned material is consistent with these observations: lower scores are made on recall tests than on recognition tests; and lower scores are made on recognition tests than by the method of relearning. In other words, although the learned material is available, and some portions of it can be brought to consciousness by the mere direction of attention upon them (recall method), other portions of it resist recall and can be brought to consciousness only through the method of recognition or through the method of relearning.

Within the unconscious range of the continuum the student is likely to have had little experience. Here it becomes necessary to refer

[10] Freud, *An Outline of Psychoanalysis,* pp. 38–9.

to clinical findings. In the process of psychoanalysis, for example, some unconscious functions are "uncovered" sooner than others; throughout the period of analysis, which may extend over several months, new unconscious material continues to find its way into the patient's consciousness. If all unconscious materials were equally accessible (or equally difficult to reinstate in consciousness), one would expect that at some point during psychoanalysis *all* of the unconscious material would *suddenly* become conscious, as if a barrier had finally collapsed. Since this sudden release does not occur—since the unconscious materials are reinstated little by little—it seems clear that the unconscious range of the continuum, like the preconscious range, is characterized by numerous degrees of accessibility to conscious perception. It becomes highly reasonable, then, to assume that there are not three but an infinite number of different levels of consciousness.

Evidences of Unconscious Functions

Since the student will have no direct knowledge of his own unconscious functions, it becomes necessary to describe some of the sources of evidence that such functions occur.

POST-HYPNOTIC SUGGESTION. A subject under hypnosis can be told that he will at a given time, or upon receiving a particular signal, carry out a prescribed act. When the hypnotic state has been abolished the subject will, in response to the predetermined signal, behave in the manner previously suggested. The behavior of the subject is said to be in response to *post-hypnotic suggestion.*

A subject who carries into action such a post-hypnotic suggestion frequently *has no conscious knowledge of his motivation for doing so.* He merely behaves in the prescribed manner without understading the basis of his behavior. The hypnotist knows, however, that this motivation involves a "mental set" which was established during the hypnotic state.

The doctor enters the hospital ward, puts his umbrella in the corner, hypnotizes one of the patients and says to him: "I'm going out now. When I come in again, you will come to meet me with my umbrella open and hold it over my head." The doctor and his assistants then leave the ward. As soon as they come back, the patient, who is no longer under hypnosis, carries out exactly the instructions that were given him while he was hypnotized. The doctor questions him: "What's this you're doing? What's the meaning of all this?" The patient is clearly embarrassed. He makes some lame remark such as: "I only thought, doctor, as it's raining outside you'd open your umbrella in the room before you went out." . . . It is clear to the spectators that he is in ignorance of his real motive. We, however, know what it is, for we were present when the suggestion was made to him which he is now carrying out, while he himself knows nothing of the fact that it is at work in him.[11]

RESISTANCE IN PSYCHOTHERAPY. The psychoanalytic theory of repression (and of the unconscious) had its origin in the observation of the *resistance* that occurs during psychotherapy.

The doctrine of repression . . . is nothing but a theoretical formulation of a phenomenon which may be observed to recur as often as one undertakes an analysis of a neurotic without resorting to hypnosis. One notices a resistance then making itself evident in opposition to the work of analysis and inducing a failure to recall memories in order to frustrate it.[12]

Freud regarded resistance as a sign of a conflict between "a force . . . which is trying to express something, and another which is striving to prevent its expression."[13] In other words, *unconscious* impulses that are about to become conscious are resisted or repressed. "The resistance can only be," according to Freud, "a manifestation of the ego, which carried through the repression at one time or other and is now endeavoring to keep it up."[14]

Resistance may take manifold forms:

The patient . . . says nothing comes into his head, then that so much comes into his head that he can't grasp any of it. Then we observe . . . that he is giving in to his critical objections, first to this, then to that; he betrays it by the long pauses which occur in his talk. At last he admits that he really cannot say something, he is ashamed to. . . . Or else, he has thought of something but it concerns someone else and not himself. . . . Or else, what he has

[11] Sigmund Freud, *Collected Papers*, edited by James Strachey (London, 1950), V, 381. Reprinted by permission of The Hogarth Press, Ltd.
[12] Sigmund Freud, *Collected Papers*, translated by Joan Riviere (London, 1950), I, 297–8. Reprinted by permission of The Hogarth Press, Ltd.
[13] Freud, *New Introductory Lectures* . . . , p. 26.
[14] *Ibid.*, p. 97.

just thought of is really too unimportant, too stupid and too absurd. . . .[15]

. . . all accidental occurrences arising during the treatment are made use of by the patient to interfere with it, anything which could distract him or deter him from it, every hostile expression of opinion from anyone in his circle whom he can regard as an authority, any chance organic illness or one complicating the neurosis; indeed, he even converts every improvement in his condition into a motive for slackening his efforts.[16]

Resistance, like repression of which it is a manifestation, operates unconsciously. The patient consciously believes that he wants to be cured, that he is co-operating as well as he can; but the resistance functions in spite of his conscious intentions.

PARAPRAXES. The term *parapraxis* refers to symptomatic actions, such as unconsciously motivated "slips" in speech or writing, inability to recall another person's name, forgetting one's promises or resolutions, mistakes in the details of one's actions, etc. Such unconsciously motivated actions have been described at length in Freud's *Psychopathology of Everyday Life*.

The individual consciously perceives such parapraxes as "mistakes" or as "failures," since he is not aware of the motivation that underlies them. Thus, the chairman of a committee may say: "The meeting will come to odor" (when he consciously intends to say "order"), on the basis of a suppressed or repressed fear that the meeting is going to "raise a stink" in relation to some issue that is embarrassing to him. The wife may lose or misplace her wedding ring and be consciously disturbed by the loss, though the loss may itself be based upon a repressed desire that the marriage be dissolved.

It was a triumph for the interpretative art of psychoanalysis when it succeeded in demonstrating that certain common mental acts of normal people . . . had a *meaning*, which was unknown to the subject but which could easily be discovered by analytic means. The phenomena in question were such events as the temporary forgetting of familiar words and names, forgetting to carry out

[15] Sigmund Freud, *A General Introduction to Psycho-Analysis* (New York, 1935), p 254. Reprinted by permission of Liveright Publishing Corporation. Copyright, R 1948, by Susie Hoch, 1935, by Edward L. Bernays.
[16] *Ibid.*, p. 257.

prescribed tasks, everyday slips of the tongue and of the pen, mis-readings, losses and mislayings of objects, certain mistakes, instances of apparently accidental self-injury . . . and so on. All of these . . . were shown to be strictly determined and were revealed as an expression of the subject's suppressed intentions or as a result of a clash between two intentions one of which was permanently or temporarily unconscious.[17]

DREAM INTERPRETATION.   Dreams were understood by Freud as symbolic attempts to gratify unconscious wishes, the tensions arising from which might interfere with the continuation of sleep. The psychoanalytic interpretation of dreams, by the method of free association, has revealed knowledge of unconscious functions. "In fact," according to Freud, "the . . . better part of what we know of the processes in the unconscious levels of the mind is derived from the interpretation of dreams." [18]

While the *manifest content* (what is remembered on waking) may provide no evidence of wish-fulfillment, the different elements of this recalled material may, through free association, reveal evidence of *symbolic* gratification of *unconscious* motives. Such symbolic gratification becomes possible on the basis of the "relaxation of repression" which occurs during sleep.

The process of free association has been described as follows:

> . . . we ask the dreamer . . . to free himself from the impression of the manifest dream, to switch his attention from the dream as a whole to individual parts of its content, and to tell us one after another the things that occur to him in connection with these parts, what associations come into his mind when he turns his mental eye on to each of them separately.[19]

The full significance of the method can hardly be understood without experiencing an actual dream in the process of being interpreted. One such example can be cited here.

> The patient, who suffered from "nervousness, numbness and muscle-ache in the back, and disturbing dreams," had been a radio operator on a bombing plane, and had endured numerous traumatic

---

[17] Freud, *Collected Papers*, V, 113.
[18] *Ibid.*, p. 114.
[19] Freud, *New Introductory Lectures* . . . , p. 20.

experiences connected with his combat missions. He reported having a recurrent dream, whose manifest content was meaningless to him, but from which he would "wake up in a cold sweat." When asked to describe his dream in detail, he said:

"I know it goes around and around. Sometimes the circles get larger, like when a raindrop drops in water and makes circles. Sometimes it goes around like a fan belt—about the size of a belt that would be used on a thrasher; it seems to be a large one. It appears gray to me. There's quite a bit of emotion attached to it; that of course means it scares me." (Pause.) "That's what it reminds me of—a raindrop hits the water and it spreads in concentric circles; there is one circle within the other."

When asked what the idea of a circle brought to his mind, the patient said: "An O is circular. The sun and moon are likewise circular. Shells are circular—and something I remember: my dreams remind me of ether! Have you ever seen the ether represented?—how a radio sends out waves in concentric circles? In fact, I wouldn't be surprised if that's what it is. I know one thing: radio is going to drive me nuts some day. I like it, but it's hard on your nerves."

This sort of insight frequently occurs when a patient is in the process of free-associating from elements of his dream. Upon the discovery by the patient of the previously unconscious meaning of a dream, or of a part of a dream, the dream is unlikely to recur. The patient whose dream is described above reported after a period of several weeks that he no longer experienced this dream.

NEUROTIC SYMPTOMS. Neurotic symptoms were interpreted by Freud as symbolic gratifications of unconscious motives, as symbolic measures to prevent such gratification, or, more usually, as compromise measures representing both aspects of conflicting motivation.[20] Symptoms, in other words, were regarded as jointly determined by conflicting motives, one or more of which functioned unconsciously. For example, symptoms might express symbolically the conflict between sexual motivation and superego motivation—that is, between sexual impulses and moral values. The meanings of the symptoms will, of course, not be consciously known to the patient.

> . . . the meaning of the symptoms is unknown to the sufferer . . . analysis invariably shows that these symptoms are derived

[20] Freud, *An Outline of Psychoanalysis*, p. 85.

from unconscious mental processes which can, however, under various favorable conditions, become conscious. . . . The fact that it is possible to find meaning in neurotic symptoms by means of analytic interpretation is an irrefutable proof of the existence —or, if you prefer it, of the necessity for assuming the existence— of unconscious mental processes.[21]

An interesting example of the symbolism that is involved in neurotic symptoms is provided by the "numbness and muscle-ache in the back" of the patient whose dream was described in the preceding section.

> Upon being asked to describe his "back trouble" in detail, the patient gave the following description: "My back did hurt right after the wreck. I couldn't pick up anything after the wreck. It didn't hurt so much—it was just a lack of ability to pick up things; of course it did hurt some too." (Some irrelevant details, referring to medical treatments and tests, were related at this point.)
>
> "Seems to me by that time my back had started hurting more. There were three or four days when it didn't give me much trouble—a sort of numbing ache—the pain isn't in one little spot. It's a dull ache, I'd say, and a sort of numbness. I believe it hurts more in the morning than at night. It keeps me conscious of it during the day now; I'm nearly always conscious of it now. I felt my tension had something to do with it too. It's just a dull ache and it feels numb. Sometimes it aches—seems to spread more than at other times.
>
> "Have you ever flown any? You've heard of the working of a beam—a radio beam. It seems on one side of a beam you have an "A" and on the other side you have an "N." Sometimes you get a background sound. When the ache is there, you have a background of numbness. One seems slightly predominant at a different time of the day. When the numbness is predominant you have a background of pain. When you're slightly off the beam, you get a background of one with a predominance of the other.
>
> "Usually it's never quite where the numbness and the ache is the same. One is always more noticeable than the other. If you were to ask me this morning, I'd say it ached; but if you were to

[21] Freud, *A General Introduction* . . . , pp. 246–7.

ask me about noon, I'd say it were numb. That's how the darn thing acts."

The patient was asked whether he had ever thought of the fact that "ache" begins with an "A" and that "numbness" begins with "N." This struck the patient as very funny; but, after he had finished laughing, he said he wondered why he had never thought of it before.

The patient's verbal intermingling of the metaphoric radio beam with the description of his symptom makes it almost impossible to avoid perceiving the symptom as a symbolic representation of his traumatic experiences as a radio operator. The particular nature of his conflict in relation to radio is of course not revealed in the above excerpt; but the fact that his symptoms were somehow connected with his experiences as a radio operator is quite evident.

OTHER EVIDENCE. A number of additional classes of evidence for unconscious functions has been outlined by Murray, who has described one type of evidence as follows:

. . . a special difficulty arises in connection with the subject who is disturbed or depressed but does not know what is wrong or what he needs. . . . For example, there is no instinct that leads a patient with scurvy to drink orange juice. He must be told what he needs. . . . Similarly it appears that many people do not know what it is they "really" want, what they "really" need for their own well-being. They recognize it only when they find it, after much fumbling about or after being shown by someone else. Parents, nurses, educators, psycho-therapists, priests and moral philosophers make it their business to tell the young, the depraved and the sick what they need. Perhaps they are wrong most of the time, but when it can be shown that such a prediction is right, that a certain heretofore unexhibited trend of action brings contentment in place of inner disturbance, then there is reason to suppose that a need has been satisfied, a need that was previously active, though entirely unconscious.[22]

In other words, what the individual consciously thinks he wants may bring little satisfaction. It can be inferred from this that his "real" need is functioning on the unconscious level; that is, its nature is unknown to him. The nature of the object that eventually yields satisfaction will provide a dependable clue to the nature of the unconscious motivation.

[22] Murray, *op. cit.*, p. 115.

ID, EGO, AND SUPEREGO FUNCTIONS

AFTER many years of psychoanalytic practice, Freud arrived at a threefold division of personality functions—a conceptual division that he regarded as basic to an understanding of human adjustment. He referred to one group of functions as the *id*, to another group of functions as the *ego*, and to another group of functions as the *superego*.

Freud frequently referred to these functional divisions as if they were entities, though a careful reading of his works should be sufficient to demonstrate that he conceived of them as broad groupings of personality *functions*. In order to avoid conveying an incorrect impression that the terms *id*, *ego*, and *superego* refer to localizable regions, or to personified entities, we shall refer to them as *id functions*, *ego functions*, and *superego functions*.

Id Functions

Id functions involve relatively unconscious motivational tendencies. Freud referred to this group of functions as ". . . a cauldron of seething excitement." [23]

> We suppose that [the id] is somewhere in direct contact with somatic processes, and takes over from them instinctual needs and gives them mental expression. . . . These instincts fill it with energy, but it has no organization and no unified will, only an impulsion to obtain satisfaction for the instinctual needs, in accordance with the pleasure-principle. . . . Contradictory impulses exist side by side without neutralizing each other or drawing apart. . . . Conative impulses which have never got beyond the id . . . are virtually immortal and are preserved for whole decades as though they had only recently occurred. . . . Naturally, the id knows no values, no good and evil, no morality. The economic, or, if you prefer, the quantitative factor, which is so closely bound up with the pleasure-principle, dominates all its processes. Instinctual cathexes seeking discharge—that, in our view, is all that the id contains. . . . In popular language, we may say that . . . the id stands for the untamed passions. [24]

[23] Freud, *New Introductory Lectures* . . . , p. 104.
[24] *Ibid.*, pp. 104–7.

In other words, id functions consist of motivational processes, which manifest none of the rational characteristics we attribute to the cognitive (intellectual) processes. They are the "untamed passions," which continually make demands in the interest of their own gratification. As Murray has pointed out, these motivational processes include primarily the innate, viscerogenic (biogenic) needs. When id functions are prominent in behavior, the individual "feels that he is overcome by irresistible forces outside himself." [25] The impersonal pronoun *id* was used by Freud to imply this "character of being foreign to the ego." [26]

In brief, then, it may be concluded that *id functions comprise the biogenic needs of the organism*—i.e., biogenic needs that are *devoid of instrumental acts or objects for their gratification*. Their gratification can, of course, be achieved only through the agency of ego functions, which alone can provide the needs with appropriate instrumental acts and appropriate objects.

Ego Functions

Ego functions may be regarded as comprising the relatively conscious perceptual-cognitive (intellectual, rational, voluntary) processes of personality. Mowrer has stated that "the ego is the conscious, voluntary, problem-solving part of the total personality." [27] Symonds has stated that "the ego has three distinct elements: one, perceiving (ego as the *knower*); two, thinking (ego as the *thinker*); and three, acting (ego as the *doer* or the *executive* or the *will*)." [28] Freud has given a comprehensive account of his conception of ego functions in his *Outline of Psychoanalysis*.

> In consequence of the relation which was already established between sensory perception and muscular action, the ego is in control of voluntary movement. It has the task of self-preservation. As regards *external* events, it performs that task by becoming aware of the stimuli from without, by storing up experiences of them (in the memory), by avoiding excessive stimuli (through

[25] Murray, *op. cit.*, p. 135.

[26] Freud, *New Introductory Lectures* . . . , p. 102.

[27] O. Hobart Mowrer, "On the Dual Nature of Learning: a Reinterpretation of 'conditioning' and 'problem solving,'" *Harvard Educational Review*, 17 (1947), 102–48. In *Learning Theory and Personality Dynamics*, O. Hobart Mowrer (New York, 1950), p. 273. Reprinted by permission of *Harvard Educational Review* and The Ronald Press Company. Copyright, 1947, by *Harvard Educational Review*, 1950, by The Ronald Press Company.

[28] Percival M. Symonds, *The Ego and the Self* (New York, 1951), p. 7. Reprinted by permission of Appleton-Century-Crofts, Inc. Copyright, 1951, by Appleton-Century-Crofts, Inc.

flight), by dealing with moderate stimuli (through adaptation) and, finally, by learning to bring about appropriate modifications in the external world to its own advantage (through activity). As regards *internal* events, in relation to the id, it performs that task by gaining control over the demands of the instincts, by deciding whether they shall be allowed to obtain satisfaction, by postponing that satisfaction to times and circumstances favorable in the external world or by suppressing their excitations completely. Its activities are governed by consideration of the tensions produced by stimuli present within it or introduced into it. The raising of these tensions is in general felt as *unpleasure* and their lowering as *pleasure*. . . . The ego pursues pleasure and seeks to avoid unpleasure. An increase in unpleasure which is expected and foreseen is met by a *signal of anxiety;* the occasion of this increase, whether it threatens from without or within, is called a *danger.* From time to time the ego gives up its connection with the external world and withdraws into a state of sleep, in which its organization undergoes far-reaching changes. . . . An action by the ego is as it should be if it satisfies simultaneously the demands of the id, of the super-ego and of reality, that is to say if it is able to reconcile their demands with one another.[29]

In his *New Introductory Lectures on Psycho-Analysis,* Freud has stated a similar conception.

. . . the ego . . . interpolates between desire and action the procrastinating factor of thought, during which it makes use of the residues of experience stored up in memory. In this way it dethrones the pleasure-principle, which exerts undisputed sway over the processes in the id, and substitutes for it the reality-principle, which promises greater security and greater success. . . . In popular language, we may say that the ego stands for reason and circumspection, while the id stands for the untamed passions. . . . [The ego] borrows its energy from the id. . . . On the whole the ego has to carry out the intentions of the id; it fulfills its duty if it succeeds in creating the conditions under which these intentions can best be fulfilled. . . . The poor ego . . . has to serve three harsh masters. . . . The . . . tyrants are the external world, the super-ego and the id.[30]

[29] Freud, *An Outline of Psychoanalysis,* pp. 15–17.
[30] Freud, *New Introductory Lectures* . . . , pp. 106–08.

Ego functions, then, may be summarized in terms of the following points:

1. Ego functions are, for the most part, relatively conscious or preconscious (capable of becoming conscious). The materials upon which the ego functions operate may consist of internal stimuli arising from biogenic needs, of external stimuli that are immediately present, of preconscious "memories" relating to internal and external stimuli, or (more usually) of a combination of all of these.

2. A major ego function is that of conscious and preconscious perception; in other words, ego functions involve perceptual processes of which the individual is aware, or of which he may become aware.

3. Other cognitive processes (thinking, memory, learning, judgment, etc.) are considered to belong among the ego functions.

4. Voluntary activity—that is, activity guided by conscious perception—is likewise considered to belong among the ego functions.

The ego functions are integrative. These perceptual-cognitive processes synthesize the data that are available to consciousness, organizing these data into a logical structure. Masserman has stated, in agreement with Freud, that "the conscious Ego utilizes the information imparted by the senses, subjects such data to the logical processes of the intellect and so evaluates the . . . milieu in terms of available sources and means of gratification as opposed to possible dangers of frustration or injury." [31]

Unfortunately, the data with which the conscious ego functions can deal are never, in the lifetime of the individual, sufficiently complete for an adequate solution of problems. In infancy and childhood, knowledge of reality and facility in integrating the data of consciousness are inadequate, even though during this period the individual may be aware of impulses that will later fall under repression. In later periods, when knowledge of reality is more adequate and when integrative facility operates at a higher level, the individual will have lost contact, through repression, with much of his earlier knowledge regarding his own needs.

[31] Jules H. Masserman, *Principles of Dynamic Psychiatry* (Philadelphia, 1946), p. 27. Reprinted by permission of W. B. Saunders Company. Copyright, 1946, by W. B. Saunders Company.

Since ego functions are integrative, they become involved in conscious conflicts; that is, ego functions frequently become concerned with the attempt to integrate incompatible data. The perception of anxiety is likewise an ego function; defensive activities are said to defend "the ego" against the conscious perception of anxiety.

The individual's conscious ego functions characteristically follow the pattern of his language. In early childhood the adequacy of his ego functions is limited by the immaturity of his language development, as well as by the immaturity of his experience. Ego functions become increasingly adequate with increasing linguistic facility. Perception, learning, thinking, etc., depend on verbal symbols for the efficient representation of relationships. The dependence of ego functions on verbal symbols has been emphasized by Freud, Watson, Sears, Guthrie, Shaffer, Dollard and Miller,[32] Murray,[33] Mowrer,[34] and others. In this connection, for example, Freud wrote:

> . . . the real difference between a Ucs [*unconscious*] and a Pcs [*preconscious*] idea (thought) consists in this: that the former is worked out upon some sort of material which remains unrecognized, whereas the latter (the Pcs) has in addition been brought into connection with verbal images. This is the first attempt to find a distinguishing mark for the two systems, the Pcs and the Ucs, other than their relation to consciousness. It would seem, then, that the question, "How does a thing become conscious?" could be put more advantageously thus: "How does a thing become preconscious?" And the answer would be: "By coming into connection with the verbal images that correspond to it." [35]

Murray has expressed a similar conception, as follows:

> Whatever a subject can report upon is considered conscious; everything else which, by inference, was operating . . . is considered unconscious. According to this convenient pragmatic criterion, consciousness depends upon verbalization.[36]

To the extent, then, that ego functions operate consciously, these functions may be regarded as essentially verbal in content and as con-

[32] John Dollard and Neal E. Miller, *Personality and Psychotherapy: an Analysis in Terms of Learning, Thinking, and Culture* (New York, 1950), p. 198.

[33] Murray, *op. cit.*, pp. 113–14.

[34] O. Hobart Mowrer, *Learning Theory and Personality Dynamics* (New York, 1950), p. 445.

[35] Sigmund Freud, *The Ego and the Id*, translated by Joan Riviere (London, 1950), p. 21. Reprinted by permission of The Hogarth Press, Ltd.

[36] Murray, *op. cit.*, pp. 113–14.

forming to the language structure.[37] This implies, of course, that perception, thinking, etc., follow grammatical principles.

Superego Functions

Id functions, as we have previously noted, involve the biogenic needs of the organism. Superego functions, on the other hand, involve the conscious and unconscious social motivation of the individual—his values, his ideals, his moral standards, and all of his other motivational tendencies of psychogenic origin.

THREE ASPECTS OF SUPEREGO FUNCTIONS. Freud explained his choice of the term *superego* as follows:

> For us the super-ego is the representative of all moral restrictions, the advocate of the impulse towards perfection; in short it is as much as we have been able to apprehend psychologically of what people call the "higher" things in human life.[38]

According to Freud, superego functions perform three major roles in the personality: (1) that of self-restriction in terms of moral prohibitions (conscience), (2) that of self-guidance in terms of aspirations for ultimate achievement (ego-ideal), and (3) that of self-observation or self-perception.

Conscience. The term *conscience* implies the negative aspects of superego motivation. Conscience motivation is concerned with the inhibition or restraint of behavior tendencies that are prohibited by moral

[37] If ego functions are to be regarded as conscious and preconscious, as they perhaps should be if we are to use the concept of ego functions in its most useful sense, then it must be admitted that Freud has omitted an important aspect of personality—namely, the integrative functions which occur on unconscious levels. Such functions as perception, thinking, judgment, etc., may occur completely or almost completely on deeply preconscious and unconscious levels. The process of creative thinking, for example, may occur while the individual is conscious of irrelevant matters—when the problem is "out of mind." Then, at an unexpected moment, the conclusion of such thinking may "burst" into consciousness. Moreover, at any given moment, the data of perception may be only partly conscious, while the rest of the total pattern remains hidden from awareness. Freud, of course, suggested that ego functions are partly unconscious, yet much of his theoretical reasoning appears to be based on the conception of ego functions as operating consciously. For this reason, in our use of the term, ego functions will imply *conscious* integrative functions. The term will imply all of the so-called cognitive or intellectual functions as they occur within the individual's awareness. To the extent that such functions are employed consciously, deliberately, or voluntarily, their rationality can be insured. To the extent, however, that they operate with insufficient data, they must lead to unrealistic interpretations, unwise choices, and other forms of maladjustive behavior.

[38] Freud, *New Introductory Lectures* . . . , p. 95.

standards—or with self-punishment on occasions when such behavior tendencies have been permitted expression.

> I feel a temptation to do something which promises to bring me pleasure, but I refrain from doing it on the ground that "my conscience will not allow it." Or I allow myself to be persuaded by the greatness of the expectation of pleasure into doing something against which the voice of my conscience has protested, and after I have done it my conscience punishes me with painful reproaches, and makes me feel remorse for it.[39]

In other words, *conscience* refers to negative psychogenic motivation. Certain actions and objects, prohibited by conscience, are negatively cathected; the individual is motivated to avoid such actions and objects.

Ego-ideal. The term *ego-ideal* refers to positive psychogenic motivation; it refers to the individual's aspirations, ideals, and ambitions; it involves positive motivation to "amount to something," to "live up to" one's expectations, to reach high goals of achievement.

> [The superego] is also the vehicle of the ego-ideal, by which the ego measures itself, towards which it strives, and whose demands for ever-increasing perfection it is always striving to fulfill. No doubt this ego-ideal is a precipitation of the old idea of the parents, an expression of the admiration which the child felt for the perfection which it at that time ascribed to them.[40]

Ego-ideal motivation involves positive cathexis of particular actions and objects; the individual is motivated to behave in terms of a high criterion of excellence.

Self-observation and Self-perception. Freud included the process of self-awareness, self-observation, or self-perception among the superego functions.[41] He conceived of the superego functions as being temporarily "split off" from the ego functions; the superego functions, after being "split off," were said to observe the ego. Just as the parents watched the child's behavior at an earlier period, the superego was said to watch the individual's behavior at a later time.

In order to emphasize the reasonableness of including self-observation among the superego functions, Freud cited the instance of psychotics who suffer from *delusions of observation.*

> They complain to us that they suffer continually, and in their most intimate actions, from the observation of unknown powers

39 *Ibid.*, p. 86.   40 *Ibid.*, pp. 92–3.   41 *Ibid.*, pp. 84–6.

or persons, and they have hallucinations in which they hear these persons announcing the results of their observations: "now he is going to say this, now he is dressing himself to go out," and so on. . . . How would it be if these mad people were right, if we all of us had an observing function in our egos threatening us with punishment, which, in their case, had merely become sharply separated from the ego and had been mistakenly projected into external reality? [42]

According to this point of view, delusions of observation would involve the projection of a *personified* superego function—that of self-observation—into the external environment.

It appears that Freud was in error when he regarded self-observation as a superego function. The organismic conception of behavior argues against the occurrence of an actual "splitting off" of functions. Whatever "splitting off" may seem to occur must be attributed to an abstracting process in the individual, who momentarily selects his own functions as the objects of observation. Both abstraction (a "thinking" process) and perception should be regarded as ego functions. Since self-observation involves both of these functions—since the "self" must be differentiated by a process of abstraction and then be perceived as an entity—self-observation should be regarded as an ego function.

In delusions of observation, a similar combination of abstraction and perception occurs: certain functions of the "self" are abstracted, personified, and perceived as external to the other functions of the "self." The *motivation* to observe one's actions and to behave autonomously should, of course, be implied in the concept of superego functions.

The *ego function* of self-observation can be, and usually will be, closely associated with superego functions; a part of the pattern of motivation which influences self-perception must consist of ego-ideal and conscience motives—that is, of positive and negative psychogenic cathexes of actions and objects. In other words, while self-observation must be regarded as an ego function, self-perception is always partially a function of the standards of conduct and attainment against which the self is evaluated. The individual will perceive himself *in terms of* the extent to which he "lives up to" his standards of perfection and morality.

SUPEREGO FUNCTIONS AS PSYCHOGENIC MOTIVES. Superego func-

[42] *Ibid.*, p. 85.

tions, as we have noted, consist of psychogenic motivation. To the extent that the individual develops psychogenic motives that conform to social standards, his self-determined behavior will be respected, approved, and valued by other people.

> . . . what was initially *external discipline* becomes *internal discipline.* . . . Loosely stated, we "trouble ourselves" in order that others will not later trouble us (more?). Thus, at a high level of abstraction, we may say that the punishing function of conscience is "rewarding." This, of course, is not to say that the "pangs" of conscience are no longer painful; instead it implies that, with sufficient personal maturity, an individual may come to respect, accept, and value these reactions and to act *upon* rather than *against* them.[43]

The superego processes, then, function to organize the individual's behavior in terms of parental and cultural expectations, since they consist of psychogenic motivational tendencies that have been developed through years of living in the cultural milieu. Just as the biogenic motives have survival value to the organism, so the psychogenic motives (superego functions) have survival value in the social setting in which the individual has developed.

Different superego motives may conflict with one another, however, if the individual has developed in a number of incompatible social settings; or they may come to interfere with the individual's survival if he leaves one social setting and takes up life in a radically different social environment. Thus, the values that have been developed in a rural setting may make survival difficult in an urban environment; or the values that have been developed in one socio-economic setting may make adjustment difficult when the individual, through education and training, "passes over" into another socio-economic class.

Parental Source of Superego Motives. The development of superego functions depends largely, according to Freud, on the relation of the child to his parents. The child is threatened with punishment for disapproved behavior and promised the reward of love and security for behaving in conformity with the parents' demands. So long as the child can conform to the parents' expectations, he can avoid punishment; if he develops psychogenic motives like those of his parents,

---

[43] O. Hobart Mowrer, *Learning Theory and Personality Dynamics* (New York, 1950), p. 587 n. Reprinted by permission of The Ronald Press Company. Copyright, 1950, by The Ronald Press Company.

these psychogenic motives will take the place of parental threats and promises in the determination of his behavior.

> The role, which the super-ego undertakes later in life, is at first played by an external power, by parental authority. The influence of the parents dominates the child by granting proofs of affection and by threats of punishment, which, to the child, mean loss of love, and which must also be feared on their own account. This objective anxiety is the forerunner of the later moral anxiety; so long as the former is dominant one need not speak of super-ego or of conscience. It is only later that the secondary situation arises, which we are far too ready to regard as the normal state of affairs; the external restrictions are introjected, so that the super-ego takes the place of the parental function, and thenceforward observes, guides and threatens the ego in just the same way as the parents acted to the child before.[44]

If the parents are consistent in the values and standards they impose upon the child, he will probably develop consistent motivation, which will serve to keep his behavior in conformity with parental expectations. He will be, that is to say, "a good boy." If parental discipline is determined by conventional values, the child can be expected to develop superego motives that will govern his behavior in conformity with the expectations of society at large.

If, however, the parents make inconsistent demands, or if their own standards are at variance with the ruling conventions of the society, then either the child will not be able to develop any dependable standards by means of which to avoid trouble with his parents, or he will "end up" with standards that will entail difficulties for him in his relations with other people. In either case, he may be said to have a "defective superego."

Other Sources of Superego Motives. Though the child's earliest psychogenic motives will develop out of his relations with his parents, his later ambitions, values, ideals, and standards may develop out of his relations with other persons. The primary requirement is that such other persons be loved or respected—that is, that such other persons can promise rewards for approved behavior and threaten punishment for disapproved behavior.

Older siblings, teachers, ministers, relatives, etc., may contribute to the individual's pattern of superego motives. Even persons whom

[44] Freud, *New Introductory Lectures . . .* , p. 89.

the individual has never actually seen may function in this respect. Thus, the individual who has never had firsthand acquaintance with a scientist, a poet, or an artist, may, through his reading, develop the ambition to become a scientist, a poet, or an artist.

UNCONSCIOUS SUPEREGO MOTIVATION. Freud clearly recognized that superego motives may function without the individual's being aware of their functioning.

> Certainly, large portions of the . . . super-ego can remain unconscious, are, in fact, normally unconscious. That means to say that the individual knows nothing of their contents and that it requires an expenditure of effort to make him conscious of them.[45]

It is probable that the psychogenic motives which owe their development to the very early relations between the child and his parents are so "deeply ingrained" that they function at an unconscious level. Such motives are developed in the early period before the child has acquired facility with language; hence they will function later at sub-vocal levels. That is to say, a conscious effort to verbalize such motives, to say what motives are functioning, will be ineffectual, since the motives, during their origin, were not associated with words. The psychogenic motives of later origin, however, may be expected to function on a conscious level.

> It is customary to consider the functions of the superego as early internalized reactions which become largely automatic and unconscious and so no longer susceptible to modification by external influences. Here again it is advisable to distinguish between more and less automatic emotional reactions and behavior rather than between a completely automatic superego and a conscious, more flexible ego.[46]

If it is clear that an important proportion of our most fundamental psychogenic motivation is relatively inaccessible to consciousness, it becomes understandable that we should experience guilt at times when we are not aware that we have done any wrong.

CONSERVATIVE NATURE OF SUPEREGO MOTIVATION. Superego motives are conservative in two senses: 1) in that, within a given personality, the psychogenic motives of earliest origin are highly resistant to

[45] *Ibid.*, p. 99.
[46] Franz Alexander, *Fundamentals of Psychoanalysis* (New York, 1948), p. 84. Reprinted by permission of W. W. Norton & Company, Inc. Copyright, 1948, by W. W. Norton & Company, Inc.

change; and 2) in that, functioning as unconscious psychogenic motives, the values of the culture are conserved in a form relatively inaccessible to the criticism and modification of rebellious spirits in each new generation.

The earliest values of the individual will function on a relatively unconscious level. Such values are resistant to change, since their influence on behavior occurs more or less automatically and usually leads the individual to regard his behavior as being the outcome of his "human nature." The individual seldom has occasion to question his behavior when it is based on such fundamental values, since almost everybody else is observed to behave in a similar manner. On the basis of this resistance to change, the cultural heritage tends to be conserved in the superego motivation of the individual.

Freud emphasized that the child acquires the parents' superego motives, rather than superego motives imitative of the parents' everyday behavior. This is based on the fact that parents often fail, in their everyday behavior, to live strictly in accordance with their superego motives; but when they discipline the child, they are more likely to be governed by these values.

> In general, parents and similar authorities follow the dictates of their own super-egos in the up-bringing of children. Whatever terms their ego may be on with their super-ego, in the education of the child they are severe and exacting. They have forgotten the difficulties of their own childhood, and are glad to be able to identify themselves fully at last with their own parents, who in their day subjected them to such severe restraints. The result is that the super-ego of the child is not really built up on the model of the parents, but on that of the parents' super-ego; it takes over the same content, it becomes the vehicle of tradition and of all the age-long values which have been handed down in this way from generation to generation.[47]

Since the child's superego motives are "built up on the model" of the parents' superego motives, the values of the culture are thereby conserved with little fundamental change from one generation to another.

CULTURAL VARIATION IN SUPEREGO MOTIVATION. Cultures vary with reference to the values they emphasize. It should be expected, therefore, that superego motivation will vary from one society to an-

---

[47] Freud, *New Introductory Lectures* . . . , p. 95.

other. Concerning this point, Masserman has made the following statement:

> Thus a child raised along fascist principles would be praised and rewarded even during its early formative years for behavior patterns that in other cultures would be regarded as ruthless, aggressive and cruel: conversely, he would be punished only for "sins against the state"—e.g., failures in group-disciplined self-sacrifice, responsibility, and idealogic allegiances. Such a child, grown to adulthood, would feel "guilty" over personal cowardice or group disloyalty, but he would see no "wrong" in lying, stealing or even murdering for the supposed good of his party. Similarly, a child raised in a democratic society, but strongly inculcated with antisocial principles by the precept and example of criminal parents, would himself tend to adopt the standards of criminality in later life; indeed, later punishment by society might make him become more wary, but would create little *internal* conflict or reorientation of values and objectives. Again, from the standpoint of the genesis of traits, a child whose natural strivings toward normal self-assertion and independence are consistently frowned upon or punished by possessive or over-strict parents may come to be so "conscientiously" diffident, modest, and retiring in later life as to prejudice his success in any sphere of emancipatory activity.[48]

Another example of cultural variation in superego motivation is to be found in the contrast between our values and the values of the Pilaga Indians in regard to interfamilial relations. Siblings in the Pilaga society learn to detest rather than to love one another; children are also expected to treat their parents as equals rather than to regard them as the proper objects of love, honor, and respect.[49]

[48] Masserman, *op. cit.*, p. 28. The question might arise: If the values of the culture are conserved in the form of superego motivation, and if the child acquires values that are in accord with the parents' superego, then how are we to account for the apparently rapid modification that occurred in the cultural values of fascist Germany? One answer might be that the amount of change that actually occurred has been overemphasized; another answer might be that strong leadership imposed new values on an entire generation of youth by promising affection and threatening punishment on the basis of principles different from those which had been current in the culture. Since the Nazi leadership could threaten greater punishment and promise higher rewards than any individual parent could threaten or promise, the superego motives of the German youth might well have been built upon that basis.

[49] Jules Henry and Zunia Henry, "Doll Play of Pilaga Indian Children," in *Personality in Nature, Society, and Culture*, Clyde Kluckhohn and Henry A. Murray, eds. (New York, 1948), p. 238.

In view of our understanding of superego functions as psychogenic motivation, it would be surprising to discover that superego functions did *not* vary with the cultures in which they develop. That they *do* vary with varying cultures is simply a corollary to familiar principles.

PSYCHOPATHIC PERSONALITY. An individual is said to have a *psychopathic personality* if he behaves as though he had no enduring standards by means of which to guide his behavior. Such a person may commit crimes, indulge in criminal sexuality, or manifest other forms of highly disapproved behavior without demonstrating any observable guilt or shame. Probably the most satisfactory interpretation of psychopathic behavior involves the conception that such behavior occurs on the basis of deficient psychogenic motivation—that is, on the basis of a failure to develop superego motivation consistent with the values of the culture.

The term *psychopathic personality* may be applied to one extreme of a continuum representing all degrees of deficient psychogenic motivation. The unconventional person is one whose values differ only slightly from the social norms; the psychopath is one whose values differ greatly from the social norms. The values of the psychopath are largely egocentric and near-biogenic; in other words, the psychopath is governed to a large extent by values that demand relatively crude and direct gratification of id motivation.

Id, Ego, and Superego as Objects of Perception

From the point of view of the psychologist, who seeks an understanding of personality functions, it is necessary to regard Freud's threefold division of the personality as a *functional* division. According to this point of view, the terms *id*, *ego*, and *superego* refer to groups of personality functions. Id functions comprise the biogenic needs; ego functions comprise the cognitive (intellectual) functions; and superego functions comprise the psychogenic motives.

From the point of view of the behaving individual, the personality functions are frequently perceived as personified entities, which may or may not be "on good terms" with one another. The individual may, for example, see his id (though he may not call it by this name) as being "foreign to his ego." Or he may perceive that his conscience makes tyrannical demands on him (his ego). The individual may regard himself as being split up into several warring "selves," each of which is trying to gain "the upper hand." As one neurotic patient has

put it: "Seems like there's two minds inside of me beating around—
the logical and the illogical. The wrong one is getting the upper hand,
too."

To the extent that individuals personify different aspects of their
personality functions, our recognition of this personification becomes
important for our understanding of their behavior. Rogers, for example, regards self-perception as the most significant aspect of human
adjustment.[50]

SUMMARY

ALLPORT's definition of personality emphasizes (1) that
the determinants of behavior are centered in the individual, (2) that
behavior is organismic, (3) that the "mental" and the "physical" are
inseparably interrelated, (4) that each person's environment and his
adjustments to it are unique, and (5) that personality functions are
continually in the process of change. An individual's personality cannot be observed directly, but it can be inferred on the basis of the observable adjustments of the individual.

Freud has emphasized the importance of recognizing that many
personality functions occur outside the individual's awareness. Freud
distinguished among three levels of consciousness—the *conscious* level,
the *preconscious* level, and the *unconscious* level. Functions that occur
in the focus of attention are said to be conscious. Functions that are
capable of becoming conscious when attention is directed upon them
are said to be preconscious. Functions that are capable of becoming
conscious only by means of specialized techniques, or that resist efforts
to direct attention upon them, are said to be unconscious.

It seems appropriate to represent levels of consciousness as an
infinite number of points along a continuum—that is, to regard any
function in terms of the degree of its accessibility to consciousness, or
the degree of effort required for its reinstatement as a conscious function. According to this point of view, the terms *conscious, preconscious,* and *unconscious* may be regarded as applying to *zones* along
the continuum.

Evidence for the occurrence of unconscious functions is provided by observations relating to post-hypnotic suggestion, resistance

[50] Carl R. Rogers, "Some Observations on the Organization of Personality,"
American Psychologist, 2 (1947), 358–68.

in psychotherapy, parapraxes, dream interpretation, neurotic symptoms, etc.

Freud has emphasized that the total organization of personality functions may be divided into three functional groupings. These may be termed *id functions*, *ego functions*, and *superego functions*.

Id functions may be regarded as comprising the biogenic needs of the organism—i.e., biogenic needs that are devoid of instrumental acts and objects for their gratification. Their gratification can be achieved only through the agency of ego functions, by means of which they become associated with gratifying instrumental acts and objects.

Ego functions may be regarded as comprising the cognitive (integrative, intellectual, rational, voluntary) functions of the personality; these functions include perception, thinking, learning, memory, judgment, and voluntary action. Though ego functions are relatively conscious, they may occur on preconscious and unconscious levels. To the extent that ego functions operate consciously, they follow the pattern of the language that is employed by the individual.

Superego functions may be regarded as comprising the positive and negative psychogenic motivation of the individual—the interests, values, ambitions, ideals, moral prohibitions, etc., that guide the individual's behavior in the direction of social conformity. The term *conscience* applies to negative superego motives, while the term *ego-ideal* applies to positive psychogenic motives. Superego motives are developed on the basis of threats of punishment for disapproved behavior and promises of reward (love, security, etc.) for approved behavior.

Superego motives may function consciously or unconsciously. Unconscious superego motives may be developed prior to the child's use of language. The child's superego motivation is built upon the model of the parents' superego motivation, rather than upon the model of the parents' actual behavior. The fundamental values of the culture are, therefore, conserved in the form of the early, relatively unconscious superego motives that are passed on, with little change, from one generation to another.

Psychopathic personality may be characterized as involving deficient psychogenic motivation. The psychopath behaves as though he had no enduring standards by which to guide his behavior—as though he were governed by id motivation rather than by superego motivation.

Although, from the psychologist's point of view, the terms id, ego, and superego properly refer to *functional* divisions of the personality, the behaving individual frequently perceives them as personified entities, which may or may not be "on good terms" with one another. To the extent that individuals personify these functional groupings, their behavior must be understood in terms of such personification.

The following chapter will be devoted to the discussion of motivational frustration and conflict. This will provide a further basis for an understanding of dynamic adjustment processes.

▶ **Suggested Readings**

DEFINITION OF PERSONALITY

Allport, G. W. *Personality: a Psychological Interpretation.* New York, 1937. Chap. ii, pp. 24–54.

Bridges, J. W. "Personality as a Work of Art," *Psychological Review, 52* (1945), 320–3.

LEVELS OF CONSCIOUSNESS

Chalfant, Eleanor M. "Conscious and Non-Conscious Mental Functions," *Journal of Clinical Psychology, 1* (1945), 77–82.

Freud, S. "The Psychopathology of Everyday Life," in *The Basic Writings of Sigmund Freud,* A. A. Brill, ed. New York, 1938.

Freud, S. "A Note on the Unconscious in Psycho-Analysis," *Collected Papers.* London, 1950. IV, 22–9.

Freud, S. "The Unconscious," *Collected Papers.* London, 1950. IV, 98–136.

Freud, S. *New Introductory Lectures on Psycho-Analysis.* New York, 1933. Chap. i, pp. 15–46.

Freud, S. "Some Elementary Lessons in Psycho-Analysis," *Collected Papers.* London, 1950. V, 376–82.

Ivimey, Muriel. "How the Unconscious Works," in *Outside Readings in Psychology,* E. L. Hartley, H. G. Birch, and Ruth E. Hartley, eds. New York, 1950. Pp. 432–40.

Lundholm, H. "Post-Mortem on a Printer's Error," *Character and Personality, 13* (1944), 22–9.

Martin, W. W. "Consciousness as Organismic Physiological Functioning," *Psychological Review, 54* (1947), 99–115.

O'Kelly, L. I. *Introduction to Psychopathology.* New York, 1949. Pp. 47–56.

Weitzenhoffer, A. M. "A Note on the Persistence of Hypnotic Suggestion," *Journal of Abnormal and Social Psychology, 45* (1950), 160–2.

Young, P. C. "Experimental Hypnotism: a Review," *Psychological Bulletin, 38* (1941), 92–104.

ID, EGO, AND SUPEREGO FUNCTIONS

Allport, G. W. "The Ego in Contemporary Psychology," *Psychological Review, 50* (1943), 451–78.

Alexander, F. *Fundamentals of Psychoanalysis.* New York, 1948. Chap. v, pp. 82–138.

Bertocci, P. A. "The Psychological Self, the Ego, and Personality," *Psychological Review, 52* (1945), 91–9.

Chein, I. "The Awareness of Self and the Structure of the Ego," *Psychological Review, 51* (1944), 304–14.

Freud, S. *The Ego and the Id.* London, 1950. Pp. 9–88.

Freud, S. *New Introductory Lectures on Psycho-Analysis.* New York, 1933. Chap. iii, pp. 82–112.

Gurvitz, M. S. "The Intelligence Factor in Psychopathic Personality," *Journal of Clinical Psychology, 3* (1947), 194–6.

Miller, D. R. and Hutt, M. L. "Value Interiorization and Personality Development," *Journal of Social Issues, 5* (1949), 2–30.

Mowrer, O. H. "The Law of Effect and Ego Psychology," *Psychological Review, 53* (1946), 321–34.

Raimy, V. C. "Self Reference in Counseling Interviews," *Journal of Consulting Psychology, 12* (1948), 153–63.

Rogers, C. R., Kell, B. L., and McNeil, Helen. "The Role of Self-Understanding in the Prediction of Behavior," *Journal of Consulting Psychology, 12* (1948), 174–86.

Symonds, P. M. *The Dynamics of Human Adjustment.* New York, 1946. Chap. xii, pp. 270–95.

Symonds, P. M. *The Ego and the Self.* New York, 1951. Chaps. ii–vi, pp. 7–120.

CHAPTER Four

Frustration and Conflict

To be or not to be; that is the question;
Whether 'tis nobler in the mind to suffer
The slings and arrows of outrageous fortune,
Or to take arms against a sea of troubles,
And by opposing end them.[1]

THOUGH few occasions arise that involve the severity of conflict which Hamlet suffered, the life of every person is continually disturbed by minor or major frustrations. It would be impossible to conceive of an environment so perfectly adjusted to human motivation that in it no frustration could occur.

The process of socialization *requires* the frustration of immature and egocentric motives. The infant or child must learn to satisfy his needs in ways that are approved in his society. As Murray has stated, society prescribes "time-place-mode-object (tpmo) formulas . . . for the expression of individual needs." [2] The child must satisfy particular needs at specified times, in specified places, by specified techniques, and in relation to specified goal objects.

The child is expected to eat at certain times, to play at certain times, to sleep at certain times; if he does any of these acts at the "wrong" time, his behavior will elicit disapproval or punishment. The child is expected to eat at the table, to play in the house or in the yard,

[1] Shakespeare, *Hamlet*, Act III, Scene i.
[2] Henry A. Murray, *Explorations in Personality* (New York, 1938), p. 136.

to sleep in his own bed; he is not permitted to eat in the bathroom, to play in the streets, or to sleep in his parents' bed. He must use "good manners" at the table, must play approved games according to approved rules, must wear pajamas when he sleeps, etc. He may eat spinach but not grasshoppers; he may kiss his parents but not strangers; he may drink milk but not rainwater; etc. His socialization involves more or less continual frustration.

Even the well-socialized, "normal" adult encounters many frustrations in his everyday life. He has but one lifetime in which to do all of the things he wishes to do, and he must frequently make choices among the possibilities available to him. He cannot hear two radio programs at once, he cannot see a ball game and a movie at the same time, he cannot have a family and remain free of responsibility, he cannot buy everything he wants with his limited income, and so on.

DEFINITION OF FRUSTRATION

WHEN the individual's behavior is goal-oriented, and when there is no frustration, his behavior will be fluent, free-flowing, and relatively effortless. When frustration occurs, however, there will be a disruption in the fluency of behavior.

Frustration Defined

Frustration involves the perception of an actual (immediate) or potential (delayed) interference with the gratification of a motive. That is to say, frustration involves either an immediately perceived interference with gratification or the anticipation of an interference that may occur in the future.

Since a given motive (need integrate) involves a *need*, an *instrumental act*, and an *object*, frustration may involve the perception of interference with any one or more of these aspects of the motive. The individual may be unable to satisfy his need in relation to a particular goal object; he may be unable to satisfy his need by means of a particular method or technique; or he may be unable to satisfy his need in relation to any goal object by any technique at this command.

Frustration as Perception

Frustrations do not occur except in terms of the individual's perception. There are some objective conditions that will function as frustrations, almost regardless of whose perception happens to be involved; some situations are relatively unambiguous in this respect. Thus, if there were no food of any kind to be found, nearly everybody would perceive the situation as frustrating.

Most situations, however, are ambiguous in this regard: they may be perceived as gratifying in various degrees, or frustrating in various degrees, depending on whose perception happens to be involved. In other words, most situations are not in themselves frustrating, but they may be perceived as frustrating in different degrees by different individuals. Some students, for example, are highly gratified when they receive C's in all of their courses, whereas others are gravely disappointed when they receive nothing better than B's.

What situations will be perceived as frustrating, and what degree of frustration they will involve, can be understood in terms of principles that apply to perception in general. The particular motives that are operative, and the long-term beliefs and attitudes of the individual, are relevant for determining the situations that will be frustrating or gratifying for the individual concerned.

Of high significance in this regard is the degree of confidence which characterizes the attitudes of the individual; the degree of confidence may, in the individual's perception, be referred to the self (self-confidence) or to the external environment (environmental confidence).

SELF-CONFIDENCE. The individual's self-confidence will, of course, be dependent on his past experiences. The individual who typically has succeeded in gratifying his motives, and who typically has succeeded in overcoming frustrations, will usually have developed an attitude of high self-confidence; he will be relatively optimistic in his self-evaluation. On the basis of this high level of self-confidence, he may be expected to perceive many new situations as gratifying or, at least, as involving only a minimum degree of frustration.

On the other hand, the individual who typically has failed to overcome frustrations will usually have developed an attitude of low self-confidence; he will be relatively pessimistic in his self-evaluation. On the basis of his low level of self-confidence, he may be expected to perceive many situations as frustrating in minor or major degrees.

The degree of self-confidence, then, is dependent on the proportion of previous situations perceived as gratifying; and the degree of self-confidence, in turn, may be expected to influence the proportion of subsequent situations to be perceived as gratifying. It becomes evident, therefore, that the experience of gratification, through its functional relationship with self-confidence, will increase the probability of gratification in the future; and, on the other hand, the experience of frustration will increase the probability of future frustration.

Of course, some motives are more significant than others in the life economy of a given individual. The relative significance of the gratified motives, as compared with that of the frustrated motives, will influence the degree of self-confidence. In other words, the mere proportion of occasions when gratification has been achieved cannot be considered apart from the significance of the particular motives that have been gratified. On the negative side, more or less continual frustration of a single important motive may be sufficient to account for an extremely low level of self-confidence, even though most of the individual's motives have been gratified regularly.

The building up of gratification on the basis of past gratification or of frustration on the basis of past frustration helps to explain the importance of childhood experiences in determining the outlook of the adult.

ENVIRONMENTAL CONFIDENCE. The perception of frustration will be influenced not only by the individual's confidence in himself but also by his confidence in the environment. To the degree that his experiences have been gratifying in relation to other people, in relation to natural resources, and especially in relation to the abiding group structures (economic, social, legal, etc.), he will have developed a high level of environmental confidence.

Environmental confidence was strongly emphasized in the stories of Horatio Alger, in which the hero, though beginning life in humble surroundings, invariably rose to a high status in a world of seemingly unlimited possibilities; the hero had but to be virtuous and industrious in order to achieve his highest ambitions (often through the operation of some extraordinary coincidence). There are, even today, strong social pressures that aim at developing high environmental confidence; indeed, so strong are these pressures that many individuals accept their failures as proof of their own limitations before considering the possibility that the environment itself may be partially responsible.

Aside from the social emphasis on opportunities that await the ambitious, the individual's own experiences of gratification and frustration will serve as a basis for the development of a given level of environmental confidence, which, in turn, will influence the individual's perception of new situations.

A high degree of environmental confidence will involve such attitudes as faith in the motives of other persons, faith in natural phenomena as manageable and predictable, faith in the justice of law, government, and other social institutions, faith in the beneficence of social regulations and moral standards, and faith in the stability of social structures. Low environmental confidence will involve such attitudes as suspicion regarding the motives of other people, the belief that natural phenomena are unpredictable or even malevolent, a distrust of law, government, and other social institutions, the belief that social regulations are arbitrary and vicious, and the belief that social structures are on the verge of collapse. Between these extremes, various degrees of environmental confidence will occur in different individuals.

The Frustration Continuum

Strictly speaking, at the moment when a need or motive becomes operative, frustration may have its beginning. The question arises: How soon after a need has become operative should we begin speaking of frustration? How strong must a need become, or how long must it exist without gratification, before we cease speaking of a need and begin speaking of frustration?

In one sense, the prolonged continuation of a need is equivalent to frustration. Yet the individual may continue to experience an ungratified motive throughout his lifetime without ever feeling that he is being frustrated; for example, a person may have a lifelong ambition, which he pursues unsuccessfully with the continued confidence that his efforts will eventually culminate in success.

Frustration may be said to begin at the moment when the individual *perceives an interference with gratification* or with the possibilities of gratification. An infant, for instance, will perceive frustration at the moment when a biogenic need first becomes operative. Moreover, immature individuals of all ages tend to perceive frustration soon after a need begins to function.

How long a need must continue before it is perceived as frustrating will depend on the individual's self-evaluation (level of self-confidence) and on his evaluation of the environment (level of environmental confidence). As long as the individual can anticipate relief before his need reaches intolerable intensity, he will probably perceive his need as nonfrustrating.

CLASSIFICATION OF FRUSTRATIONS

FURTHER understanding of the nature of frustration may be gained through a consideration of the categories into which frustrations have been classified.

Primary and Secondary Frustrations

Rosenzweig has distinguished between primary and secondary frustrations.[3] A *primary frustration* involves the "sheer existence of an active need." Such a frustration is equivalent to the perception of the discomfort that is associated with a need, and does not involve the perception of any particular interference with gratification. The perception of thirst and the perception of sleepiness are examples of primary frustrations.

A *secondary frustration,* on the other hand, involves the perception of a particular interference or obstruction that prevents gratification. A secondary frustration, then, is equivalent to frustration as it has been defined in the preceding discussion. The perception of a particular interference with going to bed when sleepy exemplifies secondary frustration, while merely being sleepy exemplifies primary frustration. The contents of the present chapter will be concerned almost exclusively with the concept of secondary frustration.

Passive and Active Frustrations

Frustrating situations have been classified by Rosenzweig in terms of whether such situations are perceived as passive or active.[4] *Passive frustrations* are interpreted by the individual as blocking the progress toward a goal, without involving any threat beyond that of merely preventing gratification. A locked door, a closed road, or a stalled car in good weather may be interpreted as a passive frustration.

Active frustrations involve the perception of danger in addition to the perception of interference with gratification. A policeman who guards an area containing food will be perceived by a hungry man as an active frustration. Similarly, in war, the continual threat of resistance and aggression by the enemy forces will be interpreted as an active frustration.

The distinction between active and passive frustration is essen-

[3] Saul Rosenzweig, "An Outline of Frustration Theory," in *Personality and the Behavior Disorders,* J. McV. Hunt, ed. (New York, 1944), p. 380.
[4] *Ibid.,* p. 381.

tially a function of the *complexity of the motivational pattern* that
undergoes frustration. When a single motive is frustrated, we are likely
to speak of *passive* frustration; but when many motives are simultaneously frustrated, we are likely to speak of *active* frustration. Thus,
a child's hunger will be frustrated if a cookie jar is placed out of his
reach; but if the mother has previously forbidden the child to eat
cookies between meals he will probably fear punishment or loss of his
mother's love in addition to suffering interference with the gratification
of his hunger.

Need, Instrumental Act, and Object Frustrations

Frustration, we have seen, may occur in relation to any aspect of
a need integrate or motive. The individual may be unable to gratify
his need by means of any form of behavior or in relation to any kind
of object; he may be unable to gratify his need by means of some preferred or customary mode of action; or he may be unable to gratify
his need in relation to some particular object. He may, in other words,
experience a *need frustration*, an *instrumental act frustration*, or an
object frustration.

Need frustrations involve temporary or permanent prevention of
gratification. If the individual is to survive, his need frustrations that
involve fundamental biogenic needs (hunger, thirst, need for oxygen,
etc.) must be of limited duration. But it is possible that psychogenic
motives may undergo permanent frustration without incurring damage
to the individual's body or to his personality. The hungry child may
undergo need frustration until the next meal, or, in unusual circumstances, for a longer period. But the pianist who loses his hands will
permanently suffer frustration of his motive to play the piano; and, of
course, he will probably survive his loss.[5]

Instrumental act frustrations involve interference with a particular
mode of gratifying a need. The instrumental act undergoing frustration may be one that is momentarily considered, or it may involve a
long-established preference. A person who considers making a trip by
air, for example, may find it impossible to obtain the desired reserva-
tions, so that he will be forced to resort to his customary mode of

[5] When psychogenic motives are involved, it may well be true that the
underlying need is biogenic; that is to say, the psychogenic aspects of any motive
may possibly involve only instrumental acts and objects. If this be the case, then
it would be improper to speak of "need frustrations" in the case of psychogenic
motivation. The pianist who has lost his hands, for example, may be able to satisfy
his fundamental need (the need for sentience?) by some other method.

travel. Or a person who is accustomed to commuting in his own car may find that his car is out of order, so that he will have to take a bus or taxicab while his car is being repaired.

Object frustrations involve interference in gratifying a need in relation to a particular cathected object. The individual may want a steak and have to settle for filet of sole; in summer he may want to cool off in a swimming-pool and have to substitute a cold shower; or he may wish to marry his childhood sweetheart and find this possibility eliminated by her unexpected death.

In general, when other factors are equal, need frustrations will be more severe than instrumental act frustrations or object frustrations. This follows from the fact that substitute actions and objects can usually be found, whereas it is difficult to conceive of a suitable substitute for the need itself.

External and Internal Frustrations

The following classification of frustrations was originally described by Rosenzweig [6] and has been slightly modified by Symonds.[7]

Frustrations are classified in terms of whether they involve interference from the *external* environment or interference that has its origin in the *internal* (personal) characteristics of the individual. These external and internal frustrations are further subclassified into *privations, deprivations,* and *obstructions.*

EXTERNAL PRIVATIONS. External privations involve the long-term lack or nonpossession of external resources that are necessary for gratification; the individual who suffers privation has never been in possession of certain desirable external resources, or he has become accustomed to their lack. Lifelong poverty, for example, may interfere with the gratification of many motives. The illiterate, having lacked the opportunity to learn to read, may be frustrated by his inability to read letters, newspapers, signs, and other forms of written communication. Lack of knowledge, which is a resource of external origin, will often interfere with an individual's gratification, since he will be an easy victim of people who wish to exploit him and since he will lack understanding of techniques that are necessary for reaching his goals. Lack of a brother or sister can be the basis of frustration for the only child.[8]

---

[6] Saul Rosenzweig, "Frustration as an Experimental Problem: VI, a General Outline of Frustration," *Character and Personality,* 7 (1938), 151–60.

[7] Percival M. Symonds, *The Dynamics of Human Adjustment* (New York, 1946), pp. 53–8.

[8] Some of these examples are not readily distinguishable from internal priva-

External privations may involve the lack of social resources or of physical resources; of the two, the lack of social resources probably functions as the more severe type of frustration. Thus, the individual who has long been without a father may suffer greater frustration than the individual who has been without certain material possessions.

EXTERNAL DEPRIVATIONS. The individual who loses some external resource, either social or material, that he once possessed is said to experience an external deprivation. The loss of a house, the loss of a job, the loss of a friend through death or through moving, the loss of any material possession or social relationship: all such losses of external resources may be classified as external deprivations.

Deprivations, as compared with privations, will usually function as the more severe frustrations; the loss of something that was once possessed may require radical readjustments, whereas the continued lack of resources (privation) may require little more than the continuation of habitual adjustments.

The severity of deprivation becomes understandable in terms of the fact that psychogenic motives will develop in connection with the use of social and material resources. Thus, a car may at first merely function as a convenient means of transportation; but the continued possession and use of a car will eventually lead to the development of interests in driving, in making side trips to out-of-the-way places, in dining at out-of-town establishments, and in many other activities difficult to carry out without the use of a car. When for some reason the car is lost, then all of these psychogenic motives, in addition to the more obvious need to possess a means of routine transportation, will undergo frustration. Probably the greater severity of deprivations, as compared with privations, then, may be accountable for in terms of this fact—that deprivations will involve frustration of a much larger segment of the individual's total pattern of motives.

EXTERNAL OBSTRUCTIONS. External obstructions involve either the interposition of a barrier between the individual and a cathected object, or an interference with an instrumental act by means of which the individual hopes to obtain gratification. The barrier or the interference may take the form of a social prohibition or of a physical obstacle. Fear of punishment and fear of social disapproval or social rejection involve external obstructions of the social variety. Physical obstructions

---

tions; for example, lack of specific knowledge at the particular time when it is necessary may function as an internal privation, though the lack may owe its origin to a deficiency in the external environment.

are exemplified by such barriers as impassable roads, locked doors or gates, and great physical distance between a person and the wanted object.

In general, social obstructions constitute more severe frustrations than do physical obstructions. Some physical obstructions, however, may function as severe threats. For example, the danger that a bomb will explode before its internal structure can be understood may act as a severe frustration to the expert who is required to discover safe ways to handle unexploded enemy bombs.

INTERNAL PRIVATIONS. Various congenital or long-standing defects or deficiencies make up the internal privations. Blindness or visual deficiency, deafness or hearing deficiency, crippled limbs, hunchback, general physical weakness, and mental deficiency are examples of internal privations. Many gratifications readily attainable by the person who has a normal complement of functions may be difficult or impossible for the individual who is deficient in any important function.

Of course, the mentally deficient person may not know what he is missing, except with respect to gratification of his biogenic needs. Indeed, situations may occur in which the individual will be guarded against frustration by virtue of his manifesting some defect or deficiency. For example, the physically defective individual will be protected from the frustrations often imposed by military service requirements. Usually, however, a defect or a deficiency will function as a frustration.

INTERNAL DEPRIVATIONS. Internal deprivations involve the loss, or the reduced adequacy, of functions that were once useful for the individual's gratification of motives. The loss of vision or hearing, the loss of health, the deterioration of abilities are examples of internal deprivations.

In general, internal deprivations function as more severe frustrations than do internal privations. Again, this is accountable for largely in terms of the operation of psychogenic motives, which will be frustrated when a function is lost or becomes deficient. Thus, a person whose fingers had always been defective would not "miss" playing the piano, whereas a pianist who loses the fingers of a hand would suffer frustration of psychogenic motives associated with his playing (the sheer enjoyment of playing, the self-esteem attendant upon success as a pianist, etc.).

INTERNAL OBSTRUCTIONS. The term *internal obstruction* refers to the simultaneous operation of incompatible motives. An internal obstruction is frequently termed a *conflict*. When a conflict occurs, the contradictory motives function to frustrate each other; the gratification of one prevents the gratification of the other. Wanting to attend two social functions that occur at the same hour, desiring something the attainment of which would interfere with some other kind of satisfaction, or wanting to escape some danger that cannot be avoided without facing a different danger—all of these are instances of internal obstructions or conflicts.

Since conflicts are especially significant in behavior dynamics, the following section will be devoted to a discussion of the classification of conflicts.

CLASSIFICATION OF CONFLICTS

CONFLICTS, as we have seen, involve the simultaneous operation of two or more incompatible motives. A conflict may occur among two or more relatively prepotent needs, among two or more techniques of gratifying the same need, or among two or more cathected goal objects. For example, a conflict may occur between hunger and the need for sleep, between the impulse to "eat on the run" and the impulse to dine leisurely, between the impulse to eat beefsteak and the impulse to eat roast pork.

In other words, a conflict may involve incompatible *needs*, incompatible *instrumental acts*, or incompatible *objects*. A conflict among instrumental acts or among objects will involve conflict among related psychogenic motives. Whether to "eat on the run" or to dine leisurely may represent a conflict between the need for achievement and the need for affiliation; whether to eat beafsteak or to eat roast pork may involve a conflict between religious scruples and the need for social acceptance; and so on.

According to Freud, conflicts are of major significance for the development of neurotic symptoms—that is, for the development of highly maladaptive defenses. Freud stated that "from the very beginning our view was that men fall ill owing to the conflict between the demands of their instincts and the internal resistance which is set up against them." [9] Since conflicts have high significance for human adjustment, a detailed discussion will be devoted to their classification.

[9] Sigmund Freud, *New Introductory Lectures on Psycho-Analysis* (New York, 1933), p. 83.

Classification in Terms of Valence or Cathexis

The following classification of conflicts is based on the work of Lewin.[10] The classification is expressed in terms of the possible combinations of valence, or cathexis, which the same object, or different objects, may have for the individual.[11] A conflict may involve two positive valences (plus-plus; adient-adient; approach-approach), a negative and a positive valence (plus-minus; adient-abient; approach-avoidant), or two negative valences (minus-minus; abient-abient; avoidant-avoidant).

PLUS-PLUS CONFLICTS. When the individual wants two or more desirable, but incompatible, ends or goals, he is said to experience a plus-plus conflict. The individual may want to attend two or more social functions that occur at the same time; he may want to hear two radio programs that occur at the same hour; he may want to take two vacation trips when he has only enough money for one; and so on.

Plus-plus conflicts may also involve two or more incompatible needs, or two or more incompatible modes of behavior for gratifying a given need. One may not, for example, satisfy hunger and the need for sleep at the same time; and one may not eat with a salad fork and a dinner fork at the same time.

Some of the major sources of plus-plus conflicts are: (1) that time is limited, (2) that the individual's energy is limited, (3) that various material and social resources are limited, (4) that the individual cannot be in widely separated places at the same time, and (5) that different activities require the use of the same parts of the body.

Since time is limited, an individual is not free to do all the things he would like to do—either during relatively brief periods or during his lifetime. The individual has only a certain amount of energy available for his activities; he must take time out to rest, to sleep, to eat, to maintain cleanliness, instead of doing many of the interesting things

[10] Kurt Lewin, *A Dynamic Theory of Personality* (New York, 1935), pp. 88–94.

[11] Although this classification appears to apply only to conflicts among objects, it should be noted that, from the point of view of the individual's perception, an instrumental act may function as an object. Moreover, it seems probable that, in unconscious as well as in conscious perception, the gratification of needs must be represented in terms of instrumental acts (perceived as objects) and in terms of objects. The conflict is likely to be represented in terms of whether to eat (beefsteak or roast pork?) or to drink (water or beer?), rather than in terms of whether to relieve hunger or to relieve thirst. In other words, the individual— unless he be a hypochondriac—is likely to think in terms of what he should do in order to become comfortable, rather than in terms of the quality and location of his discomfort.

he would like to be doing; he must limit his activities and thereby become involved in plus-plus conflicts.

The individual with limited financial resources must choose among the many desirable goods and services he would like to enjoy. Likewise, an individual's social resources will always be limited: he cannot enjoy intimacy with many different persons at the same time; he cannot have more than one wife at a time; he cannot be wholeheartedly friendly and sympathetic toward different persons who are themselves mutually antagonistic. One obviously cannot be in more than one place at a time; he cannot, for instance, be with his hometown sweetheart when he is away at college, or at work, or in the military service.

Finally, there are many different actions that are incompatible, since they utilize the same sensory, motor, or integrative equipment of the organism: one cannot listen simultaneously to a radio play and to conversation; one cannot whistle a melody while eating; one cannot pay attention to one's memories of the evening before while listening to the professor's lecture.

Plus-plus conflicts are frequently of minor significance for the psychology of adjustment. They will usually incur relatively little anxiety, since they can easily be resolved. The individual can usually make a choice among desirable goals, for, whatever his choice may be, some degree of gratification will be forthcoming. Oftentimes such a choice need not be a permanent choice among alternatives, since each of the conflicting motives may be gratified in its turn; though the individual cannot gratify them simultaneously, he may gratify first one and then the other.

Though plus-plus conflicts are usually of minor significance, they may infrequently become extremely severe; this is especially true in the case of lifetime ambitions or in the case of goals that cannot be achieved except through the concentrated efforts of the individual over a long period of time. Masserman, for instance, has reported the case of a senior medical interne who had difficulty choosing between two highly desirable residencies, which were located in New York and San Francisco, respectively.

> Either appointment was eminently desirable, but, since with the dramatic fatality of youth, the interne imagined that the decision "would alter his whole future"—which should he choose? In his dilemma he looked up every scrap of information that might serve

to tip the balance. . . . He made tables of comparisons, and tried ineffectively to weigh each item quantitatively and then assay the totals. He spent hours in restless rumination, paced the floor nights, and could find no surcease in any of his usual recreations. He at first plagued his faculty acquaintances with requests for advice until he himself realized that this might undermine their respect for him, and that the decision must be his own. He began to regret that he had ever studied medicine, and indulged in regressive phantasies as to how much better off he would have been had he entered his father's business where he would have been assured of a career that did not require sweeping and hazardous decisions.[12]

When plus-plus conflicts require a permanent decision, as in the case above, the individual may later become obsessed with doubt and regret at having made his unalterable choice. Since he cannot know how the other choice would have turned out, it may, in retrospect, come to seem preferable; and the choice that he actually made may lose, under conditions of familiarity, some of its positive cathexis, and indeed may become endowed with negative cathexis.

PLUS-MINUS CONFLICTS. The plus-minus conflict requires either losing a desired (positively cathected) object or accepting along with it an undesirable (negatively cathected) object. In order to approach a desired goal, the individual is required to approach another goal that he would prefer to avoid. Oftentimes the same goal is both positively and negatively cathected; in order to enjoy the positive features of the goal, the individual must be frustrated by its negative features.

This might be termed the "mixed blessing" conflict; some "bitter" must be taken along with the "sweet," if the "sweet" is to be had at all. For example, one may like to see football games but, in order to do so, one may have to suffer the discomforts of inclement weather. Or, in order to be eligible to participate in college athletics, the aspiring athlete may have to undergo the (to him) unpleasant rigors of classroom attendance and study. Or, in order to marry the woman (or man) of one's choice, it may be necessary to accept along with her (or him) an intolerable mother-in-law.

When plus-minus conflicts are relatively strong—that is, when both the positive and the negative features of a situation are relatively strong and of approximately equal strength—the individual may either

[12] Jules H. Masserman, *Principles of Dynamic Psychiatry* (Philadelphia, 1946), p. 137.

become immobile or vacillate in his approach-avoidant reactions.[13] As the individual approaches the desirable goal he will simultaneously approach the undesirable goal; eventually, the negative features of the situation will be perceived to be as strong as, or stronger than, the positive features; the individual, therefore, will be trapped in a region where the positive and negative features appear to be approximately equal. He may be trapped into immobility or he may be trapped into a ceaseless oscillation toward and away from the goal.

Vacillation is understandable in terms of the analogy to momentum: the momentum of approach will carry the individual to a point where repulsion is much greater than attraction; following this, the momentum of repulsion will carry the individual to a point where attraction is much greater than repulsion. Thus the individual will vacillate, swinging back and forth in relation to the positive-negative goal. An example of such vacillation in relation to a plus-minus conflict is afforded by the college student who enjoys the social life of the campus but finds academic work difficult and unattractive: he may think of dropping out of school, but as he thinks along this line the attractive features of his social activities will regain ascendance; then, as he thinks of staying in school to retain these enjoyments, the thoughts of arduous examinations and dull classes will become uppermost in awareness. Thus he will vacillate in terms of the positive and negative features, as these alternately capture his attention.

Plus-minus conflicts are generally of major significance for the psychology of adjustment, since they are relatively difficult to resolve. Whatever the individual eventually decides, if indeed an eventual decision occurs, some frustration will be involved. Either he will lose something desirable or he will gain something undesirable.

The blocking and immobility, or the vacillation, which occurs with the prolonged plus-minus conflict will entail much anxiety; if the conflict cannot be resolved to the individual's ultimate satisfaction, the anxiety will be reduced by means of defense mechanisms.

MINUS-MINUS CONFLICTS. The minus-minus conflict requires a choice among two or more negatively cathected goals. In order to escape one such danger, difficulty, or frustration, it will be necessary to fall into an equally serious danger, difficulty, or frustration. The phrase "from the frying pan into the fire" implies such a conflict. The minus-minus conflict is sometimes called a *dilemma*.

[13] Neal E. Miller, "Experimental Studies of Conflict," in *Personality and the Behavior Disorders*, J. McV. Hunt, ed. (New York, 1944), pp. 436-41.

Severe minus-minus conflicts are typically the basis of war neuroses. In order to avoid endangering his life or his health, the combat soldier would have to desert or otherwise exhibit "cowardly" behavior, thus risking disgrace or court martial. When both alternatives become sufficiently strong, the soldier's only escape may be through the development of a war neurosis.

Minus-minus conflicts are characteristacally reacted to by some form of withdrawal or by vacillation. Miller has illustrated the withdrawal reaction by the example of the individual who finds himself between two vicious dogs; his most direct route of escape would be along a line which is perpendicular to that connecting the two dogs.[14] If the individual were "hemmed in," as he usually would be in a genuine conflict situation, or as he would be if he were in a narrow corridor between the two dogs, he would either vacillate between the two choices or make some sort of *symbolic withdrawal.* Hamlet's conflict ("to be or not to be") may be considered an instance of the minus-minus conflict, involving vacillation between undesirable alternatives.

When the individual has a genuine minus-minus conflict, he *perceives inescapable alternatives;* to his perception, there is no way out except to choose one or the other, either of which will involve serious frustration. As he considers escaping one alternative, the necessity of facing an equally frustrating alternative will gain ascendance in his perception. Thus he will vacillate between the two, and he will suffer severe anxiety. As the combat soldier considers the possibility of saving his life, he will become more and more aware of the disgrace or punishment that would ensue; and, as he considers escaping disgrace or punishment by continuing in combat, the danger to his life will loom in his perception; he will vacillate between the catastrophic alternatives and will suffer agonizing anxiety.

The minus-minus variety of conflicts is typically the most severe. If the conflict is genuine, the individual can see no other alternative than that of eventually choosing one of the anticipated frustrations. If both alternatives are endowed with high negative cathexis, the individual will be, so to speak, "between the devil and the deep blue sea." Escaping one will require being trapped by the other.

COMPLEX COMBINATIONS. Few conflicts experienced by an individual are so simple as the preceding classification would imply. Usually conflicts involve complex combinations of positive and negative cathexis. Thus, a conflict may occur between several positive goals and

[14] *Ibid.,* pp. 442–6.

several other contradictory positive goals, or between one strong positive goal and several minor positive goals. The child who has six pennies to spend may want everything in the candy case, but he will be limited to a few things; or he may have to choose between one (to him) expensive item and several less expensive items. Or the conflict may occur between two positive goals, one or both of which involve some negative cathexis. Thus, the boy may want, for his limited money, both a pack of cigarettes and a comic book; but his parents disapprove of both. This example illustrates what some writers have termed a *double approach-avoidant conflict*.

The attempt to classify conflicts is complicated by the fact that, even in the case of the simple plus-plus conflict, the necessity of losing one goal in order to have the other will render the alternatives, to a certain extent, undesirable.

It is oftentimes, too, a matter of arbitrary decision whether a given conflict should be considered an example of one class or of another, since, even in the case of the combat soldier's minus-minus conflict, positive features may be involved; he may risk his life in order to *maintain* the respect of other persons rather than in order to *escape* disgrace. It may be that the awareness of positive features (an optimistic attitude) distinguishes the soldier who can "take it" from the one who develops a neurosis.[15]

Since conflict is a function of the individual's perception, what may represent one class of conflicts for one individual may represent another class of conflicts for another individual.

Classification in Terms of the Origin of Conflicting Motives

This classification is expressed in terms of the origin of the motives that conflict with each other. Different id motives or biogenic motives may conflict with each other (id-id conflict); an id motive may conflict with a superego motive or psychogenic motive (id-superego conflict); and different superego motives may conflict with each other (superego-superego conflict).

ID-ID CONFLICTS. Id-id conflicts involve the simultaneous operation of two or more incompatible biogenic needs. Hunger (n Food) may conflict with n Sex, n Urination, n Defecation, n Heatavoidance, or n Harmavoidance: eating would interfere with the sexual act; it

---

[15] In actuality, it is not so much a matter of the difference in ability to "take it" as of the difference between what they are called upon to take. What the individual must endure depends on his perception of the situation.

would be considered "dirty" to eat in the bathroom; it may sometimes be impossible to find a cool place or a safe place in which to eat; and so on. The need for sex (n Sex) may conflict with n Urination or n Defecation, for obvious reasons; n Sex may conflict with n Harm-avoidance, since fear of venereal disease may be involved.

Under ordinary circumstances, id-id conflicts will be of minor significance for the individual's adjustment. Though many biogenic needs are not amenable to simultaneous gratification, they can usually be gratified successively.

ID-SUPEREGO CONFLICTS. The superego motives of the individual are frequently incompatible with his biogenic (id) motives. In infancy and early childhood, the individual typically expresses his biogenic needs in a simple and straightforward manner—uncomplicated by considerations of time, place, mode, or object. When a biogenic impulse arises, it is likely to be expressed immediately, either in the form of appropriate action (as in the case of n Urination, n Defecation, n Inspiration, etc.) or in the form of crying, for example (as in the case of n Food and n Water).

On the basis of training, however, the child will develop psychogenic motives that are in conflict with the immediate expression of his impulses. Many instrumental acts and objects, and certain needs *per se* (such as n Sex), will become negatively cathected. The child may also develop positive psychogenic motives (ego-ideals) that, on occasion, will conflict with the adequate satisfaction of his biogenic needs.

Sexual and aggressive impulses will quite frequently conflict with moral standards. Other biogenic needs may at times conflict with moral (negative psychogenic) values. For example, the unemployed person who is driven by hunger may be tempted to accept the aid of a social welfare agency, but this temptation may conflict with his negative attitude toward accepting charity.

Biogenic needs may conflict with duties and ambitions (positive psychogenic motives) as well as with negative superego motives. The mother may have to undergo partial starvation—or, much more frequently, loss of sleep and rest—in order that her children may be adequately fed and cared for. An individual may wish to spend his limited money on present "creature comforts," but, having an ambition to prepare for a profession, he must either save his money and sacrifice present comforts or forego the education required to fulfill his ambition.

Id-superego conflicts are frequently of severe intensity; the theory of psychopathology is replete with discussions of this type of conflict. Freud's theory of neurosis, in particular, has emphasized the significance of conflicts between sexual impulses and the demands of conscience.

When biogenic deprivation is sufficiently intense, there will usually occur, as we have seen, a regression to biogenic motivation; the conflict will be resolved in favor of biogenic gratification, even though the attendant frustration of psychogenic motives will give rise to guilt and inferiority feelings.

SUPEREGO-SUPEREGO CONFLICTS.   The individual will frequently develop psychogenic motives that are in conflict with each other. He may develop incompatible ambitions, incompatible moral standards, incompatible duties. His ambitions may conflict with his moral standards; and his ambitions or his moral standards may conflict with his conception of duty.

The individual may have difficulty in choosing between two possible professions or two possible ways of life; he may be required to choose between science and art, between marriage and a successful career, between a high income and the enjoyment of his work.

The individual may have to choose between the moral standards of his parents and the moral standards that prevail in a different social class or in a different geographical region. This will be true especially in the case of the individual who rises to a higher social class, and in the case of the individual of foreign-born parentage.

Some marriages are troubled by the conflict that the husband experiences between his duty as a breadwinner and his duty as a companion to his wife and children. Conflicts may also occur between duties toward different persons or toward different "causes." Thus, according to Grinker and Spiegel, the flight surgeon may be faced with the problem of considering the safety of the pilot or gunner who has developed a neurosis and of considering the sometimes incompatible demands of the service for active combat personnel.[16]

An individual's ambition to attain wealth, power, or prestige may conflict with his moral values concerning the techniques that are often employed for attaining these ends.

An individual's ambition to complete his education may conflict with the belief that his duty requires him to volunteer for military service. And the "borderline" conscientious objector to military serv-

[16] Roy R. Grinker and John P. Spiegel, *Men under Stress* (Philadelphia, 1945), p. 152.

ice may suffer a conflict between his moral standards and his conception of duty.

Often superego-superego conflicts will develop into conflicts of severe intensity. It seems likely that many of the major discontents of present-day men and women can be attributed to conflicts involving ambitions, moral values, duties, etc. Many marriages, for example, will become a source of torment through their frustration of ideals concerning the "good way of life"; such marriages may then be held together on the basis of moral obligation. One or both parties to such marriages will continually suffer from inner conflict: whether to risk a gnawing sense of guilt for having dissolved the marriage in order to live according to one's ego-ideal, or to risk a sense of defeated inferiority for having maintained the marriage in order to live up to one's moral obligations.

It appears that contemporary theories of neurosis have given insufficient emphasis to the significance of incompatible superego motives—that is, to the significance of superego-superego conflicts.

SOME TYPICAL FRUSTRATIONS

SOME frustrations occur in our society with sufficient frequency to be termed *typical frustrations*. These will be discussed briefly as an aid to further definition of the concept of frustration.[17]

The child is often highly sensitive to indications of love, or its absence, in the behavior of his parents and others. He may interpret brief separation from his parents (being left alone at home, or being left with baby-sitters) as a sign that his parents do not love him. He will also be likely to interpret harsh treatment of any kind as an indication that he is not loved.

Shifting from breast-feeding to bottle-feeding, which may occur during the first few weeks of life, and weaning, which inevitably occurs at an early age, are typical examples of feeding frustrations.

Children learn about their environment by means of various exploratory activities—manipulating objects, putting things in the mouth, running about, etc. In the interest of the child's safety, parents often restrict these exploratory activities and thus, unavoidably, they frustrate the child's impulses.

[17] This discussion is adapted from a similar discussion by Symonds, *op. cit.*, pp. 64–9.

Toilet training and training in habits of cleanliness require frustration of the child's impulses to "do what comes naturally." The child must await the proper time and the proper place for gratifying his needs to eliminate; he must wait till his hands are washed before eating; he must be bathed, etc., before going to bed.

Different children in the family may compete for the parents' attention and affection. As the child notes the devotion of the parents to a younger sibling, he may feel frustrated at losing their attention.

As the child grows older, he is required to develop independence and self-sufficiency. The process of losing his dependence on the parents may frustrate his need for dependence, which has had psychogenic development during earlier years.

Children are frustrated in their impulses to gain auto-erotic gratification. At later ages, they are frustrated in their efforts to gain other forms of sexual gratification.

Boys are required to behave "like boys" and girls to behave "like girls." The culture maintains different expectations regarding members of the two sexes. Frustrations will be involved to the extent that the individual desires to behave in ways regarded as appropriate to the opposite sex.

When he goes to school, the child is separated from persons on whom he has previously been dependent, and he is forced to accept restrictions of freedom. Many children find schoolwork too difficult (if they have lower than average ability) or too easy and uninteresting (if they have higher than average ability). Yet they are required to spend their allotted time in school, in spite of the intensity of their frustration.

In addition to the obvious sexual frustrations of the adolescent, he may be frustrated in his efforts to become self-sufficient and to prepare for the eventual responsibility of economic competition, independence from parents, and the management of a family.

The adult may be frustrated in his efforts to make a living and to become economically secure. He may be frustrated in his efforts to maintain a particular social status. Accidents and illness may occur to render his struggle more than normally difficult.

The death of a member of one's family or of a friend is a deprivation that may occur at any time. Frustrations of this type are often quite severe, since they involve a serious disruption of the individual's way of life.

To the extent that the individual's level of aspiration is incompatible with the reality of his opportunities and his personal limitations, he may be expected to meet failure in some of his efforts. Since society is highly competitive, it is almost inevitable that each person will at times be a loser; each person will encounter failure in some of his projects.

SOME PRINCIPLES OF FRUSTRATION AND CONFLICT

THE PRECEDING discussion has dealt with the nature and characteristics of frustration and conflict. The following discussion will deal with interrelations that occur among different frustrations, and with interrelations that occur among frustrations and other personality functions.

Frustration and Motivation

Frustration involves all of the principles that relate to motivation itself. Primary frustrations involve the continued operation of needs; secondary frustrations, or frustrations proper, involve anxiety, which itself functions as a need. The principles of motivation, then, may be rephrased to emphasize their application to frustration and conflict.

1. Frustration and conflict are experienced as distressing and unpleasant.
2. Frustration and conflict involve muscular tension.
3. An increase in activity frequently accompanies frustration and conflict.
4. The behavior that accompanies frustration and conflict is partially *motivated* (determined) by the nature and intensity of frustration and conflict.
5. When the intensity of frustration or conflict is reduced, there will occur a decrease in conscious distress, in muscular tension, in the vigor of activity, and so on.
6. Frustration and conflict may occur unconsciously; the individual may not be aware that he is frustrated or that he has conflicting motives.
7. The total organization (the pattern) of frustrations and conflicts will determine the nature of reactions to frustration and conflict; a single frustration or conflict seldom functions independently.

Strength of Frustration and Conflict

The relative strength or severity of frustration or conflict will be a function of the length of time during which the frustration or conflict continues, of the degree of anxiety evoked, and of the strength of other reactions that are elicited. Some factors that must be considered for the evaluation of the strength of frustration or conflict will be discussed below.

EQUALITY OF "OPPOSING FORCES." A frustration or conflict will be of minor significance unless the motive and its frustration are of *approximately equal strength*. If a motive is weaker than its frustration, the individual will be unlikely to strive for its gratification. If a motive is decidedly stronger than its frustration, the individual will be likely to overcome the frustration in short order.

If, in the case of a conflict, one motive is definitely stronger than the other, the stronger motive will readily win over the other. Thus, if a child dreads a spanking more than he wants to cross the street, he will restrain his impulse to cross the street; but, if he wants to cross the street more than he dreads a spanking, he will readily decide to make the perilous crossing. Or, if a child would rather read than eat, he will continue to read until other factors (hunger and social pressure) intervene to render a change in his preference.

It is only when a motive and its frustration are of approximately equal strength that the frustration or conflict will continue sufficiently long to become significant for the individual's adjustment.

STRENGTH OF "OPPOSING FORCES." For a frustration or a conflict to be of significance at all, it is necessary that the opposing forces be of approximately equal strength. Once this condition has been met, the relative strength of the frustration or conflict will be dependent on the relative strength of the opposing forces themselves.

Thus, if a motive is relatively weak, and if its frustration is equally weak, the frustration or conflict will be relatively minor in severity. But when the motive is very strong, and when its frustration is equally strong, the frustration or conflict will be intense. The individual who only mildly wants to go to a movie, and who has found nobody who is willing or free to accompany him, can take such a frustration in his stride. But the man who is madly in love with a girl, and who cannot marry her because of her parents' objections, will experience a major frustration.

PREPOTENCE OF MOTIVES. Certain motives—notably the biogenic

motives—will, with extended periods of deprivation, become much stronger than others. When such biogenic needs as hunger, thirst, the need for oxygen, undergo continued frustration, the strength of frustration may reach catastrophic intensity. When, however, a conflict occurs between two motives, one of which is biogenic, the biogenic motive will eventually become prepotent, so that the conflict will be resolved in its favor.

> It is certainly true in a general way that the importance of an instinctual desire is mentally increased by frustration of it. Suppose one made the experiment of exposing a number of utterly different human beings to hunger under the same conditions. As the imperative need for food rose in them all their individual differences would be effaced, and instead the uniform manifestations of one unsatisfied instinct would appear.[18]

Any motive that is prepotent at a given time will win in the competition for gratification. But when frustrated by agents other than competing motives, such relatively prepotent motives will become involved in relatively severe frustrations.

THE ACCUMULATION OF MINOR FRUSTRATIONS. If the individual experiences over a relatively short period of time a number of frustrations, each of minor significance, he may eventually react as if in response to a single major frustration. To the external observer, who perceives only the last in the series of minor frustrations, the individual's reaction will appear to be unreasonably violent in relation to the immediate provocation. Thus a schoolteacher who has been able to maintain her composure through several hours of minor frustrations may suddenly "explode like a bombshell" in response to a child's misbehavior.

Interdependence of Frustrations

Frustrations are dynamically interrelated in the same sense that the underlying motives themselves are interrelated. The severity of the total interacting pattern of frustrations is not likely, in any case, to be equal to the summation of the strengths of the particular frustrations that make up the pattern. The strength of the total pattern will sometimes be less than the sum, and sometimes greater than the sum, of the strengths of all the particular frustrations, as these might be considered individually. This is only one of the many specific instances

[18] Sigmund Freud, *Collected Papers* (London, 1950), IV, 213–14.

of the principle that any complex whole will exhibit characteristics that are different from those of component parts.

Sometimes one frustration will function to *lessen* the severity of another frustration. A wound received in battle, for example, will lessen the strength of the minus-minus conflict of the soldier who is driven to endure danger in order to avoid disgrace, for no disgrace will be implied when the soldier is taken from the lines to become hospitalized; and the frustrative value of the wound itself may be lessened in terms of the fact that it has provided an indirect escape from the previous dilemma. Similarly, the conflict experienced by an individual whose conscience interferes with the attainment of a desired goal will be reduced when to conscience is added the support of active social prohibitions. For example, the presence of a chaperone may relieve young people of the conflict that will otherwise probably be experienced in relation to sexual temptations.

It is also true that one frustration may function to *increase* the strength of a co-existing frustration. Thus the person who has physical or mental limitations may have an increased perception of frustration when his motives are also denied gratification through the agency of external factors. The handicapped individual who cannot obtain employment because of the employer's prejudice against employing handicapped workers is a case in point. His difficulty in obtaining an income sufficient for his needs will, in any case, be greater than average (involving greater fatigue to achieve the same output, for instance), but the added frustration connected with the prejudice will increase his difficulties.

The solution of a particular conflict, or the removal of a particular frustration, may serve to decrease or increase the severity of the remaining conflicts or frustrations. Often the solution itself will involve the individual in new conflicts or frustrations. Thus the individual who has resolved a marriage-related conflict by means of divorce may encounter frustrations that did not occur during marriage or that were counteracted, during marriage, by other frustrations in the total pattern.

Cultural Sources of Frustration and Conflict

Most complex societies, since they foster mutually incompatible values, will make contradictory demands on the individual. When these incompatible values are introjected by the individual—when these become components of his psychogenic motivation—he will frequently become involved in situations in which his values are in conflict. The individual will also frequently suffer frustration from external sources, if he has introjected ambitions, ideals, and standards incompatible with the material and human resources provided by his environment.

The Christian ideals of brotherly love and humility may conflict with the current standards of economic competition. The child is taught to believe that anybody can accomplish anything he sets out to accomplish, if only he works hard enough and maintains seriousness of purpose; this he later discovers to be completely at variance both with individual limitations and with environmental opportunities. Moreover, persons are censured if they fail to develop high ambitions, yet the society cannot provide opportunities for the widespread achievement of such ambitions. Likewise, some agencies of the society stress the ideal of providing equal opportunities for all human individuals, regardless of their origin, while other agencies foster racial and minority-group prejudices.[19]

Generalization of Frustration and Conflict

Miller has demonstrated that frustrations and conflicts tend to become generalized—that is, frustrations will spread from the original situation to new situations.[20] This concept becomes understandable as a function of the lowered self-confidence of the individual who has experienced a severe, or long-enduring, conflict. This lowered self-confidence will function as a basis for the perception of frustration in new situations.

Moreover, the influence of a severe conflict will function to lower the individual's efficiency in dealing with various situations, so that situations ordinarily interpreted as gratifying may now be interpreted as frustrating. For example, the student who is frustrated by financial difficulties, or who suffers from a conflict relating to his family or to

[19] "Our educational agencies, in other words, are inconsistent in what they teach and are therefore frustration inducing. They create veritable never-never lands which abound with frigidaires, yachts, television sets, glamorous exotic women, and men of distinction. We are taught to want them, and to want them, we are taught, is proof of our enterprise and our sound Americanism. And then we are prevented by our economic organizations and practices, by our church and our parents and our neighbors from getting them. There is much in our culture that induces frustration." (David Krech and Richard S. Crutchfield, *Theory and Problems of Social Psychology* [New York, 1948], p. 492. Reprinted by permission of McGraw-Hill Book Company, Inc. Copyright, 1948, by McGraw-Hill Book Company, Inc.)

[20] Miller, *op. cit.*, pp. 462–3.

a love affair, will be likely to have unusually great difficulty in his studies or in his social relations. Both his efficiency and his self-confidence will, under conditions of frustration or conflict, have been reduced below their normal level.

Frustration of Unconscious Motives

The motives operative in an individual will vary along a continuum from clearly conscious to deeply unconscious. The individual will be clearly aware of some motives, only vaguely and intermittently aware of other motives, and completely unaware of still other motives. Frustration may occur in the case of any motive, regardless of the degree of awareness associated with its operation.

Sometimes, when the motive is a clearly conscious one, the individual will know what motive is being frustrated. Perhaps more frequently, since motives may be involved that are not clearly conscious, the individual will be aware only that he is frustrated, or only that he suffers anxiety, but will be unable to identify the motive or motives that are being frustrated.

It is to a large extent the function of psychoanalysis, and of other forms of therapy, to aid the individual in discovering the particular motives that are being frustrated or are in conflict with one another.

Frustration Tolerance

The concept of *frustration tolerance* was developed by Rosenzweig, who defined frustration tolerance as "an individual's capacity to withstand frustration without failure of psychobiological adjustment, *i.e.*, without resorting to inadequate modes of response." [21] Rosenzweig regarded the term *frustration tolerance* as approximately equivalent to the psychoanalytic term *ego strength*.[22]

Freud seems to have been referring to frustration tolerance when he wrote that "there may exist for every one a limit beyond which his psyche fails in the attempt to cope with the demands which the excitation in question makes upon him," [23] and when he wrote that "the capacity to withstand neurotic illness . . . depends upon the *amount* of un-

[21] Rosenzweig, "An Outline of Frustration Theory," *op. cit.*, pp. 385–7.
[22] The psychoanalyst regards therapy as consisting, in part, of procedures that "strengthen the ego"; the concept of ego strength will be treated in a subsequent chapter.
[23] Sigmund Freud, *The Problem of Anxiety* (New York, 1936), p. 91. Reprinted by permission of *The Psychoanalytic Quarterly* and W. W. Norton & Company, Inc. Copyright, 1936, by The Psychoanalytic Quarterly Press.

discharged libido that a person can hold freely suspended." [24] The terms *excitation* and *undischarged libido* may roughly be translated into the term *primary frustration;* these terms imply the continuation of an ungratified need.

The development of frustration tolerance may be considered analogous to the development of tolerance of drugs. Tolerance will develop most adequately when the dosage of a drug is gradually increased, but will be unlikely to develop at all when too much is taken at a particular time.

The development of frustration tolerance follows a similar principle: frustration tolerance will develop most satisfactorily through gradually increased exposure to frustration. The person who has been "overprotected" or "pampered"—that is, protected against a normal amount of frustration—will have low tolerance for the frustrations that will inevitably occur when the protection has been removed. Likewise, the person who has been subjected to more frustration than he can tolerate will have low frustration tolerance, since it will have been necessary for him to employ maladaptive defensive reactions (which become habitual).

Probably frustration tolerance, as defined by Rosenzweig, is concerned only with primary frustration—that is, with frustrations involving the sheer continuation of ungratified needs.[25] When high frustration tolerance is manifested, it is probably based on confidence in eventual gratification—an attitude that implies the absence of secondary frustration. In other words, frustration tolerance (which might preferably be termed *need tolerance*) is apparently dependent on self-confidence and environmental confidence.

It is probable that each individual at a given stage in his development has a specific degree of frustration tolerance. To an external observer, a person's level of frustration tolerance may appear to fluctuate greatly from time to time, depending on such conditions as fatigue, physical illness, the kind of day he has had, etc. This fluctuation is probably apparent rather than real, since fatigue, illness, etc., will

[24] Sigmund Freud, *A General Introduction to Psycho-Analysis* (New York, 1935), p. 327.
[25] As we shall have occasion to note subsequently, however, anxiety and aggressive motivation arise with the occurrence of secondary frustrations. Both anxiety and aggressive motivation will function as primary frustrations—that is, as continued motivational excitations. The capacity to delay the relief of anxiety and of aggressive motivation would properly come under the concept of frustration tolerance.

themselves function as frustrations, whose strength will approach the upper limit of the individual's tolerance. Under such conditions, an additional minor frustration may be sufficient to elicit extreme reactions. This interpretation seems to be consistent with what has been said regarding the cumulative effect of minor frustrations, the interdependence of frustrations, and the generalization of frustration.

Our present-day society continually exerts pressure on the individual to develop frustration tolerance. From the time of St. Paul, who exhorted us to "put away childish things," to modern times, when we are admonished to "be our age," our culture has been imbued with propaganda for frustration tolerance. Thus, one of the powerful motivations during childhood involves the pressure to be a "big boy" or a "big girl." And adults feel that it is shameful to "show their weakness" in public by the exhibition of uncontrolled reactions to frustration; the same individuals, however, may exhibit these reactions in the privacy of their homes.

GENERAL REACTIONS TO FRUSTRATION AND CONFLICT

THIS section will deal with some of the general reactions to frustration and conflict. The treatment here will be relatively brief, since subsequent chapters will treat these reactions in detail.

Direct Removal of Frustration

The direct removal of frustration, which leads to gratification of the original motive, is the expected reaction to frustration, if the individual can perceive this as a possibility. Such direct removal of frustration may be achieved in different ways.

One method involves increasing one's effort to overcome the barrier that obstructs progress toward a goal. This is exemplified by the individual who runs in order to catch a bus he is about to miss, or by the individual who studies harder in order to pass a course.

Another method involves a re-evaluation of the positive and negative features in the situation—i.e., a reinterpretation of the situation so that it will be perceived as nonfrustrating. Thus, a child whose ball is lodged in a tree, and who has been forbidden to climb trees, may discover that he can dislodge the ball by throwing rocks at it.

Aggression

It is the thesis of Dollard and his collaborators that the invariable response to frustration will be aggression in some form.[26] Whoever or whatever is perceived to be the source of frustration will regularly be perceived as a suitable object of aggression. As Freud has stated, "the ego hates, abhors and pursues with intent to destroy all objects which are for it a source of painful feelings." [27]

This does not imply that aggression will be directly or crudely expressed, for aggression may be displaced and disguised in various ways. Since direct aggression against the perceived source of frustration may represent a danger to the individual, such aggression may be displaced onto less dangerous objects, or it may be changed into socially approved or symbolic forms. A more detailed treatment of aggression will be given in Chap. V.

Anxiety

The occurrence of anxiety is a regular accompaniment of frustration or conflict. Since anxiety itself functions as a motive, and since defensive activities are employed to reduce anxiety, the psychology of adjustment is focused upon the anxiety reaction and methods for its reduction. A subsequent chapter will be devoted to the discussion of anxiety.

ADJUSTIVE IMPLICATIONS

THIS section, and those similarly titled in subsequent chapters, will deal with the "applied psychology" of adjustment. Traditionally this has been termed "mental hygiene."

The implications of such terms as "mental hygiene," "mental health," etc., are incorrect in a number of respects. In the first place, the term "mental" implies a dichotomy between "mental" and "physical," when in reality there is no such dichotomy. The organism functions psychosomatically, as the discussion of a previous chapter has emphasized. Moreover, terms such as "hygiene" and "health" had their origin in medicine and therefore carry implications that do not really apply to the phenomena of adjustive behavior.

[26] John Dollard, Leonard W. Doob, Neal E. Miller, O. Hobart Mowrer, and Robert R. Sears, *Frustration and Aggression* (New Haven, 1939), pp. 1–54.
[27] Freud, *Collected Papers*, IV, 81.

The terms "adjustment" and "adjustive," however, carry no such incorrect implications. When we speak of *adjustive implications,* there should be no misleading connotations, since the term implies merely the application of adjustive principles to the problems of everyday living. Few will be misguided by this term, as persons frequently have been by terms such as "mental hygiene" and "mental illness." [28]

It should be emphasized that there can be no simple rules for the achievement of effective adjustment. Adjustive behavior should be understood to involve extremely complicated interrelations; and, though it is true that general principles can be discovered, the concrete manifestation of these general principles in a unique personality cannot be described except on the basis of an intensive study of the individual personality. There can be no free and easy statements as to what *all* individuals should or should not do in order to become effectively adjusted.

Frustration Unavoidable

In previous sections it has been emphasized that frustration is unavoidable. The socialization process requires frustration of the child's originally uncontrolled impulses. Limitations that occur in the external environment and in the potentialities of the person also imply that frustration is inevitable.

Since frustration is unavoidable, there can be little value in advocating its elimination. Even if this were possible, it would probably not be desirable, for, as we have previously seen, the pleasures of life consist in activities that reduce motivation; and if motivation were not frustrated at all—that is, if motivation were not allowed to build up to appreciably high levels—little pleasure would be derived from living.

Frustration Necessary for Learning

O'Kelly has pointed out that frustration is probably a necessary condition for the occurrence of learning.[29] If the individual could achieve gratification immediately upon the arousal of each motive, there would be no adaptation to be accomplished. The individual learns new responses only upon the basis of frustration, which itself

[28] That such misunderstanding has occurred from the use of misleading terms is evident from the statement by physicians, as well as by laymen: "It's all in your mind"—as if to imply that symptoms arising from adjustive difficulties are imaginary rather than real.

[29] Lawrence I. O'Kelly, *Introduction to Psychopathology* (New York, 1949), p. 41.

will occur only by virtue of the inadequacy of pre-existing behavior patterns. The individual who has been excessively protected against frustration will, on the basis of his immature behavior patterns, be unprepared to gratify his motives when at last he is forced to depend on his own devices.

Frustration within Limits

Any person who holds an authoritative position in relation to children, or, for that matter, in relation to other adults, should be sensitive to the level of frustration tolerance which characterizes each individual over whom he exerts authority. The procedures of socializing, teaching, and supervising should involve no more frustration than the subordinate individual can reasonably tolerate. Since frustration is an inevitable accompaniment of these procedures, the parent, the teacher, or the supervisor should limit the amount of frustration to that which is essential for achieving the immediate purpose.

The use of forms of gratification (rewards, praise, the display of friendliness or affection, etc.) will aid in keeping the level of frustration to a minimum; thus, while any educative procedure will necessarily involve the frustration of particular impulses, the other motives of the individual need not be frustrated in the process.

Level of Aspiration (Ego-Ideal)

An individual's level of aspiration, or ego-ideal, embodies the standards of achievement which the individual has adopted for himself. Obviously, frustration is largely a function of the incompatibility between the level of aspiration and the individual's realistic possibilities in relation to his environment. Lewin has made the following statement regarding level of aspiration:

A successful individual typically sets his next goal somewhat, but not too much, above his last achievement. In this way he steadily raises his level of aspiration. Although in the long run he is guided by his ideal goal, which may be rather high, nevertheless his real goal for the next step is kept realistically close to his present position. The unsuccessful individual, on the other hand, tends to show one of two reactions: he sets his goal very low, frequently below his past achievement—that is, he becomes intimidated and gives up reaching out toward higher goals—or he sets his goal far above his ability. . . . To develop and to maintain high goals and, at the same time, to keep the plan for the next action realistically within the limits of what is possible, seems to be one of the basic objectives for and a criterion of high morale.[30]

Johnson has stressed that the source of much maladjustment is to be understood in terms of the "I-F-D formula," which involves a development "from idealism to frustration to demoralization." [31] Keeping the level of aspiration realistically within the limits of one's possibilities of achievement, then, is a guiding principle that can aid in preventing the occurrence of frustration beyond the limit of one's frustration tolerance.

Hierarchy of Values (Philosophy of Life)

If the individual has established a hierarchy among his values (motives)—if his values are ordered in terms of their relative importance—if he has developed, in other words, a reasonably consistent philosophy of life, then many of his conflicts will resolve themselves more or less automatically, and many of his frustrations will have little significance for him. When a conflict occurs between two motives the preference order of which has already been established, the conflict will immediately be resolved, since the individual will choose to gratify one motive in preference to the other. Moreover, frustration of motives that are evaluated as relatively unimportant will arouse little anxiety, since motives of greater importance will be gratified with some degree of regularity. The achievement of a hierarchy of values is one of the significant indications of a mature personality.

SUMMARY

FRUSTRATION and conflict pervade human living. Frustration involves the perception of an actual (immediate) or potential (delayed) interference with the gratification of a motive, or with some special way of gratifying a motive. The perception of frustration is significantly related to the individual's self-confidence and to his confidence in the environment. The continuation of a motive becomes a

[30] Kurt Lewin, "Time Perspective and Morale," in *Civilian Morale*, Goodwin Watson, ed. (Boston, 1942), p. 59. Reprinted by permission of The Society for the Psychological Study of Social Issues, and Henry Holt and Company, Inc. Copyright, 1942, by The Society for the Psychological Study of Social Issues.

[31] Wendell Johnson, *People in Quandaries: the Semantics of Personal Adjustment* (New York, 1946), pp. 3-20. Reprinted by permission of Harper & Brothers. Copyright, 1946, by Harper & Brothers.

frustration as soon as the individual perceives an interference with gratification.

Frustrations may be classified in a number of ways. *Primary frustrations* involve the sheer continuation of needs, while *secondary frustrations* involve the perception of some particular interference with gratification.

Passive frustrations involve the mere perception of an interference with gratification, while *active frustrations* involve a threat to the individual's safety; in other words, active frustrations involve a larger pattern of motives than is involved in passive frustrations.

Need frustrations involve the temporary or permanent prevention of gratification; *instrumental act frustrations* involve interference with a particular mode of achieving gratification; *object frustrations* involve interference with gratification in relation to a particular cathected object.

Frustrations may also be classified, in terms of their source, as *external* and *internal;* external and internal frustrations may be further subdivided into *privations* (lacks or defects), *deprivations* (losses), and *obstructions* (barriers between the individual and his goals). Internal obstructions are termed *conflicts*.

Conflicts may be classified in terms of the possible combinations of valence or cathexis—in terms of whether they are predominantly plus-plus, plus-minus, or minus-minus.

Plus-plus conflicts require a choice between incompatible goals that are positively cathected. Plus-plus conflicts are usually relatively minor, since either choice will bring some gratification; they may, however, be of major importance when they require a relatively permanent or irrevocable choice.

Plus-minus conflicts require a choice between losing some desired goal in order to avoid its negative features and accepting the negative features in order to attain the desired goal. Immobility and vacillation frequently occur in response to plus-minus conflicts. Plus-minus conflicts are likely to be of severe intensity, since they are difficult to resolve, and since either solution will involve frustration.

Minus-minus conflicts require a choice between negatively cathected goals; in order to escape one frustration, the individual must become the victim of another. The typical reactions to minus-minus conflicts are withdrawal and vacillation. Minus-minus conflicts are typically severe; they are difficult to resolve, since escaping one frustration will involve being trapped by another.

Conflicts usually involve complex combinations of positive and negative cathexis; the above classification of conflicts, therefore, should be regarded as an oversimplification.

Conflicts may also be classified in terms of the origin of the motives that conflict with each other. *Id-id conflicts* involve the operation of two or more incompatible biogenic motives. *Id-superego conflicts* involve the operation of psychogenic motives that are incompatible with biogenic motives. *Superego-superego conflicts* involve the operation of incompatible psychogenic motives. Id-id conflicts are usually of minor significance, but id-superego and superego-superego conflicts may be at the root of most instances of human maladjustment.

Human living is beset with frustrations that are typical at different stages of development. Among these typical frustrations are loss of love, feeding frustrations, exploration restrictions, cleanliness training, rivalries within the family, lessening dependence, sexual restrictions, sex patterning, school frustrations, adult frustrations in striving for economic security and social status, death of family members and friends, and failures in various enterprises.

Frustration involves all of the principles that relate to motives. The concepts of discomforting stimuli, increased muscular tension, increased activity, and unconscious motivation apply as much to frustration as to the original motives that are frustrated.

For a frustration or a conflict to be significant, it must involve relatively strong motives. Both the motive and its frustration—both of the incompatible features of a conflict—must be of equal strength if the frustration or conflict is to become significant for adjustment. Of the motives involved in conflict, those which are prepotent will eventually win out. If prepotent motives are frustrated by agencies other than incompatible motives, the frustration is likely to be severe. The response to a series of minor frustrations may be similar to that which is induced by a single major frustration.

Frustrations are dynamically interrelated. The severity of the total interacting pattern of frustrations will not necessarily be equal to the summation of the separate strengths of each component frustration; the strength of the total pattern of frustrations will sometimes be less than, sometimes more than, and sometimes equal to, this sum.

In a complex society, contradictory demands may be made on the individual; he may introject values that are mutually conflicting, or he may introject ambitions, ideals, or standards that are incompatible with the resources available in his environment.

Frustrations may generalize from one situation to another. On the basis of previous frustrations, the individual may develop a low level of confidence in himself or in his environment, and he may become less than normally efficient; therefore he will be more likely to perceive any given situation as frustrating.

Since many motives operate on a relatively unconscious level, the frustration of relatively unconscious motives will occur; the individual may be aware that he is frustrated, or merely aware of anxiety, without knowing what motives are being frustrated.

Frustration tolerance (or need tolerance) is defined as the individual's capacity to delay gratification. It will develop most adequately when the frustration required of the individual increases gradually within the limit of pre-existing tolerance. Too little frustration or too much frustration at any given time will interfere with the development of frustration tolerance.

General reactions to frustration include the direct removal of frustration through gratification of the original motive, the development of aggressive motivation, and the development of anxiety.

The principles of frustration have the following adjustive implications: (1) that frustration is unavoidable; (2) that frustration is necessary for learning; (3) that the level of aspiration should be maintained reasonably near the level of the individual's previous achievement; (4) that persons in authority over others should be sensitive to the frustration tolerance of those who are subordinate to them, and should strive to socialize, teach, or supervise in such a manner that the induced frustration will be within the limits of frustration tolerance; and (5) that many conflicts are readily resolved, and many frustrations rendered unimportant, if the individual has developed a stable hierarchy, or ordered system, of values.

Aggression, which is one of the general reactions to frustration, and punishment, which involves aggression, will be discussed in the following chapter.

► Suggested Readings

Bayton, J. A. and Whyte, Esther C. "Personality Dynamics during Success-Failure Sequences," *Journal of Abnormal and Social Psychology*, 45 (1950), 583–91.

Bitterman, M. E. "Behavior Disorder as a Function of the Relative Strength of Antagonistic Response-Tendencies," *Psychological Review, 51* (1944), 375–8.

Brown, J. S. and Farber, I. E. "Emotions Conceptualized as Intervening Variables—with Suggestions toward a Theory of Frustration," *Psychological Bulletin, 48* (1951), 465–95.

Cameron, N. *The Psychology of Behavior Disorders.* Boston, 1947. Pp. 130–40.

Cameron, N. and Magaret, Ann. *Behavior Pathology.* Boston, 1951. Chap. ix, pp. 246–75.

Child, I. L. "Children's Preference for Goals Easy or Difficult to Obtain," *Psychological Monographs, 60,* No. 4 (1946).

Child, I. L. and Whiting, J. W. M. "Determinants of Level of Aspiration: Evidence from Everyday Life," *Journal of Abnormal and Social Psychology, 44* (1949), 303–14.

Child, I. L. and Whiting, J. W. M. "Effects of Goal Attainment: Relaxation versus Renewed Striving," *Journal of Abnormal and Social Psychology, 45* (1950), 667–81.

Crandall, V. J. "Induced Frustration and Punishment-Reward Expectancy in Thematic Apperception Stories," *Journal of Consulting Psychology, 15* (1951), 400–4.

Dollard, J. and Miller, N. E. *Personality and Psychotherapy.* New York, 1950. Chap. x, pp. 127–56.

Guthrie, E. R. *The Psychology of Human Conflict.* New York, 1938. Chaps. xxiv–xxvi, pp. 320–55.

Kaplan, L. and Baron, D. *Mental Hygiene and Life.* New York, 1952. Chap. x, pp. 253–82.

Lewin, K. *A Dynamic Theory of Personality.* New York, 1935. Chap. iii, pp. 66–113.

Lewin, K., Dembo, Tamara, and Festinger, L. "Level of Aspiration," in *Personality and the Behavior Disorders,* J. McV. Hunt, ed. New York, 1944. Chap. x, pp. 333–78.

Lindzey, G. and Riecken, H. W. "Inducing Frustration in Adult Subjects," *Journal of Consulting Psychology, 15* (1951), 18–23.

Loomis, S. D. and Green, A. W. "The Pattern of Mental Conflict in a Typical State University," *Journal of Abnormal and Social Psychology, 42* (1947), 342–55.

McKinney, F., Strother, G. B., Hines, Ruth R., and Allee, Ruth A. "Experimental Frustration in a Group Test Situation," *Journal of Abnormal and Social Psychology, 46* (1951), 316–23.

Maslow, A. H. "Conflict, Frustration, and the Theory of Threat," *Journal of Abnormal and Social Psychology, 38* (1943), 81–6.

Maslow, A. H. and Mittelmann, B. *Principles of Abnormal Psychology.* New York, 1951. Chaps. iv–vii, pp. 45–86.

Miller, D. R. "Responses of Psychiatric Patients to Threat of Failure," *Journal of Abnormal and Social Psychology, 46* (1951), 378–87.

Mowrer, O. H. "Discipline and Mental Health," *Learning Theory and Personality Dynamics.* New York, 1950. Chap. xvi, pp. 455–71.

Murphy, G. *Personality.* New York, 1947. Chap. xiii, pp. 296–328.

O'Kelly, L. I. *Introduction to Psychopathology.* New York, 1949. Pp. 38–47.

Orlansky, H. "Infant Care and Personality," *Psychological Bulletin, 46* (1949), 1–48.

Steisel, I. M. and Cohen, B. D. "The Effects of Two Degrees of Failure on Level of Aspiration and Performance," *Journal of Abnormal and Social Psychology, 46* (1951), 79–82.

Symonds, P. M. *The Dynamics of Human Adjustment.* New York, 1946. Chaps. iii and xv, pp. 50–80, 336–61.

Vaughan, W. F. *Personal and Social Adjustment.* New York, 1952. Chap. vii, pp. 236–84.

Yarrow, L. J. "The Effect of Antecedent Frustration on Projective Play," *Psychological Monographs, 62,* No. 6 (1948).

Zander, A. F. "A Study of Experimental Frustration," *Psychological Monographs, 56,* No. 3 (1944).

CHAPTER Five

Aggression and Punishment

Thou shalt not kill.[1]

The limitation of aggression is the first and perhaps the hardest sacrifice which society demands from each individual.[2]

*W*HENEVER the individual is frustrated, aggressive motivation will arise. This aggressive motivation will usually undergo frustration, not only through external (usually social) prohibitions but also through prohibitions of conscience. The frustration of aggressive motivation will arouse further aggressive motivation, and so a self-maintaining sequence will occur: aggressive motivation will continually increase in intensity until it is finally gratified in a direct, displaced, disguised, or symbolic manner.

DEFINITION OF AGGRESSION

AGGRESSION may be defined as *an act intended to frustrate, injure, or destroy* another individual or an object.[3] An act that *accidentally* injures another person or an object need not be interpreted as aggression. Since, however, the aggressive motive may function unconsciously, it is always difficult, if not impossible, to determine

---

[1] Exodus xx–13.

[2] Sigmund Freud, *New Introductory Lectures on Psycho-Analysis* (New York, 1933), p. 151.

[3] Aggression should be distinguished from dominance, which involves controlling or influencing the behavior of other persons or objects.

whether a given act is accidental or the outcome of aggressive motivation. Aggression involves activity that *aims at frustrating or injuring* an object; it is accompanied by a conscious or an unconscious attitude of hostility. Aggression does not always eventuate in frustration or injury to an object, even though its goal is to achieve such frustration or injury.

Forms of Aggression

Aggression may assume many forms. It may be expressed through overt physical attack, through overt attack against the personality, or through subtle and indirect forms of attack.

OVERT PHYSICAL AGGRESSION. The most obvious forms of aggression involve doing physical damage or injury to another person, to his possessions, or to things that he values.

Attacks against the body of another person may involve hitting, slapping, scratching, biting, or pushing him; pulling his hair; using weapons—sticks, stones, knives, guns, blackjacks, lead pipes and other "blunt instruments"—against him; tying him with ropes; locking him in dark closets; burning his house while he is asleep; lynching him; tar-and-feathering him; etc.

Attacks against the individual's property may involve damaging, burning, stealing, or otherwise destroying his possessions; or they may involve "cutthroat" competition to drive him out of business.

Attacks against things that another person values may involve kicking his dog, putting up billboards to interfere with his "view," scaring his children, or defacing monuments or symbols of a patriotic or religious nature.

OVERT AGGRESSION AGAINST THE PERSONALITY. Aggressive actions that damage the personality, through injury to the individual's reputation, are usually verbal in nature. Such attacks may involve cursing, denouncing, accusing, blaming, criticizing, ridiculing, belittling, insulting, or slandering the object of aggression; they may involve telling malicious jokes at his expense, using foul language in his presence, making irritable or nonsensical (e.g., punning) replies to his serious remarks, using sarcasm against him, or making him the object of malicious gossip. Such verbal attacks on another's personality or reputation may eventuate in his embarrassment, his loss of self-esteem, his loss of social approval, or even his disgrace.

INDIRECT FORMS OF AGGRESSION. Indirect forms of aggression may damage the object of aggression even though the aggressor may not be aware of the aggressive intention of his acts; or the aggression may do no real harm to the object of aggression, since it makes use of such unrealistic techniques as fantasy, magic, sorcery, or witchcraft.

In the first class are to be mentioned those acts which have given rise to the adage that "hell is paved with good intentions." The individual who harbors unconscious aggressive needs will frequently do harm to the persons whom he consciously strives to benefit. This is frequently the case when parents or teachers punish children with the *conscious* goal of preparing them for a better-adjusted life in the future. Being too lenient with children may serve a similar aggressive aim. In other words, as much genuine damage may be done through the expression of unconscious aggressive motivation as through the realization of a conscious aggressive design.

When aggression is expressed in fantasy, as in the case of the child who dreams of the time when he can retaliate for a spanking, or as in the case of the pupil who imagines his teacher in an embarrassing situation or in a serious accident, no real damage will be done to the object of aggression. Likewise, when an individual gratifies his hostility by means of such a technique as magic, sorcery, or witchcraft, he will do no actual damage to his intended victim, unless the latter happens to believe in the power of such techniques and happens to have knowledge that one of them is being used against him.

CHANGE IN FORM OF AGGRESSION. When the individual is prevented, either by external pressures or by introjected standards, from committing aggression in a direct and obvious form, he will ordinarily substitute a less direct form. Thus, if he cannot use physical aggression, he may give vent to verbal methods of attacking the personality; when even this form of expression is prevented, he may indulge in aggressive fantasies. Such projective techniques as finger-painting and play therapy are based on the principle that individuals who are not free to express their hostility in a direct form may express it through these indirect media.

Feelings and Attitudes Associated with Aggression

Aggression, as previously indicated, implies an *action*. Certain feelings and attitudes are, in general, associated with aggressive behavior. Among these feelings and attitudes may be mentioned anger, resentment, hostility, hatred, anxiety, and guilt.

Anger implies an emotional process that is aroused during frustration. In terms of the total need integrate—which may be termed *hostil-*

ity or *aggressive motivation*—anger may be regarded as involving the combination of a need (tension) with imagined instrumental acts (injurious modes of action), but with no recognized or definite object. When anger is experienced, the individual will be able to gratify his aggressive need by means of aggressive action against almost any object that happens to be in his way. Anger has sometimes been called "free-floating aggression," implying its lack of a definite object. The term *resentment* implies a prolonged state of anger, which continues to be experienced when the individual cannot find suitable aggressive outlets.

Hostility involves the total need integrate that we have previously called aggressive motivation. That is to say, hostility involves a need (tension) in combination with imagined instrumental acts (injurious modes of action) in relation to a definite person or object. An individual may be angry or feel resentment without knowing what he is angry at or resentful toward, but an individual's hostility is always directed toward some particular person or thing.

Hatred implies an established and long-continuing hostility that is maintained in relation to a particular object. One may have a momentary attitude of hostility, but one only hates those objects in relation to which hostility has become a firmly established attitude.

When, through repression, both the object and the instrumental act have been lost to consciousness, the bare need (tension) that remains in consciousness will be experienced as *anxiety*.

When, through repression and displacement, the original object of hostility is lost to consciousness and hostility is consciously turned against the self, *guilt* will be experienced.

Sadism and Masochism

When aggressive needs become relatively generalized, and become permanent personality traits, it is customary to classify such personality traits under *sadism* or *masochism*. Originally, following the practice of Kraft-Ebing, Freud treated sadism and masochism as sexual perversions.[4] According to Freud, "we use the word 'sadism' when sexual satisfaction depends upon the sexual object suffering pain, ill-treatment, and humiliation, and the word 'masochism' when the subject himself has to suffer such treatment." [5]

[4] Sigmund Freud, "Three Contributions to the Theory of Sex," in *The Basic Writings of Sigmund Freud*, A. A. Brill, ed. (New York, 1938), pp. 569-71.
[5] Freud, *New Introductory Lectures* . . . , p. 143.

In modern usage these terms have come to imply a generalized tendency to inflict pain and suffering on others (sadism) or to gain gratification from the suffering of pain and humiliation (masochism). The pleasure associated with inflicting or suffering pain is not necessarily related to gratification of the biogenic sexual drive. Murray, for example, states that sadism "describes pleasure that is felt when an object is hurt or belittled. It leads to the maltreatment of others: unjustly dominating, bullying, hurting or torturing a younger child or animal." [6] Murray lists masochism under the *need for abasement*, which is defined as the need to "surrender . . . comply and accept punishment . . . apologize, confess, atone. . . ." [7]

The sadist—the person who has developed a consistent need to commit aggression against external objects—manifests various forms of cruelty. The masochist—the person who has developed a consistent need to displace aggression onto himself—enjoys various forms of martyrdom, humiliation, and self-depreciation. Both sadistic and masochistic tendencies are often expressed in the behavior of the same individual. [8]

TYPICAL AGGRESSIVE EXPRESSIONS

IN OUR own society, some forms of aggression are severely prohibited, while other forms are approved and encouraged. Thus, "aggressiveness leading to the destruction of life and property is strongly prohibited by our code of laws and penal system. On the other hand, rivalry and competition are encouraged, and have become the accepted pattern of our culture." [9] The present section will deal with some major areas in which aggression is expressed by present-day Americans.

Economic Competition

Indirect forms of aggression are continually practiced in economic competition. Individuals compete against one another for jobs; retailers compete against consumers and against one another for the consumer's limited income; manufacturers compete against other manufacturers—in short, almost every phase of our economic life is competitive.

To the extent that one person or corporation wins in such eco-

[6] Henry A. Murray, *Explorations in Personality* (New York, 1938), p. 340.
[7] *Ibid.*, p. 82.
[8] Freud, "Three Contributions . . . ," *op. cit.*, p. 570.
[9] Percival M. Symonds, *The Dynamics of Human Adjustment* (New York, 1946), p. 97.

nomic competition, other competitors will lose. Successful economic competition involves an indirect aggression against the less successful competitors. Regardless of the degree of success in economic competition, the competitive activity itself will involve various forms of aggression. Economic forms of aggression, when practiced within the limits of legal and moral standards, are highly approved in our society; as a matter of fact, the noncompetitive individual is often regarded as "abnormal."

Political Competition

Our political system involves continual competition among rival parties, and among rival candidates, for positions of dominance. There are, even between elections, many expressions of hostility against members of opposite parties; during pre-election campaigns such aggression reaches its height, with the contending candidates making true and false accusations against one another, one impugning another's character, and so on. Most of this political competition is approved by the majority; indeed, it is widely believed that representative government would be impossible without it.

Crime and Delinquency

Although our society disapproves, and often punishes, the individual who commits a criminal form of aggression, crime and delinquency are widely practiced. Many crimes involve aggression, sometimes against the frustrating agent himself (as in the case of some murders) and sometimes against objects other than the frustrating agent (as in the case of delinquent behavior that has its origin in home and family frustrations). Frequently, crimes involve aggression against the property of the frustrating agent (as in the case of arson "for spite") or against symbols highly valued by the frustrating agent (as in some cases of treason). Obviously many crimes gratify the hostile needs of the criminal even though they may, at the same time, gratify other forms of motivation.

Industrial Conflicts

Industrial conflicts (strikes, lockouts, etc.) frequently involve aggression. Krech and Crutchfield have pointed out that "the worker does not perceive a strike as a passive refusal to work—he sees it as a *positive technique of force.*" [10] The strike, in other words, is seen as a

[10] David Krech and Richard S. Crutchfield, *Theory and Problems of Social Psychology* (New York, 1948), p. 554.

form of aggression against management. Such aggression may have its origin in the frustrations that occur outside the work situation as well as in frustrations relating to the conditions of employment. It is probable, however, that frustrations occurring outside the work situation have been overemphasized in this connection. Thus, according to Krech and Crutchfield,

> . . . it is safe to hazard a guess that most instances of industrial conflict can properly be characterized as constructive and healthy frustration reactions. That is, specific, consciously identified needs are frustrated. The worker, thus frustrated, recognizes management policies as the barriers intervening between him and his goals, and he reacts by direct action against these barriers through striking or other forms of industrial conflict.[11]

War

For some of the individuals involved, the waging of war will gratify aggressive motivation. But it would be incorrect to assume—even though the activities of soldiers do injure and destroy the enemy and his property—that soldiers themselves are necessarily engaged in gratifying aggressive needs. "Many, perhaps most, people are forced to engage in war despite their own lack of desire for it or even active opposition to it." [12] This coercion in itself may function as a frustration, which, along with other frustrations necessarily associated with military life, may arouse aggressive needs that can be expressed in action against the enemy.

Exposure to propaganda may also lead to the canalization (displacement) of aggression onto the specific enemy that happens to be in vogue at a particular period in history. Propaganda, likewise, may induce individuals to perceive the enemy as a frustrating agent, so that their need for aggression against the enemy will be increased. Thus, one of Hitler's favorite techniques was to "inform" his subjects that they were about to be attacked by some bordering state, thus preparing them for the "necessity" of striking the first blow.

Prejudice

Minority groups provide approved objects against which to direct aggression. Aggressive needs that have been initiated by frustrations arising from other sources are frequently expressed, through displace-

[11] *Ibid.*, p. 547.   [12] *Ibid.*, p. 576.

ment, against members of minority groups. When members of a minority group happen to be the actual agents of frustration, aggression will more readily be committed against them than against frustrating agents who are not members of a minority group.[13]

SOME PRINCIPLES OF AGGRESSION

THE PRECEDING discussion has dealt mainly with the definition and description of aggression. The following discussion will deal with the dynamic interrelations between aggression and other personality processes.

Sources of Aggression

Questions that relate to the sources of aggression are highly significant not only for the psychology of adjustment but also for some of the broader problems in social psychology. Thus, Frank has written:

This question is of the utmost importance socially and educationally, since the answer involves the future of our society and of the civilized world. If man is innately hostile and aggressive, prone to destructive antagonisms and rivalries, then the prospects for a better, more humanly desirable society are not very bright. If human nature, as theological tradition and many of our . . . students of personality tell us, is born wicked, sinful, and hostile and must be forced to be social, co-operative, and altruistic, the task of education is essentially a coercive one, that of curbing the hostility, of teaching individuals to "handle their aggressiveness." If, on the other hand, human nature is essentially plastic, subject to educational direction toward friendliness, co-operativeness, gentleness, and genuine group or social activity, then the task of education is to prevent the early distortions and unnecessary deprivations that arouse resentment and aggressiveness, by providing as much affectionate reassurance and toleration of individual, temperamental differences as possible for the children who have been ill treated or neglected by their parents.[14]

---

[13] *Ibid.*, pp. 443–98.
[14] Lawrence K. Frank, "The Fundamental Needs of the Child," *Mental Hygiene, 22* (1938), p. 372. Reprinted by permission of The National Association for Mental Health, Inc. Copyright, 1938, by The National Committee for Mental Hygiene, Inc.

As has been suggested by Frank, both biogenic and psychogenic interpretations of the sources of aggression have been advocated.

BIOGENIC VERSUS PSYCHOGENIC INTERPRETATIONS. In his later years, Freud believed that "the tendency to aggression is an innate, independent, instinctual disposition in man." [15] This conception was connected with Freud's concept of the "death instinct" or "instinct of self-destruction"; aggression was believed to be accounted for in terms of the displacement of self-destructive impulses onto the external world. At an earlier time, however, Freud believed aggression to be the "primordial reaction" to frustration.[16]

> When the object becomes a source of pleasurable feelings, a motor tendency is set up which strives to bring the object near to and incorporate it into the ego; we then speak of the "attraction" exercised by the pleasure-giving object, and say that we "love" that object. Conversely, when the object is the source of painful feelings, there is a tendency which endeavors to increase the distance between object and ego and to repeat in relation to the former the primordial attempt at flight from the external world with its flow of stimuli. We feel a "repulsion" from the object, and hate it; this hate can then be intensified to the point of an aggressive tendency towards the object, with the intention of destroying it. . . . The ego hates, abhors and pursues with intent to destroy all objects which are for it a source of painful feelings. . . .[17]

Freud viewed aggression as a biogenic reaction: in his later interpretation he regarded aggression as the direct expression of a basic need, while in his earlier interpretation he regarded aggression as *a biogenic reaction to the frustration of any need*. In other words, Freud believed that the tendency to aggression, whether independent of, or secondary to, frustration, must be considered a biogenic process.

Modern students of behavior dynamics are, for the most part, in agreement with Freud's earlier view that aggression occurs as a reaction to frustration. Dollard and his collaborators have organized much evidence in support of this point of view.[18] Some writers maintain that the aggressive response to frustration is itself a *learned* reaction; others,

---

[15] Sigmund Freud, *Civilization and Its Discontents*, translated by Joan Riviere (London, 1951), p. 102. Reprinted by permission of The Hogarth Press, Ltd.

[16] Sigmund Freud, *Collected Papers*, translated by Joan Riviere (London, 1950), IV, 79–81, 162–3.

[17] *Ibid.*, pp. 79–81.

[18] John Dollard, Leonard W. Doob, Neal E. Miller, O. Hobart Mowrer, and Robert R. Sears, *Frustration and Aggression* (New Haven, 1939), pp. 1–54.

like Freud, regard aggression as a biogenic reaction. It seems highly probable that aggression functions as *a biogenic process that occurs in response to frustration*—that is to say, the aggressive response to frustration does not have to be learned by the individual.[19]

FRUSTRATION-AGGRESSION HYPOTHESIS. The frustration-aggression hypothesis was given its first systematic treatment by a group of psychologists working at Yale University. In their book, *Frustration and Aggression*, this hypothesis is succinctly stated: ". . . the occurrence of aggressive behavior always presupposes the existence of frustration and, contrariwise . . . the existence of frustration always leads to some form of aggression." [20]

This does not imply that direct aggressive behavior will always occur in conjunction with frustration, since aggression may be expressed in devious and indirect ways; yet ". . . although these reactions may be . . . compressed, delayed, disguised, displaced, or otherwise deflected from their immediate and logical goal, they are not destroyed." [21]

When the authors of *Frustration and Aggression* speak of frustration as *an instigation to aggression,* they mean that the occurrence of frustration *will develop a need for aggression*. This need, like any other need, will continue to function until it is gratified in some way. If the aggressive need remains ungratified, the occurrence of further frustration will increase its strength. Factors associated with the strength of aggressive motivation will be discussed in a subsequent section.

The first contention of the frustration-aggression hypothesis— that aggression occurs only as a reaction to frustration—has met with little criticism. There have been, however, a number of criticisms against the second contention—that frustration always leads to aggression. Such criticisms usually begin by interpreting aggression as *overt aggression,* without taking adequate account of the devious, indirect, and substitute methods by which the aggressive need may be gratified.

[19] We have indicated, in Chap. II, that anger may be regarded as a biogenic emotion; we have also noted that, except for its lack of a definite object, anger is equivalent to aggressive motivation or hostility. If anger can be considered a biogenic emotion, then aggressive motivation should likewise be regarded as biogenic; in any given instance, all that remains to be learned—the only psychogenic aspect —is the identity of the frustrating agent (a suitable object of aggression). Of course, this does not imply that anger or hostility will always function consciously in response to frustration, nor that aggression will always occur in a recognizable form, if indeed it occurs at all.

[20] John Dollard, Leonard W. Doob, Neal E. Miller, O. Hobart Mowrer, and Robert R. Sears, *Frustration and Aggression* (New Haven, 1939), p. 1. Reprinted by permission of Yale University Press. Copyright, 1939, by Yale University Press.

[21] *Ibid.,* p. 2.

Strength of Instigation to Aggression

Since in the course of everyday living the individual is continually experiencing the frustration of his motives, the aggressive need will, at all times, be operative in some degree. This, of course, does not mean that the individual will continually be in the process of expressing aggression; it means only that the *need* will be functioning. This need will, in different individuals and on different occasions, build up to a certain strength before being "discharged." The strength of aggressive motivation which can be tolerated before "discharge" will depend upon the degree of frustration tolerance of the individual, as well as upon the situation.

Dollard and his collaborators have discussed three objective variables that may be interrelated with the strength of instigation to aggression (or strength of aggressive motivation). These three variables are: "(1) *the strength of instigation to the frustrated response*, (2) *the degree of interference with the frustrated response, and* (3) *the number of frustrated response-sequences*." [22]

STRENGTH OF INSTIGATION TO FRUSTRATED RESPONSES. This variable involves the strength of the frustrated motive and the strength of cathexis in relation to a particular goal object. In the case of thirst, for example, the stronger the thirst, the stronger will be the impulse to aggression if water is unavailable. Or if the thirsty individual is intent on having a glass of beer, he will, upon being offered a glass of water instead, develop stronger aggressive motivation than if he were merely thirsty and had no particular goal object in mind. The authors of *Frustration and Aggression* have pointed out, in exemplification of this principle, that the violence of lovers' quarrels is greater than the violence of quarrels between mere acquaintances, since in the case of lovers the need for affectionate behavior between them is greater, so that any interference "produces a more serious frustration."

DEGREE OF INTERFERENCE WITH FRUSTRATED RESPONSE. This variable involves the degree of frustration which is perceived by the individual.[23] One study that bears on the relation between the strength of the aggressive need and the strength of frustration (objectively in-

---

[22] *Ibid.*, pp. 28–38.

[23] In the objective or peripheral frame of reference, which is maintained by the authors of *Frustration and Aggression*, the perceptual process is not, of course, embodied in this variable. The concept of objective frustration, however, apart from the individual's perception of it, can have little value for the understanding of behavior dynamics. For example, the loss of a five-dollar bill would constitute a different frustration to a millionaire than to a typical college student or professor.

terpreted) revealed a high inverse relationship between economic conditions in the South and the annual number of lynchings; lynchings occurred with higher frequency in years of relatively great economic frustration.[24]

NUMBER OF FRUSTRATED RESPONSE-SEQUENCES. This variable refers to the accumulation of aggressive motivation which, awaiting gratification, will continue to grow with each successive frustration. "Minor frustrations add together to produce an aggressive response of greater strength than would normally be expected from the frustrating situation that appears to be the immediate antecedent of the aggression."[25] In other words, each frustration will give rise to a certain degree of aggressive motivation; the aggressive motivation will continue to increase in strength and, when it is finally discharged in action, the aggressive response will be disproportionate to the final frustration in the sequence.

AGGRESSIVE CATHARSIS. A significant principle related to the accumulation of aggressive motivation is that *"the occurrence of any act of aggression is assumed to reduce the instigation to aggression.* In psychoanalytic terminology, such a release is called *catharsis.*"[26] This principle is similar to that involved in the gratification of any motive; any form or degree of gratification will reduce the need.

Aggressive catharsis is exemplified by the fact that an emotional outburst will be followed by relief or relaxation. This "blowing off of steam" amounts to gratification of the aggressive need that has developed through a succession of minor frustrations. For example, Baruch found that children became better adjusted to their home situations after engaging in play therapy that involved the mutilation of clay models of their parents—that is, after symbolic gratification of their need for aggression.[27]

INTEGRATIVE SUMMARY. The three objective variables that were discussed by Dollard and others[28] can be embodied in a single principle: *the strength of aggressive motivation varies directly with the strength of frustration.* When frustration is viewed in terms of the

[24] Carl I. Hovland and Robert R. Sears, "Minor Studies of Aggression: VI. Correlation of Lynchings with Economic Indices," *Journal of Psychology, 9* (1940), 301–10.

[25] Dollard *et al., op. cit.,* p. 31.

[26] Dollard *et al., op. cit.,* p. 50.

[27] Dorothy W. Baruch, "Therapeutic Procedures as a Part of the Educational Process," *Journal of Consulting Psychology, 4* (1940), 165–72.

[28] Dollard *et al., op. cit.,* pp. 28–38.

individual's perception, all three of these variables are included in the concept of frustration. Thus, the stronger the individual's need and its objective interference are, and the greater the amount of accumulated aggressive motivation, the stronger will be the individual's perception of frustration in a given situation; and hence the stronger will be his aggressive motivation.

In addition to the three factors mentioned above, some other factors that may influence the perception of frustration have been noted by Symonds.[29]

1. If an equally attractive substitute for the original goal or for the original instrumental act is available, the degree of frustration is likely to be minimal. For example, if the hungry child wants an ice-cream cone, his frustration will be less if he is given candy instead of ice-cream than if he is forbidden to eat anything at all.

2. Frustration will be greater if the blocked goal or the blocked instrumental act functions as an end in itself than if it functions merely as one of several possible sub-goals or as one of several possible means for achieving the end. Thus, if the individual's ultimate goal is to reach Chicago, his frustration will not be extreme if he finds that he must go by train rather than by air; however, if his main desire is to enjoy an airplane trip, while reaching Chicago is incidental, his frustration will likely be extreme if he finds air transportation to be unavailable. This principle, of course, involves merely a specific instance of the preceding principle: when the goal or instrumental act functions as an end in itself, no substitute is likely to be available.

3. If the perceived interference with gratification is immediately present, greater frustration will be perceived than if the interference is merely a vaguely anticipated future possibility. "As long as there is life, there is hope." For example, when an individual goes shopping for a coat and finds that none is available, his frustration will be greater than if he is merely planning to buy a coat and anticipates the possibility that he will be unable to find one which he considers suitable. The degree of frustration, in other words, is related to the perceived degree of probability that an interference of some kind will actually occur.

[29] Symonds, *op. cit.*, pp. 61–2.

4. Frustration will less likely be perceived if the individual is "emotionally secure." The factor of "emotional security," however, involves a combination of factors which have been mentioned previously; it is a function of frustration tolerance, of the strength of previously accumulated aggressive motivation, and of confidence in the self and in the environment.

5. The degree of "ego-involvement" is related to the degree of frustration. Allport has defined "ego-involvement" as a "condition of total participation of the self . . . when [the individual] is behaving personally, perhaps excitedly, seriously committed to a task. . . ." [30] Thus, the individual will perceive greater frustration when he fails to achieve a goal which is important to him (e.g., a high intelligence test score) than when he fails to achieve a goal of little significance (e.g., the solution of a cross-word puzzle).

6. When "momentum"—*conative perseveration*, in Allport's terminology [31]—has developed, frustration will be greater than when there is no such "momentum" in operation. That is to say, once an activity has been initiated, there will be a stronger tendency to complete it—and hence stronger frustration when it is interfered with—than when the activity has not yet been initiated. This principle may involve the preceding one, since the development of "momentum" implies that the individual has become "seriously committed to a task."

In summary, it may be said that the strength of instigation to aggression—that is, the strength of aggressive motivation—is a function of the strength of frustration. The strength of frustration is, in turn, a function of such factors as the strength of the need being frustrated, the strength of the objective interference with gratification, the number of occasions on which satisfaction is prevented, the difficulty in substituting a new form of gratification, the degree to which a given goal or action functions as an end in itself, the immediacy of interference with satisfaction, the degree of "emotional insecurity," the degree of ego-involvement, and the degree of "momentum" already developed in a course of action.

[30] Gordon W. Allport, "The Ego in Contemporary Psychology," *Psychological Review, 50* (1943), p. 459. Reprinted by permission of American Psychological Association, Inc.

[31] Gordon W. Allport, *Personality: a Psychological Interpretation* (New York, 1937), p. 198.

General Direction of Aggression

The strength of aggressive motivation should be distinguished from the direction in which aggression is expressed. The direction of aggression relates to the object against which aggression is expressed, or toward which a hostile attitude is directed.

AGGRESSION AGAINST THE FRUSTRATING AGENT. When frustration is attributed to the external environment—when external privations, deprivations, or obstructions are involved—the aggression will probably be directed against the person or object that is perceived to be the frustrating agent.[32] The child who attributes economic privation to shortcomings of his parents will be likely to direct his aggression against the parents. The student who can no longer get a date with a particular girl, and who has lately seen her in the company of another man, will be likely to direct his aggression against this rival. The child whose parent has forbidden him to gratify some need will be likely to direct his aggression against the parent.

Frequently, however, the frustrating agent will be feared, respected, or loved, so that the frustrated individual will not be free to express his hostility. Other inhibiting influences—e.g., laws, customs, moral standards—may similarly operate to prevent the direct expression of hostility against the frustrating agent.

When the direct expression of hostility is prevented, this in itself will constitute a further frustration. A secondary increase in aggressive motivation will then occur. "Obviously this vicious circle—frustration, aggression, interference with aggression, more frustration—tends to be repeated as long as successive acts of aggression suffer interference." [33]

If aggression is prevented by some influence other than the original frustrating agent, then the aggression may be directed against this new source of frustration. For example, if one child takes another's candy, and if the latter is prevented by a parent from "beating up" the offender, the parent may then become the object of aggression.

When internal frustrations occur—that is, when frustrations arise from personal defects, losses of function, or conflicts with other motives—aggression will probably be directed against the self. The individual may castigate himself because his "mental ability" is too low to

[32] ". . . the strongest instigation, aroused by a frustration, is to acts of aggression directed against the agent perceived to be the source of the frustration and progressively weaker instigations are aroused to progressively less direct acts of aggression." (Dollard *et al.*, *op. cit.*, p. 39. Italics removed.)

[33] Dollard *et al.*, *op. cit.*, p. 40.

permit his doing passing work in a college course; or the individual may feel inferior after he has lost a limb; or he may commit suicide when he suffers from an insoluble conflict.

DISPLACED AGGRESSION. When direct aggression against the perceived source of frustration is prevented, the aggression may be displaced onto some other object, or it may take the form of "free-floating" aggression. Hostility that was originally directed against an external source of frustration may be displaced onto another external object. The parent who is frustrated by his child's behavior in public may redirect his aggression against unoffending salespeople. The teacher who is frustrated by a substandard income, and who cannot express his hostility against the school board, may take it out on his pupils. The soldier who is frustrated by the humiliating treatment that issues from superiors may direct his aggression against the enemy; his superiors who have been frustrated by *their* superiors may express their hostility against him; or the first sergeant who has been denied a weekend pass may give his subordinates a "bad time."

Hostility may also be displaced from an external frustrating agent onto the self. Suicide involves an extreme instance of displacing aggression onto the self. There occur, of course, many milder manifestations of aggression against the self—tearing the hair, beating the head, feelings of inferiority, guilt feelings, and other forms of self-accusation and self-punishment.

On the other hand, hostility that was originally directed against the self as frustrating agent may be displaced onto external objects. For example, the student who is frustrated by his low ability-level may commit verbal aggression against his instructors, accusing them of making unfair demands, and so on. Whenever the individual blames another person for a self-induced frustration, he will be displacing aggression from himself onto an external object.

When aggression is prevented, either through fear of punishment, or through inability to recognize the source of frustration (e.g., when *unconscious* motives are frustrated), "free-floating" aggression may be manifested; aggression becomes so generalized and indiscriminate that any near-by object may become the target of aggression. "Free-floating" aggression is not directed against any particular feature of the environment; it is characterized by a high level of irritability and by the tendency to strike out against anything that happens to be available. In everyday language, "free-floating" aggression has been termed "having a chip on the shoulder."

Cultural Canalization of Aggression

Since frustration is an unavoidable accompaniment of living, and since frustration gives rise to aggressive motivation, it should be clear that aggressive motivation will be unavoidable. Aggression must be expressed in some form. The modes of aggressive expression which are most likely to occur in any given society will depend on societal encouragements and limitations; the forms of aggression which are approved in one society will not necessarily be those which are approved in another society. That is to say, social pressures will be effective in *canalizing aggression.* Social control of aggression is, of course, necessary if social organization itself is to be maintained.

If each human being were a law unto himself, as an animal in a state of nature tends to be, then capacity to behave in an effectively aggressive manner would be precious indeed. But the fact is that human beings live socially and are, therefore, often dependent upon the very persons who frustrate them. Without careful control of in-group aggression, even the simplest forms of social organization, to say nothing of civilization, would not be possible.[34]

DIFFERENCES AMONG SOCIETIES. Societies differ with respect to the kinds of aggression they encourage and discourage. As previously noted, aggression in our own society is acceptable when it takes certain forms (e.g., economic or political competition) and unacceptable when it takes other forms (e.g., direct physical assault). Moreover, it is acceptable for parents to punish their children, but wrong for the children to strike back.

In contrast to our own cultural norms in this regard, it is of interest to quote descriptions of two other societies.

. . . the Dobuans are lawless, treacherous, suspicious, and constantly fighting with each other. The tribe is divided into localities, and these are organized as war units. The dominant theme running through all their social institutions is that of possession of material goods at someone else's expense. No two individuals within the group are on really intimate terms, since one is con-

---

[34] O. Hobart Mowrer and Clyde Kluckhohn, "Dynamic Theory of Personality," in *Personality and the Behavior Disorders,* J. McV. Hunt, ed. (New York, 1944), I, 114. Reprinted by permission of The Ronald Press Company. Copyright, 1944, by The Ronald Press Company.

stantly plotting or suspected of plotting the downfall of the other. Treachery and cheating are regarded as virtues.[35]

Among the Dobuans, in other words, direct physical aggression is approved and encouraged. The Saulteaux exhibit another extreme:

> To the casual observer, co-operation, laughter, harmony, patience, and self control appear to be the key notes of Saulteaux interpersonal relations. These people have never engaged in war with the whites nor with other Indian tribes. There are no official records of murder; suicide is unknown; and theft is extremely rare. Open expressions of anger or quarrels ending in physical assault seldom occur. . . . Broadly speaking, the culturally sanctioned channels for hostility are of two kinds. . . . Gossip is as rife among the Saulteaux as among any other people. . . . The second channel for the expression of aggression [is] sorcery and magic. . . .[36]

These two societies manifest marked differences in approved forms of aggression. Anthropologists have described many other societies exhibiting variations in this regard.

DOMINANT VERSUS MINORITY GROUPS. Within a given society, the forms of aggression that are approved in members of the dominant group will usually differ from the forms that are approved in members of the nondominant (minority) groups. Members of the dominant group are usually free to commit aggression against minority group members, but members of minority groups may not reciprocate. For example, when the Nazis became the dominant group in Germany they felt free to aggress against members of any other group, but the persecuted minorities could commit counter-aggression only in fantasy or in secret conversations among themselves.[37]

Similar observations have been made regarding Negro-white re-

[35] Steuart H. Britt, *Social Psychology of Modern Life* (rev. ed., New York, 1949), p. 49. Reprinted by permission of Steuart H. Britt and Rinehart & Company, Inc. Copyright, 1941, 1949, by Steuart Henderson Britt.

[36] A. Irving Hallowell, "Aggression in Saulteaux Society," *Psychiatry, 3* (1940), 395–407. In *Personality in Nature, Society, and Culture,* Clyde Kluckhohn and Henry A. Murray, eds. (New York, 1948), pp. 205–9. Reprinted by permission of A. Irving Hallowell, The William Alanson White Psychiatric Foundation, Inc., and Alfred A. Knopf, Inc. Copyright, 1940, by The William Alanson White Psychiatric Foundation, Inc., 1948, by Alfred A. Knopf, Inc.

[37] Gordon W. Allport, J. S. Bruner, and E. M. Jandorf, "Personality under Social Catastrophe: Ninety Life-Histories of the Nazi Revolution," in *Personality in Nature, Society, and Culture,* Clyde Kluckhohn and Henry A. Murray, eds. (New York, 1948), p. 363.

lations in the South. While the whites may even go so far as to lynch Negroes with impunity, the Negro rarely dares to commit any form of aggression against the white caste; he frequently must displace his white-inspired hostility onto other Negroes.[38]

AGGRESSION TOWARD OUT-GROUPS.   Aggression against minority groups will often be discouraged when the country is at war; that is to say, there will be an attempt to canalize hostile-aggressive expressions in the direction of the current outside enemy. Racial tolerance will be advocated with a fervor seldom achieved in times of peace. The dominant group in the society will characteristically prohibit violent aggression among its own members, while disregarding, condoning, or encouraging aggression against out-groups (minority groups in time of peace and enemy nations in time of war or preparation for war).

> In many respects man is the most ruthlessly ferocious of beasts. . . . And killing off a neighboring tribe from whom no good thing comes, but only competition, may materially better the lot of the whole tribe. Hence the gory cradle . . . in which our race was reared; hence the fickleness of human ties, the ease with which the foe of yesterday becomes the ally of to-day, the friend of to-day the enemy of to-morrow. . . .[39]

SEX DIFFERENCES IN AGGRESSIVE EXPRESSION.   There is little reason to believe that either sex is subjected to less total frustration than the other; hence, the aggressive motivation of the sexes should be approximately equal. The forms of aggression which are approved in males, however, are different from the forms which are approved in females.

In our own society the male is expected to be aggressive, while the female is expected to be meek and submissive. From very early childhood this difference in sex roles is impressed upon the child. With respect to aggressive behavior, the female in our culture occupies a position in relation to the male which is analogous to the position of the minority group member in relation to the dominant group. We should therefore expect female expressions of hostility to take subtle and indirect forms.

[38] Hortense Powdermaker, "The Channeling of Negro Aggression by the Cultural Process," in *Personality in Nature, Society, and Culture*, Clyde Kluckhohn and Henry A. Murray, eds. (New York, 1948), pp. 473–84.

[39] William James, *The Principles of Psychology* (New York, 1890), II, 409–10. Reprinted by permission of Henry Holt and Company, Inc. Copyright, 1890, by Henry Holt and Company, Inc.

Aggression as a Source of Anxiety

The experience of frustration alone will be, as we have seen, sufficient to arouse anxiety. But the degree of anxiety may become disproportionate to the degree of original frustration, through the functional interrelations that occur among frustration, aggressive motivation, and anxiety. In the first place, the aggressive motivation itself may be frustrated, thereby increasing the total frustration. In the second place, aggressive impulses become functionally related with anxiety, through the early association of aggression with punishment.

Since there are legal and social sanctions against overt aggression, and since parents begin early to enforce such sanctions by punishing the child for aggressive acts, the child will soon begin to associate aggressive impulses (before their expression) with fear of punishment. Eventually, the socialized individual in our society will come to experience anxiety (fear without the knowledge of what he fears) whenever *unconscious* aggressive impulses arise. He will, in other words, come to experience anxiety a part of whose strength derives from (unconscious) hostile impulses of which he is unaware. The strength of his anxiety will be disproportionate to the strength of the frustration he consciously experiences.

Horney regards hostile impulses as the main source of neurotic anxiety. "It is well known," she writes, "that an acute hostile impulse may be the direct cause of anxiety, if its pursuit would mean defeating the purposes of the self." [40] In a child, aggressive actions will ordinarily "defeat the purposes of the self"; his parents are his main source of frustration, while they are at the same time the source of his gratification and of his security. Aggressive acts (and impulses to commit aggressive acts) against the parents will therefore function as threats to his own security.

PUNISHMENT

PUNISHMENT involves the expression of aggressive impulses. Murray considers punishment to be an environmental press that is motivated by the fusion of aggressive and dominant needs; [41] in other

[40] Karen Horney, *The Neurotic Personality of Our Time* (New York, 1937), pp. 63–78. Reprinted by permission of W. W. Norton & Company, Inc. Copyright, 1937, by W. W. Norton & Company, Inc.

[41] Murray, *op. cit.*, p. 305.

words, punishment is motivated by the simultaneous operation of dominant needs and aggressive needs in the person who administers the punishment. Symonds defines punishment as "the infliction of pain or loss on another in order to prevent certain behavior." [42] Similarly, Maier writes that "any activity that leads to pain, failure, or ego degradation may be considered punished." [43]

The common denominators among these statements seem to be (1) that punishment is administered for the purpose of controlling another person's behavior (need for dominance), and (2) that it involves a frustration to the individual who is punished (need for aggression). In other words, *punishment involves the use of aggression in order to control another's behavior.*

Forms of Punishment

Punishment may be manifested in various forms. The classification of unique actions into a limited number of categories involves, of course, an oversimplification. In addition, there is the difficulty that the frustration intended by the person who administers punishment may not be the same as the frustration actually experienced by the recipient: what is intended as punishment may be perceived as no punishment at all, and what is intended as mild punishment may actually be interpreted as relatively severe.

The forms of punishment may be classified in terms of the categories that have been used for the classification of frustrations; that is to say, the recipient may perceive a given instance of punishment as an external or internal privation, as an external or internal deprivation, or as an external or internal obstruction. *External* categories will apply to cases in which the individual is punished by another person; *internal* categories will apply to cases that involve self-punishment.

Murray has classified punishments into the following categories: [44]

1. Verbal reprimand or censure.
2. Striking or spanking.
3. Restraint or limitation of action.
4. Coercion or enforced action.
5. Dispossession.

[42] Symonds, *op. cit.*, p. 113.
[43] Norman R. F. Maier, *Frustration* (New York, 1949), p. 194. Reprinted by permission of McGraw-Hill Book Company, Inc. Copyright, 1949, by McGraw-Hill Book Company, Inc.
[44] Murray, *op. cit.*, pp. 305–6.

Symonds has classified punishments as follows: [45]

1. Infliction of pain.
2. Injury to a loved object.
3. Forced labor.
4. Physical restraint.
5. Deprivation.
6. Exclusion from the group.
7. Depreciation.
8. Threats.
9. Neglect.

Both of these classifications are useful for indicating the multiplicity of forms that punishment may take, when regarded from an objective point of view; both, however, neglect to consider punishment from the standpoint of the recipient's perception.

Since punishment must ultimately be understood in terms of its relation to the behavior dynamics of the recipient, it seems appropriate to classify punishments from the point of view of the recipient's perception—that is, in terms of the categories of frustration.

EXTERNAL PRIVATIONS. Verbal reprimands, threats, depreciation, and exclusion from the group may be interpreted by the recipient as the continued frustration of his need for self-esteem. Spankings, restraint, and coercion may be seen by the child as demonstrations of his continued lack of autonomy. When the child is denied a money allowance (which he never has had) on the grounds that it would make him lazy or dependent, or when his parents neglect him or give him little attention, he may see this as an indication that he is not loved by his parents. Any objective form of punishment, then, will function as an external privation for the individual who is on the receiving end, if he happens to interpret it as the continued withholding of some long-wanted form of gratification.

EXTERNAL DEPRIVATIONS. The recipient of a spanking may interpret the spanking as an indication that he is no longer loved, or as an indication that he is unworthy or inferior. Almost any instance of punishment may be interpreted in a similar manner. Restraint, confinement, forced labor, coercion, etc., may be interpreted as indicating the loss of autonomy or the loss of freedom. Dispossession and deprivation, when interpreted as the punisher intends, will obviously come under this classification. Exclusion from the group (being expelled, sent to

[45] Symonds, *op. cit.*, pp. 116–18.

bed, sent to one's room, or made to stand in a corner) may be interpreted as loss of love, loss of self-esteem, or loss of a feeling of belongingness. In general, again, any specific punishment may function as an external deprivation if the recipient so interprets it.

EXTERNAL OBSTRUCTIONS. The recipient of punishment is likely to consider it an obstruction to the future gratification of whatever impulse led to the punishment. If, for example, the child has just been punished for going across the street, the punishment may be perceived as an obstruction to the gratification of future impulses to cross the street. To the extent that punishment is interpreted specifically in relation to the occasion for the punishment, it will be interpreted as the punisher intends; this, however, will be only one of the many possible interpretations.

Motivation of Punishment

To a limited extent it is possible to accept at face value the parent's (or teacher's) conscious belief that punishment is motivated by consideration of the child's welfare. This is undoubtedly part of the motivational pattern of the sincere parent or teacher. To the extent that the parent or teacher identifies with the child, the present and future welfare of the child will be one of his important goals. But such a goal may be achieved with a minimum of punishment; and it should be emphasized that punishment involves additional motivation that the parent or teacher will not so willingly admit.

In defining punishment we have explicitly noted that the punisher is motivated both by the need for dominance and by the need for aggression. In other words, dominant and aggressive needs are involved in the parent's (or teacher's) motivation. When the dominance need, or any other motive, is frustrated by the child this will, as we have seen, instigate aggressive motivation in the parent or teacher. This statement does not imply any depreciation of the parent or teacher who is himself well socialized—that is, who has introjected the significant standards of his culture. In such a case, behavior that is in conflict with the cultural standards will always be perceived by the parent or teacher as a frustration. If the parent or teacher happens not to be well socialized, of course, it follows that the child will frustrate egocentric motives, and that he may receive punishment merely because his behavior constitutes an annoyance.

When punishment is exceptionally severe, it may be suspected that the punisher has been severely frustrated by the recipient of the punishment, or that aggressive motivation arising from other sources of frustration has been displaced onto the recipient. In either case, the external observer may be inclined to interpret the punishment as needlessly severe, since the external observer will not usually know how the recipient's behavior has been interpreted by the punisher, and how much accumulated aggressive motivation preceded the punishment.

Reactions to Punishment

Whether, and to what degree, punishment will function as a frustration to the recipient will depend upon the nature of his motivation. Sometimes what a parent intends as punishment will be perceived as a gratification. Symonds, for example, has pointed out that on some occasions the child may perceive punishment as a demonstration that the parent cares enough about him to attempt to correct his behavior; punishment is likely to be preferred to neglect, which might constitute for the child a more significant frustration than the punishment itself.[46]

When punishment is perceived in this manner, the child's need for affection is probably more important to him than the motive that is being frustrated by punishment; in other words, the amount of gratification outweighs the amount of frustration involved. In such a case —when the child suffers frustration of his love needs—the child may indulge in minor forms of misbehavior in order to insure that he will receive punishment.

Many authorities are in agreement that punishment will be perceived as gratifying when the recipient has developed a *need for punishment*.[47] This need is associated with guilt, which occurs after the development of superego motives. The need for punishment becomes a persistent personality trend when the individual has developed masochistic motivation. If the recipient is either momentarily or persistently motivated by a need for punishment, then what is intended as punishment will be perceived as a gratification; in fact, the withholding of punishment will be interpreted as frustrating.

Behavior that has been referred to as "testing reality"—that is, finding out how far one can go before being punished, or testing the limits of the parent's frustration tolerance—may, in many cases, be understood in terms of the child's striving to gratify his need for punishment.

[46] Symonds, *op. cit.*, p. 121.
[47] For example, Franz Alexander, *Fundamentals of Psychoanalysis* (New York, 1948), pp. 118–21; Freud, *New Introductory Lectures* . . . pp. 149–50; Maier, *op. cit.*, pp. 212–13.

When punishment is interpreted as frustrating, the reactions to punishment will be the same as the reactions to frustration, which were discussed in the preceding chapter. That is to say, the reactions may involve direct removal of frustration through constructive efforts to modify behavior in conformity with social demands; they may involve aggressive actions against the punisher (the frustrating agent), against the self (guilt, self-criticism, feelings of inferiority, etc.), or against some other object (displacement); or they may involve anxiety reactions, which in turn are likely to be relieved by means of defensive mechanisms.

ADJUSTIVE IMPLICATIONS

SINCE aggressive motivation develops on the basis of frustration, it follows that aggression can be reduced through the reduction of frustration. It follows, also, that all of the adjustive implications that were derived from principles of frustration (Chap. IV) are applicable to aggression. These may be restated as follows:

1. Since frustration is unavoidable, aggressive motivation is likewise unavoidable.
2. Since frustration is a necessary condition for learning, certain aspects of the learning process will involve aggressive motivation; this motivation will be reduced to the extent that the learning process leads to gratification.
3. The level of aggressive motivation in children, pupils, employees, and other subordinates may be kept at a minimum if the parent, teacher, or supervisor avoids imposing more frustration than the subordinate individual can tolerate.
4. If the individual maintains a reasonable adjustment of his level of aspiration to his capacities and environmental opportunities, the degree of frustration—and, hence, the degree of aggressive motivation—can be minimized.
5. The development of an ordered system of values (philosophy of life) can be a basis for the reduction of frustration and, therefore, for the reduction of aggressive motivation.

In general, then, it may be said that any procedure effective for reducing frustration will have value for reducing aggressive motivation.

Emphasis on Co-operative Activities

May has pointed out that competitive ambition—the tendency to strive for economic status in competition with others—is one of the dominant characteristics of our present-day society.

> Social prestige goals are dominant in our culture, social prestige being defined as success and this success in turn being defined chiefly in economic terms. . . . Since success is measured against the status of others, the striving for success is essentially competitive: one is successful if one excels and triumphs over others. . . . Being the dominant cultural value, competitive success is likewise the dominant criterion of self-evaluation; it is . . . the means of validating the self in one's own eyes as well as in the eyes of others. . . .[48]

The ideal of competitive success can function as a source of severe frustration and, hence, of aggressive motivation. It has been suggested by Mowrer and Kluckhohn that "frustration and ensuing tendencies toward aggression can be reduced if the principle of co-operation rather than coercion and competition be used in teaching and in structuring social relationships generally." [49]

These authors add, however, that "the encouragement of co-operation can succeed only to a limited extent so long as it is against the major trends of our society." [50] In other words, the sincere efforts of a few understanding parents and teachers cannot achieve much in the way of fostering habits of co-operation while the majority seek, and foster the ideal of, competitive success.

To the extent, however, that individuals can be encouraged to participate in co-operative community projects, the level of frustration should be reduced and the need for aggression accordingly diminished.[51] Through such co-operation, the individual may gratify his need for affiliation and achieve a sense of belonging; his level of security and

---

[48] Rollo May, *The Meaning of Anxiety* (New York, 1950), pp. 181–2. Reprinted by permission of The Ronald Press Company. Copyright, 1950, by The Ronald Press Company.

[49] Mowrer and Kluckhohn, *op. cit.*, p. 115.

[50] Mowrer and Kluckhohn, *op. cit.*, p. 115.

[51] Frequently such time-consuming activities will conflict with the individual's (often stronger) motivation to "get ahead." Typically, also, individuals use such co-operative projects as a means of achieving competitive success; for example, the salesman may become active in church affairs in order to meet potential customers.

his confidence level may be increased, so that aggressive motivation can be held to a minimum.

Frustration Tolerance in Parent-Child Relations

High frustration tolerance in the parent will serve as a basis for the development of frustration tolerance in the child. The parent's behavior will function as a model for the behavior of the child; this will be dependent for its effectiveness on the child's identification with his parent—a process that can be expected to occur during some period in the child's development. In other words, to the extent that the parent can be seen to endure frustration with equanimity, the child will strive to do likewise.

Perhaps even more significantly, the parent's frustration tolerance will be related to the level of frustration which the child will have to experience. If the parent has low frustration tolerance, a vicious circle will become operative: the child's behavior (including aggressive expression) will easily frustrate the parent beyond his tolerance; the child will receive punishment; the punishment will frustrate the child; the child will become aggressive; the aggression of the child will frustrate the parent beyond his limit; and the frustration-punishment cycle will continue with ever increasing intensity.

If, on the other hand, the parent has high frustration tolerance, he will not quickly reach the point of punishing the child; since a minimum of punishment will be added to the frustration that the child must endure for his socialization, conditions will be maintained that are favorable for the development of frustration tolerance. Thus, the parent-child relationship can become mutually adjustive if the parent himself manifests high frustration tolerance.

Permissive Human Relationships

The parent-child relationship constitutes only one of the many human relationships in which frustration tolerance may function in the service of mutual adjustment. Permissiveness in human relationships implies the operation of maximal frustration tolerance in the individuals who are concerned. Any two individuals—two friends, husband and wife, employer and employee, counselor and client, teacher and pupil, etc.—can develop and maintain mutually adjustive relationships to the extent that they are mutually tolerant of each other's behavior; if free expression of aggression (at least verbally) and of differences in point of view are mutually permitted, the frustration of each will be kept within limits.

Permissiveness in the counseling relationship has been given central importance in the client-centered therapy of Rogers.[52] According to this conception of counseling, the individual should be accepted as a person who has much aggressive motivation that must be expressed freely before he will be able to approach his problems constructively. During the early part of the therapeutic period, much of the client's expression will deal with hostile attitudes toward his family, his friends, and his other associates. After this hostile motivation has been adequately gratified (verbally or symbolically), the individual can devote his attention to more basic frustrations; in other words, the superstructure of aggressive motivation must be torn away before the foundations can be viewed. This accounts, in large part, for the value of any confessional activity or expression of confidence in a permissive atmosphere; it permits aggressive catharsis.

Constructive Canalization of Aggression

Since aggressive motivation is unavoidable, it must be expressed in some way. The problem is not one of finding ways to eliminate aggression completely, but one of finding channels of expression which will not disrupt human relationships or disorganize the individual's personality. Such channels of expression can be utilized by the parent or teacher who is faced with the problem of providing children with acceptable outlets for aggression. A few of the possibilities will be discussed.

Aggressive outlets are available in the form of play activities, games, sports, and recreations. In this connection, there has been an incorrect emphasis on the notion that aggressive play is maladjustive— for example, that playing soldier will *develop* an undesirable liking for violence.

The implications of the concept of aggressive catharsis have often been overlooked. To the extent that aggressive play is successful in gratifying aggressive needs that arise from unavoidable frustrations, this activity will provide a wholesome outlet for aggression that might otherwise be used destructively.

Even adults can find satisfying release for their aggressive motiva-

[52] Carl R. Rogers, *Counseling and Psychotherapy: Newer Concepts in Practice* (Boston, 1942); *Client-Centered Therapy: Its Current Practice, Implications, and Theory* (Boston, 1951).

tion through active participation in games, sports, and other forms of recreation. Indeed, it is probable that *passive* participation in violence (as in reading fiction, seeing boxing-matches, attending movies) may have some value for the relief of aggressive tensions.

Another channel for the constructive expression of hostility involves the displacement of aggression onto non-human features of the environment. Aggression does not have to be displaced onto other persons, as in war, prejudice, crime, etc. It may be displaced onto the material aspects of nature—that is, expressed in the form of activities aimed at gaining mastery over natural resources (aggression combined with dominance); or it may be displaced onto evil features of human relations and thus be utilized for bringing about improvements in social organization.

When aggression is directed against the self, it may function in the interest of effective self-control. But when too much aggression is displaced onto the self conditions will be created that are conducive to high frustration. A vicious circle will ensue: aggression against the self → frustration → further need for aggression → further aggression against the self—and so on.

Psychoanalysts regard the displacement of too much aggression onto the self as a foundation of the neuroses. It is equivalent to the development of a "harsh and demanding superego." [53]

Effective Socialization of Parents and Teachers

We saw earlier that the kind of child behavior that frustrates the parent or teacher is dependent on the latter's motivation; and that, when the parent or teacher is well socialized, he will be frustrated by behavior that deviates from the norm prevailing in society at large. Thus, the well-socialized parent or teacher will be likely to administer punishment on just those occasions when the child's behavior requires, for the child's own future adjustment, some correction or modification.

It is perhaps in this connection that the adjustment of parents or teachers has most significance for the future adjustment of children. In other words, when parents or teachers are themselves well socialized, the children in their care will not be punished for behavior that happens to frustrate an elder's selfish or egocentric motivation.

Adjustment of Punishment to the Child's Perception

Frequently, as we have seen, the child will perceive punishment in a very different way from that which is intended; thus, what may be

[53] Freud, *New Introductory Lectures* . . . , pp. 148–52.

intended as relatively mild punishment may affect the child as a frustration of great severity; or, conversely, what may be intended as severe punishment may be taken by the child as involving hardly any frustration at all.

This is why the parent is often bewildered by the child's reaction to punishment. It is, therefore, important for the parent to become sensitive to the meaning the child derives from punishment, in order that on future occasions he may employ methods of punishment which achieve neither more nor less than the intended outcome. A few suggestions that may be helpful in this connection are discussed below.

PUNISHMENT OF BEHAVIOR AS DISTINGUISHED FROM PUNISHMENT OF THE CHILD. The failure to distinguish the *punishable acts* of the child from *the child as a personality* can have catastrophic influences on the child's self-perception. Too frequently, the child will get the impression that *he* is bad or mean or worthless, rather than that *some of his actions* are unacceptable. The impression will be given that the *child*, rather than his *behavior*, is disliked.

This impression will be reinforced by the language habits of the parent, who will often have a tendency to say: "You are naughty!" or: "You are a mean little so-and-so!" rather than to say: "You are too nice a person to do that sort of thing." In other words, the effective adjustment of the child will be insured, rather than endangered, by emphasizing that he is loved or appreciated as a person although some aspects of his behavior require improvement.

Sometimes the child can be helped to make this distinction if the parent warns him that the repetition of a certain act will be punished; then, on a subsequent occasion, if punishment is administered, the child will be more clearly aware of its basis. When such a warning has been previously given, the occurrence of punishment, as promised, will reaffirm the child's confidence in the parent's reliability. Obviously, then, when punishment has been promised it should not be withheld.

AVOIDANCE OF DESIRABLE BEHAVIOR AS A FORM OF PUNISHMENT. When coercion is used as a form of punishment, this should not involve behavior that the child enjoys or that the parent hopes to develop into a future motivation of the child. If the child enjoys the form of behavior he is forced to carry out, the coercion will be interpreted as only mildly punishing, if indeed it is regarded as punishing at all.

On the other hand, if the parent forces the child to work, as punishment for some offense, the child may come to dislike work; if he forces the child to go to bed, as punishment, the child may come to dislike going to bed; if he forces the child to take cod liver oil as punishment, the child may develop an intense dislike for cod liver oil; and so forth. In other words, the child may associate these forms of behavior with punishment, so that they will acquire negative cathexis.

AVOIDANCE OF DISPLACED AGGRESSION IN PUNISHMENT. If the child becomes the object of displaced aggression, the child is almost certain to interpret his punishment as a demonstration that he is hated by his parents, since he cannot be expected to understand the dynamics of displacement. This is a point of which the parent should become especially aware, since the punishment of children often provides a highly convenient occasion for such displacement.

The displacement of aggression involves the additional danger that the child will not be provided with a dependable means of distinguishing between himself and his acts, or of learning the relative cultural evaluation of different forms of behavior; in cases involving displacement, the punishment is likely to be highly severe regardless of the nature of the immediate occasion for it.

Guidance versus Punishment

Some writers have distinguished between punishment and "more positive" forms of guidance or direction.[54] When such a distinction is made, it is formulated in terms of the parents' intention rather than in terms of the child's perception.

As we have previously pointed out, the adjustive implications of punishment must be viewed in terms of the behavior dynamics of the recipient. From this point of view, all forms of discipline or guidance will almost inevitably be perceived by the child as punishment.

Persuasion, for example, is frequently of such a character that the child is made to feel that the love of his parents will depend on his conformity; this involves frustration, since the child will feel that he must either modify his behavior or lose his place in the parents' affection.

In all forms of guidance, the child is made aware of future frustrations that may occur unless he foregoes some present form of behavior; even in conforming, he will be accepting frustration of a present motive in order to avoid frustration in the future.

While it is probably true that the "positive" methods may involve less severe punishment than other forms, they will nevertheless operate as punishments from the child's point of view. These methods are,

[54] For example, Symonds, *op. cit.,* pp. 129–32.

however, to be recommended over many other forms of punishment, since they will usually involve less disruption of the parent-child relationship.

SUMMARY

AGGRESSION involves an action that is intended to frustrate another individual or object. Aggression may be manifested as an overt physical attack, as an overt attack against another's personality or reputation, or as an indirect or symbolic form of attack.

Various feelings and attitudes—anger, resentment, hostility, hatred, anxiety, guilt, etc.—accompany aggressive behavior. When aggressive motivation has become functionally autonomous, so that it operates as a consistent personality-trend in the individual, the terms *sadism* and *masochism* become applicable.

Aggressive motivation is frequently expressed in economic and political competition, in criminal and delinquent behavior, in industrial conflicts, in war, and in prejudice. Some of these forms of expression are socially encouraged, while others are discouraged, but all of them occur with relatively high frequency in modern American society.

Aggression is believed to have its source in the frustration of motives; that is to say, aggressive motivation is said to arise whenever the individual experiences frustration. The degree of instigation to aggression is a function of such objective factors as the strength of the motive that undergoes frustration, the strength of the interference with gratification, and the number of occasions on which the individual is frustrated within a given period of time.

If frustration is viewed in terms of the individual's perception, only one factor—*the strength of frustration*—is necessary to account for the strength of aggressive motivation.

Aggressive catharsis involves the reduction of aggressive motivation through *any* act of aggression; this principle may be viewed as a special instance of the general principle that the strength of a motive will be reduced through any of its possible forms of gratification.

Aggression will be directed against the person or object perceived to be the frustrating agent, provided that the aggression is not prevented by the frustrating agent, by the individual's conscience, or by social sanctions.

When direct aggression against the frustrating agent is prevented, aggression may occur in a less direct form against the frustrating agent, or it may be displaced onto some other object. Either an external object or the self may be perceived as the frustrating agent; displacement may involve the direction of aggression onto the self or the direction of aggression onto an external object.

Aggression is canalized by social pressures that encourage some forms and directions of expression, while discouraging others. Societies differ in terms of the forms of aggression which are approved and disapproved. Dominant groups in any society are free to express aggression against minority groups, while minority groups are prevented from reciprocating.

In-group relations are often fostered through the encouragement of displacement onto out-groups. Societies encourage different forms of aggression by members of the two sexes. Since disapproved forms of aggression frequently incur punishment, the occurrence of aggressive impulses may give rise to anxiety.

Punishment involves the use of aggression in order to control another's behavior. Forms of punishment are best understood when considered from the recipient's point of view. Whatever the punisher's intention may be, it is the perception of the recipient that is most relevant for the understanding of behavior dynamics.

Punishment is motivated by the combination of aggressive and dominant needs in the parent or teacher. Behavior in the child which frustrates the parent or teacher will give rise to aggressive motivation, which may be expressed in the form of punishment.

The reaction of the recipient to punishment depends on his motivation. Sometimes punishment will be perceived as gratifying—as a demonstration of the parent's concern for the child, or as a gratification of the need for punishment. Frequently the child will perceive punishment as involving a frustration the parent has not intended to impose.

Adjustive implications include all of those which follow from the principles of frustration, since aggressive motivation is a function of frustration. Since competitive ambition is at the source of much frustration, it is suggested that aggressive motivation may be reduced by an increased emphasis on co-operative activities. Frustration tolerance in parents, and permissive human relations in general, are suggested as aids to the reduction of aggressive motivation. Aggressive motivation may be canalized into nondestructive, or even into constructive, activities—thus relieving aggressive motivation that might otherwise be expressed in ways disruptive of human relations.

The well-socialized parent or teacher will be frustrated by, and therefore will punish, behavior whose continuance by the child would interfere with his future adjustment.

Since the child will perceive punishment as a function of his own unique motivation, the parent or teacher should make an effort to adjust punishment to the child's perception. The child may perceive punishment as a sign that he, as a person, is disliked, or he may come to dislike desirable forms of behavior if these are forced upon him in the form of punishment. Punishment will be unreasonably severe if it involves the displacement of aggression.

While guidance and persuasion may be preferable to other forms of punishment, the child will nevertheless perceive them as punishment or as threats of future punishment.

The following chapter will deal with anxiety, guilt, and inferiority feelings—processes that often require the development of defensive mechanisms.

▶ Suggested Readings

Albee, G. W. "Patterns of Aggression in Psychopathology," *Journal of Consulting Psychology, 14* (1950), 465–8.

Alexander, F. *Fundamentals of Psychoanalysis.* New York, 1948. Pp. 63–75.

Axline, Virginia M. "Play Therapy and Race Conflict in Young Children," *Journal of Abnormal and Social Psychology, 43* (1948), 300–10.

Baldwin, A. L., Kalhorn, Joan, and Breese, Fay H. "Patterns of Parent Behavior," *Psychological Monographs, 58,* No. 3 (1945).

Bettelheim, B. "The Dynamism of Anti-Semitism in Gentile and Jew," *Journal of Abnormal and Social Psychology, 42* (1947), 153–68.

Cass, Loretta K. "Parent-Child Relationships and Delinquency," *Journal of Abnormal and Social Psychology, 47* (1952), 101–4.

Counts, R. M. and Mensh, I. N. "Personality Characteristics in Hypnotically-Induced Hostility," *Journal of Clinical Psychology, 6* (1950), 325–30.

Crider, B. "The Hostility Pattern," *Journal of Clinical Psychology, 2* (1946), 267–73.

Dollard, J., Doob, L. W., Miller, N. E., Mowrer, O. H., and Sears, R. R. *Frustration and Aggression.* New Haven, 1939. Chaps. i–iii, pp. 1–54.

French, R. L. "Changes in Performance on the Rosenzweig Picture-Frustration Study following Experimentally Induced Frustration," *Journal of Consulting Psychology, 14,* (1950), 111–15.

Gatling, F. P. "Frustration Reactions of Delinquents Using Rosenzweig's Classification System," *Journal of Abnormal and Social Psychology, 45* (1950), 749–52.

Golightly, C. L. and Scheffler, I. " 'Playing the Dozens': a Note," *Journal of Abnormal and Social Psychology, 43* (1948), 104–5.

Greco, M. C. "Clinical Psychology and Penal Discipline," *Journal of Clinical Psychology, 1* (1945), 206–13.

Grinker, R. R. and Spiegel, J. P. *Men under Stress.* Philadelphia, 1945. Chap. xiii, pp. 307–26.

Horney, Karen. *Our Inner Conflicts.* New York, 1945. Chap. xii, pp. 191–216.

Meals, D. W. and Summerskill, J. "A Technique for Dealing with Hostility in Activity Therapy," *Journal of Clinical Psychology, 7* (1951), 376–8.

Morlan, G. K. "A Note on the Frustration-Aggression Theories of Dollard and his Associates," *Psychological Review, 56* (1949), 1–8.

Mowrer, O. H. "Discipline and Mental Health," *Learning Theory and Personality Dynamics.* New York, 1950. Pp. 455–71.

Mowrer, O. H. "Pain, Punishment, Guilt, and Anxiety," in *Anxiety,* P. H. Hoch and J. Zubin, eds. New York, 1950. Pp. 27–40.

Newcomb, T. M., Hartley, E. L., *et al.,* eds. *Readings in Social Psychology.* New York, 1947. Pp. 257–82.

Rogers, C. R. *Client-Centered Therapy.* Boston, 1951. Chap. ii, pp. 19–64.

Rosenzweig, S. "Types of Reaction to Frustration," in *Outside Readings in Psychology,* E. L. Hartley, H. G. Birch, and Ruth E. Hartley, eds. New York, 1950. Pp. 492–4.

Sargent, S. S. "Reaction to Frustration—a Critique and Hypothesis," *Psychological Review, 55* (1948), 108–14.

Symonds, P. M. *The Dynamics of Human Adjustment.* New York, 1946. Chaps. iv–v, pp. 81–132.

Tyson, R. "Current Mental Hygiene Practice: an Inventory of Basic Teachings," *Journal of Clinical Psychology, 7* (1951), 21–2.

Veltfort, Helene R. and Lee, G. E. "The Cocoanut Grove Fire: a Study in Scapegoating," *Journal of Abnormal and Social Psychology, 38,* No. 2, Suppl. (1943), 138–54.

CHAPTER Six

Anxiety, Guilt, and Inferiority Feelings

. . . the problem of anxiety is a nodal point, linking up all kinds of most important questions; a riddle, of which the solution must cast a flood of light upon our whole mental life.[1]

*T*HE CONTEMPORARY period has been referred to as the "age of anxiety." Since 1914 we have experienced two major world wars, two periods of economic inflation, and one severe economic depression. A third world war is predicted to be imminent. We are threatened with the possibility of atom bombs, hydrogen bombs, bacteriological warfare, and a host of other improved techniques of mass extermination. It is not difficult to account for the widespread occurrence of anxiety.

But mankind has never been completely free of pervasive threats to its security. Anxieties in relation to the supernatural, in relation to epidemic diseases, and in relation to floods, earthquakes, and other natural disasters have plagued man at various times during his difficult social and technological evolution.

Anxieties of a uniquely personal nature have troubled man in all periods of history, regardless of the stability or instability of the age.

[1] Sigmund Freud, *A General Introduction to Psycho-Analysis* (New York, 1935). p. 341.

It is probably a rare person who is as free of anxiety as he superficially appears to be. The pressure of the culture, which emphasizes self-reliance and the importance of "keeping up a front," is reflected in the overt behavior of individuals who feel that they must keep their anxieties under cover in order to maintain their social status.

The problems that relate to anxiety, to its sources, and to its dynamics are highly significant for the psychology of adjustment. These problems are generally recognized by clinical psychologists and by therapists, as they were by Freud, to be the central problems of behavior dynamics.

DEFINITION OF ANXIETY

THE TERM *anxiety* is applied to one aspect of the interrelated emotional processes that occur during frustration and conflict; anxiety, in other words, functions as one aspect of what may be termed the *frustration syndrome*, which involves a complex pattern of motives along with a complex pattern of frustration.

The conscious aspects of anxiety have been given such labels as apprehension, dread, anxious expectation, distress, feelings of helplessness, guilt feelings, and remorse. May has emphasized the conscious aspects of anxiety in his statement that "anxiety is the apprehension cued off by a threat to some value which the individual holds essential to his existence as a personality." [2]

Anxiety, like other emotional processes, involves a complex of interrelated functions, many aspects of which operate outside the individual's awareness. Therefore anxiety must be defined in such a way that all of the interrelated processes, rather than just the conscious aspects of them, will be implied.

Masserman has defined anxiety as "a state of apprehensive tension which arises during motivational and adaptational conflicts." [3] This is an acceptable definition from the organismic point of view, since it emphasizes that anxiety is an aspect of a more inclusive organization of motivational and emotional processes. Moreover, the term *apprehensive tension* is adequate to imply both the conscious and the unconscious aspects of anxiety.

[2] Rollo May, *The Meaning of Anxiety* (New York, 1950), p. 191.
[3] Jules H. Masserman, *Principles of Dynamic Psychiatry* (Philadelphia, 1946), p. 266.

Varieties of Anxiety

According to Freud, there are "three main varieties of anxiety—objective anxiety, neurotic anxiety and moral anxiety—[which can] be related to the three directions in which the ego is dependent, on the external world, on the id and on the super-ego." [4]

OBJECTIVE ANXIETY. When the individual perceives the source of danger to be external to himself, he is said to experience *objective anxiety*.

> You will understand me . . . when I describe this form of anxiety as objective anxiety, in contrast to neurotic anxiety. Now *real* anxiety or dread appears to us a very natural and rational thing; we should call it a reaction to the perception of an external danger, of an injury which is expected and foreseen. . . . The occasions of it, i.e., the objects and situations about which anxiety is felt, will obviously depend to a great extent upon . . . the person's knowledge and feeling of power regarding the outer world. It seems to us quite natural that a savage should be afraid of a cannon or of an eclipse of the sun, while a white man who can handle the weapon and foretell the phenomenon remains unafraid in the same situation. At other times it is knowledge itself which inspires fear, because it reveals the danger sooner; thus a savage will recoil with terror at the sight of a track in the jungle which conveys nothing to an ignorant white man, but means that some wild beast is near at hand; and an experienced sailor will perceive with dread a little cloud on the horizon because it means an approaching hurricane, while to a passenger it looks quite insignificant. [5]

Freud applied the term *objective anxiety* to the emotional attitude we shall term *fear*. Objective anxiety (fear) is perceived in relation to some specific object or situation. In other works Freud has used the terms *reality anxiety*, *true anxiety*, and *normal anxiety* to refer to "anxiety in face of the external world." [6] Horney has employed the term *fear* with a similar meaning. [7]

NEUROTIC ANXIETY. According to Freud, neurotic anxiety may be manifested in three main forms: (1) in the form of free-floating,

[4] Sigmund Freud, *New Introductory Lectures on Psycho-Analysis* (New York, 1933), p. 119.
[5] Freud, *A General Introduction* . . . , p. 342.
[6] Sigmund Freud, *The Problem of Anxiety* (New York, 1936), pp. 112–15.
[7] Karen Horney, *The Neurotic Personality of Our Time* (New York, 1937), p. 41; *New Ways in Psychoanalysis* (New York, 1939), pp. 194–5.

general apprehensiveness; (2) in the form of a phobic reaction to some definite object or situation; and (3) in the form of "anxiety attacks," or anxiety in relation to the symptoms of hysteria or some other form of severe neurosis.[8]

Free-floating anxiety, or general apprehensiveness, may be regarded as anxiety in its purest form, since it is not specifically related to any particular object, but may be related momentarily first to one object and then to another, without apparent discrimination. As Freud has described it, free-floating anxiety is

> . . . ready to attach itself to any thought which is at all appropriate, affecting judgments, inducing expectations, lying in wait for any opportunity to find a justification for itself. We call this condition "*expectant dread*" or "anxious expectation." People who are tormented with this kind of anxiety always anticipate the worst of all possible outcomes, interpret every chance happening as an evil omen, and exploit every uncertainty to mean the worst. . . .[9]

Phobic reactions involve the perception of some definite object, situation, or action as the occasion of anxiety. In other words, a phobia may be regarded as an instance of objectified anxiety; it is perceived by the individual as *fear*. An external observer will regard the intensity of the fear (objectified anxiety) as disproportionate to the degree of danger actually represented by the object or situation; indeed the object of the phobia may, from the viewpoint of most persons, represent hardly any danger at all. The phobia will often function to the advantage of the individual, since, to the extent that he is able to avoid the object of his phobia, his conscious experience will be relatively anxiety-free.

In the case of hysteria and other severe neuroses, *anxiety may be objectified in terms of the symptoms*. In other words, the individual may experience anxiety about his symptoms—from his point of view, his anxiety will become reasonable. Again, anxiety may be manifested in the form of an "anxiety attack."

> The whole attack can be represented . . . by a single intensively developed symptom—shuddering, faintness, palpitation of the heart, inability to breathe—and the general feeling which we rec-

---

[8] Freud, *New Introductory Lectures* . . . , pp. 114–15; *A General Introduction* . . . , pp. 345–8.

[9] Freud, *A General Introduction* . . . , p. 345.

ognize as anxiety may be absent or may have become unnotice-able.[10]

MORAL ANXIETY OR GUILT.   Moral anxiety, or guilt, arises when superego motives undergo frustration. Since guilt and its relations with superego motives will be treated at greater length in a subsequent section, it is sufficient at this point to mention that guilt, like neurotic anxiety, may occur in several distinguishable forms. It may be experienced in free-floating form, without awareness of the occasion for the guilt feelings; it may be manifested as a phobic reaction; it may be experienced in relation to the symptoms of a neurosis, and so forth. To the individual who experiences it, guilt may be recognizable as guilt; or it may be consciously represented as anxiety, so that it becomes indistinguishable from the anxiety arising from other sources.

Objective Anxiety (Fear) as Compared with Neurotic Anxiety

The comparison of objective anxiety with neurotic anxiety amounts to *a comparison of fear with anxiety*. The fundamental distinction between fear and anxiety involves the fact that fear always occurs in relation to some particular object, while anxiety is "objectless." An individual *fears* something in particular, but he suffers *anxiety* without knowing what he is anxious about. In other words, fear functions as an *attitude*, since it is experienced in relation to some object, while anxiety functions as an *emotional process* that is not related to a specific object. According to May, "it is agreed by students of anxiety —Freud, Goldstein, Horney, to mention only three—that anxiety is a *diffuse* apprehension, and that the central difference between fear and anxiety is that fear is a reaction to a specific danger while anxiety is unspecific, 'vague,' 'objectless.' " [11] Thus, either anxiety or fear may become operative when the individual perceives danger; in the case of fear, the source of the danger will be recognized; in the case of anxiety, the source of the danger will not be consciously perceived.

A *real* danger is a danger which we know, a true anxiety the anxiety in regard to such a known danger. Neurotic anxiety is anxiety in regard to a danger which we do not know.[12]

From the point of view of an external observer, anxiety will seem disproportionate to the danger represented in a situation; fear will seem proportionate to the danger.

[10] *Ibid.*, pp. 347–8.
[11] May, *op. cit.*, p. 190.
[12] Freud, *The Problem of Anxiety*, p. 113.

Horney has emphasized three distinctions between fear (objective anxiety) and anxiety (neurotic anxiety).[13]

1. In anxiety the individual experiences a "quality of diffuseness and uncertainty," which involves "something of the horror of the unknown"; in fear the object is known and its dangerous qualities understood.
2. Anxiety involves danger to "the essence or the core of the personality." Some vital value of the individual is felt to be endangered. What this vital value may be will differ among individuals: it may be "his body, his possessions, his reputation, his convictions, his work, his love relationships," etc. In the case of fear, no such vital value is endangered.
3. In anxiety, though not in fear, there occurs a "feeling of helplessness toward the danger."

It is probable that all of these characteristics of (neurotic) anxiety are manifestations of the more fundamental principle that the object of anxiety has been repressed and is therefore unknown to the individual —i.e., that anxiety is "objectless."

Symonds has also discussed some additional distinctions between fear and anxiety;[14] these distinctions may, again, be considered to follow from the primary distinction that fear is related to a specific object, while anxiety is "objectless."

Thus, according to Symonds, anxiety is diffuse, fear is concentrated; anxiety involves muscular tension, fear involves the motor reaction of escape; anxiety is persistent, fear is momentary; and anxiety involves helplessness or impotence, fear does not.

Since anxiety does not involve consciousness of a specific danger —that is, since anxiety is objectless—it cannot be concentrated on any particular object; it cannot organize behavior effectively for a motor reaction of escape; it will persist over relatively long periods of time; and, in view of its failure to organize behavior in terms of escaping from a specific danger, it will involve feelings of helplessness or impotence.

Since fear, on the other hand, involves awareness of a specific danger—that is, since it involves an attitude toward a particular object—

[13] Karen Horney, *New Ways in Psychoanalysis* (New York, 1939), pp. 194–5. Reprinted by permission of W. W. Norton & Company, Inc. Copyright, 1939, by W. W. Norton & Company, Inc.
[14] Percival M. Symonds, *The Dynamics of Human Adjustment* (New York, 1946), pp. 136–8.

it can organize behavior effectively in terms of a ready escape from the recognized danger; it will, therefore, be momentary in duration, and its quick termination will probably be accompanied by feelings of competence rather than by feelings of helplessness.

Manifestations of Anxiety

Since anxiety is a complex emotional process, it is likely to be manifested not only in forms of conscious experience but also in forms of "physiological" activity. The aspects of the total process which happen to be uppermost in the individual's conscious perception at any given time will vary.

In the case of the "anxiety attack," as it was described by Freud, the focus of the individual's perception will be on purely "physiological" aspects of the anxiety process; in the case of a phobia, his attention will be focused on the object of his displaced anxiety; in the case of free-floating anxiety, his attention will be focused primarily on the diffuse experience of general apprehensiveness; etc.

In whatever form the anxiety may be experienced, the process itself will involve various "symptomatic" manifestations. Among such manifestations may be mentioned muscular tension, muscular tremors, chronic fatigue, irritability and "jumpiness" (tendency to be startled by stimuli), insomnia or difficulty in going to sleep, profuse sweating, general restlessness, inability to concentrate, confusion and doubt or indecision, and various "physiological" disturbances in respiration, pulse, blood pressure, digestive and alimentary functions, etc.

When such symptomatic manifestations are focal in consciousness, and awareness of apprehension is absent, these may be termed "anxiety equivalents." [15] All of these manifestations become understandable as different aspects of frustration and conflict; the relations of frustration and conflict with the anxiety process will be discussed in a subsequent section.

SOURCES OF ANXIETY

THE PRECEDING discussion has been concerned mainly with the description and definition of anxiety. The present section is primarily concerned with the sources of anxiety—that is, with the dynamic relations that occur between anxiety processes and the other

[15] Freud, *A General Introduction* . . . , pp. 347–8.

functions of personality. Some of the hypotheses that have been advanced to account for the origin of anxiety will be discussed, as a basis for the attempt to derive an integrated conception of anxiety.

Freud's Hypotheses

Freud's conception of the origin of anxiety underwent successive changes during his mature period of psychoanalytic investigation. His early hypotheses differ sufficiently from his later conceptions to justify their treatment under separate sections.

FREUD'S EARLY HYPOTHESES. Freud considered two distinct problems in relation to the sources of anxiety: (1) What was the nature of the first occasion of anxiety in the lifetime of the individual? (2) What are the relations between anxiety and other personality processes? Freud's early answer to the first question was that the *experience of birth* constitutes the earliest occasion of anxiety—in other words, that the birth experience is the "prototype for all occasions on which life is endangered."

> . . . we believe we know what this early impression is which is reproduced as a repetition in the anxiety affect. We think it is the experience of *birth*—an experience which involves just such a concatenation of painful feelings, of discharges of excitation, and of bodily sensations, as to have become a prototype for all occasions on which life is endangered, ever after to be reproduced again in us as the dread or "anxiety" condition. The enormous increase in stimulation effected by the interruption of the renewal of blood (the internal respiration) was the cause of the anxiety experience at birth—the first anxiety was therefore toxically induced. . . . It is very suggestive too that the first anxiety state arose on the occasion of the separation from the mother. We naturally believe that the disposition to reproduce this first anxiety condition has become so deeply ingrained in the organism, through countless generations, that no single individual can escape the anxiety affect; even though, like the legendary Macduff, he "was from his mother's womb untimely ripped" and so did not himself experience the act of birth.[16]

Thus, in this early period, Freud believed that anxiety is originally a reaction to the toxic conditions arising during birth—a physiological, environmental interpretation; but, at the same time, Freud believed that

[16] *Ibid.*, p. 344.

the anxiety experience is innately ready to function in the organism as soon as it is set off by the perception of some danger situation—a hereditary, instinctual interpretation.

The second problem—that of the relation between anxiety and other personality processes—was treated in terms of the concept of libido. Anxiety, according to this view, arises when libido is prevented from discharging normally.

> . . . expectant dread or general apprehensiveness stands in intimate relation to certain processes in the sexual life—let us say, to certain modes of libido-utilization. The simplest and most instructive case of this kind arises in people who expose themselves to what is called frustrated excitation, i.e., when a powerful sexual excitation experiences insufficient discharge and is not carried on to a satisfying termination. . . . Under these conditions the libidinal excitation disappears and anxiety appears in place of it, both in the form of expectant dread and in that of attacks and anxiety-equivalents. . . . The more "temperament," i.e., the more inclination for sexual intercourse and capacity for satisfaction, a woman has, the more certainly will she react with anxiety manifestations to the man's impotence or to *coitus interruptus;* whereas such abuse entails far less serious results with anaesthetic women or those in whom the sexual hunger is less strong. . . . How anxiety develops out of sexual desire is at present obscure; we can only ascertain that desire is lacking and anxiety is found in its place.[17]

Even though Freud at this point denied that he understood the relation between anxiety and libido (sexual desire), there was a strong suggestion that he believed anxiety to consist of *transformed* libidinal excitation. Freud pointed out, for example, that children who "have inherently a greater amount of libidinal need in their constitution than others" are more amenable to training in apprehension of objective dangers than are children who have less "libidinal need." [18] In his later work, indeed, Freud stated that he had previously "assumed that libido (sexual excitation) rejected by the ego or not utilized by it found direct discharge in the form of anxiety." [19]

FREUD'S LATER HYPOTHESES. Freud's conceptions of the origin of anxiety and of the relations of anxiety to other personality processes

[17] *Ibid.*, pp. 348–9.
[18] *Ibid.*, p. 354.
[19] Freud, *The Problem of Anxiety*, p. 107.

were modified in his later writings. With reference to the birth experience, Freud no longer gave exclusive emphasis to this occasion of anxiety. Rather, he emphasized that there are danger situations appropriate to particular stages of development:

> . . . every stage of development has its own particular conditions for anxiety: that is to say, a danger-situation appropriate to it. The danger of mental helplessness corresponds to the stage of early immaturity of the ego; the danger of loss of object or of love corresponds to the dependence of the early years of childhood; the danger of castration to the phallic phase; and finally, fear of the super-ego, which occupies a special position, to the period of latency.[20]

In his later works Freud also continued to stress the importance of libidinal transformation as a source of anxiety, but this process was no longer given exclusive emphasis. Some of the conceptions Freud discussed in his *New Introductory Lectures* and in his *Problem of Anxiety* are given here, with little attempt, at this point, to clarify Freud's understanding of their interrelations.

1. Freud still maintained that neurotic anxiety may arise "through direct transformation of libido." He added to this the possibility that hostility may similarly be transformed into anxiety. "It is the idea that undergoes repression and may be distorted so as to become unrecognizable; its associated affect is always turned into anxiety, regardless of its nature, whether, that is to say, it is aggression or love." [21]

2. Freud maintained that what is feared in the case of neurotic anxiety "is obviously one's own libido. The difference between this and objective anxiety lies in two points—that the danger is an internal instead of an external one, and that it is not consciously recognized." [22] Neurotic danger was said to have its source in "instinctual demand." [23]

3. But libido (instinctual demand) represents danger "only because it involves an external danger"; this external danger is said to be the child's fear of castration, the threatened punishment of the boy for being in love with his mother (Oedipus complex).[24]

[20] Freud, *New Introductory Lectures* . . . , pp. 122–3.
[21] *Ibid.*, p. 116.
[22] *Ibid.*, p. 117.
[23] Freud, *The Problem of Anxiety*, pp. 115–16.
[24] Freud, *New Introductory Lectures* . . . , pp. 120–1.

4. Anxiety arising from instinctual demands (since they evoke "well-remembered danger-situations") eventuates in repression (loss of awareness) of the impulse: ". . . the ego anticipates the satisfaction of the questionable impulse, and enables it to reproduce the painful feelings which are attached to the beginning of the dreaded danger-situation. Thereupon the automatic mechanism of the pleasure-pain principle is brought into play and carries through the repression of the dangerous impulse." [25]

5. The true significance of a danger situation involves "the estimation of our strength in comparison with its magnitude, the admission of our helplessness in the face of it." A situation that arouses the perception of helplessness is called a *traumatic situation*.[26]

6. Anxiety functions as a signal that a traumatic situation is about to be experienced; a danger situation, in other words, arouses anticipation of a traumatic situation of helplessness. The anxiety, which was an original reaction to helplessness, is displaced onto the present danger situation.[27]

The above account of Freud's hypotheses relating to the sources of anxiety will be supplemented in a subsequent section, in which an attempt will be made to integrate different conceptions into a consistent hypothesis.

Horney's Hypothesis

Horney developed the hypothesis that "basic anxiety" consists of the child's feeling of "being isolated and helpless in a potentially hostile world."

A wide range of adverse factors in the environment can produce this insecurity in a child: direct or indirect domination, indifference, erratic behavior, lack of respect for the child's individual needs, lack of real guidance, disparaging attitudes, too much admiration or the absence of it, lack of reliable warmth, having to take sides in parental disagreements, too much or too little responsibility, over-protection, isolation from other children, injustice, discrimination, unkept promises, hostile atmosphere, and so on and so on.[28]

[25] *Ibid.*, p. 124.
[26] Freud, *The Problem of Anxiety*, pp. 113–14.
[27] *Ibid.*, pp. 114–15.
[28] Karen Horney, *Our Inner Conflicts* (New York, 1945), p. 41. Reprinted by permission of W. W. Norton & Company, Inc. Copyright, 1945, by W. W. Norton & Company, Inc.

In passing, it may be noted that Horney postulated three "neurotic trends"—moving *toward* people, moving *against* people, and moving *away from* people—which correspond to the three elements of her anxiety concept: helplessness (dependence), hostility (aggressiveness), and isolation (withdrawal).[29]

According to Horney, the anxiety experience is intimately associated with hostility.[30] First, there may be a direct connection, in the sense that one may have hostile impulses that are directed against a person on whom one is dependent—a case in which the actual expression of aggression would defeat "the purposes of the self."

Second, the repression of hostility may cause an individual to become more defenseless against those who already frustrate him or take unfair advantage of him—here, his failure to "fight back" would put him even more seriously at the mercy of others. As he becomes more and more victimized (frustrated) by other persons who take advantage of his overt submissiveness, the repressed hostility itself will become intensified.

Third, the individual may project his repressed hostile impulses onto other persons, so that they will become, in his perception, more hostile toward him than they really are—he will then feel even more helpless in his efforts to overcome the sources of frustration.

Fourth, a "retaliation fear may get hold of the repressed impulse"; that is to say, the individual may fear retaliation from the persons toward whom his hostile impulses are directed. In all of these ways, according to Horney, anxiety and hostility are interrelated.

May's Hypothesis

According to May, anxiety develops through the maturation of the organism, and thus has its basic source in hereditary potentialities.[31] First to appear is "the *startle pattern*, a pre-emotional, innate reflexive reaction"; next to appear is "*anxiety*, the undifferentiated emotional response"; last to appear is "*fear*, a differentiated emotional reaction." Fear is interpreted by May as "anxiety objectivated"—that is, as anxiety that has become related to some specific object.

> It is here suggested that the capacity for anxiety is not learned, but the quantities and forms of anxiety in a given individual are learned. This means that normal anxiety is a function of the or-

[29] *Ibid.*, pp. 42–3.
[30] Horney, *The Neurotic Personality* . . . , pp. 60–78.
[31] May, *op. cit.*, pp. 190–234.

ganism *qua* organism; every human being would experience anxiety in situations of threat to its vital values. But *what* the individual regards as a situation of threat to vital values *is* largely due to learning.[32]

Anxiety, according to May, will thus appear whenever a vital value is threatened. May believes that frustration or conflict will generate anxiety, provided that the frustration or conflict should endanger such a vital value. For May, the fundamental value is to be found in the relation of the individual to his community (parents, family, friends, etc.). The individual's growth problem comprises the difficulties involved in developing independence and autonomy without, at the same time, losing effective interrelationships with other people.

> In the individual who is characterized by independence without corresponding relatedness, there will develop hostility toward those whom he believes to be the occasion of his isolation. In the individual who is symbiotically dependent, there will develop hostility toward those whom he regards as instrumental in the suppression of his capacities and freedom. In each case, the hostility increases the conflict and anxiety. Another mechanism will also be present, namely repression. . . . It is well known . . . that the mechanism of repression itself decreases autonomy and increases helplessness and conflict.[33]

It will be noted that May[34] follows Horney with regard to the close association of hostility with anxiety.[35] He also stresses, as does Horney, that the basis of anxiety is to be found in the relationship of the individual with other people.

Mowrer's Hypothesis

Mowrer has advocated a "guilt theory" of neurotic anxiety.[36] According to Mowrer, *normal anxiety* "is associated with a conflict in which the contending forces are consciously recognized."[37] But *neurotic anxiety* arises when guilt (fear of conscience) has been repressed; in other words, through repression, fear will be converted into anxiety, since the object of fear will have been lost from awareness.

---

[32] *Ibid.*, p. 208.   [33] *Ibid.*, pp. 213–14.   [34] *Ibid.*, pp. 222–3.

[35] May, however, believes that anxiety is more basic than hostility—in other words, that hostility arises after the individual experiences anxiety.

[36] O. Hobart Mowrer, *Learning Theory and Personality Dynamics* (New York, 1950), pp. 537–9.

[37] *Ibid.*, p. 559.

. . . anxiety is merely fear which has been converted into anxiety by the act of repression. Or, more precisely said, anxiety is merely fear (anticipation of punishment, guilt, bad conscience) which has been repressed as such and which, incapable of being kept completely repressed . . . periodically breaks forth into consciousness, there to be experienced, not as what it is, namely social fear and guilt, but as anxiety.[38]

According to Mowrer, repression is concerned mainly with superego motivation, rather than, as Freud maintained, with id motivation. "Anxiety comes, not from repressed sexuality or pentup hatred, but from a denial and defiance of the forces of conscience." [39]

Neurotic anxiety, according to Mowrer, thus has its origin in the repression of superego motivation: anxiety, by this interpretation, occurs when *fear of conscience* arises in consciousness as *fear of something unknown*.

. . . . Freud's theory holds that anxiety comes from evil wishes, from acts which the individual would commit if he dared. *The alternative view here proposed is that anxiety comes, not from acts which the individual would commit but dares not, but from acts which he has committed but wishes that he had not. It is, in other words, a "guilt theory" of anxiety rather than an "impulse theory."* [40]

The aim of psychotherapy, from this point of view, becomes that of turning anxiety into "ordinary guilt and moral fear, to which realistic readjustments and new learning can occur." [41] In other words, the problem in psychotherapy is concerned with helping the individual to recognize that what he fears is his own conscience, rather than, as Freud has maintained, his biogenic motives or instinctual demands. According to either conception, of course, the function of psychotherapy is *to convert anxiety into fear*.

Strictly speaking, according to Mowrer, Freud's three varieties of anxiety—objective, moral, and neurotic—can be reduced to two cate-

---

[38] *Ibid.*, p. 539.

[39] O. Hobart Mowrer, "Biological vs. Moral 'Frustration' in the Causation of Personality Disturbances," *Progressive Education*, 26 (1949), 65–69. In *Learning Theory and Personality Dynamics*, O. Hobart Mowrer (New York, 1950), p. 568. Reprinted by permission of *Progressive Education* and The Ronald Press Company. Copyright, 1949, by American Education Fellowship, 1950, by The Ronald Press Company.

[40] Mowrer, *Learning Theory and Personality Dynamics*, p. 537.

[41] *Ibid.*, pp. 539–40.

gories: fear and anxiety. Objective anxiety and moral anxiety should be called *fear;* and the term *neurotic anxiety* "is redundant, for there is no other kind" of anxiety.[42]

Integrative Interpretation

Much of the disagreement among hypotheses relating to the sources of anxiety may, it seems, be attributed to the frequent failure to distinguish between fear and anxiety, and to the failure to distinguish among different aspects of what we term the frustration syndrome. This syndrome, as we have seen, involves at least four distinguishable aspects: motivation, frustration, anger (or hostility), and anxiety (or fear). Some of the major points that were considered by Freud, Horney, May, and Mowrer may be interpreted in terms of the frustration syndrome.

ANXIETY AS A FUNCTION OF MATURATION AND LEARNING. May has stated that anxiety occurs as a function of maturation, and that the maturational sequence includes: first, the startle pattern; second, anxiety; and finally, fear. It seems probable that, in this connection, May has made no distinction between anxiety and the reaction to motivational discomfort (pain?).

Perhaps no distinction *should* be made. We have seen in a previous chapter (Chap. II) that motivational discomfort involves tension, just as anxiety involves tension. There occurs, indeed, a fundamental similarity between the primary motivational process and anxiety: in either case, no instrumental act is consciously anticipated, and no goal object is consciously cathected. As a matter of fact, in the infant, before object cathexis has occurred, no distinction can properly be made between motivation, frustration, and anxiety: to the infant's perception, apparently, motivation *is* frustration and motivation *is* anxiety.

It may well be that the problem of the origin of anxiety can best be treated by first redefining anxiety to imply *any motivational process that occurs without conscious anticipation of a gratifying instrumental act and without conscious cathexis of a gratifying object*. According to this interpretation, May's "anxiety" should be termed *primary anxiety* or, in Horney's terminology, *basic anxiety;* while Mowrer's "anxiety," which is conceived to occur after repression, should be termed *secondary anxiety*.

The following developmental sequence may now be hypothesized:

[42] *Ibid.,* p. 18 n.

1. Primary motivation or primary anxiety occurs as soon as the individual becomes conscious of a motivational discomfort— that is, when the individual becomes motivated by any of the biogenic needs—and before he has associated any specific objects or actions with the relief of motivational discomfort (prior to the development of object cathexis). This primary anxiety occurs as a function of the "organism *qua* organism," in the words of May; it occurs as a natural function of the organism and is not dependent on learning. When Freud emphasized that anxiety is "deeply ingrained in the organism," he referred to *primary anxiety*. Horney's point that "basic anxiety" occurs whenever the individual feels helpless or isolated is consistent with this interpretation: the individual feels helpless in terms of the fact that he does not know what to do in order to relieve his discomfort; he feels isolated, since nobody seems immediately available to provide him with the external help he needs.

2. After object cathexis has been established through learning, the individual will "love" the persons, actions, and objects that have been positively cathected, or that have been associated with gratification; he will hate and fear persons, actions, and objects that have been associated with frustration. In other words, the individual must *learn* what to love, what to feel hostile toward, and what to fear. Love, hostility, and fear, then, involve object cathexis, and are dependent on learning.

3. Through repression, the attitudes of love, hostility, and fear become (consciously) objectless and devoid of gratifying instrumental acts; when their emotional counterparts occur in consciousness, they are experienced as *secondary anxiety*. Thus, conscious anxiety—that is, conscious anxiety of *secondary* origin—arises as a function of the prior repression ("learning to forget") of positive or negative object-cathexes.

According to this view, hostility and fear may be regarded as biogenic processes that occur in relation to frustrating objects; what particular objects will arouse hostility and fear in the individual will depend on learning, as a function of his previous unique experiences with frustrating objects. Likewise, love may be regarded as a biogenic process that occurs in response to gratification; but what objects will arouse an individual's love will, again, depend upon his previous experiences with gratifying objects.

In any case, before objects (including instrumental acts) have been cathected, and after their cathexis has been lost through repression, the individual will experience "objectless" motivation, which we have termed *anxiety*.

DANGER AS THE OCCASION OF ANXIETY. Anxiety arises when there is a perception of danger. This seems to be a point of agreement. But there is disagreement about *what* danger involves. Freud's treatment of the birth experience as the prototype of all danger situations can be considered to involve the conception of primary anxiety in response to a primary danger; in this case, the danger will involve sheer motivational discomfort, arising from oxygen want before the infant has associated breathing with relief from the discomfort.

A primary danger, then, might be defined as the perception of motivational discomfort which occurs prior to the establishment of object (and instrumental act) cathexis; in other words, the concept of primary danger is equivalent to Rosenzweig's concept of primary frustration. In this connection, Freud has explicitly stated the meaning of danger to the infant:

> If the infant longs for the sight of the mother, it does so, surely, only because it already knows from experience that she gratifies all its needs without delay. The situation which the infant appraises as "danger," and against which it desires reassurance, is therefore one of not being gratified, of an *increase of tension arising from non-gratification of its needs*—a situation against which it is powerless. I believe that from this standpoint everything falls into place; the situation of privation, in which stimuli reach an unpleasurable magnitude . . . without an ability to cope with them . . . and thus provide for their discharge, must represent to the infant a situation analogous to the birth experience, a repetition of the danger situation. . . .[43]

Freud has clearly implied here that anxiety consists of motivational discomfort that is experienced without knowledge of how to bring about relief (except through the indirect agency of the mother).

Danger situations that are consciously recognized by the individual should be regarded as the objects of *fear* and of *hostility*, rather than of anxiety, since anxiety is "objectless." When a "vital value" of the individual is threatened (Cf. May and Horney), presumably the danger

[43] Freud, *The Problem of Anxiety*, p. 76.

is an object of fear (and hostility); the danger is, in other words, associated with the perception of a recognized frustrating agent.

The relation between hostility and anxiety may be a more direct one than either Horney or May has indicated, though such indirect relations as those which were conceived by Horney must also occur. When knowledge of the object of hostility is repressed, and when conscious anticipations of aggressive action are repressed, this hostility will presumably be converted into conscious anxiety. This accords well with Mowrer's theory of secondary, or neurotic, anxiety, in which fear is conceived to be converted into anxiety through an act of repression.

Secondary dangers that function as the occasions of anxiety will clearly involve *unknown* frustrating agents—that is, objects of fear and hostility which have been lost from awareness through repression, or objects of love which have similarly been lost in view of their functioning as frustrating agents or in view of their being associated with frustrating agents.

The perception of danger, then, becomes equivalent to the perception of frustration; some danger to some value (motive) of the individual will be perceived, regardless of how mild or how temporary the frustration may be. Frustrations are easier to overcome when the individual has conscious awareness of the frustrating agent; thus, it should be expected that fear, as compared with anxiety, will involve less of a "sense of helplessness."

ANXIETY AS UNDISCHARGED LIBIDO. Undischarged libido, if interpreted strictly as sexual motivation in the biological sense, may be considered the equivalent of frustration of the sexual impulse. This should, in our interpretation, be accompanied by anxiety. According to the present interpretation, however, *any* frustration should be accompanied by anxiety. If the term *libido* be interpreted broadly to imply any instance of positive cathexis, or as the equivalent of love, then undischarged libido must involve frustration.

If the frustrating agent is known, it will be an object of hostility or fear. If the frustrating agent has been lost from consciousness by repression, the hostility and fear will be experienced as anxiety; if the object of love has been repressed, the love should be experienced as anxiety.

ANXIETY AS RELATED TO HOSTILITY. If hostility (aggressive impulse directed toward an object) is an invariable aspect of frustration, we should expect hostility and anxiety to be closely related. The tracing of (secondary) reciprocal relations between hostility and anxiety (Cf. Horney and May) aids our understanding of the development of severe anxiety, which to an external observer will seem disproportionate to the occasion of anxiety. If the original frustration were maintained at a given level, as it likely would be if the frustrating agent were unknown, the intensity of anxiety should be expected to remain at a relatively constant and "reasonable" level.[44]

Since anxiety and hostility are aspects of the frustration syndrome, their reciprocal relations will lead to a high level of frustration, and hence a high level of anxiety. Since hostility is normally frustrated, the frustration of hostility will be added to the frustration of the original motive, with an accompanying increase in hostility, which will undergo further frustration, with a further increase in hostility, etc. Eventually, through repression, the hostility will be converted into anxiety.

But anxiety, too, will function as a need; and, since there is no specific way to relieve it, the occurrence of anxiety will further increase the individual's frustration, with accompanying increases in hostility and anxiety; and so on.

These vicious-circle relations will operate to build up an ever increasing level of frustration and of anxiety.

FURTHER PRINCIPLES OF ANXIETY

ONE of the major principles relating anxiety to other aspects of the functioning personality has already been treated—namely, the principle that anxiety occurs as an aspect of the frustration syndrome. Some further principles of a general nature will next be discussed.

Anxiety as Related to Consciousness

As we have seen, many processes operate outside the individual's awareness; they operate, that is, even though the individual has no awareness, or only vague awareness, of their operation. Different aspects of the frustration syndrome may similarly function outside awareness, or at unconscious levels.

Sometimes the individual will be aware of frustration without

---

[44] Of course, it must also be recognized that, especially in the case of biogenic needs, the degree of frustration will also increase with an increase in the period of deprivation.

knowing what it is that frustrates him, or without knowing what motives are undergoing frustration. Sometimes the individual will be aware of "anxiety equivalents"—rapid pulse, difficult breathing, profuse perspiration, etc.—without conscious recognition of the fact that he is anxious; the individual may be quite surprised, for example, when his physician informs him that his psychosomatic symptoms are a manifestation of anxiety. Sometimes the individual will be aware of hostility, or resentment, or anger without awareness of being anxious. In brief, any aspect or combination of aspects of the frustration syndrome may function on a conscious level while the remaining aspects function unconsciously.

It is a major function of psychotherapy—regardless of the particular system that is employed—to aid the individual in gaining conscious recognition of the (to him) hidden aspects of this syndrome; until this has been achieved, the individual will be in no position to solve his problem effectively. The individual must have knowledge concerning the particular motives that are being frustrated, and concerning the particular agencies of frustration, before he can take adequate measures to insure gratification.

Anxiety Tolerance

The capacity to endure anxiety without resorting to maladaptive defensive measures may be termed *anxiety tolerance*. When anxiety is understood to function as one aspect of a syndrome that includes frustration, it becomes clear that anxiety tolerance is equivalent to frustration tolerance, which was discussed in a previous chapter.

Anxiety as a Need

The anxiety experience, in its free-floating form, is a distressing experience. This general apprehensiveness, or objectless fear, functions as a need. The individual's behavior during anxiety will be organized mainly in terms of efforts to relieve or reduce his anxiety. Thus, when anxiety is strong it will dominate the individual's motivational pattern, so that other motives will take a secondary position in relation to anxiety.

Since anxiety is fundamentally objectless, the problem of reducing it cannot be solved in a direct and forthright manner. The individual will be driven to try various forms of behavior; he will manifest the random, vigorous behavior characteristic of an organism that is motivated by needs that can be satisfied only by accidental means.

As a result of this procedure the individual will "hit upon" methods that, for him, are effectual in reducing anxiety.[45] These methods, as previously mentioned, are termed *defensive activities, defensive mechanisms*, etc., since they function to defend the conscious ego functions against anxiety—that is, they relieve the individual from the conscious perception of anxiety.

Defenses against Anxiety

Many of the commonly employed defenses against anxiety have been briefly mentioned in Chap. I; and some of the major defensive mechanisms will be described in detail in subsequent chapters. It is sufficient here to reiterate that some defensive activities are more adaptive, or less maladaptive, than others; and that the extent to which a defensive method is maladaptive (or maladjustive) can be evaluated in terms of the extent to which the defensive measure itself functions as a source of subsequent frustration, and hence of subsequent anxiety.

Frustration of Defenses

Defensive activities themselves may be frustrated, or their use may entail other frustrations for the individual. Such defensive activities, entailing further frustrations for the individual, have previously been termed *maladaptive defenses*. To the extent that defensive activities are socially disapproved, the attempt to use them may bring punishment upon the individual.

Overt aggression, for example, may be frustrated. (Aggression may function as a defense, since it prevents the development of intense anxiety, through the reciprocal relations between hostility and anxiety.) As overt aggression is frustrated, the individual may develop anxiety that must be defended against by some other means—usually by some more acceptable form of aggression. If the overt aggression is not frustrated, its expression may interfere with amicable social relationships, thereby frustrating other important motives of the individual.

[45] The fact that the individual must depend on random efforts to hit upon a successful method of relieving anxiety follows from the fact that he does not consciously know the nature of the underlying motivation; this should not be taken to imply that just any method will be successful in relieving anxiety. The appropriate instrumental acts and objects, or substitutes for them, must eventually be employed in order to relieve the underlying motivation. While the individual may be conscious only of anxiety or of "anxiety equivalents," aggressive actions must be employed to relieve the anxiety remaining in consciousness after the repression of hostility; escape reactions must be employed to relieve anxiety arising from the repression of fear; and positive reactions must be employed to relieve anxiety arising from the repression of love or sexuality.

When symptoms of a neurotic nature are interfered with in the course of therapeutic procedures, this may again be regarded as a frustration of defensive activities; the symptoms have functioned as defensive measures against anxiety. Freud has stated that when obsessive patients are restrained from carrying out their obsessive performances "they are forced by an appalling dread to yield to the compulsion and to carry out the act. We perceive that the anxiety was concealed under the obsessive act and that this is only performed to escape the feeling of dread." [46]

Similarly, it has been noted that psychoanalytic procedures frequently meet with resistance, since their purpose is largely to frustrate defenses against anxiety. When such resistances are broken down, anxiety will return; so that the appearance of anxiety may be regarded as a sign that the therapeutic procedure is meeting with success.[47]

Horney has suggested that individuals may develop a superstructure of defenses: primary defenses will be frustrated, with accompanying anxiety; further defenses will be resorted to in order to alleviate the anxiety that was generated as a function of the secondary frustration; thus the individual will develop "defenses against defenses against defenses," and so on.

> It is a commonplace that one lie usually leads to another, the second takes a third to bolster it, and so on till one is caught in a tangled web. . . . So it is with neurotic attempts to solve the basic conflict; and here, as elsewhere, nothing is of . . . avail but a radical change in the conditions out of which the original difficulty arose. What the neurotic does instead—and cannot help doing—is to pile one pseudo solution upon another.[48]

The use of any maladaptive defense, then, will bring with it frustration and anxiety; further defenses will be employed to alleviate the secondary anxiety; these in turn will entail frustration and anxiety, which must be defended against by further defenses; the original conflict will become so deeply embedded in this tangled structure of defenses that psychotherapy can bring it to light only through the long and tedious procedure of tearing away a defense, or, more commonly, a piece of a defense at a time.

[46] Freud, *A General Introduction . . .* , p. 350.

[47] This anxiety, however, as we have seen, must subsequently be converted into love, fear, or hostility; the patient must know what he loves, what he fears, and what he hates before he can make successful readjustments.

[48] Horney, *Our Inner Conflicts*, p. 131. (Cf. Mowrer, *Learning Theory and Personality Dynamics*, pp. 446–50.)

"Physiological" Manifestations of Anxiety as Related to Conflict

In a previous section, it was noted that anxiety involves various symptomatic manifestations, such as muscular tension, muscular tremors, chronic fatigue, irritability, insomnia, profuse sweating, restlessness, inability to concentrate, indecision, confusion and doubt, and disturbances in respiration, pulse, blood pressure, alimentary functions, etc. These manifestations become understandable in terms of the underlying conflict of motives. A conflict, as we have seen, involves tendencies to carry out mutually incompatible actions with reference to a goal object or objects—that is, tendencies to approach and to avoid or destroy such objects.

The muscular tensions that occur can be understood as the operation of preparatory sets in antagonistic muscle groups; when such muscular tensions are operative, tremors will occur, as the student can easily verify by tensing his arm and fist.

Muscular tensions that are continued over long periods of time will eventuate in fatigue; this fatigue will occur chronically, since no adequate rest can be achieved without relaxation. Tensions will likewise interfere with sleep, since relaxation is a necessary condition for adequate sleep.

Tension, being a state of readiness to react, will be manifested also in the form of irritability, "jumpiness," and susceptibility to startle. Restlessness is a function of inability to concentrate attention and to relax; and the inability to concentrate is a function of the division of attention that occurs with respect to different aspects of the conflicting (positive and negative) features of the situation.

Sweating will be associated with muscular effort, regardless of whether it involves actual movements of the body or just muscular tension. Indecision, confusion, and doubt are manifestations of uncertainty regarding the nature of the appropriate action to be taken in relation to goal objects. The various "physiological" disturbances have been described by Cannon in terms of the organism's preparation for an emergency.[49]

GUILT AND INFERIORITY FEELINGS

IT HAS previously been pointed out that superego motives function as a major source of conflicts. *Guilt* involves an anxiety-like

[49] Walter B. Cannon, *Bodily Changes in Pain, Hunger, Fear and Rage* (New York, 1915).

process that accompanies the self-frustration of superego motives. *Inferiority feelings* may also be related to the frustration of superego motives.

Definition of Guilt

The term *guilt* is frequently applied to what Freud has termed *moral anxiety*.[50] We may say, then, that guilt comprises the anxiety-like process deriving from the *self-frustration of conscience*—that is, the self-frustration of negative superego motivation.[51] Guilt arises when the individual has an impulse, or acts on an impulse, to behave in a manner contrary to his introjected moral standards.

Masserman has defined guilt as "conscious or unconscious dread of loss of love or retributive punishment for impulses or deeds forbidden in earlier experiences." [52] Our previous treatment of the origin of conscience is consistent with Masserman's definition. Guilt is seen, then, to be the successor of objective anxiety; after moral standards have been introjected, the occurrence of "immoral" impulses will frustrate (will be in conflict with) these standards, and hence guilt will begin to function.

When guilt is extremely severe, it may be experienced as *depression*.

> If the depression is severe enough, the patient manifests a "delusion of sin and guilt." He is utterly dejected; he condemns himself, and says that he has committed the unpardonable sin. He is convinced that the whole world considers him a sinner, that God has rejected him and will punish him, that he is more worthless than a worm before God and man.[53]

This excerpt emphasizes the continuity of guilt and depression, and stresses the relation of guilt to superego motives (conscience).

The individual experiences *shame* when someone has discovered,

---

[50] Freud, *New Introductory Lectures* . . . , p. 119.

[51] It seems appropriate to refer to guilt as an anxiety-like process, rather than to refer to it as a variety of anxiety, since guilt, when it is perceived as such, involves *fear* of punishment, often without clear consciousness of the nature of the agency from which punishment may issue, but sometimes with awareness that it is one's conscience from which the punishment will come. Of course guilt may, as we have seen, be converted into anxiety; but when this has occurred we should, according to Mowrer, speak of anxiety rather than of guilt.

[52] Masserman, *op. cit.*, p. 278.

[53] Abraham H. Maslow and Bela Mittelmann, *Principles of Abnormal Psychology: the Dynamics of Psychic Illness* (New York, 1941), p. 139. Reprinted by permission of Harper & Brothers. Copyright, 1941, by Harper & Brothers.

or seems about to discover, that he has committed an act contrary to his conscience. Shame will be experienced by the small child, for example, when his parents discover that he has done something that, in terms of their standards, is judged to be "naughty." And this may occur before the child himself has thoroughly introjected these standards.

Shame appears, then, to consist of a mixture of objective anxiety and guilt, since its occurrence is associated with anticipated or actual discovery, and since it apparently does not occur prior to the (at least) partial introjection of parental (cultural) standards. In other words, shame involves fear of punishment, with some recognition that the source of punishment will be an agency external to the self. But shame will not occur until the individual has learned, to some degree, to recognize which of his actions are regarded as punishable.

Guilt Compared with Inferiority Feelings

Both Freud and Alexander have treated the distinction between guilt and inferiority feelings. Freud had the following to say in this regard:

> The sense of inferiority has a strong erotic basis. The child feels itself inferior when it perceives that it is not loved, and so does the adult as well. . . . The sense of inferiority and the sense of guilt are exceedingly difficult to distinguish. Perhaps we should do better if we regarded the former as the erotic complement to the sense of moral inferiority. We have paid but little attention to such questions of conceptual differentiation in psycho-analysis.[54]

Alexander has dealt with the same problem, as follows:

> The psychological content of guilt feelings can be verbalized about as follows: "I am no good. What I want to do or what I have done is mean and objectionable. I deserve contempt and punishment." In contrast, the emotional content of inferiority feelings is: "I am weak, I am not as strong, as clever, as efficient as the other fellow. I am ashamed on account of my weakness." In inferiority feelings, the self-condemnation is the result, not of wrongdoing, but of a shameful recognition of weakness. Accordingly, inferiority feelings stimulate competition and aggression. The only way to eradicate them is to show one's superiority in competition. Guilt feelings, on the contrary, inhibit competition. . . . To get rid of guilt

[54] Freud, *New Introductory Lectures* . . . , pp. 93-4.

feelings, one must renounce competition. . . . Guilt feelings require the opposite of the competitive attitude, namely subordination, self-abasement, and even punishment.[55]

Although both of the foregoing treatments have suggested the nature of the fundamental distinction between guilt and inferiority feelings, they fail to make this distinction explicit. The fundamental distinction probably should be made in terms of the classes of motives which undergo frustration.

In brief, guilt may be said to arise when *negative* superego motives (conscience motives) are frustrated, while inferiority feelings may be said to arise when *positive* superego motives (ego-ideals) are frustrated.

According to this point of view, guilt involves fear of danger—originally, an objective danger, and, after introjection, a moral danger. Thus guilt arises entirely in terms of negative motivation (negative cathexis); it functions to protect the individual from harm. When the individual lives up to the demands of his conscience, he will achieve nothing more than safety or security.

When the individual lives up to his ego-ideal, he will achieve something highly positive; he will approach some high level of achievement, through the guidance of his aspirations. When the individual fails to live up to his ego-ideal, he will feel inferior in comparison with his level of aspiration—and inferior to others who appear to be more successful in this regard.

The person who feels inferior (rather than experiencing guilt) for failure to live up to his moral standards will be a person whose ego-ideal involves a high moral aspiration; for example, he may be a great moral or religious leader.

Freud hinted that inferiority feelings arise from the frustration of ego-ideals when he stated: "The child feels itself inferior when it perceives that it is not loved"; to receive love implies a positive achievement.

Alexander's treatment of inferiority feelings as a function of the recognition of weakness has offered a similar suggestion; weakness implies a positive standard of judgment. Moreover, Alexander has agreed with this point of view in his denial that inferiority feelings arise with consciousness of wrongdoing.

[55] Franz Alexander, *Fundamentals of Psychoanalysis* (New York, 1948), p. 123.

Relation of Guilt to Hostility

With the occurrence of extreme degrees of guilt, as in cases of depression, guilt and hostility may become interrelated in a mutually reinforcing manner. In a general way, it may be seen that in all cases of guilt, even in its milder forms, a component of hostility is involved. Whenever superego motives undergo frustration, hostility (aggressive motivation) can be expected to occur, as in all instances of frustration. In this case, the hostility will properly be directed against the self, which is perceived to be the frustrating agent.

If the hostility is displaced onto other persons, either in the form of aggressive impulses or in the form of overt aggression, this will function as a further frustration of moral motivation: hence, guilt will increase; hostility will increase; hostility will be displaced again; guilt will be further increased; etc.

This mutually reinforcing interrelation between hostility and guilt (as between any form of anxiety and hostility) may eventuate in a great intensification of guilt, so that it will appear to be unreasonably strong in relation to its original basis.

Need for Punishment

When certain aspects of the guilt process are repressed, it becomes possible to speak of an unconscious *need for punishment*.

> . . . this unconscious need for punishment . . . behaves like a part of the conscience, like the prolongation of conscience into the unconscious; and it must have the same origin as conscience, that is to say it will correspond to a piece of aggressiveness which has been internalized and taken over by the super-ego. If only the words were less incongruous, we should be justified, for all practical purposes, in calling it "an unconscious sense of guilt." [56]

The incongruity Freud has referred to involves the conception of an *unconscious* guilt *experience* that is recognizable as such; conceived in these terms, of course, the idea of unconscious guilt can have little logical congruity. But no incongruity need be implied if we postulate that *certain aspects* of the total guilt process will continue to function unconsciously after they have undergone repression.

It is necessary to recognize that the total guilt process involves both a *need for punishment* and a *fear of punishment*. Prior to the de-

[56] Freud, *New Introductory Lectures* . . . , pp. 149–50.

velopment of conscience—that is, prior to the development of negative superego motivation—the child must have felt *hostility* and *fear* in relation to his parents, who, by virtue of their punishing activities, were perceived as his original frustrating agents.[57]

With the development of conscience motivation, the hostility and fear that were originally related to the parents will have been displaced onto certain aspects of the child's personality. If the child *personifies* his conscience and his ego—as he normally can be expected to do—he will perceive his ego as *fearing his conscience*, and he will perceive his conscience as *hostile toward his ego*.

Then, by a process of integration, the child may come to *accept his conscience as a part of himself*; so that, whenever he acts, or is tempted to act, in a manner contrary to the demands of his conscience he will experience the *need for punishment*, as well as the *fear of punishment*.

This combination of need for punishment and fear of punishment occurs as the consciously recognizable form of guilt. This sense of guilt, as we usually know it, will operate as a punishing experience of such intensity that it will gratify, at least in part, the *need for punishment*.

As a function of repression, however, both the fear of punishment and the need for punishment may be represented in consciousness as anxiety, which can be relieved by any form of punishment—by an external agency, by means of punishing symptoms, by means of "accident proneness," or by means of any of the other forms of masochism.

> . . . we are dealing with . . . a sense of guilt, which is finding atonement in the illness and is refusing to give up the penalty of suffering. . . . But as far as the patient is concerned this sense of guilt is dumb; it does not tell him he is guilty; he does not feel guilty, he simply feels ill. This sense of guilt expresses itself only as a resistance to recovery which it is extremely difficult to overcome. . . . Nothing can be done against it directly, and nothing indirectly but the slow procedure of unmasking its unconscious repressed roots, and of thus gradually changing it into a conscious sense of guilt. . . .[58]

---

[57] The child will, of course, also *love* his parents on the basis of their gratifying activities in relation to him. With the development of superego motives, some of this love will be displaced onto the child's ego-ideal; and, with the development of mastery and autonomy, some of this love will be directed onto the ego itself, since in this case the child acts as his own source of gratification.

[58] Sigmund Freud, *The Ego and the Id* (London, 1950), pp. 71–2, 72 n.

Special Defenses against Guilt and Inferiority Feelings

In a preceding section, the quotation from Alexander has suggested that compensation is frequently employed as the main defense against inferiority feelings. A subsequent chapter will treat compensation in connection with other defenses against anxiety.

As defenses against guilt, a number of activities are especially appropriate. Apology, atonement, restitution, etc., are frequently effective in relieving guilt feelings. Fundamentally, all of these activities function as self-punishment; they involve suffering—that is, they involve self-imposed frustrations of various kinds.

The need for punishment may also be gratified by many subtle forms of suffering which are the proper subject matter of psychopathology. For example, Freud [59] and Alexander [60] have explained some instances of crime in terms of the unconscious need for punishment. According to this interpretation, individuals will engage in petty crimes, which are "less objectionable than the forbidden desire they harbor in the unconscious," in order that they may be apprehended and punished, and thus relieve their need for punishment.

ADJUSTIVE IMPLICATIONS

SINCE anxiety may become operative whenever the individual is frustrated, it follows that the adjustive implications that were discussed in relation to frustration and conflict (Chap. IV) and in relation to aggression (Chap. V) are also applicable in relation to anxiety. Any procedure that will aid in the reduction of frustration or in the constructive expression of hostility should aid in the reduction of anxiety. Some further adjustive implications may be derived from principles relating to anxiety.

Social Tolerance of Fear and Hostility

Fear and hostility should become accepted as normal forms of human motivation. If mild and verbalized expressions of fear and hostility are tolerated in children—and in friends, husbands, wives, colleagues, subordinates, etc.—an important source of anxiety will lose much of its potency.

Unfortunately, both fear and hostility are regarded, in our society,

[59] Sigmund Freud, *Collected Papers* (London, 1950), IV, 342; V, 233.
[60] Alexander, *op. cit.*, pp. 238–9.

as manifestations of weakness, of lack of courage, or of immorality. The strong social pressure that operates to counteract the expression of fear and hostility will eventuate in the introjection of superego motives incompatible with the individual's more fundamental tendencies. When fear or hostility arises, then, the individual will experience guilt or inferiority feelings. He will probably repress his fear and hostility and become conscious of intensified anxiety. He may then employ maladaptive defenses, so that the insightful management of fear and hostility, in terms of their sources in frustration, will become unnecessarily difficult.

Increased social tolerance of fear and hostility would provide a firmer basis for individual adjustment. If the individual could accept his own fear and hostility as normal human processes he would be in a much better position to function efficiently in dealing with his fundamental frustrations.

Rest as Related to Anxiety

The conception of rest as a means of alleviating anxiety may have had its origin in the common belief that overwork is the basis of "nervous breakdowns." There seems to be some validity in this belief. Overwork as such may be related to anxiety in terms of the fact that fatigue will render the individual less than normally able to cope with frustrating situations, and more than normally ready to perceive situations as frustrating. Moreover, it is true that concentration on one kind of activity may serve as a frustration of many motives that are incompatible with the work itself.

Rest, then, as a specific remedy for fatigue, will function as a partial relief of anxiety, since the individual will, as a function of rest, become less susceptible to frustration and more able to overcome the frustrations that occur.

But rest alone may in many cases be insufficient; if, however, the rest is accompanied by psychotherapy with the aim of uncovering the specific sources of anxiety, or if it is accompanied by activities that gratify the previously frustrated motives, anxiety reduction will be more nearly adequate than if rest alone were involved.

Anxiety as Related to Self-Actualization

Since frustration and conflict are inevitable accompaniments of normal living, anxiety itself cannot be avoided. Living constructively and creatively involves the necessity of tolerating anxiety. May, for example, writes:

To the extent that an individual seeks to avoid anxiety, responsibility, and guilt feeling by refusing to avail himself of his new possibilities, by refusing to move from the familiar to the unfamiliar, he sacrifices his freedom and constricts his autonomy and his self-awareness. Availing oneself of possibilities, confronting the anxiety, and accepting the responsibility and guilt feeling involved result in increased self-awareness and freedom and enlarged spheres of creativity. . . . *In fine, the positive aspects of selfhood develop as the individual confronts, moves through, and overcomes anxiety-creating experiences.*[61]

Living up to one's ego-ideal or level of aspiration—in other words, self-actualization—inevitably involves frustration and conflict. In order to reach high levels of achievement, the individual must tolerate anxiety without resorting to maladaptive defenses.

The individual's realization that he must endure such anxiety in order to develop his potentialities can be, in itself, a source of strength to the individual. (It is, of course, assumed that the individual's level of aspiration should be reasonably well adjusted to the level of his actual capacities and opportunities.)

SUMMARY

THE PROBLEM of anxiety is a central problem of behavior dynamics. The term *anxiety* refers to one aspect of the interrelated emotional processes that occur during frustration or conflict. Anxiety is differentiated from fear in that fear relates to a consciously recognized object, while anxiety involves diffuse apprehension (apprehensive tension) without relation to a clearly defined object.

Objective anxiety relates to external dangers; it may be regarded as equivalent to fear. Neurotic anxiety may occur as free-floating apprehensiveness, as a phobic reaction, or as the symptoms of a severe neurosis. Free-floating anxiety is not related specifically to an object, but may be momentarily and indiscriminately related to any object that happens to be perceived. Phobic reactions involve the perception of some specific object, situation, or action as the occasion of anxiety; phobic reactions involve the objectification of anxiety. In severe neurosis, the individual may experience anxiety in relation to his symptoms or he may experience an anxiety attack, in which "physiological"

[61] May, *op. cit.*, p. 234.

disturbances capture the focus of his attention. Moral anxiety, or guilt, occurs when superego motives undergo frustration.

Anxiety may be manifested in consciousness as general apprehensiveness, as a phobic reaction, as an anxiety attack, etc. The particular aspects of the anxiety process which are predominantly conscious will vary from individual to individual, and from time to time in the same individual.

Hypotheses relating to the source of anxiety have been described —specifically, the hypotheses advanced by Freud, by Horney, by May, and by Mowrer. Some of the major points in the several hypotheses have been integrated in terms of the conception that anxiety involves an aspect of the frustration syndrome, which also includes motivation, frustration or conflict, and anger or hostility.

Anxiety may be redefined as any motivational process that occurs without conscious anticipation of a gratifying instrumental act and without conscious object cathexis. Primary anxiety occurs before the establishment of object cathexis; secondary anxiety occurs after the repression of object cathexis.

The developmental sequence, then, is believed to consist of: (1) the occurrence of primary anxiety before the establishment of object cathexis; (2) the occurrence of love, fear, and hostility—involving positive and negative object cathexes that were established on the basis of gratifying and frustrating experiences; and (3) the occurrence of secondary anxiety—involving motivational tensions that have been dissociated from their objects and their instrumental acts by means of repression.

Danger, when it functions as the occasion of anxiety, involves the perception of motivational discomfort or the perception of frustration, without awareness of an appropriate way to relieve the discomfort and without awareness of the nature of the frustrating agent.

Different aspects of the frustration syndrome are manifest to consciousness at different times; many aspects, at any given time, function unconsciously. Tolerance of anxiety is equivalent to frustration tolerance. Anxiety functions as a need; when strong anxiety occurs, the individual's behavior will be organized primarily in terms of attempts to relieve his anxiety.

Defenses against anxiety are methods that are employed for the relief of anxiety; some of the major defensive methods will be considered in subsequent chapters. Defensive activities may themselves undergo frustration, and their use may function to frustrate other motives; the frustrating nature of maladaptive defenses may eventuate in the development of a complex superstructure of defenses.

Guilt, or moral anxiety, occurs when negative superego motives undergo frustration; inferiority feelings have their source in the frustration of positive superego motives (ego-ideals).

When the degree of guilt is extreme, depression is said to occur. Shame may be regarded as a mixture of objective anxiety (fear) and guilt, since it usually arises when discovery of one's wrongdoing is anticipated or actual.

Guilt and hostility may interact in a mutually reinforcing manner, leading to great intensification of guilt.

When guilt functions unconsciously, it may be understood as an unconscious *need for punishment;* it may be relieved through accidents and self-injury, through punishing symptoms, through masochistic personality trends, or through the occurrence of subtle psychopathological processes.

Guilt that functions consciously may be relieved through apology, restitution, atonement, or any other form of retributive self-punishment.

Expressions of fear and hostility should be accorded social tolerance, since they function as normal human processes; the motivation to avoid such expressions may be introjected as a superego motive, whose frustration will tend to intensify the anxiety that the individual must tolerate (if he is to avoid the development of maladaptive defense mechanisms).

Rest can be effective in reducing anxiety, especially if it is combined with psychotherapy or with activities that gratify motives frustrated during periods of overwork.

Self-actualization—making the most of one's potentialities—can be achieved only through facing and overcoming unavoidable anxieties. Recognition of this fact can be a source of strength.

Chap. VII will deal with repression and related defensive processes.

▶ Suggested Readings

Cameron, N. *The Psychology of Behavior Disorders.* Boston, 1947. Chap. ix, pp. 246–77.

Cameron, N. and Magaret, Ann. *Behavior Pathology.* Boston, 1951. Chaps. x–xi, pp. 276–336.

Dollard, J. and Mowrer, O. H. "A Method of Measuring Tension in Written Documents," *Journal of Abnormal and Social Psychology, 42* (1947), 3–32.

Freud, Anna. *The Ego and the Mechanisms of Defense.* New York, 1946. Chap. v, pp. 58–70.

Freud, S. *New Introductory Lectures on Psycho-Analysis.* New York, 1933. Chap. iv, pp. 113–52.

Freud, S. *A General Introduction to Psycho-Analysis.* New York, 1935. Pp. 341–56.

Freud, S. *The Problem of Anxiety.* New York, 1936. Chap. viii, pp. 69–84.

Freud, S. *Civilization and Its Discontents.* London, 1951. Chaps. vii–viii, pp. 104–44.

Goss, A. E. "Stuttering Behavior and Anxiety as a Function of the Duration of Stimulus Words," *Journal of Abnormal and Social Psychology, 47* (1952), 38–50.

Hebb, D. O. "On the Nature of Fear," *Psychological Review, 53* (1946), 259–76.

Horney, Karen. *New Ways in Psychoanalysis.* New York, 1939. Chaps. xii, xiv, xv, pp. 193–206, 232–75.

Jenkins, R. L. "Guilt Feelings—Their Function and Dysfunction," in *Feelings and Emotions,* M. L. Reymert, ed. New York, 1950. Chap. xxviii, pp. 353–61.

Liddell, H. S. "Animal Origins of Anxiety," in *Feelings and Emotions,* M. L. Reymert, ed. New York, 1950. Chap. xv, pp. 181–8.

May, R. *The Meaning of Anxiety.* New York, 1950. Chaps. i–vi, pp. 3–234.

Mead, Margaret. "Some Anthropological Considerations Concerning Guilt," in *Feelings and Emotions,* M. L. Reymert, ed. New York, 1950. Chap. xxix, pp. 362–73.

Mowrer, O. H. *Learning Theory and Personality Dynamics.* New York, 1950. Chaps. iii, xvii, xix, pp. 65–83, 472–82, 531–61.

Mowrer, O. H. "Pain, Punishment, Guilt, and Anxiety," in *Anxiety,* P. H. Hoch and J. Zubin, eds. New York, 1950. Chap. iii, pp. 27–40.

Rado, S. "Emergency Behavior, with an Introduction to the Dynamics of Conscience," in *Anxiety,* P. H. Hoch and J. Zubin, eds. New York, 1950. Chap. ix, pp. 150–75.

Symonds, P. M. *The Dynamics of Human Adjustment.* New York, 1946. Chaps. vi, xvi, pp. 133–68, 362–404.

Tyson, R. "Current Mental Hygiene Practice," *Journal of Clinical Psychology,* 7 (1951), 17–18.

Washburne, Annette C. "Tension States," in *An Introduction to Clinical Psychology,* L. A. Pennington and I. A. Berg, eds. New York, 1948. Chap. ix, pp. 178–99.

Welch, L. and Kubis, J. "The Effect of Anxiety on the Conditioning Rate and Stability of the PGR," *Journal of Psychology, 23* (1947), 83–91.

CHAPTER Seven

Repression and Related Processes

To tear deep-rooted passion from the breast,
To still the inward strife. . . .[1]

WE HAVE seen, in Chap. III, that psychosomatic functions may operate at various levels of consciousness, and that the degree of their accessibility to consciousness may roughly be indicated by the terms *conscious, preconscious,* and *unconscious.* The present chapter will deal with repression and repression-like processes, which are concerned with rendering psychosomatic functions less accessible to consciousness or less amenable to conscious control.

DEFINITIONS

THE CONCEPT of repression may be differentiated from a number of related concepts.

Repression

The term *repression* refers to a relatively automatic, relatively unconscious process by which conscious and preconscious functions be-

[1] Edwin Arnold, *The Light of Asia.*

come, and are made to remain, unconscious. It is a process by which the "unthinkable" becomes truly *unthinkable*—that is, it may not, under ordinary conditions, be reinstated as a conscious function.

> . . . *the essence of repression lies simply in the function of rejecting and keeping something out of consciousness.*[2]

> . . . the essence of the process of repression lies, not in abrogating or annihilating the ideational presentation of an instinct, but in withholding it from becoming conscious.[3]

> *Repression* . . . is the process by which a mental act capable of becoming conscious (that is, one which belongs to the preconscious system) is made unconscious and forced back into the unconscious system. And we also call it *repression* when the unconscious mental act is not permitted to enter the . . . preconscious system at all. . . .[4]

These quotations from some of the works of Freud should make a number of points clear:

1. That repression refers to a psychological process that functions more or less continuously;
2. That repression does not destroy any psychosomatic function, but merely removes its operation from conscious perception;
3. That repressed functions continue to operate even though the individual has lost awareness of them.

Alexander has explicitly stated that the process of repression is an *unconscious* function:

> Repression consists in excluding impulses and their ideational representations from consciousness. It always occurs when a wish, impulse, or idea would on becoming conscious cause unbearable conflict resulting in anxiety. . . . The whole act takes place outside of consciousness. The rejection is automatic; otherwise the . . . content could not remain unconscious.[5]

We may summarize, then, by saying that repression functions as an unconscious process; that repression operates continuously to prevent

[2] Sigmund Freud, *Collected Papers* (London, 1950), IV, 86.
[3] *Ibid.*, p. 98.
[4] Sigmund Freud, *A General Introduction to Psycho-Analysis* (New York, 1935), p. 299.
[5] Franz Alexander, *Fundamentals of Psychoanalysis* (New York, 1948), p. 96.

conscious perception of impulses and their ideational representations; and that, in spite of repression, the unacceptable impulses continue to operate, though outside the individual's awareness.

Dissociation

Dissociation is a descriptive term that, according to Freud, refers to "a splitting of the content of consciousness"; [6] this comes about through the process of repression. Certain "groups of ideas" become dissociated, or split off, from other "groups of ideas," in the sense that some of them are repressed or excluded from conscious perception while others retain their conscious character.

When it happens that a group of ideas remains in the unconscious, psycho-analysis . . . maintains that an active antagonism of certain groups of ideas has caused the isolation of another group in the unconscious. The process which imposes such a fate upon a given group is termed . . . "repression.". . .[7]

Prior to Freud's conception of repression, dissociation was postulated by Janet in order to account for the symptoms of hysteria. Janet "assumed that certain mental processes go on in the subconscious independently of (dissociated from) the main stream of consciousness." [8] He accounted for dissociation in terms of a "weakness of psychic tension."

Suppression

While, as we have seen, the term repression refers to an unconscious process, the term *suppression* refers to a conscious process.

In excluding certain tendencies from consciousness there is . . . a conscious and voluntary selective process, called "suppression," which eliminates everything even loosely connected with unconscious material. Suppression also eliminates all kinds of irrelevancies which would distract attention from the topic which is at the focus of interest at any given moment.[9]

When we suppress an idea, we do so with conscious recognition that it is desirable, from some point of view, to stop thinking about it, or to

[6] Sigmund Freud, *Collected Papers* (London, 1950), V, 27.
[7] Sigmund Freud, *Collected Papers,* translated by Joan Riviere (London, 1950), II, 107. Reprinted by permission of The Hogarth Press, Ltd.
[8] Kenneth E. Appel, "Psychiatric Therapy," in *Personality and the Behavior Disorders,* J. McV. Hunt, ed. (New York, 1944), II, 1109.
[9] Alexander, *op. cit.,* p. 279.

avoid remembering it. Suppression, then, occurs as a function of attentive effort or concentration; it involves the deliberate exclusion of ideas from consciousness by rendering them temporarily preconscious.

Inhibition

Inhibition, like repression, refers to an unconscious process; but, unlike repression, inhibition refers to the prevention of overt action rather than to the prevention of ideas or impulses from entering, or remaining in, consciousness. Repression and inhibition may function at the same time, although they do not necessarily do so.

> . . . repressions that stop thinking are likely to be correlated with inhibitions that stop action. . . . Whenever the conditions for learning or unlearning them are different, however, they will be expected to vary independently. Thus, it is often observed in the course of psychotherapy that a person may have "insight," *i.e.*, have the correct sentences to describe his behavior, but may still be "sick," *i.e.*, be unable to make the responses that would relieve the misery of conflict.[10]

Restraint

The term *restraint* refers to the conscious or deliberate avoidance of some action—that is, to the deliberate prevention of an impulse from being carried into action. Restraint may be accompanied by suppression, or it may occur without suppression. Thus an individual may "put out of mind" an impulse to strike a superior, at the same time that he restrains himself from doing so; or he may remain conscious of his impulse but nevertheless avoid expressing it in action.

Isolation

Isolation involves a temporary exclusion from consciousness of certain ideas or impulses. According to Freud, isolation exhibits qualitative features similar to both those of repression and those of suppression. Isolation is similar to repression in that it functions more or less automatically (unconsciously); but it is similar to suppression in that the ideas and impulses that are subjected to isolation become preconscious rather than unconscious.

[10] John Dollard and Neal E. Miller, *Personality and Psychotherapy: An Analysis in Terms of Learning, Thinking, and Culture* (New York, 1950), p. 221. Reprinted by permission of McGraw-Hill Book Company, Inc. Copyright, 1950, by McGraw-Hill Book Company, Inc.

Isolation frequently involves a dissociation of the emotional from the cognitive (ideational) aspects of impulses. The individual may, upon directing his attention appropriately, become aware of the ideational contents without having any conscious perception of the emotional experiences that were once associated with them. He may remember that he was angry and aggressive in his behavior toward another person, without perceiving the quality of the anger itself; or he may recall that he once loved another, without being able to reinstate the quality of the erotic emotion.

> . . . the experience is not forgotten but it is stripped of its affect and its associative connections are suppressed or interrupted, so that it stands apart, as if isolated, and furthermore fails to be reproduced in the course of one's mental activity. The effect of this isolation is the same, then, as in repression with amnesia.[11]

Freud has compared isolation with the normal process of concentration, which functions to keep irrelevant or distracting memories from entering the consciousness.

Denial or Negation

The concept of *denial* or *negation* is very similar to the concept of repression. Repression, as we have seen, refers to an automatic process, the function of which is to deny the reality of an internal process that was once consciously perceived. Denial or negation, on the other hand, refers to an (often unconscious) intellectual process whose function is to deny the reality of an *external* process that was once the object of perception. While repression "blinds" the individual to internal realities, denial "blinds" the individual to external realities.

> A negative judgment is the intellectual substitute for repression. . . . The function of judgment is concerned ultimately with two sorts of decision. It may assert or deny that a thing has a particular property; or it may affirm or dispute that a particular image . . . exists in reality.[12]

One may deny that a situation is dangerous, and thus avoid the necessity of fearing it; or one may deny that a situation exists (or has existed) in reality at all, so that there will be no need to deny its dangerous properties.

[11] Sigmund Freud, *The Problem of Anxiety* (New York, 1936), p. 55.
[12] Freud, *Collected Papers*, V, 182–3.

Restriction of Ego Functions

The conscious, integrative ego functions may be restricted through repression or through withdrawal from active participation with external reality. As we have noted in a previous chapter, ego functions involve the integration of internal and external features of reality through such processes as perception, learning, and reasoning. To the extent that any aspect of reality is avoided, the integrative adequacy of ego functions will be reduced.

Anna Freud has used the term *restriction of the ego* to imply a withdrawal from dangerous features of external reality.[13] It seems appropriate, however, to generalize the term *to imply any kind of limitations imposed upon ego functions,* regardless of whether these limitations occur through repression or through avoidance of external reality. The adequacy of ego functions will be reduced, for example, if the individual withdraws from social contact with members of the opposite sex, or if he represses the impulses that could render such social contacts dangerous.

FUNCTIONS COMMONLY REPRESSED

ANY impulse that arouses anxiety may undergo repression. Such anxiety-arousing impulses include: (1) impulses whose gratification would involve frustration of superego motives; (2) superego motives that are weaker than the impulses which conflict with them; and (3) impulses that are frustrated through the operation of other factors.

Sexual Impulses

Freud has emphasized especially the repression of sexual impulses. Sexual motives are particularly amenable to repression in view of their relative weakness and insignificance for the individual's survival, and in view of the cultural regulations that are imposed on sexual expression.

Some biogenic motives—hunger and thirst, for example—are highly resistant to repression, since their gratification is essential for the organism's survival.[14]

[13] Anna Freud, *The Ego and the Mechanisms of Defense* (New York, 1946), pp. 100–13.

[14] It is reasonable to assume that the entire need-integrate does not undergo repression. But instrumental acts and objects, as these are represented in ideation,

On the other hand, the repression of sexual impulses, rather than their gratification, will often have *social survival value* for the individual. Parents in our society are perhaps more disturbed by evidences of sexuality in their children than by any other form of "misbehavior." The child learns at an early age to equate sexual expression with punishment, and therefore to suppress (and eventually to repress) his interest in sexuality.[15] His negative psychogenic motivation (conscience) becomes especially strong with reference to sexual impulses and their possible expression.

Aggressive Impulses

Aggression, like sexual behavior, is subjected to punishment and to relatively strict social regulation. Individuals usually develop negative superego (conscience) motives that conflict with aggressive impulses, so that repression of aggressive impulses may occur as a means of alleviating the conflict. As Horney has pointed out, however, the repression of hostility (aggressive motivation) may become a source of intensified anxiety.[16]

Other Id Functions

Among the clearly biogenic motives, other than sexuality and aggression, fear may be regarded as the most highly amenable to repression. However, though consciousness of fear as such (and consciousness of anxiety in the form of general apprehensiveness) may be repressed, certain "anxiety equivalents"—the so-called "physiological manifestations"—may persist in conscious perception.

Other biogenic motives, though they may not be repressed as such, may become involved in repression; that is to say, the original time, place, mode, or object of their expression may be repressed. Thus,

---

in verbal expression, and in imagery, can and do frequently undergo repression. When it is said that hunger and thirst are highly resistant to repression, it is implied that the underlying needs are so insistent that the instrumental acts of eating and drinking must eventually be employed in the interest of survival. There are, of course, some pathological exceptions. In anorexia, for example, there must be an element of repression in relation to hunger. Also, in severe psychotic withdrawal the patient must be tube-fed in order to maintain his life; here again, the repression of aspects of the hunger motive must be assumed to occur.

[15] It seems probable that the conscious process of suppression, as this becomes habitual, may gradually become an unconscious process of repression. This is similar to any other case of habituation: conscious awareness of the response decreases as it becomes habitual and "automatic."

[16] Karen Horney, *The Neurotic Personality of Our Time* (New York, 1937), pp. 66 f.

everybody must eat; but, in a given culture, there are conventionally inappropriate times, places, and modes of eating, just as there are inappropriate things to eat.

The socialized individual has repressed his immediate impulses to gratify his biogenic needs in a primitive or infantile fashion. Though he may be "hungry enough to eat a horse," it will never occur to him that he should satisfy his hunger in this particular way.

In early childhood, during socialization, the individual will have employed a conscious process of suppression in relation to disapproved times, places, modes, and objects of gratification; but in adulthood the process can be expected to have become automatic—that is, to have become a process of repression.

Superego Functions

While the main emphasis of Freud and his followers has been on the repression of id functions, especially the sexual and aggressive motives, Mowrer has stressed the possibility—indeed, the probability—that superego functions are more commonly repressed than are id functions.[17]

> For Freud the unconscious was populated with impulses of forbidden lust and hostility; here we are exploring the thesis that what falls under repression is far more likely to be man's "nobler" impulses, rather than those of the "id.". . .[18]

In other words, Mowrer has held that when conscience and sexual or aggressive motivation are in conflict, conscience will be the more likely to fall under repression. This is consistent with the principle of regression to biogenic motivation, discussed in a previous chapter.

Mowrer's point of view implies that sexual and aggressive motives are much more powerful than Freud has considered them to be. Were it otherwise, these id impulses, rather than the moral prohibitions against them, would be expected to undergo repression.

If we take the position that sexual and aggressive motives are relatively weak when compared with other biogenic motives, we are likely to agree with Freud that these id impulses are more likely to be repressed than are superego motives.

[17] O. Hobart Mowrer, *Learning Theory and Personality Dynamics* (New York, 1950), pp. 518, 552, 559, 601 f., 622, 638.
[18] *Ibid.*, p. 638.

On the other hand, it is still possible to agree with Mowrer that the superego functions will fall under repression when these happen to be weaker than the biogenic motives to which they are opposed. Thus, what will be repressed—whether id impulses or superego functions—becomes, as Freud has stated, an "economic" problem: [19] *the relative strengths of conflicting motives will determine which will be repressed.*

It becomes clear, then, that either id impulses or superego motives may be repressed, and that their relative strengths will determine which of these will undergo repression.

FUGUES INVOLVING AMNESIA.   In the literature of abnormal psychology, numerous instances have been described in which the patient manifests a *fugue*. A fugue characteristically involves a "flight," lasting from several days to several years, during which the individual, who has previously lived a "respectable" life, lives the life of a reprobate or immoral character, only to "awaken" suddenly in an environment that offends his recovered moral sensibility.

During such a fugue, id motivation has apparently occupied the individual's conscious perception, while superego motivation has been repressed; before and after the fugue, superego motivation has apparently occupied conscious perception, while id motivation has been repressed. In other words, the individual's total behavior seems to be a manifestation of the alternate repression of id and superego motives.

MULTIPLE PERSONALITIES.   A similar interpretation may apply to cases of multiple personality. In many of these cases, large systems of motivation are dissociated from one another, and each system will alternately occupy a place in conscious perception. In other words, the individual will be conscious of only one "personality" at a time.

> When dissociation occurs it is but natural that one personality should be lively and not too scrupulous while the other exhibits puritanical tendencies. Study of most of the reported cases of multiple personality shows this difference of moral characteristics.[20]

This implies that at one time, when one "personality" is dominant, id motives are repressed; while at another time, when another "personality" is dominant, superego motives are repressed.

---

[19] Freud, *A General Introduction* . . . , pp. 311–12, 326–7.
[20] Charles D. Fox, *The Psychopathology of Hysteria* (Boston, 1913), p. 332. Reprinted by permission of Chapman & Grimes, Inc. Copyright, 1913, by Richard G. Badger.

DYNAMIC INTERRELATIONS WITH ANXIETY

ANXIETY and repression are dynamically interrelated functions. The nature of their interrelations will be discussed in terms of (1) the ego functions as related to anxiety and repression, (2) the anxiety process as a basis of repression, and (3) the repression process as a basis of anxiety.

Ego Functions as Related to Anxiety and Repression

The integrative ego functions may be restricted either as a function of anxiety or as a function of repression.

EGO RESTRICTION AS A FUNCTION OF ANXIETY. As we have seen, the conscious perception of anxiety is a distressing experience; when this experience reaches a certain intensity, perception will become "flooded," as it were, with anxiety. The integrative ego functions will be left with little data to work upon, other than anxiety and objects to which it may be related (through displacement).

In earlier discussions, it has been pointed out that perception, learning, thinking, etc., are organized in terms of the motivational pattern operative at a given time. When anxiety is prepotent as a motivating factor, these ego functions will become organized in terms of anxiety and its possible relief. But since anxiety is not consciously related to its object, the ego functions will be relatively ineffectual in relieving anxiety; necessary data have become unavailable (through repression).

So long, then, as anxiety occupies perception, the integrative ego functions will be restricted and limited; this is what is meant by the statement that "the ego is overwhelmed by anxiety." When anxiety reaches an extreme intensity, as it may in the case of the combat soldier, the ego functions will be restricted to an extraordinary degree.

> In the severe anxiety states occurring in ground combat troops, the ego has regressed to such an extent that it is incapable of dealing with any environment, and such men need hospital care. . . . They are characterized by varying degrees of mutism, stupor, amnesia or bizarre behavior . . . sometimes accompanied by signs of somatic regression involving loss of normal coordinated . . . activity. . . .[21]

[21] Roy R. Grinker and John P. Spiegel, *Men under Stress* (Philadelphia, 1945), p. 95. Reprinted by permission of The Blakiston Company. Copyright, 1945, by The Blakiston Company.

The patient was agitated and trembled constantly. His face betrayed persistent fright and bewilderment. He was unable to speak, producing only syllables in a whisper or low voice. He could not give his name and was apparently unable to recall what had happened to him, or even to make the effort to recall. . . . He started with terror at any sudden noise or motion made toward him by the attendants.[22]

In order to resume normal functioning, the ego must "defend itself against anxiety." But repression, though it may (in combination with other defensive techniques) succeed in relieving the conscious perception of anxiety, will likewise restrict the ego functions, and therefore become the basis of further anxiety.[23]

EGO RESTRICTION AS A FUNCTION OF REPRESSION. To the extent that repression occurs, the individual will lose insight into some of his motivation; that is to say, his conscious ego-functions will lose some of the important data necessary for the adequate integration of the demands of external reality, of id motives, and of superego motives. To the extent that any relevant aspects of these are absent from conscious perception, the adequacy of the integrative ego-functions will be restricted. "The loss of such knowledge," according to Freud, "means for the ego a surrender of power and influence; it is the first tangible sign that the ego is being constricted and hampered by the demands of the id and of the superego." [24] Freud has similarly stated that "by the act of repression [the ego] renounces a portion of its organization, and is obliged to allow the repressed impulse to remain permanently withdrawn from its influence." [25]

Since the child's integrative powers are weak, his ego can only exclude from consciousness impulses which it cannot control and

[22] *Ibid.*, pp. 95–6.

[23] Repression alone, as we have suggested in Chap. VI, cannot operate adequately for the relief of anxiety; in fact, it appears to function as an essential mechanism for the production of anxiety. Other defensive techniques have as their main function the relief of the original motivation, by substitution of instrumental acts and objects for those which have undergone repression. They can serve, therefore, to relieve anxiety (the need tension remaining in consciousness) and can function to maintain repressions that otherwise could not be maintained against the intensity of anxiety. "Failure of repression," which is subsequently to be discussed, involves the reinstatement in consciousness of original instrumental acts and objects when no adequate substitutes have become available through the development of defensive techniques.

[24] Sigmund Freud, *An Outline of Psychoanalysis* (New York, 1949), p. 70.

[25] Sigmund Freud, *New Introductory Lectures on Psycho-Analysis* (New York, 1933), pp. 128–9.

harmonize. . . . This weakens the ego's dynamic resources but saves its unity. Tendencies alien to the ego are repressed because they cannot undergo necessary modification. . . . The ego must take defensive measures against them which drain the ego's dynamic resources and make it less able to exercise its adaptive function of grappling with external reality.[26]

Just as repression will remove from conscious perception some of the necessary data for conscious integration, *inhibition* will remove from voluntary control many responses that are necessary for adequate functioning. "Many inhibitions," according to Freud, "are an obvious renunciation of function, because the exercise of the function would give rise to anxiety." [27] Such inhibitions represent a "limitation and restriction of ego functions." [28]

Denial of external reality will likewise function to restrict the data available to the ego processes. Such denial—such repudiation of the unacceptable features of external reality—will reduce the amount of relevant material for integration. The individual will therefore draw misleading conclusions, which will prepare him for voluntary actions of a maladaptive nature.

EGO STRENGTH. The concept of *ego strength* implies the functioning of the ego processes (perception, thinking, learning, memory, voluntary action, etc.) at the highest level of integrative efficiency, unimpaired by the restrictive processes of repression, inhibition, or denial. More correctly, ego strength should be regarded as *a quantitative concept referring to the degree of integrative efficiency with which the ego functions are able to operate.*

High ego-strength should be positively correlated with the employment of the conscious functions of restraint and suppression, and negatively correlated with the employment of repression, inhibition, and denial. An important therapeutic aim is that of improving the individual's ego strength through helping him gradually to abandon the use of repression, inhibition, and denial.

Anxiety as a Basis of Repression

Repression was originally conceived to be a process employed for the relief of anxiety.[29] Freud stated in 1911 that "any operation which

---

[26] Alexander, *op. cit.*, p. 99.
[27] Freud, *The Problem of Anxiety*, p. 12.
[28] *Ibid.*, p. 16.
[29] Strictly speaking, fear and hostility are converted, in consciousness, to anxiety; repression, therefore, defends against fear and hostility, rather than against

might arouse unpleasantness ('pain')" is likely to be repressed.[30] Later (1914) Freud was beginning to develop his conception of what he finally called the superego. Accordingly, he wrote that "libidinal impulses are fated to undergo pathogenic repression if they come into conflict with the subject's cultural and ethical ideas." [31] At this time, Freud referred to the ego-ideal and conscience as significant factors in the repression process. In other words, anxiety arising from the frustration of superego motives was thought to form the basis of repression. In 1933 Freud wrote:

> How can we picture the process of repression carried out under the influence of anxiety? I think this is what happens: the ego becomes aware that the satisfaction of some nascent instinctual demand would evoke one among the well-remembered danger-situations. . . . In the case of repression . . . the impulse is still a part of the id, and the ego feels weak. In such a contingency, the ego calls to its aid a technique, which is, at bottom, identical with that of normal thinking. Thinking is an experimental dealing with small quantities of energy, just as a general moves miniature figures about over a map before setting his troops into motion. In this way, the ego anticipates the satisfaction of the questionable impulse, and enables it to reproduce the painful feelings which are attached to the beginning of the dreaded danger-situation. Thereupon the automatic mechanism of the pleasure-pain principle is brought into play and carries through the repression of the dangerous impulse.[32]

In brief, then, any impulse that (indirectly) arouses anxiety may be repressed. Id impulses will probably be repressed if the combination of objective anxiety (fear of punishment) and moral anxiety (fear of conscience) is stronger than the anxiety that would arise from repression of the id impulse itself. If, however, the combination of objective anxiety and moral anxiety should be less intense than the anxiety that would arise from repression of the id impulse, the individual may *deny* the objective danger or *repress* the conflicting superego motivation. The student will recognize in this the operation of the quantitative or

anxiety. As previously noted, other defensive techniques must be employed in order to relieve anxiety, which has been "created" by the act of repression.

[30] Freud, *Collected Papers*, IV, 14.
[31] *Ibid.*, pp. 50 f.
[32] Freud, *New Introductory Lectures* . . . , p. 124.

"economic" principle, which was mentioned in a previous section.[33]

Another approach is to consider the impulse ambivalent—having both positive and negative cathexis. If the positive cathexis is the greater, the impulse will be *expressed* in action; if the negative cathexis is the greater, the impulse will be repressed.

Repression as a Basis of Anxiety

There are at least three ways in which repression has been interpreted to function as a basis of anxiety: (1) Repression may function to liberate the "affective components" of impulses in the form of consciously perceptible anxiety. (2) Repression may "fail"—that is, repressed impulses may become conscious, so that their perception is associated with the rearousal of anxiety (in place of an original fear). (3) Ego functions may, through repression, become restricted—that is to say, less effective in overcoming frustrations. Each of these functional relationships will be discussed separately.

REPRESSION AND THE LIBERATION OF "AFFECTIVE COMPONENTS." Freud believed that when repression occurs there is a dissociation of the idea from the affective component of the impulse. According to Freud, "it is the idea that undergoes repression and may be distorted so as to become unrecognizable; its associated affect is always turned into anxiety, regardless of its nature, whether, that is to say, it is aggression or love." [34] In other words, when hostile or sexual impulses (and we would add, fear) become repressed, the emotional element in each will be perceived as conscious anxiety.

> . . . we have treated repression at some length, but in so doing we have been concerned exclusively with the fate of the *idea* to be repressed. . . . But we have so far ignored the question of what happened to the *affect* attached to this idea, and now we learn for the first time that it is the immediate fate of the affect to be converted into anxiety, no matter what quality of affect it would otherwise have been had it run a normal course. This transformation

---

[33] This "economic" principle can be stated as follows: When conflicting motives or conflicting combinations of motives occur, the weaker motive or the weaker combination of motives will be the more likely to undergo repression. Stated in terms of anxiety, the principle may be formulated as follows: The motive or the combination of motives whose repression will leave in consciousness the lesser degree of anxiety will be the more likely to undergo repression. The strength of the motive should be equal to the strength of the anxiety "liberated" when the motive undergoes repression.

[34] *Ibid.*, p. 116.

of affect is, moreover, by far the more important effect of the process of repression.[35]

Perhaps this process will become more readily understandable if we think of the organism as being in a state of motivated readiness to commit an action—for example, a sexual or an aggressive action. If awareness of the goal or intention is suddenly lost (through repression), the internal tension states will continue to function; but, since the different emotional processes are perceptually distinguishable from one another primarily in terms of their goal orientation, it is clear that when such goal orientations are lost, these internal processes can now be perceived only as undifferentiated *anxiety*. This interpretation is consistent with Mowrer's hypothesis, discussed in Chap. VI, of the origin of anxiety.

FAILURE OF REPRESSION.   Mowrer's conception also involves the second general interpretation of repression as a basis of anxiety. This has to do with the *failure of repression*. Freud has stated that "if a repression does not succeed in preventing feelings of 'pain' or anxiety from arising, we may say that it has failed, even though it may have achieved its aim as far as the ideational element is concerned." [36] Mowrer has interpreted "failure of repression" as follows :

> The repudiated impulse retains its vitality; and, at periods when the impulse is particularly strong or the repressing forces somewhat weakened, it may break through the "membrane" separating it from consciousness, not with sufficient force to be fully recognizable but far enough to arouse great fear. And since this fear is experienced without knowledge of what caused it . . . the fear is nameless, objectless, mysterious, terrifying—that is to say, *anxiety*.[37]

EGO RESTRICTION.   The ego restriction that occurs in relation to repression has been described in a previous section. Since the ego functions will lose relevant data through repression, these functions will become less effective for the individual's adjustment. This "impoverish-

---

[35] Freud, *A General Introduction* . . . , p. 355.
[36] Freud, *Collected Papers*, IV, 92.
[37] Mowrer, *op. cit.*, p. 621. (As we have previously noted, it is likely that such a "failure" of repression must occur on the basis of the failure of other defenses to provide substitute gratification for the original motive. Strictly speaking, it is not possible clearly to distinguish "failure of repression" from "liberation of affective components." Probably these are simply different verbal expressions to denote one and the same dynamic relationship between repression and anxiety.)

ment" of the ego may become the source, then, of frustration and anxiety. We have seen, in Chap. VI, how the repression of hostile impulses may function to lower the individual's level of confidence—to give him a "feeling of helplessness," as Horney would say.

The repression of any impulse will remove from consideration factors that are relevant to the individual's adjustment; his behavior will become maladjustive, since needs of which he is unaware cannot be integrated effectively with his conscious knowledge of reality.

> It is . . . important that the conflicting desires should become conscious. Some must be radically modified, others renounced in their original form so that more important interests can be safeguarded. The final solution is a compromise reconciling different needs in the light of their relative importance and practicality under the . . . circumstances. The ego must therefore get a full report from within concerning subjective needs and must know the conditions upon which their gratification depends. . . . Repressed wishes and desires are excluded from this process of mediation and compromise. Since they are lodged in the unconscious, they are inaccessible for adjustment either to other needs or to the environment.[38]

The individual's behavior will continue to be organized partly in terms of unconscious motives, but since the nature of these are unknown to him his behavior may become maladjustive or irrational.

REPRESSION AS A BASIS FOR ALL DEFENSES

ACCORDING to Anna Freud, repression is "not only the most efficacious, it is also the most dangerous, mechanism. The dissociation from the ego entailed by the withdrawal of consciousness from whole tracts of instinctual and affective life may destroy the integrity of the personality for good and all." [39] Sigmund Freud wrote, similarly, that "repression is something quite peculiar, more sharply differentiated from the other mechanisms than these are from one another." [40]

Repression is probably involved in some degree in each of the ego's

[38] Alexander, *op. cit.*, pp. 196–7.
[39] Anna Freud, *The Ego and the Mechanisms of Defense* (New York, 1946), p. 54. Reprinted by permission of International Universities Press, Inc. Copyright, 1946, by International Universities Press, Inc.
[40] Freud, *Collected Papers*, V, 338.

defensive measures against anxiety. The defensive efficacy of the different mechanisms is usually based on repression or denial of some aspect of the original data of consciousness; for, if all of these data were to remain conscious, the individual would perceive the irrational quality of his behavior when it involves displacement, regression, projection, reaction formation, etc. Freud developed the following analogy to clarify the relation between repression and the other defenses:

> Let us imagine what might have happened to a book at the time when books were not printed in editions but written out separately by hand. We will imagine that such a book contained statements which at a later time were regarded as undesirable. . . . Single words here and there were left out or replaced by others and whole new sentences were interpolated; at best, the passage was completely erased and replaced by another in exactly the opposite sense. When the book was next transcribed the text aroused no suspicion, but had, in fact, been falsified. It no longer contained the author's statement and very probably the correction was not in the interests of truth.
>
> Without pressing the analogy too closely we may say that repression is to the other methods of defense what the omission of words or passages is to the corruption of a text.[41]

In other words, repression can function to give defensive activities the appearance of rationality and sincerity, though they no longer contain the "author's statement"—that is, though their true motivation has been lost from conscious perception.

REPRESSION AS RELATED TO OTHER PERSONALITY FUNCTIONS

REPRESSION is dynamically related to anxiety and to various defenses against anxiety. Repression may also be related to such other personality functions as energy level and intelligence level.

Energy Level

Repression, according to Freud, is a continuous process, rather than a process that operates only at the time when an impulse is first rendered unconscious. Freud has stressed the point that repression will make demands upon the energy of the organism.

[41] *Ibid.*, pp. 338–9.

The process of repression is not to be regarded as something which takes place once for all, the results of which are permanent . . . on the contrary, repression demands a constant expenditure of energy, and if this were discontinued the success of the repression would be jeopardized, so that a fresh act of repression would be necessary.[42]

The following considerations should aid our understanding of the continued demand on energy which occurs with repression. Repression does not *solve* the underlying conflict; it merely eliminates it from conscious perception. The conflict continues to function, even though the individual has lost his awareness of it. Conflicts, as we have previously noted, consume energy; they involve tensions in muscles, and such tensions involve energy expenditure, and lead to fatigue. The therapeutic abrogation of repression—that is, its nullification by therapy—is followed by a saving of energy, not as a function of the abrogation as such, but as a function of the *solution* of the conflict, which becomes possible only after the repressed impulses have become conscious.

Since repression continues at the cost of great energy expenditure, it is clear that energy-level itself is related to repression. If the individual is characterized by a high energy-level, he can be expected to maintain his repressions effectively, while still having at his disposal sufficient energy for constructive work and for enthusiastic social activities. If, however, the individual is characterized by a low energy-level, his repression may use most of his available energy, leaving him especially susceptible to frustrations in his work and in his everyday living. The chronically tired person is frequently one who must expend much of his available energy in maintaining the tensions associated with unresolved (repressed) conflicts.[43]

Intelligence Level

In our previous discussions of intelligence level, we have regarded intelligence as the degree of competence with which the individual is able to gratify his motives—that is, the degree of competence with which he can integrate his whole motivational pattern (including id and superego motives) with the demands of external reality. The con-

[42] Freud, *Collected Papers*, IV, 89.
[43] The assumption is made here, of course, that the basic energy-level of the individual is hereditary or constitutional in origin.

cept of intelligence, then, may be regarded as equivalent to the concept of ego strength.

To the extent that repression occurs, and to the extent that denial occurs, the level of the individual's intelligence will be reduced. On the other hand, to the extent that the individual's intelligence level is high at the outset, repression and denial will less probably be resorted to for the relief of anxiety. Unfortunately for the individual, *intelligence level is always low at the outset*—that is, during infancy and early childhood. This is Freud's implication when he writes of the "immature, feeble ego" of early childhood.

> We come to see that the first years of infancy (up to about the age of five) are, for a number of reasons, of special importance. This is, in the first place, because they contain the first expansion of sexuality, which leaves behind decisive determinants for the sexual life of maturity; and, in the second place, because the impressions of this period come up against an unformed and weak ego, upon which they act like traumas. The ego cannot defend itself against the emotional storms which they call forth except by repression, and in this way it acquires in childhood all the predispositions to subsequent illnesses and disturbances of function.[44]

It is, of course, a well-known fact that "intelligence," as it is measured by tests, functions at a low level in early childhood, and that it increases with age.[45] Therapy occurring during adolescence and adulthood will aid in making available to consciousness repressed data that the individual is then able to integrate more efficiently than he could at the time of the initial repression. This accounts, in large part, for the observed fact that the therapeutic outlook (prognosis) is more favorable for patients of high intelligence than for patients of low intelligence levels.

ADJUSTIVE IMPLICATIONS

SOME significant adjustive implications can be inferred from the principles of repression.

[44] Freud, *New Introductory Lectures* . . . , pp. 200–1.
[45] Intelligence tests, in their present forms, do not "measure" all that is included in the concept of intelligence, since they provide stimuli of limited and special kinds, and since they fail to engage the individual's total motivational pattern in the complex everyday environment.

Suppression Preferable to Repression

It will be recalled that suppression is a conscious process, while repression functions automatically and unconsciously. Moreover, suppression removes data from consciousness only temporarily, so that it remains capable of becoming conscious whenever needed, whereas repression removes such data to an unconscious level, so that it becomes, for long periods, inaccessible to consciousness.

Since repression operates unconsciously, it can, like any habitual process, occur without attentive effort; but the very fact of its unconscious operation renders it a dangerous process. Since repression becomes habitual, it may frequently occur even when it is relatively unnecessary for the prevention of fear and hostility—that is, even after the integrative ego functions have become relatively competent in the solution of problems and, therefore, in the prevention of long-standing frustrations.

The adult ego with its greater strength continues to defend itself against dangers which no longer exist in reality and even finds itself impelled to seek out real situations which may serve as a substitute for the original danger, so as to be able to justify its clinging to its habitual modes of reaction. Thus the defensive mechanisms produce an ever-growing alienation from the external world and a permanent enfeeblement of the ego . . .[46]

The adult individual can adjust his behavior to the requirements of reality by means of the less radical process of suppression. He can remain aware of, and accept, his impulses; but at the same time he can restrain them and suppress consciousness of them when their expression would be inappropriate. When the occasion is judged to be appropriate, the individual will then be able to express his impulses in a gratifying manner.

The problem of sexual impotence or frigidity is relevant here. When sexual impulses, even in their mature form, have been subjected to repression, the individual may, on attaining the social status (marriage) appropriate for sexual expression, find that he is sexually unresponsive. In cases, however, where sexual impulses have merely been suppressed or restrained there should be little difficulty in arriving at a free expression of them when the occasion has become appropriate.

Security in Childhood

Since the ego functions are relatively inadequate in early child-hood, the use of repression can be kept to a minimum only if the child is provided with adult support in the solution of problems arising dur-ing his socialization. This implies that adults must provide for the child a secure environment, keeping their demands for socialized behavior within the frustration tolerance of the child.

To the extent that the child is accepted as a child—to the extent that he is permitted to be himself, in spite of the limitations of his im-mature ego functions—he should have a minimum need to resort to re-pression. He will be able to solve his problems as they arise, if they are not made too difficult for him to manage in his own way. Such a secure environment—such freedom to be a child while he *is* a child—should provide the individual with a basis for making happy and suc-cessful adjustments in his later years.

Insight in Psychotherapy

One of the major aims of psychotherapy is the achievement of in-sight. This involves not only the nullification of repression—the bring-ing back of previously repressed impulses to conscious perception—but, what is equally important, the understanding of them (their inte-gration with relevant aspects of reality).

> . . . analysis enables the mature ego, which by this time has at-tained a greater strength, to review these old repressions, with the result that some are lifted, while others are accepted but recon-structed from more solid material. These new dams have a greater tenacity than the earlier ones; we may be confident that they will not so easily give way before the floodtide of instinct. . . .[47]

Not all of the repressions will be lifted permanently; some impulses, after intelligent examination, will be perceived as infantile or impracti-cal; but the new repressions, being based on more realistic considera-tions, will be unlikely to "fail" again. The impulses that are now sub-jected to repression will be weak as compared with conflicting con-scious motives, and so will not make excessive demands on the energy of the individual who maintains the repression.

But impulses that, examined in the light of adult experience, are

[47] *Ibid.,* p. 329.

found to be relatively unobjectionable, or that are found to be appropriate for some occasions and inappropriate for other occasions, will be kept at preconscious levels—that is, available for expression at suitable times and places. Thus the ego functions will be strengthened, since more data will have become available for perception, thinking, and action.

The Case against Libertinism

A common misconception concerning the psychoanalytic concept of repression is that it provides an apology for libertinism—that is, for the unrestrained expression of impulses without regard for the established moral values of society.

The reasoning that underlies this misconception is that since repression may be detrimental to adjustment, then the free expression of impulses can be the only acceptable alternative. As our previous discussion has implied, however, libertinism is not the only, nor the best, alternative.

> It is out of the question that part of the analytic treatment should consist of advice to "live freely"—if for no other reason because we ourselves tell you that a stubborn conflict is going on in the patient between libidinal desires and sexual repression, between sensual and ascetic tendencies. This conflict is not resolved by helping one side to win a victory over the other. It is true we see that in neurotics asceticism has gained the day. . . . If we were to make victory possible to the sensual side instead, the disregarded forces repressing sexuality would have to indemnify themselves by symptoms. Neither of these measures will succeed in ending the inner conflict: one side in either event will remain unsatisfied. . . .[48]

What Freud seems to have suggested in the above statement is that either superego motives or id motives are likely to be repressed when these are in conflict, and that "living freely" will require the repression of superego motives, just as asceticism will require the repression of id impulses.

The recommended course of action, as mentioned in a previous section, is not to repress either id motives (excepting infantile and impractical ones) or superego motives, but to *suppress and restrain im-*

[48] Freud, *A General Introduction* . . . , p. 375.

pulses when the occasion demands. This rational management of impulses in terms of external reality and superego motivation is quite a different procedure from that which is implied by libertinism.

SUMMARY

Repression refers to an automatic process by which conscious functions become, and are made to remain, unconscious. *Dissociation* refers to the "splitting" of a unitary conscious function through the repression of a part of it. *Suppression* refers to the conscious process of rendering conscious functions preconscious. *Inhibition* refers to an automatic process that prevents the occurrence of overt actions. *Restraint* refers to the conscious process of avoiding some action. *Isolation* may be regarded as an automatic process that renders a conscious function, or a part of a conscious function, preconscious. *Denial* refers to the process of negating, or becoming "blind" to, aspects of external reality. Repression, inhibition, and denial serve to restrict or limit the ego functions.

Sexual impulses, aggressive impulses, other id impulses, and superego motives are commonly amenable to repression. Fugues involving amnesia, and multiple personalities, provide evidence for the hypothesis that what undergoes repression depends on the relative strength of conflicting tendencies.

Rational behavior is dependent upon the capacity of ego functions to integrate the data of consciousness; both anxiety and repression will limit the data of consciousness and therefore restrict the ego functions, with accompanying reduction in the rationality of behavior. Pre-existing anxiety may function to motivate repression, which in turn may function as the basis for the development of subsequent anxiety.

Repression is involved in some degree in each of the defenses against anxiety; it functions to prevent the other defensive activities from seeming irrational to the individual who employs them. (On the other hand, the other defenses would probably be unnecessary in the absence of prior repression.)

Energy level and intelligence level are dynamically interrelated with repression. To the extent that these levels are high, repression will become relatively unnecessary; on the other hand, repression will decrease the effective level of both energy and intelligence.

Suppression is preferable to repression as a defensive measure, since suppression does not "weaken" the ego functions; the individual can accept the reality of his impulses but at the same time restrain them when their expression would be inappropriate.

Since ego functions are relatively inadequate in early childhood, parents can keep repression at a minimum by providing a secure environment, in which the child's problems are kept within the limits of his problem-solving capacity.

Insight that is achieved during psychotherapy involves the temporary nullification of repression and the integration of the previously unconscious data with the other data of consciousness, at a time when the individual's ego functions are more adequate than when repression was originally instigated.

Contrary to common misconception, libertinism is not the recommended alternative to repression.

The following chapter will deal with developmental aspects of personality, an understanding of which will prepare the student for a consideration of the defensive functions of fixation, regression, and progression.

▶ Suggested Readings

Belmont, Lillian and Birch, H. G. "Re-individualizing the Repression Hypothesis," *Journal of Abnormal and Social Psychology,* 46 (1951), 226–35.

Cameron, N. *The Psychology of Behavior Disorders.* Boston, 1947. Chaps. xi–xii, pp. 318–87.

Cameron, N. and Magaret, Ann. *Behavior Pathology.* Boston, 1951. Chap. xii, pp. 337–71.

Dollard, J. and Miller, N. E. *Personality and Psychotherapy.* New York, 1950. Chap. xii, pp. 198–221.

Eriksen, C. W. "Perceptual Defense as a Function of Unacceptable Needs," *Journal of Abnormal and Social Psychology,* 46 (1951), 557–64.

Freud, Anna. *The Ego and the Mechanisms of Defense.* New York, 1946. Chaps. vi–viii, pp. 73–113.

Freud, S. "Psychopathology of Everyday Life," in *The Basic Writings of Sigmund Freud,* A. A. Brill, ed. New York, 1938. Chaps. i–iii, pp. 35–61.

Freud, S. "Repression," *Collected Papers.* London, 1950. IV, 84–97.

Freud, S. *A General Introduction to Psycho-Analysis.* New York, 1935. Lect. xix, pp. 253–65.

Freud, S. *The Problem of Anxiety.* New York, 1936. Chaps. i, vi, pp. 11–16, 53–8.

Horney, Karen. *Our Inner Conflicts.* New York, 1945. Chap. x, pp. 154–78.

Lazarus, R. S. and McCleary, R. A. "Autonomic Discrimination without awareness: a Study of Subception," *Psychological Review, 58* (1951), 113–22.

Levine, J. M. and Murphy, G. "The Learning and Forgetting of Controversial Material," *Journal of Abnormal and Social Psychology, 38* (1943), 507–17.

Rosenstock, I. M. "Perceptual Aspects of Repression," *Journal of Abnormal and Social Psychology, 46* (1951), 304–15.

Sears, R. R. "Survey of Objective Studies of Psychoanalytic Concepts," *Social Science Research Council Bulletin,* No. 51 (1943). Chap. vi, pp. 105–20.

Shoben, E. J., Jr. "Psychotherapy as a Problem in Learning Theory," *Psychological Bulletin, 46* (1949), 366–92.

Taylor, W. S. and Martin, Mabel F. "Multiple Personality, "*Journal of Abnormal and Social Psychology, 39* (1944), 281–300.

Torrance, P. "The Phenomenon of Resistance in Learning," *Journal of Abnormal and Social Psychology, 45* (1950), 592–7.

Zeller, A. F. "An Experimental Analogue of Repression: I. Historical Summary," *Psychological Bulletin, 47* (1950), 39–51.

CHAPTER Eight

Developmental Aspects of Personality

A mature person is not one who has come to a certain level of achievement and stopped there. He is rather a maturing person—one whose linkages with life are constantly becoming stronger and richer because his attitudes are such as to encourage their growth rather than their stoppage.[1]

FIXATION and regression—which are to be discussed in the following chapter—involve, respectively, stoppages and backward tendencies that occur in the course of development. Freud originally formulated the concepts of fixation and regression with reference to psychosexual development, though it is now understood that many fixations and regressions involve behavior not primarily psychosexual in nature.

Accordingly, as a background for the discussion of fixation and regression, the present chapter will deal with two developmental aspects of personality: with the normal course of psychosexual development, as it was understood by Freud; and with the general criteria of behavior maturity and immaturity, as these were outlined by Lewin.

[1] H. A. Overstreet, *The Mature Mind* (New York, 1949), p. 43. Reprinted by permission of W. W. Norton & Company, Inc. Copyright, 1949, by W. W. Norton & Company, Inc.

PSYCHOSEXUAL DEVELOPMENT

FREUD'S conception of psychosexual development differed from previous conceptions in two major respects: (1) in that sexual motivation was regarded as beginning in infancy rather than at puberty; and (2) in that sexual motivation and sexual behavior were generalized to include functions in addition to those which are involved in reproduction.

(a) Sexual life does not begin only at puberty, but starts with clear manifestations soon after birth.
(b) It is necessary to distinguish sharply between the concepts of "sexual" and "genital." The former is the wider concept and includes many activities that have nothing to do with the genitals.
(c) Sexual life comprises the function of obtaining pleasure from zones of the body—a function which is subsequently brought into the service of that of reproduction. The two functions often fail to coincide completely.[2]

We do not . . . believe that there is a single sexual instinct, which is from the first the vehicle of the impulse towards the aim of the sexual function, that is, the union of the two sex cells. On the contrary, we see a large number of component instincts, arising from various regions of the body, which strive for satisfaction more or less independently of one another, and find this satisfaction in something that may be called "organ-pleasure." The genitals are the latest of these *erotogenic zones;* and their organ-pleasure must certainly be called "sexual." Not all of these pleasure-seeking impulses are incorporated in the final organization of the sexual function.[3]

In other words, from Freud's point of view, *almost any impulse to achieve pleasurable stimulation in any region of the body should be considered sexual.* The pleasure so achieved was regarded as erotic or sexual in quality. This generalized conception should be understood, as a basis for interpreting Freud's treatment of sexuality.

Freud distinguished among three aspects of the sexual impulse: (1)

[2] Sigmund Freud, *An Outline of Psychoanalysis* (New York, 1949), p. 26.
[3] Sigmund Freud, *New Introductory Lectures on Psycho-Analysis* (New York, 1933), p. 135.

the *source*—that is, the part of the body in which excitation is experienced and in which pleasurable (relieving) stimulation is sought; (2) the *aim*—that is, the kind of activity through which gratification is achieved or anticipated; and (3) the *object*—that is, the object from which pleasurable stimulation is anticipated or "the person from whom the sexual attraction emanates."[4] An effort will be made to maintain these distinctions in our discussion of Freud's conception of psychosexual development.

Primary Narcissism (Autoerotism)

According to Freud, the earliest object-choice (cathexis) is narcissistic or autoerotic; the first pleasurable stimulation is said to occur through the agency of ego functions. The mother also, during this early period, is said to function as a sexual object, since her care of the child will involve stimulation of erotogenic zones.

We say that the human being has originally two sexual objects: himself and the woman who tends him, and thereby we postulate a primary narcissism in everyone, which may in the long run manifest itself as dominating his object-choice.[5]

Originally . . . the ego's instincts are directed to itself and it is to some extent capable of deriving satisfaction for them on itself. This condition is known as narcissism and this potentiality for satisfaction is termed auto-erotic.[6]

We have had to infer that at the beginning of its development the libido (all the erotic tendencies, all capacity for love) in each individual is directed towards the self. . . . It is only later that, in association with the satisfaction of the chief natural functions, the libido flows over beyond the ego towards objects outside the self. . . . Thus we look upon the development of the individual as a progress from narcissism to object-love. . . . A certain amount of libido is always retained in the ego; even when object-love is highly developed, a certain degree of narcissism continues.[7]

On the basis of the above quotations, it becomes clear that Freud considered the child's first love-object to consist of his own ego functions—which, in the child's perception, are objectified and personified.

[4] *Ibid.*, pp. 132–3.
[5] Sigmund Freud, *Collected Papers* (London, 1950), IV, 45.
[6] *Ibid.*, pp. 77–8.
[7] *Ibid.*, pp. 349–50.

It is also clear that Freud regarded all positive cathexes (or love) as ultimately libidinal or erotic—that is, Freud's concept of sexuality was
sufficiently inclusive to imply all instances of pleasurable relations with
positively cathected objects.

The status of the mother as a sexual object during the narcissistic
period may be clarified by the following statement:

> A child's first erotic object is the mother's breast that feeds him,
> and love in its beginning attaches itself to the satisfaction of the
> need for food. *To start with, the child certainly makes no distinc-
> tion between the breast and his own body;* when the breast has to
> be separated from his body and shifted to the "outside" because he
> so often finds it absent, it carries with it, now that it is an *"object,"*
> part of the original narcissistic cathexis.[8]

What Freud has stated here is essentially what every modern child
psychologist knows: that in infancy the child does not distinguish between himself and what he later comes to regard as the world external
to himself.[9] Thus, according to Freud, the mother is for the child, during the early autoerotic period, *a narcissistic object.*

Freud distinguished among three major developmental phases said
to occur during the autoerotic period. These phases correspond to
different sexual sources—that is, to different parts of the body (erotogenic zones) in which sexual stimulation may be sought by the child.
The three phases were termed the *oral phase,* the *anal phase,* and the
phallic phase.

ORAL PHASE. The mouth, according to Freud, is the earliest part
of the body to function as an erotogenic zone. Though at first serving
only as a means of receiving nutrition, the mouth becomes an erotogenic zone "in its own right"; sucking and other forms of oral stimulation are sought for their own sake.

> The first organ to make its appearance as an erotogenic zone and to
> make libidinal demands upon the mind is, from the time of birth
> onward, the mouth. . . . The baby's obstinate persistence in suck-
> ing gives evidence at an early stage of a need for satisfaction
> which, although it originates from and is stimulated by the taking

---

[8] Freud, *An Outline of Psychoanalysis,* pp. 89–90. (Italics added.)
[9] Freud's conception, however, differed from the modern view. Freud regarded the ego as a primary object, from which objects in the external world are
later differentiated; the modern view is that the primary object of perception is
the external world, from which the ego is later differentiated.

of nourishment, nevertheless seeks to obtain pleasure independently of nourishment and for that reason may and should be described as "sexual." [10]

According to Freud, the oral phase may be subdivided into an earlier "oral incorporation" stage and a later "oral sadistic" stage.[11] During the former stage, the child is said to manifest unconditional positive cathexis in relation to the mother's breast; during the latter stage, the child is said to manifest ambivalence (both a tendency to seek and a tendency to injure through biting).

ANAL PHASE. The second erotogenic zone to become functional is, according to Freud, the anal region.

> Children utilizing the erogenous sensitiveness of the anal zone, can be recognized by their holding back of fecal masses until through accumulation there result violent muscular contractions; the passage of these masses through the anus is apt to produce a marked irritation of the mucous membrane. Besides the pain, this must also produce a sensation of pleasure.[12]

During this phase the child is also said to gain pleasurable stimulation through the function of urination.[13] The anal phase is sometimes called the *sadistic-anal* (or anal-sadistic) phase, since Freud associated this developmental period with the child's manifestation of aggressive outbreaks.[14]

The anal phase, like the oral phase, has been subdivided into two periods.

> In the former of these the destructive tendencies to annihilate and to get rid of things have the upper hand, while in the latter those tendencies predominate which are friendly to the object, and seek to possess things and hold them fast. In the middle of this phase, then, there appears for the first time a consideration for the object, which is the forerunner of a later relation of love towards the object.[15]

---

[10] *Ibid.*, p. 28.

[11] Freud, *New Introductory Lectures* . . . , pp. 136–7.

[12] Sigmund Freud, "Three Contributions to the Theory of Sex," in *The Basic Writings of Sigmund Freud*, A. A. Brill, ed. (New York, 1938), p. 589. Reprinted by permission of Sigmund Freud Copyrights, Ltd. Copyright, 1938, by Random House, Inc.

[13] Sigmund Freud, *A General Introduction to Psycho-Analysis* (New York, 1935), p. 287.

[14] Freud, *An Outline of Psychoanalysis*, p. 28.

[15] Freud, *New Introductory Lectures* . . . , p. 136.

Freud's concept of the so-called "anal character," involving a complicated system of interrelationships between anal erotism and other aspects of personality, will be treated in a subsequent chapter.

PHALLIC PHASE. The third autoerotic phase is termed the *phallic phase;* during this period, sexual excitation is said to become centered in the male genital organ. It was Freud's view that during the early phallic phase the child assumes that girls and boys manifest no differences in the nature of their genital organs.

> It is to be noted that what comes in question at this stage is not the genitals of both sexes but only those of the male (the phallus). The female genitals long remain unknown. . . . With the phallic phase and in the course of it the sexuality of early childhood reaches its height and approaches its decline. Thenceforward boys and girls have different histories.[16]

> The little boy undoubtedly perceives the distinction between men and women, but to begin with he has no occasion to connect it with any difference in the genitals. It is natural for him to assume that all living beings, persons and animals, possess a genital organ like his own; indeed we know that he investigates inanimate objects with a view to discovering something like his member in them. . . . The driving force which this male portion of his body will generate later at puberty expresses itself in childhood essentially as an impulsion to inquire into things—as sexual curiosity.[17]

Freud believed that the so-called *Oedipus complex* appears during the phallic phase, and that the fear (of castration) associated with the Oedipus complex motivates the sexual repression that occurs during the latency period of later childhood.

Oedipus Complex

During the phallic phase of psychosexual development the child is said to manifest the *Oedipus complex.* The Oedipus complex consists in the child's being in love with the parent of opposite sex and having an attitude of jealousy toward the like-sexed parent.[18] That such an at-

---

[16] Freud, *An Outline of Psychoanalysis*, p. 29.
[17] Sigmund Freud, *Collected Papers* (London, 1950), II, 246.
[18] This is complicated, however, by the consideration that the child is "bisexual," so that he also loves the parent of the same sex and is jealous of the parent of the opposite sex. (Cf. Sigmund Freud, *Collected Papers* (London, 1950), V, 230.)

titudinal complex occurs in relation to the parents has probably been demonstrated adequately.

How such a complex arises, and how it finally disappears, however, involve difficult problems. Since Freud treated these problems differently with reference to boys and with reference to girls, his hypotheses concerning the origin and the disappearance of Oedipal attitudes will be described separately for each of the sexes.

OEDIPUS COMPLEX IN BOYS. At the age of two or three, at the beginning of the phallic phase, the boy is said to become his mother's lover.[19]

> . . . his early awakened masculinity makes him seek to assume, in relation to her, the place belonging to his father, who has hitherto been an envied model on account of the physical strength which he displays and of the authority in which he is clothed. His father now becomes a rival who stands in his way and whom he would like to push aside. If when his father is absent he is able to share his mother's bed and if when his father returns he is once more banished from it, his gratification when his father vanishes and his disappointment when he reappears are deeply felt experiences.[20]

It is not especially difficult to understand that the child should love his mother in the sense of wanting her affection, and perhaps of wanting to be the passive recipient of bodily stimulation that he has experienced during her care of him. It is difficult, however, to understand how the child could have perceived any relation between his genitals and the nature of the love relationship (mutual affection) that he has been able to observe between his parents.

It is probable that Freud never intended to imply any more than that the child had perceived a qualitative difference between the experience of self-stimulation and the experience of being stimulated by the mother during her care of him. Since the latter experience must be much the more pleasurable, it becomes possible to conceive that the child should begin actively to seek such stimulation from the mother. This need not imply that the child, at this early period, has formed any

---

[19] A difficulty arises in connection with Freud's conception of the phallic phase: he regards it as an autoerotic period and at the same time as a period of object love (for the mother). This again raises the question of which is primary in development—narcissism or love for the mother. If the phallic phase were truly narcissistic, it would be difficult to account for the occurrence of Oedipal attitudes during this period.

[20] Freud, *An Outline of Psychoanalysis,* p. 91.

conception of the function of the genitals in sexual intercourse; it implies only that the child, on the basis of his prior experience, will desire to monopolize the mother as an agency of erogenous stimulation.

Having regarded the Oedipus complex, then, as a genuine phenomenon, Freud had the problem of accounting for its later disappearance and for the fact that, as adults, we have no conscious memory of it. This he accounted for in terms of a postulated fear of castration (the so-called "castration complex").

> The boy's mother understands quite well that his sexual excitement refers to her. Sooner or later she thinks to herself that it is wrong to allow this state of things to continue. She believes she is acting rightly in forbidding him to manipulate his genitals. The prohibition has little effect and at the most brings about some modification in his method of self-gratification. At last his mother adopts the severest measures: she threatens to take away from him the thing he is defying her with. As a rule, in order to make the threat more terrifying and more credible, she delegates its carrying out to the boy's father, saying that she will tell him and that he will cut the penis off. Strangely enough, this threat only operates if another condition is fulfilled, either before or afterwards. In itself it seems quite inconceivable to the boy that anything of the sort could happen. But if when he is threatened he is able to recall the appearance of female genitals, or if shortly afterwards he has a glimpse of them—of genitals, that is to say, which really lack this supremely valued part, then he takes what he has heard seriously and, coming under the influence of the castration complex, experiences the severest trauma of his youthful existence.[21]

The fear of castration will, according to Freud, induce the boy to fear and hate his father even more intensely than before. The Oedipus complex will then undergo repression—the fear and hatred (of the father) surviving as guilt. It is possible that the love (for the mother) may survive in the form of "secondary narcissism"—that is, as love of the ego-ideal.

OEDIPUS COMPLEX IN GIRLS. The girl, like the boy, originally receives much stimulation through the mother's care, so that her first love-object (aside from her personified ego-functions) may be said to be the mother. Her Oedipus complex is said to begin during the same period as that in which the boy's attitudes undergo repression.

[21] *Ibid.*, pp. 91–2.

According to Freud, the girl does not experience *fear* of castration; instead, through comparison of her genitals with those of boys, and through her unsatisfactory experiences with attempted masturbation, she will conclude that her own castration *is an accomplished fact.* She will hold her mother responsible for her inferiority in this regard; and she will therefore develop hostility toward her mother and substitute the father (in place of the mother) as a love object.

> . . . the daughter, under the influence of her envy for the penis, cannot forgive her mother for having sent her into the world so insufficiently equipped. In her resentment she gives her mother up and puts someone else in place of her as the object of her love—her father. . . . It does little harm to a woman if she remains in her feminine Oedipus attitude. . . . She will in that case choose her husband for his paternal characteristics. . . .[22]

The girl, according to this point of view, may retain her Oedipal attitudes more or less permanently, since she will experience no severe trauma in relation to them.

Latency Period

The phallic phase of psychosexual development is followed, in many cases, according to Freud, by a *latency period.* The latency period may have its beginning between the ages of six and eight; and it will terminate at puberty. The latency period is characterized by a minimum of conscious sexual interest; it is a period during which sexual impulses have, to a large extent, undergone repression. In boys, the repression is accounted for in terms of castration fear; in girls, it is accounted for in terms of disappointment in connection with sexual experimentation.[23]

Freud did not, as is frequently believed, assert that the latency period occurs in all cases, or that it functions with respect to all aspects of sexuality.

> From about the sixth or eigth year onwards a standstill or retrogression is observed in the sexual development, which in those cases reaching a high cultural standard deserves to be called a *latency period.* This latency period, however, may be absent; nor does it necessarily entail an interruption of sexual activities and

[22] *Ibid.*, pp. 98–9.
[23] *Ibid.*, pp. 29–30.

sexual interests over the whole field. Most of the mental experiences and excitations occurring before the latency period then succumb to the infantile amnesia . . . which veils our earliest childhood from us and estranges us from it.[24]

Since repression occurs, adults will seldom have any conscious memory of their own sexual experiences during early childhood. This is said to account for their astonishment and disbelief in connection with Freud's conception of infantile sexuality.

Secondary Narcissism

With the occurrence of the latency period may come manifestations of secondary narcissism. The child's ego-ideal—his standards of perfection, his positive values, his ambitions and ideals—may become the object of his love (his sexuality). His love will be directed toward the achievement of an admirable status in self-perception and in the perception of others. In fantasy he will imagine himself to be a famous cowboy, bandit, circus performer, engineer, or aviator; in his play, he will act as if his immature ego-ideal were an accomplished fact.

> To this ideal ego is now directed the self-love which the real ego enjoyed in childhood. The narcissism seems to be now displaced on to this new ideal ego, which, like the infantile ego, deems itself the possessor of all perfections. . . . He is not willing to forego his narcissistic perfection in his childhood; and if, as he develops, he is disturbed by the admonitions of others and his own critical judgment is awakened, he seeks to recover the early perfection, thus wrested from him, in the new form of an ego-ideal. That which he projects ahead of him as his ideal is merely his substitute for the lost narcissism of his childhood—the time when he was his own ideal.[25]

This secondary narcissism, which is said to begin in the latency period, may continue throughout the lifetime of the individual. The positive cathexis may alternately be displaced from the ego-ideal onto other persons and from other persons back onto the ego-ideal.[26] When the individual is in love his work will suffer; and when his life work monopolizes his attention his "love life" will suffer.

[24] Freud, *A General Introduction* . . . , p. 286.
[25] Freud, *Collected Papers*, IV, 51.
[26] Freud, *An Outline of Psychoanalysis*, pp. 23-4.

Genital Phase

The repressions maintained during the latency period will lose their effectiveness with the great intensification of sexual excitation that occurs at puberty. This period was regarded by Freud as the final stage of sexual development; it was referred to as the *genital phase*. All of the "component impulses" of earlier developmental periods were said to become organized in terms of the "primacy of the genitals." If development has proceeded normally, a heterosexual object will be cathected.

> In the earlier phases the separate component instincts set about their pursuit of pleasure independently of one another; in the phallic phase there are the first signs of an organization which subordinates the other trends to the primacy of the genitals and signifies the beginning of a co-ordination of the general pursuit of pleasure into the sexual function. The complete organization is not attained until puberty, in a fourth, or genital, phase. A state of affairs is then established in which (1) many earlier libidinal cathexes are retained, (2) others are included in the sexual function as preparatory or auxiliary acts, their satisfaction producing what is known as fore-pleasure, and (3) other tendencies are excluded from the organization, and are either entirely suppressed (repressed) or are employed in the ego in some other way, forming character-traits or undergoing sublimation with a displacement of their aims.[27]

Inversions, perversions, and abnormal sexual attachments (for example, fetishism) were interpreted by Freud as manifestations of fixation or regression, either with respect to the sexual object or with respect to the sexual source.

Integrative Summary

According to Freud, then, the successive sexual objects that will normally be chosen by the individual are: (1) the ego functions that are involved in self-stimulation (autoerotic period), (2) the mother, (3) the opposite-sexed parent (Oedipus complex), (4) the immature ego-ideal (secondary narcissism of the latency period), and (5) contemporaries of the opposite sex (genital phase of puberty).

Some degree of narcissism (ego or ego-ideal as sexual object) was believed to occur at all ages, except in the brief periods during which

[27] *Ibid.*, pp. 30–1.

the individual can be said to love another person exclusively—when, according to Freud, there is "sexual over-estimation of an object." [28] The individual's choice of his ego-ideal may be in conflict with his heterosexual object choice when the two objects make incompatible demands on him.

The source of sexual excitation, according to Freud, is expressed in four different developmental phases: the oral, the anal, the phallic, and the genital.

Certain aspects of Freud's formulation of psychosexual development require, we feel, reinterpretation.

NARCISSISM AS A SECONDARY MANIFESTATION. While Freud recognized that the child must *learn* to differentiate his ego functions from external reality, he probably erred in assuming that the child's perception of ego functions *precedes* his perception of other aspects of reality.

It is much more probable that the child will, at first, perceive his own ego functions (movements of parts of the body, and so forth) as undifferentiated from the rest of *external* reality. He must *learn* that his own hand is *his own*, for example. He will gradually differentiate his body and its parts from other objects—since his experience, in the two cases, has been different. The parts of his body have always been available, while other objects have sometimes been absent. Moreover, the *quality* of his experience with parts of his own body has been different from the quality of this experience with external objects. For example, the quality of his experience when he bit his finger was not the same as that when he bit a teething ring.

In other words, then, it is probable that the ego must be differentiated from the external environment, rather than that the external environment must be differentiated from the ego.

If the foregoing interpretation is correct, it seems improbable that the child's first love-object can be the personification of his own ego functions. The child's first love-object will probably be his mother's breast, and later will become generalized to include the mother as a whole. Still later, after the ego functions have become perceptually differentiated, the sexual cathexis can be displaced onto the ever available, though less pleasurable, ego functions.

Narcissism, then, must be regarded as secondary rather than primary; the earliest sexual expression must involve object-choice rather than autoerotism. The earliest instances of self-stimulation, which the external observer might be inclined to regard as autoerotic expressions,

[28] Freud, *Collected Papers*, IV, 51.

must involve, *from the child's point of view,* instances of object-choice, even though the chosen object be nothing more pleasurable than a convenient thumb. As long as his thumb seems an external object over which he can exert little voluntary control, it will remain as pleasurable as any other external stimulation of his oral region; when he perceives it as his own, he will find it an unworthy substitute for the stimulation arising from external sources.

DOUBTFUL VALIDITY OF THE OEDIPUS COMPLEX. Freud encountered difficulties in relation to his concept of the Oedipus complex. A major difficulty is concerned with the likelihood that the Oedipus complex may demand more sexual knowledge on the part of the boy than he can be expected to have during the phallic phase. The concept of the Oedipus complex seems to imply that, at this stage, the boy will understand the functions of the genitals in sexual intercourse—though at this stage the boy, as well as the girl, is said to believe that the genitals of the two sexes exhibit no differences in structure. As a matter of fact, Freud accounted for the *dissolution* of the Oedipus complex in boys in terms of castration fear; and this castration fear was said, even then, to lack reality to the boy until after he had *discovered* the difference in appearance between the male and the female genitals. If it be true that the Oedipus complex requires such knowledge as its basis, then the Oedipus complex could not make its appearance before the approach of its dissolution.

It is probable, however, that the Oedipus complex involves nothing more (in the case of boys) than a continued attachment to the mother, on the basis of the pleasurable stimulation that, through her activities in caring for his needs, she has provided from the beginning. But when the phallic phase begins, the *mother* might be expected to perceive for the first time that her son's activities in relation to her are sexual in nature. Prior to that time it may not have occurred to her that he has been getting *sexual* stimulation from her activities. Once she has begun to perceive this, she may be expected to punish him regularly (not necessarily with a threat of castration) for any behavior she interprets as sexual. Such punishment may motivate repression and thus account for the occurrence of the latency period. Many modern parents, feeling themselves to be among the "enlightened," may disregard such sexual manifestations; their children will manifest no obvious latency period.

Freud assumed that the basis of the girl's Oedipus complex—her withdrawal from the mother, with subsequent attachment to the father—was her discovery of "genital inferiority" and her consequent resentment toward the mother for bringing her into the world "so insufficiently equipped." But such as explanation does not seem necessary to account for the occurrence of inferiority feelings when the girl compares herself with boys. Boys enjoy greater independence and are subjected to less frustration in their everyday activities. Since the mother is at home much of the time, she is likely to appear as the source of the little girl's comparatively greater frustration.

The father, however, being himself heterosexual, will frequently be more lenient with his daughter, and will frequently show more affection toward her than that shown by the mother—he will then come to seem more lovable than the mother. This apparently is sufficient to account for the origin of the girl's Oedipal attitudes.

Probably it is during the phallic phase and the early latency period that the girl becomes most acutely aware of the favored status of boys and of the more severe restrictions imposed upon her behavior. This is also the period when boys begin to discriminate against girls in their selection of playmates.

Both boys and girls will probably be given more attention and affection by the opposite-sexed parent than by the like-sexed parent, since the parents will normally be heterosexual in their preferences. The reciprocation of such affection could account, at least partially, for the observed Oedipal attachments in children.

Mowrer has taken the position that the Oedipus complex is "an expression of familial pathology rather than an inevitable stage of development." [29] He has accounted for the development of heterosexual object-choice in terms of *identification* with the like-sexed parent. In object-choice, as well as in many other respects, the son can be expected to become like the father and the daughter can be expected to become like the mother. The process of developmental identification, which is implied here, will be discussed in more detail in Chap. XI.

GENERAL CRITERIA OF BEHAVIOR MATURITY AND IMMATURITY

IN TERMS of the ahistorical (dynamic) conception of regression (which will be discussed in the following chapter), any par-

[29] O. Hobart Mowrer, *Learning Theory and Personality Dynamics* (New York, 1950), p. 611.

ticular instance of behavior must be considered regressive or progressive on the basis of its qualitative characteristics. It becomes necessary, then, to develop criteria by means of which to distinguish among different degrees of behavioral maturity.

Lewin has formulated five criteria for differentiating the behavior characteristics of different age levels.[30] These criteria have been formulated in terms of (1) the variety of behavior, (2) the organization of behavior, (3) the extension of areas of activity, (4) the interdependence of behavior, and (5) the degree of realism.

Variety of Behavior

The variety of behavior increases with age. More and more different types of activities are manifested as the child grows older. "The *behavior* of the newborn is more or less confined to sleeping, crying, drinking, eliminating, and lying awake." The only motives of the newborn are biogenic, his emotions primitive and undifferentiated, the extent of his knowledge and his social relations very limited.

As the child grows older, he develops an increasing variety of behavior forms: he develops complex psychogenic motivation; he develops differentiated emotions; he develops broad knowledge; and he develops complicated and specific social relationships.

Immaturity, then, is characterized by a limited variety of responses. The individual may be said to regress on those occasions when he manifests a decrease in the variety of his behavior.

Organization of Behavior

It will be recalled that the molar behavior-unit, which was discussed in a previous chapter, is organized in terms of the motivational pattern of the individual. The complexity of the behavior unit, the degree to which it is hierarchically organized, and the degree to which its organization is complicated constitute criteria for determining the relative maturity of behavior.

The *complexity of units* is a function of the "number of subparts and the variety of subparts contained in one unit of action." The number of blocks a child uses to form a pattern, and the length of time a child spends in continuous play, are particular instances of this criterion.[31]

---

[30] Kurt Lewin, "Regression, Retrogression, and Development," in *Field Theory in Social Science: Selected Theoretical Papers*, Dorwin Cartwright, ed. (New York, 1951), pp. 98–113.
[31] *Ibid.*, p. 101.

Hierarchical organization refers to the organization of molar sub-units of behavior in terms of more inclusive molar units. For example, the aim of passing a single college course may be a goal in terms of which behavior is organized over a short period of time; this goal may function in the service of the more inclusive goal of being graduated from college; this more inclusive goal may function in the service of the still more inclusive goal of succeeding in a profession; etc.

Such hierarchical organization is also manifested in problem-solving; the hierarchy of hypotheses, from most inclusive to least inclusive, might be as follows for the solution of a particular problem: (1) that the problem can be solved; (2) that it can be solved by the application of a mechanical principle; (3) that it can be solved by manipulating a system of levers; and (4) that it can be solved by a particular series of manipulations. Ordinarily, the more inclusive the hypothesis, the longer it will be maintained without modification. The degree of hierarchical organization can be expressed in terms of the number of hierarchical levels involved.

Complicated organization may involve (1) the occurrence of a behavior unit that will be resumed after interruption by other behavior units, (2) the more or less simultaneous occurrence of different behavior-units that are organized in terms of unrelated motives, or (3) the occurrence of a behavior unit that involves more than one level of meaning. The writing of a book, by a professor for example, will involve numerous interruptions (to teach classes, to attend committee meetings, to eat meals, to hold conferences with students, to engage in recreation, etc.), yet it will be resumed after each of the interruptions. Eating lunch with a group that has met to discuss some business matter affords an example of the second variety of complicated organizations; it achieves two unrelated goals—that of satisfying hunger and that of solving some business problem. Such activities as "lying, joking, showing overfriendly behavior out of hate," involve more than one level of meaning.[32]

Extension of Area of Activity

As the child grows older, his *life space* and his *space of free movement* are increased. The life space of the individual is co-extensive with his perceptual environment; it includes all of the actions the individual

[32] *Ibid.*, p. 102.

can imagine himself carrying out in those areas of space and time which have become available to his perception. The space of free movement involves all of the activities that are *possible* for the individual at any given time.

Both the activities that are conceivable by the individual, and the activities that are possible for the individual, will broaden in scope with increasing maturity. As the child matures, he can envisage an ever broadening range of activities in an ever broadening geographical area; his activities can be oriented in terms of larger sectors of the past and of the future. Moreover, as a function of increased personal autonomy and increased ability, there will occur an increase in the range of activities possible for the individual.

Interdependence of Behavior

Any one function of the infant-in-his-environment is directly dependent on all of his other functions. The movement of an arm will be accompanied by movements throughout the body. A need or emotion will immediately be expressed in overt behavior. The satisfaction of one need will bring "all-over" satisfaction of the whole child. A change in the environment will bring immediate reactions on the part of the child. The infant may be likened to a colloidal blob of protoplasm in a liquid medium: any event in the blob or in the medium will be followed by compensatory (equilibrating) events in all other parts of the system. In other words, the different psychosomatic functions will manifest *direct interdependence*.

With increasing maturity, the different functions will become more nearly independent of one another; they will become differentiated, so that they can operate with a minimum of simple interdependence. Movements of fingers may occur when the arm is relatively motionless; needs and emotions may occur without overt manifestations; when one need is satisfied, other needs will continue to be operative; when changes occur in the environment, the child may manifest hardly any overt reaction to them; and so on.

Along with this increasing differentiation of functions, there will also occur, with increasing maturity, an increase in secondary organization among the functions; maturity is characterized by *organizational interdependence*. In other words, the original direct interdependence, manifesting functional interrelations like those in a chunk of gelatin that shakes all over when touched by a spoon, *will be replaced by an interdependence that is the outcome of secondary organization among the differentiated functions.* This secondary organization or co-ordination of functions will correspond more adequately to the demands of reality, since it is based on learning.

Degree of Realism

The young child fails to discriminate clearly between reality and fantasy; with increasing maturity, the *realism of perception* will increase. External reality will become clearly differentiated from the merely imagined. In early childhood, for example, the child may have an imaginary playmate, with whom he talks and plays games and to whom he may attribute remarkable qualities. As the child grows older, he can distinguish between imagined experiences and real experiences.

Integrative Summary

According to Lewin, as the individual matures he will manifest an increase in the variety of his skills, his emotional reactions, his needs and goals, his knowledge, and his social interrelations with other people. His behavior will become organized into more inclusive molar units, which are more highly integrated in terms of hierarchies of value, and which are more resistant to disturbance by the interposition of unrelated activities. His perceptual environment (his life space) will be extended, and the range of activities possible to him (his space of free movement) will be broadened. His previously undifferentiated functions will be differentiated and reorganized, through learning, into activities more adequately adjusted to the requirements of reality. And his perceptual realism will increase, so that he will become more competent in distinguishing between external reality and the products of his fantasy.

According to these criteria, the individual's behavior will manifest immaturity (fixation or regression) when it exhibits any or all of the following characteristics:

1. When it is restricted to a narrow range of activities—when it involves relatively few activities and interests.
2. When it appears to be relatively inconsistent from time to time —when it is organized in terms of short-term goals, or when it is easily disrupted and disorganized by interruptions and obstructions.
3. When it is based on a limited outlook—when it is organized in

terms of restricted areas of the temporal and spatial environment.

4. When it is not well adjusted to the requirements of present reality—when it is impulsive; when it involves "too much" of the personality; when it involves "overreaction" to minor changes in the environment.

5. When it is based on a failure to distinguish between reality and fantasy—when it involves "taking too seriously" the products of imagination.

In brief, immaturity will be manifested when the individual engages in only a few activities—when he does little else than his work, when he knows about little else than what is involved in his daily activities, when his "wants are simple and his needs are few"; when the individual "lives from hand to mouth," and flits rapidly from one activity to another, as if he were unmotivated by any long-term ideals or values; when he lives as if he were bound for life to a particular place, and as if the future were completely unpredictable or "of no consequence"; when he acts impulsively, when he is totally disabled by minor disappointments, when his emotional responses are "too strong" in relation to the kind of situations that arouse them; and when he depends too much on imaginary gratifications and behaves as if the world of his fantasy were the real world.

SUMMARY

AS A background for the subsequent discussion of fixation and regression, the present chapter has dealt with two developmental aspects of personality: with the normal course of psychosexual development, as it was understood by Freud; and with the general criteria of behavior maturity and immaturity, as these were outlined by Lewin.

Freud believed that sexual motivation begins in infancy rather than at puberty, and that any impulse to obtain pleasurable stimulation should be considered sexual.

Freud distinguished among three aspects of the sexual impulse: (1) the source—the part of the body in which pleasurable stimulation is sought; (2) the aim—the kind of activity through which gratification is achieved; and (3) the object—the person or agency that provides pleasurable stimulation.

According to Freud, the successive sexual objects are: (1) the ego functions (primary narcissism), (2) the mother, (3) the opposite-sexed parent (Oedipus complex), (4) the immature ego-ideal (secondary narcissism of latency period), and (5) contemporaries of the opposite sex (genital phase of puberty).

Four different phases were distinguished with respect to source of sexual excitation—the oral, the anal, the phallic, and the genital. The oral, anal, and phallic phases were said to occur during the period of primary narcissism (the ego as sexual object); the genital phase was said to occur at puberty, when the sexual object normally becomes an opposite-sexed contemporary.

The Oedipus complex (being in love with the opposite-sexed parent) was said to occur during the phallic phase; it was said to be repressed in boys on the basis of castration fear, and to begin in girls on the basis of their discovery that they were "insufficiently equipped."

The Oedipus complex was said to be followed by a latency period (a period of more or less complete sexual repression), during which secondary narcissism (being in love with the ego-ideal) appears. At puberty, with the occurrence of the genital phase and the choice of an opposite-sexed contemporary, sexual development was said to reach maturity.

It seems reasonable to reinterpret Freud's treatment of psychosexual development in two respects: (1) by considering the mother to be the earliest sexual object, and by considering the ego functions to be *secondarily* differentiated from the mother and the external environment; and (2) by considering the origin and the dissolution of the Oedipus complex to occur as a function of the parents' behavior toward the child, rather than considering these occurrences to be inherent in the biology or the psychology of the child.

Lewin formulated five criteria for determining the relative maturity of behavior. According to these criteria, the process of maturing is characterized by: (1) an increase in the variety of behavior; (2) an increase in the inclusiveness of molar behavior-units, with hierarchical and complicated organization; (3) an extension in the range of the "life space" (perceptual environment) and of the "space of free movement" (kinds of possible activities); (4) a differentiation of functions and a reorganization of these functions on the basis of learning; and (5) an increase in the realism of perception, with the development of ability to distinguish between fantasy and reality.

The following chapter will deal with the defensive functions of fixation, regression, and progression.

See the end of Chap. IX for suggested readings relevant to the material of this chapter.

CHAPTER Nine

Fixation, Regression, and Progression

When I was a child, I spake as a child, I felt as a child, I thought as a child: now that I am become a man, I have put away childish things.[1]

IT IS doubtful that any living person has sufficient ego strength to live in complete accordance with the above principle. Indeed, such strict adherence to a principle is not expected, or even approved, in the ordinary individual. We are all childish in some of our behavior some of the time, and there are respects in which all of us have failed to "grow up." The problem of the individual's struggle to "be his age" is the problem of fixation, regression, and progression.

DEFINITIONS

THE CONCEPTS of fixation, regression, and progression relate to the degree of maturity in behavior. *Fixation* implies remaining at an immature stage of development; *regression* implies returning to behavior that is characteristic of an earlier stage of development; and

[1] I Corinthians, xiii-11.

progression implies the adoption of behavior more mature than that which has previously been manifested.

Fixation

Fixation may be treated either in terms of a *special definition* or in terms of a *general definition*. The special definition relates to Freud's conception of psychosexual development, which was discussed in the preceding chapter.

SPECIAL DEFINITION OF FIXATION. According to Freud's special use of the term, fixation refers to an arrest of certain components of the sexual impulse at an early stage of development.

> . . . we consider it possible that single portions of every separate sexual impulse may remain in an early stage of development, although at the same time other portions of it may have reached their final goal. . . . We will . . . decide at this point to call this *arrest* in a component impulse at an early stage a FIXATION (of the impulse).[2]

According to Freud, the sexual impulse is divisible into several components, each of which may develop in the direction of mature expression; but each of these components may be arrested at any stage in this developmental process.[3] Freud's analogy will help to clarify his conception of fixation:

> When a whole people leaves its dwellings in order to seek a new country, as often happened in earlier periods of human history, their entire number certainly did not reach the new destination. Apart from losses due to other causes, it must invariably have happened that small groups or bands of the migrating people halted on the way, and settled down in these stopping-places, while the main body went further.[4]

Freud likened these groups which "halted on the way" to components of the sexual impulse which become fixated at points along the course of development toward maturity.

GENERAL DEFINITION OF FIXATION. Fixation has, in the course of time, come to have a broader meaning than that which was originally

---

[2] Sigmund Freud, *A General Introduction to Psycho-Analysis* (New York, 1935), p. 298.

[3] These different "components" of the sexual impulse were said to correspond to the different "sexual sources" or to the different erotogenic zones—particularly, to the oral, anal, phallic, and genital zones.

[4] *Ibid.*, p. 297.

implied. The term is no longer restricted to instances that involve arrest of psychosexual development. Fixation, according to this generalized definition, implies a cessation in the normal development of any form of behavior; that is, fixation is said to occur whenever any form of behavior persists in spite of a change in conditions which will justify a change in behavior.

> Conditions change, and owing to growth the organism itself changes. Changed conditions require fresh adaptation. The adult cannot, like the infant, satisfy his needs by relying upon maternal help. . . . Growth requires continuous learning. The principle of inertia impels the organism to cling to automatic behavior which was satisfactory in the past but which is no longer adequate. This indolence was recognized by Freud who called it *fixation*.[5]

> In the course of adaptation, behavior patterns which have proved useful are repeated, become automatic, and thus consume less energy. Since the organism's fundamental tendency is to preserve homeostatic equilibrium with the least possible expenditure of energy, it clings tenaciously to successful automatisms.[6]

Murray has implied the generalized meaning of fixation in his treatment of the *sameness/change* variable of personality. This personality variable is concerned with the degree to which fixation consistently characterizes a given person's behavior.

> The characteristic finding is that the same object, or the same class of objects, is cathected from year to year. These are some of the signs: to adhere to one place (the same room, house, neighborhood, city); to select a few chosen pathways and haunts (the same streets, restaurants, shops); to like and associate with the same people (members of the family, school and college friends); to maintain the same tastes, sentiments and beliefs (political party, preferred authors, creed); to wear the same clothes, smoke the same brand of cigarettes, like the same dishes, enjoy the same music, etc.[7]

Fixation, then, implies the rigid maintenance of a particular relationship with a goal object; it implies also the continuation of a particular kind of behavior in relation to the object.

[5] Franz Alexander, *Fundamentals of Psychoanalysis* (New York, 1948), p. 38.
[6] *Ibid.*, pp. 128–9.
[7] Henry A. Murray, *Explorations in Personality* (New York, 1938), p. 203.

Regression

Just as there are special and general definitions of fixation, there are also special and general definitions of regression. The special definition of regression relates to Freud's conception of psychosexual development.

SPECIAL DEFINITION OF REGRESSION. Regression, as defined in terms of psychosexual development, refers to a return of the libido "to its earlier pregenital cathexes." [8] Regression, in other words, refers to the *reinstatement of former sexual attitudes*, or the recurrence of immature sexual impulses in relation to previously cathected, but now "outgrown," sexual objects.

> . . . those portions [of the sexual impulse] which have proceeded further may easily revert in a backward direction to these earlier stages. The impulse will find occasion to *regress* in this way when the exercise of its function in a later and more developed form meets with powerful external obstacles, which thus prevent it from attaining the goal of satisfaction.[9]

Freud believed that, when psychosexual regressions occur, the reinstated sexual tendencies are ones that have been fixated during some previous period.

GENERAL DEFINITION OF REGRESSION. The meaning of regression has been generalized in two respects: (1) in that regression has come to imply forms of behavior not necessarily phychosexual in nature; and (2) in that regression has come to imply not only the reinstatement of behavior that an individual has previously manifested, but also the adoption of any behavior pattern less mature than the behavior pattern it replaces.

Freud generalized the meaning of regression in the first respect; he used the term *ego-regressions* to imply regressions that are not specifically psychosexual in character.[10] For example, the transformation, in dreams, of ideas into visual images was believed by Freud to involve ego-regression.[11]

Mowrer has employed the term *habit regression* to imply the reinstatement of any form of earlier behavior.

[8] Sigmund Freud, *An Outline of Psychoanalysis* (New York, 1949), p. 32.
[9] Freud, *A General Introduction* . . . , p. 298.
[10] *Ibid.*, p. 312.
[11] Sigmund Freud, *New Introductory Lectures on Psycho-Analysis* (New York, 1933), p. 31.

. . . habit regression . . . is merely the converse of habit *progression,* which may be defined as the development of a new mode of need gratification as a consequence of disruption of or interference with a previously established mode of adjustment. . . . [The behavior that] appears when a given level of adjustment is regressed to is almost never exactly the same as the behavior that occurred previously, before this level of adjustment was abandoned. Changes in physical size and appearance, altered status in the community or family . . . rearousal of anxieties that were used to produce habit progression, and a number of other factors may so confuse any given instance of regression as to render it almost unrecognizable as such.[12]

Lewin has generalized the meaning of regression in the second respect. Lewin used the term *retrogression* to imply the reinstatement of a previously employed mode of behavior, and reserved the term *regression* to imply the adoption of any behavior pattern that the individual has characteristically (or recently) employed.[13] In Lewin's usage, then, regression does not necessarily imply a reinstatement of behavior that the individual has manifested at any previous time.

Progression

Progression involves a modification of behavior in the direction of maturity. Although progression, like fixation and regression, may refer specifically to psychosexual development, it may refer, as well, to the development of any other kind of behavior. Whenever the individual adopts a new pattern of behavior that is qualitatively more mature than his previous behavior, he can be said to manifest progression or to make a progressive adjustment.

CLASSIFICATIONS OF REGRESSIVE BEHAVIOR

FURTHER definition of the concepts of fixation, regression, and progression may be achieved by considering the different classifications of regressive behavior. Although these classifications will be dis-

[12] O. Hobart Mowrer, "An Experimental Analogue of 'Regression' with Incidental Observations on 'Reaction Formation,'" *Journal of Abnormal and Social Psychology,* 35 (1940), 56–87. In *Learning Theory and Personality Dynamics,* O. Hobart Mowrer (New York, 1950), pp. 366–7. Reprinted by permission of The Ronald Press Company and the American Psychological Association, Inc. Copyright, 1950, by The Ronald Press Company.

[13] Kurt Lewin, "Regression, Retrogression, and Development," in *Field Theory in Social Science: Selected Theoretical Papers,* Dorwin Cartwright, ed. (New York, 1951), pp. 93–6.

cussed specifically in relation to regression, it should be apparent that they are equally applicable to fixation and to progression.

Need, Object, and Instrumental Act Regression

Sears has put regressive behavior into three categories: (1) drive regression, which we prefer to call *need* regression, (2) *object* regression, and (3) *instrumental act* regression.[14] These categories are distinguished in terms of the particular aspect of the need integrate (motive) which undergoes regression.

Need (or drive) *regression* involves a change in the need that is related to a given object. For example, genital sexual need may regress to anal or oral sexual need. Such psychosexual regressions will be discussed in a subsequent section.

Object regression involves the return to an object that has previously been cathected in relation to a given need. "If a man had had a strong attachment to his mother but then made the customary shift to a wife, he might regress to the earlier object (mother) if he were frustrated in his efforts to gain gratification from the later one (wife)." [15]

Instrumental act regression involves a change in the quality or character of behavior employed to gratify a particular need in relation to a given object. "For example, a five-year-old may resume his crawling to wrest parental attention from a younger sib, or an author accustomed to a typewriter may revert to longhand on a difficult piece of writing." [16]

Temporary and Permanent Regression

Regression may be relatively temporary or relatively permanent.

Regression may last only a few minutes, for instance in a case of a slight shock, disturbance, or emotion, or it may last many years, for example as a result of sickness. Regression may be a slow sinking or a sudden drop. The individual may stay regressed, he may slowly or suddenly regain his previous level, or he may return to an intermediate level.[17]

[14] Robert R. Sears, "Survey of Objective Studies of Psychoanalytic Concepts," *Social Science Research Council Bulletin*, No. 51 (1943), pp. 76–104.
[15] *Ibid.*, p. 76. Reprinted by permission of Social Science Research Council.
[16] *Ibid.*, p. 77.
[17] Kurt Lewin, "Regression, Retrogression, and Development," in *Field Theory in Social Science: Selected Theoretical Papers*, Dorwin Cartwright, ed. (New York, 1951), p. 97. (Reprinted from *University of Iowa Studies in Child Welfare*, *18* [1941], 1–43.) Reprinted by permission of Harper & Brothers and Iowa Child Welfare Research Station. Copyright, 1951, by Harper & Brothers.

Temporary regressions are involved in most recreational activities, in rest and sleep, in temporary emotional outbursts, etc. Relatively permanent regressions may occur in severe neuroses and psychoses, in change of occupation, in chronic illness, etc.

Every individual will manifest temporary regressions, some of which can be regarded as necessary for the maintenance of effective adjustment. Even in cases of permanent ego-ideal regression, individuals may become better adjusted in terms of a lowered level of aspiration than they could have been in terms of their previous unrealistic ideal.

Situational and Established Regression

Lewin has distinguished between regressions that are manifested only in relation to a particular situation (situational regressions) and regressions that are manifested without reference to the nature of the situation (established regressions).[18] In cases of situational regressions the individual will gain his previous (more mature) level of behavior when the situation undergoes a favorable change; in cases of established regression, however, the individual's behavior will remain at the re-gressed-to level even though conditions become highly favorable for progression to mature behavior-patterns.

Partial and General Regression

Regressions may also be classified in terms of the extent of the personality organization that regresses to a given immature stage of development.

Regression may affect more or less restricted areas of a person. For example, regression may affect only the motor functions, or the emotional life of a person, without much change in his intel-lectual capacities. Psychopathology gives many examples of dif-ferent patterns of regression of specific areas of the person as well as general deterioration. Of course any regression of specific areas does, to some degree, affect all behavior of the individual.[19]

Partial regressions, then, will involve only certain aspects of the individual's behavior, while general regressions will involve many as-pects. Probably every individual has regressed, at one time or another, to an immature stage of development with respect to some of the as-

18 *Ibid.*, pp. 97–8.
19 *Ibid.*, p. 98.

pects of his behavior. General regressions, however, occur with relative infrequency.

HISTORICAL AND AHISTORICAL (DYNAMIC) CONCEPTS OF REGRESSION

IT IS controversial whether regression involves the reinstatement of behavior patterns that were formerly manifested by the individual, or whether regression involves merely the adoption of behavior patterns that have immature characteristics.

Freud recognized both possibilities when he classified regressions into topical (topographical), temporal, and formal categories.[20] *Topographical regression* referred to the transformation of unconscious "thoughts" into conscious visual images during dreams; this transformation was regarded by Freud as "a return to the primitive level of hallucinatory wish-fulfillment." [21] Visual images, in other words, will be interpreted by the dreamer as if they represented something *really there in fact*—an interpretation that involves a failure to differentiate between reality and fantasy. *Formal regression* referred to "primitive modes of expression and representation," [22] and so did not necessarily imply a reversion to behavior that had been manifested during the individual's previous history. *Temporal regression*, however, did refer to a reinstatement of earlier behavior-patterns—this classification of regressions arose in the context of the historical conception of regression.

The historical conception of regression was clearly stated by Freud, in connection with the treatment of psychosexual behavior.

It is a short step to assume that fixation and regression are not independent of each other; the stronger the fixations in the path of development the more easily will the function yield before the external obstacles, by regressing on to those fixations; that is, the less capable of resistance against the external difficulties in its path will the developed function be. If you think of a migrating people who have left large numbers at the stopping-places on their way, you will see that the foremost will naturally fall back upon these

[20] Sigmund Freud, "The Interpretation of Dreams," in *The Basic Writings of Sigmund Freud*, A. A. Brill, ed. (New York, 1938), p. 497.
[21] Sigmund Freud, *Collected Papers* (London, 1950), IV, 143.
[22] Freud, "The Interpretation of Dreams," *op. cit.*, p. 497.

positions when they are defeated or when they meet with an enemy too strong for them. And, again, the more of their number they leave behind in their progress, the sooner will they be in danger of defeat.[23]

Mowrer has insisted on the validity of the historical conception of regression—that regression involves a return to previously fixated behavior-patterns. He states that "regression is historically conditioned (by the presence or absence of prior fixations) and that it is primarily in the *genetic* sense that this concept has greatest usefulness and meaning." [24] It is Mowrer's belief that "behavioral changes are always *progressive* in the dynamic sense" [25]—behavior, even though it may appear primitive *to an outside observer*, will none the less be, from the individual's own point of view, an adaptive adjustment to his environment. The historical concept of regression has also been stressed by Dollard and Miller,[26] by Masserman,[27] by Alexander,[28] and by others.

Lewin, as we have seen, preferred to use the term *retrogression* to imply the reinstatement of any behavior pattern that was formerly used by the individual.[29] He reserved the term *regression* to imply the primitivation of behavior—that is, to imply a change from relatively mature to relatively immature behavior-patterns. His criteria of maturity have been treated in the preceding chapter. Lewin's conception of regression may be termed an *ahistorical* or *dynamic* conception, in order to distinguish it from the historical conception.

It seems probable that both the historical and the dynamic conceptions possess validity, and that the two need not be regarded as mutually exclusive. Some instances of regression may involve primarily the reinstatement of former behavior-patterns (which are not necessarily more primitive than the patterns they replace), while other instances may involve primarily the primitivation of behavior patterns (without necessarily reinstating any pattern that was previously manifested). Most instances of regression will probably involve both the

[23] Freud, *A General Introduction* . . . , pp. 298–9.

[24] Mowrer, *op. cit.*, p. 383.

[25] Mowrer, *op. cit.*, p. 382.

[26] John Dollard and Neal E. Miller, *Personality and Psychotherapy: An Analysis in Terms of Learning, Thinking, and Culture* (New York, 1950), pp. 171–2.

[27] Jules H. Masserman, *Principles of Dynamic Psychiatry* (Philadelphia, 1946), p. 63.

[28] Alexander, *op. cit.*, p. 129.

[29] Lewin, *op. cit.*, pp. 93–6.

reinstatement of earlier patterns and the primitivation of behavior; in other words, the reinstatement of earlier patterns will usually *involve* primitivation.

FORMS OF EXPRESSION

ALTHOUGH every instance of behavior must involve fixation, regression, or progression, the present section will be limited to a discussion of some common fixations and regressions that occur in relation to psychosexual behavior and in relation to behavior in general.

Psychosexual Fixations and Regressions

On the basis of Freud's treatment of sexual development, various forms of behavior have been interpreted to involve psychosexual fixation or regression. Psychosexual fixations and regressions may involve behavior within the "normal" range, as well as behavior that is referred to as "abnormal."

PERVERSIONS. Perversions involve relatively general, relatively well established fixations or regressions with respect to sexual source (or need). The utilization of the mouth, tongue, or lips for the attainment of sexual gratification has been interpreted as an oral fixation or regression; while the utilization of the anal region has been interpreted as an anal fixation or regression. Perverted sexuality is generally regarded as abnormal.

ORAL FIXATIONS AND REGRESSIONS. Many of the activities of the otherwise mature adult may function as partial, or situational, regressions. Among such activities may be mentioned chewing on pencils, nail-biting, smoking, chewing gum, drinking, talking excessively, singing. These regressive activities are partial in that they involve only a small segment of the individual's total behavior; they are situational in that they are employed most extensively during periods of stress or frustration. Thus, smoking may be carried to excess whenever the individual is disturbed by some minor or major frustration.

An oral fixation that occurs in most children is thumb-sucking. When left alone, in the absence of the mother, the child will be likely to engage in this passifying activity—as he frequently will when he is tired or otherwise frustrated. Many mothers, as though jealous, are disturbed when their children indulge in thumb-sucking, though, according to Brill, normal children will usually give up this pleasurable activity when they begin to gain satisfaction from playing with other children.[30]

ANAL FIXATIONS AND REGRESSIONS. Anal fixations and regressions, aside from their expression as perversions, are frequently sublimated and otherwise modified before being permitted expression in adult life. The so-called "anal character" (involving compulsive orderliness, obstinacy, and parsimony) is, according to Freud, a sublimated expression of anal sexuality; reaction formation, as well as sublimation, may be involved in this "anal character" syndrome.[31]

The direct utilization of the sense of smell in order to achieve sexual stimulation is, according to Brill, a manifestation of anal sexuality; the sublimated expression of this tendency may account for the widespread use of perfume.[32] Certain psychosomatic symptoms—including constipation and diarrhea—have also been regarded as expressions of anal sexuality.

NARCISSISTIC FIXATIONS AND REGRESSIONS. Continued masturbation during childhood and youth, or the return to masturbation at puberty, involves fixation at, or regression to, the narcissistic object level. Excessive vanity may be interpreted as a regression to the narcissistic level, involving perhaps the mechanism of sublimation.[33]

INVERSION. According to one interpretation, inversion (homosexuality) involves the choice of a narcissistic object. That is to say, the chosen love-object, being of the same sex, will manifest physical features and personality characteristics similar to those of the individual himself. As Freud has expressed it, homosexuals are "plainly seeking themselves as a love-object and their type of object-choice may be termed *narcissistic*." [34] In terms of this interpretation, inversion implies a fixation at, or a regression to, the narcissistic stage. The problem of inversion is, however, extremely complicated, involving many factors that cannot be discussed at this point.

OTHER OBJECT FIXATIONS AND REGRESSIONS. When the child clings to a favored toy, persistently taking it to bed with him until it becomes worn and dilapidated, the child is manifesting an object fixation. Most children have some such "fetish," which becomes the main

[30] A. A. Brill, *Lectures on Psychoanalytic Psychiatry* (New York, 1946), p. 171.
[31] Freud, *Collected Papers* (London, 1950), II, 47–8.
[32] Brill, *op. cit.*, pp. 181–2.
[33] Percival M. Symonds, *The Dynamics of Human Adjustment* (New York, 1946), p. 214.
[34] Freud, *Collected Papers*, IV, 45.

object of affection at times when the parents are absent or when they have, as punishment, temporarily withdrawn their affection. Even after the toy has been in disuse for many months, the child may, during periods of insecurity, insist on retrieving the dependable "fetish" as a love-object and as a bedtime companion; that is to say, the child may regress to his earlier object-choice.

Soldiers, prisoners, and other men who have long shown heterosexual object attachments may, in the absence of women, regress to homosexual object choice. If the regression is relatively complete, overt homosexual practices may occur. The regression, however, will usually be expressed in sublimated forms—as, for example, in a depth of comradeship that can seldom occur under ordinary circumstances.

At times when the frustrations associated with marriage become more impressive than the satisfactions, the individual may, in fantasy, look back with nostalgia toward the women (or men) who were the love-objects of his (or her) past. Or he may go back to the first love-object—his mother.

Grief has been interpreted by Freud as an instance of object fixation. "Grief is a prototype and perfect example of an affective fixation upon something that is past, and, like the neurosis, it also involves a state of complete alienation from the present and the future." [35] Nostalgia or homesickness—the longing for familiar objects in the past or in a distant place—may be given a similar interpretation.

General Fixations and Regressions

The preceding discussion has been concerned with a few of the many behavior manifestations that have been interpreted as psychosexual fixations or regressions. We come now to a consideration of fixations and regressions of a more general character, which may require ahistorical (dynamic) interpretations as well as historical (though not necessarily psychosexual) interpretations.

SLEEP. It is generally agreed that sleep involves a state of regression—perhaps the most general state of regression that can occur within the normal range of behavior. Freud, for example, has stated:

> Sleep is a condition in which I refuse to have anything to do with the outer world and have withdrawn my interest from it. I go to sleep by retreating from the outside world and warding off the stimuli proceeding from it. . . . Thus the biological object of

[35] Freud, *A General Introduction* . . . , p. 244.

sleep seems to be recuperation, its psychological characteristic the suspension of interest in the outer world. Our relationship with the world which we entered so unwillingly seems to be endurable only with intermission; hence we withdraw again periodically into the condition prior to our entrance into the world: that is to say, into intrauterine existence. At any rate, we try to bring about quite similar conditions—warmth, darkness and absence of stimulus —characteristic of that state.[36]

If sleep be regarded as a return to the intrauterine condition, the historical conception of regression should apply. In any case, Lewin's criteria, which were formulated in terms of the dynamic point of view, imply that sleep involves a very general regression: the variety of behavior is reduced to a minimum; the organization of behavior is greatly simplified; the life space is greatly reduced; the degree of realism is so diminished that dream perceptions are interpreted as real; etc.

DREAMS. The condition of sleep, as we have seen, is itself a regressive manifestation; it constitutes a temporary denial of many aspects of reality. Freud believed that the main function of dreaming is to prevent the interruption of sleep. This was said to be achieved by means of hallucinatory wish-fulfillments (gratifications), with the attendant relief of tensions that would, if continued, interfere with sleep.

During his sleep a need for food stirs in the dreamer. He has a dream of a delicious meal and sleeps on. . . . The sleeper must wake up in order to be in time for his work at the hospital. But he sleeps on, and has a dream that he is at the hospital—but as a patient, who has no need to get up. . . . We shall be taking all our observations into account if we say that every dream is an *attempt* to put aside a disturbance of sleep by means of a wish-fulfillment. The dream is thus the guardian of sleep.[37]

In addition to the fact that dreams may help to maintain a regressive condition (i.e., sleep), the dreams themselves involve regressive manifestations. The hallucinatory wish-fulfillment will be accepted at its face value by the dreamer; and such a confusion of fantasy with reality, as Lewin and others have pointed out, is regressive: it represents a stage of development characteristic of early childhood.

[36] *Ibid.*, p. 79.
[37] Freud, *An Outline of Psychoanalysis*, pp. 55-7.

In dreams and reveries, indeed, nearly everyone escapes from the usual fetters of time and space, and reconstitutes the universe according to his own imagery.[38]

Considered from the point of view of psychological dynamics, unreality, the land of dreams and air castles, presents a soft and easily movable medium. It is characterized by the fact that in it one can do whatever he wishes.[39]

Dreams are regressive also in that the quality of thinking in dreams is similar to that which is characteristic of young children. "Dreaming is," in Alexander's words, "a return to infantile forms of thought." [40] One of the manifestations of infantile thought involves the visual representation of ideas that in mature thinking are verbally represented.

In this process thoughts are transformed into images, mainly visual; that is to say, verbal ideas are reduced to the ideas of the corresponding things, on the whole as if the process were controlled by considerations of *suitability for plastic representation.*[41]

On account of the same process of regression ideas are turned into visual pictures in the dream; the latent dream-thoughts are, that is to say, dramatized and illustrated.[42]

Punning, or play upon words, and other immature processes of thinking are also involved in dreams.

FANTASY. Daydreams or fantasies are also said to function as wish-fulfillments. But, unlike dreams, they will not be accepted by the normal person at their face value; only in the case of psychotic hallucinations will such fantasies be accepted with the naïveté that characterizes the dreamer. Moreover, fantasies may involve little regression in the character of the thinking processes, except to the extent that they manifest a temporary disregard for reality.

. . . when the human being grows up and ceases to play he only gives up the connection with real objects; instead of playing he

---

[38] Masserman, *op. cit.,* p. 37.
[39] Kurt Lewin, "Education for Reality," *A Dynamic Theory of Personality: Selected Papers* (New York, 1935), p. 174. Reprinted by permission of McGraw-Hill Book Company, Inc. Copyright, 1935, by McGraw-Hill Book Company, Inc.
[40] Alexander, *op. cit.,* p. 130.
[41] Freud, *Collected Papers,* IV, 143.
[42] Freud, *New Introductory Lectures . . . ,* p. 31.

then begins to create phantasy. He builds castles in the air and creates what are called day-dreams. . . . The relation of phantasies to time is altogether of great importance. One may say that a phantasy at one and the same moment hovers between three periods of time—the three periods of our ideation. The activity of phantasy in the mind is linked up with some current impression, occasioned by some event in the present, which had the power to rouse an intense desire. From there it wanders back to the memory of an early experience, generally belonging to infancy, in which this wish was fulfilled. Then it creates for itself a situation which is to emerge in the future, representing the fulfillment of the wish —this is the day-dream or phantasy, which now carries in it traces both of the occasion which engendered it and of some past memory.[43]

Different levels of realism may be involved in fantasy. Creative or constructive thinking depends upon the integration of fantasy with realistic perception; the attainment of any goal will depend upon its prior representation in fantasy.

RECREATION. Temporary regressions are involved in all forms of recreation—in hobbies, sports, games, rest, etc. As Alexander has stated, "the business man who plays cards or golf after a strenuous day in the office behaves in a sense like a child. He competes innocuously and finds gratification in physical or mental accomplishments which have no significance in his daily struggle for existence." [44]

Recreation, while it differs in no essential respect from the play of children, is held in high esteem in our society, though the adult who "plays" or "daydreams" rather than "engaging in recreation" will encounter disapproval.

The child's best loved and most absorbing occupation is play. Perhaps we may say that every child at play behaves like an imaginative writer, in that he creates a world of his own or, more truly, he rearranges the things of his world and orders it in a new way that pleases him better. It would be incorrect to think that he does not take this world seriously; on the contrary, he takes his play very seriously and expends a great deal of emotion on it. The opposite of play is not serious occupation but—reality.[45]

[43] Freud, *Collected Papers*, IV, 175-7.
[44] Alexander, *op. cit.*, p. 130.
[45] Freud, *Collected Papers*, IV, 173-4.

The adult, like the child at play, takes his recreation seriously. Games must be played according to the rules; hobbies must be among the acceptable and standardized ones; a person must not "play at" a game but must "put his heart into it"; etc. Recreation, like play, however, involves a temporary rearrangement of the world in order to give it a pleasing structure—a structure that differs as much as possible from the structure of reality, within which life's major adjustments must be made.

ALCOHOLISM. The state of intoxication induced by alcohol is a regressive condition.

> Many of the behavior patterns that thus find expression are, as may be expected, regressive in nature: thus, the alcoholic titillates his "oral" desires from his bottle, becomes maudlin and sentimentally dependent while drunk and may continue to intoxicate himself into an autistic, fantasy-ridden torpor.[46]

> During this state the individual will behave childishly, since he has temporarily lost some of the psychogenic motivation that ordinarily participates in the determination of his behavior. There may occur sexual and aggressive expressions that during the "sober" state are kept under control by suppression, restraint, inhibition, or repression.[47]

REPUDIATION OF MARITAL RESPONSIBILITIES. When husband and wife perceive that their marital difficulties are on the increase, and when they see little prospect of future compatibility, one or both may indulge in regressive behavior. One form this regressive behavior may take is the repudiation of marital responsibilities. The wife may become slovenly in her standards of housekeeping, may neglect the children, or may take an extra-marital lover. The husband may stay away from home, may lose ambition in his profession, or may abandon his wife and children.

> Thus, a man who is dissatisfied with a contentious and unsuccessful marriage and who longs for his pre-marital freedom, might act as though he were again a bachelor by not supporting his wife, keeping his own hours, having extra-marital affairs, and so on.[48]

[46] Masserman, *op. cit.*, p. 149.
[47] Donald Horton, "The Functions of Alcohol in Primitive Societies," in *Personality in Nature, Society, and Culture*, Clyde Kluckhohn and Henry A. Murray, eds. (New York, 1948), pp. 540–50.
[48] Masserman, *op. cit.*, p. 63.

Responsibilities that are related to other major areas of adjustment may likewise be repudiated, if conditions of unusual frustration occur in connection with them.

ENURESIS. The insecure child may continue to wet his bed for many years; in such cases, enuresis will involve fixation. It is a common observation, also, that many children who have developed socialized habits in this respect may, for example, upon the birth of another child, revert to enuresis.

> The older child, who previously felt secure, now feels seriously threatened in regard to the affection and love of his parents. The bed-wetting is partly a direct expression of anxiety, partly an attempt to show his need of parental attention and help, and partly an attempt to be a helpless infant and thus get all of the parents' affection. In such a situation the child may also want the bottle or the breast again.[49]

WITHDRAWAL. Ego restriction, as we have seen, can occur as a function of repression or of denial. One form of denial involves physical withdrawal from situations that are frustrating. The normal course of development requires increasing participation with broader and broader aspects of reality; the life space and the space of free movement become more and more extensive. Withdrawal from (avoidance of) any aspect of reality will interfere with such expansion: the ego functions will be restricted by failure to gain the knowledge and the skills that can only be acquired through active participation.

The child may avoid certain games in which he is outclassed; he may avoid social relations in which he is at a disadvantage; he may avoid attempting school tasks in which the other children are superior. There may occur an increasing tendency for the individual to avoid activities and situations in which he senses any possibility of failure.

NEUROSES AND PSYCHOSES. It is generally agreed that neuroses and psychoses involve regression. In the first place, the processes by which the neuroses and the psychoses develop involve regression (as well as frustration, conflict, repression, etc.); in the second place, the symptomatic manifestations are themselves regressive in character.

> . . . the psychological content of neurotic symptoms would appear "normal" if the patient were a child. Fear of the dark or of being alone in crowded places or the streets of a big city are com-

[49] Abraham H. Maslow and Bela Mittelmann, *Principles of Abnormal Psychology: the Dynamics of Psychic Illness* (New York, 1941), pp. 166–7.

mon reactions of the small child. The fear of great open spaces is also universal when the child is learning how to walk. . . . The regressive nature of psychotic symptoms is self-evident. According to Freud, the hallucinatory gratification of needs is characteristic of the infant who has not yet differentiated between the inner and outer worlds. . . .[50]

Neurotic and psychotic symptoms involve much more general and much more firmly established regressions than those which are involved in the regressive behavior of "normal" individuals.

DYNAMIC RELATIONS WITH ANXIETY

FIXATION and regression are based on anxiety; and they may function as a basis for the development of subsequent anxiety. That is, fixation and regression, like repression and other defensive mechanisms, manifest complicated interrelations with anxiety.

Anxiety as a Basis of Fixation, Regression, and Progression

Whenever the individual anticipates that progression to a new level of adjustment will involve an increase in frustration and anxiety, he will likely remain fixated at the level he has already attained. If the individual's present adjustment and the progressive adjustments that he is able to imagine threaten frustration beyond the limit of his tolerance, he will be likely to regress to an older or a simpler mode of adjustment. When ego-ideals or social pressures render fixation or regression more frustrating than the change to some new mode of adjustment, progression will be likely to occur.

Thus, the possibilities of adjustment at any given moment will include fixating at the present mode of adjustment, regressing to an earlier or more primitive mode of adjustment, and progressing to a new and more mature form of adjustment. Whether the individual will, at a particular time, fixate, regress, or make a progressive adjustment will depend on the relative amounts of frustration (and anxiety) involved in the different possibilities.

Some examples should aid in making clear how fixation and regression may be motivated by anxiety, and how these reactions can function to relieve anxiety. Bettelheim has described the case of a boy

[50] Alexander, *op. cit.*, pp. 206–07.

who tried to avoid learning to read (fixation at the illiterate level). He
believed that, as a little boy, he had killed another child. He feared that
when he grew up he might do the same again, and that "if he knew
how to read and write, everybody would say that he knew what he'd
been doing, while if he remained a dumbbell, no one could hold him
responsible." [51]

Anna Freud has described the case of a girl who regressed after a
humiliating experience at her first dance.

> . . . she fell in love at first sight with the handsomest and most
> distinguished-looking boy at the party. . . . She made advances to
> him but met with no encouragement. In fact, when they were
> dancing together, he teased her about her clumsiness. This disap-
> pointment was at once a shock and a humiliation. From that time
> on she avoided parties, lost her interest in dress and would take no
> trouble to learn to dance. . . . Gradually she came to regard all
> this side of her life with supreme contempt.[52]

These ego-restrictive withdrawals involved the use of relatively
severe measures for the relief of anxiety. The temporary wish-fulfillments that may be achieved through dreams and fantasy, and the
equally temporary indulgence in recreational activities, involve less
radical measures for the relief of anxiety. These temporary regressions
will function to gratify motives that cannot be gratified in the realistic
world of mature adjustment.

> You know that the ego in man is gradually trained by the influence
> of external necessity to appreciate reality and to pursue the reality-
> principle, and that in so doing it must renounce temporarily or
> permanently various of the objects and aims—not only sexual—of
> its desire for pleasure. But renunciation of pleasure has always
> been very hard to man; he cannot accomplish it without some kind
> of compensation. Accordingly he has evolved for himself a mental
> activity in which all these relinquished sources of pleasure and
> abandoned paths of gratification are permitted to continue their
> existence, a form of existence in which they are free from . . .
> what we call the exercise of "testing reality." Every longing is

[51] Bruno Bettelheim, *Love Is Not Enough: the Treatment of Emotionally
Disturbed Children* (Glencoe, Ill., 1950), p. 144. Reprinted by permission of The
Free Press. Copyright, 1950, by The Free Press.
[52] Anna Freud, *The Ego and the Mechanisms of Defense* (New York, 1946),
p. 108.

soon transformed into the idea of its fulfillment; there is no doubt that dwelling upon a wish-fulfillment in phantasy brings satisfaction, although the knowledge that it is not reality remains thereby unobscured. In phantasy, therefore, man can continue to enjoy a freedom from the grip of the external world, one which he has long relinquished in actuality. He has contrived to be alternately a pleasure-seeking animal and a reasonable being; for the meagre satisfaction that he can extract from reality leaves him starving.[53]

Recreations, like fantasy, will provide an escape from the demands of reality; they will function to gratify motives that might otherwise remain frustrated. This will aid in keeping the intensity of such motives sufficiently low for the individual to tolerate their frustration in the course of the everyday adjustments required by routine working and living.

Alcoholism also has its source in anxiety; the motivation for continued drinking is to be found in the relief it affords.

> . . . the primary function of alcohol is reduction of anxiety. The greater the amount of alcohol consumed, other conditions being equal, the more completely anxiety is reduced; and conversely, the greater the initial anxiety, the greater the amount of alcohol required to reduce it. Anxiety-reducing acts are inherently rewarding and, therefore, tend to be habit-forming.[54]

To the extent that this interpretation is correct, the best "cure" for alcoholism will involve the adoption of some other means of relieving anxiety.

Psychosexual regressions (or fixations), like other fixations and regressions, may function to relieve anxiety. Mowrer and Kluckhohn, for example, have pointed out that "children resort to thumb- or finger-sucking most frequently when they are lonely, disappointed, or apprehensive."[55] These writers suggest that the relief of anxiety may

[53] Freud, *A General Introduction* . . . , pp. 324–5.

[54] Donald Horton, "The Functions of Alcohol in Primitive Societies," *Quarterly Journal of Studies on Alcohol,* 4 (1943), 292–303. In *Personality in Nature, Society, and Culture,* Clyde Kluckhohn and Henry A. Murray, eds. (New York, 1948), p. 541. Reprinted by permission of *Quarterly Journal of Studies on Alcohol* and Alfred A. Knopf, Inc. Copyright, 1943, by Journal of Studies on Alcohol, Inc., 1948, by Alfred A. Knopf, Inc.

[55] O. Hobart Mowrer and Clyde Kluckhohn, "Dynamic Theory of Personality," in *Personality and the Behavior Disorders,* J. McV. Hunt, ed. (New York, 1944), p. 117.

be based on the fact that the oral, anal, and genital activities are functions of the parasympathetic division of the autonomic nervous system, while anxiety is a function of the sympathetic division. These divisions of the autonomic nervous system function antagonistically; action in one tends to inhibit action in the other. Anxiety and anger "have a paralyzing effect on sexuality"; but sexual stimulation may have a similar "paralyzing effect" on anxiety. Thus the relief of anxiety as a function of psychosexual regression may be accounted for in terms of a physiological relationship.

This is only partially correct, however, since *mature* sexual functioning manifests a similar physiological relationship with anxiety; so that, in order to account for the anxiety-reducing value of *regression*, it becomes necessary to consider interrelations that occur on the level of overt adjustments.

If regression, rather than mature sexual expression, is to function in the service of relieving anxiety, it must be based on the prior frustration of mature sexuality. In other words, psychosexual regression will relieve anxiety to the extent that regressive sexual gratification can more easily be achieved than mature sexual gratification.

Fixation and Regression as Sources of Anxiety

While fixation and regression are motivated by anxiety, and while their immediate function is to relieve anxiety, they may, like other defensive measures, become the sources of further conflict and anxiety. Fixation or regression may arouse anxiety as a function of (1) the reactivation of early conflicts, (2) the frustration of immature motivation by the social pressure to "act one's age," and (3) the conflict between immature motivation and superego motivation. Each of these possibilities will be discussed separately.

REACTIVATION OF EARLY CONFLICTS. Progression is motivated, in the first place, by anxiety; the fact that anxiety was previously associated with immature motivation and immature behavior accounted for the development of a more mature form of adjustment.

If, on later occasions, anxiety eventuates in regression to an earlier form of motivation, this regression will reactivate the anxiety that was previously associated with the older adjustment. Since the regressed-to motivation was once progressed-from on the basis of anxiety, this same anxiety will again become operative. Freud believed, for example, that cases of neurosis in adults involve the regression to (or fixation on) a neurosis that had occurred in childhood.

When a neurosis breaks out in later life analysis invariably reveals it to be a direct continuation of that infantile neurosis, which had . . . been expressed in a veiled and incipient form only; as has been said, however, there are cases in which the childish nervousness is carried on into lifelong illness without a break.[56]

Regression to a previous pattern of motivation, or the continuation of such a pattern (fixation), will reinstate or maintain the anxieties that have been associated with this motivation.

. . . this is how neurotics behave. Although in their mental apparatus there have long since developed all the agencies necessary for dealing with a wide range of stimuli, although they are mature enough to be able to gratify the greater part of their needs themselves . . . they nevertheless behave as though the old danger situation still existed, they remain under the spell of all the old causes of anxiety.[57]

In this connection, Mowrer has taken the position that fixation, rather than regression, is usually involved in neurosis—that neurotic individuals suffer from "*immaturities* which they have never surmounted. They are, in other words, individuals who are *developmentally fixated;* but the fixation is not, as Freud supposed, libidinal, save incidentally; it can be more correctly described as 'moral.' " [58]

SOCIAL FRUSTRATION OF IMMATURE MOTIVATION. The social pressures that emanate from adults and contemporaries are such that they support and approve progression ("growing up," "being one's age," etc.) while they disapprove fixation or regression. If a child continues overlong to behave in an immature fashion, or if an adult regresses (in disapproved ways) to immature behavior, he will come in conflict with social pressure and so will experience anxiety.

As an example of this, Horton has stated, in his discussion of alcoholism, that "anticipation of punishments for the personally or socially unacceptable consequences of drinking is the chief counteracting response." [59] Social punishments will ensue from the alcoholic impairment of functions (which renders the individual unable to earn his living or to support his family) and from the unrestrained expression of sexuality and aggression.

[56] Freud, *A General Introduction* . . . , p. 318.
[57] Sigmund Freud, *The Problem of Anxiety* (New York, 1936), pp. 89–90.
[58] Mowrer, *op. cit.*, p. 361.
[59] Horton, *op. cit.*, p. 542.

CONFLICT BETWEEN IMMATURE MOTIVATION AND SUPEREGO MOTIVATION. Fixation and regression are frequently followed by guilt feelings and feelings of inferiority, since immature motivation and its expression will come into conflict with the individual's standards of morality (conscience) and his ideals of achievement (ego-ideal); ". . . what was at one time a satisfaction must to-day arouse resistance or horror." [60]

> This regression creates new emotional problems. Shame may develop and express the tension between the regressive behavior and adult standards, which are not wholly relinquished. To relieve this shame and sense of inferiority, other neurotic attitudes may develop. . . .[61]

Since the individual has developed psychogenic motives more or less consistent with the values of his society, the retention of immature fixations or the regression to immature modes of behavior will arouse guilt and inferiority feelings.

REPRESSION AS RELATED TO FIXATION, REGRESSION, AND PROGRESSION

FIXATION, regression, and progression manifest interrelations with other defensive mechanisms. In the present section, a brief consideration will be given to their interrelations with repression. Subsequent chapters will include discussions of the interrelations of fixation, regression, and progression with other defenses.

Behavior involving fixation or regression probably requires repression of the particular superego motives that conflict with the immature motivation being expressed. Progression, on the other hand, probably requires the repression of immature impulses.

Yet, although *conflicting* superego motives may be repressed when fixation or regression occurs, and although *conflicting* immature motives may be repressed when progression occurs, the possibility should not be overlooked that fixation or regression may *gratify* or be "motivated" by other (nonconflicting) superego motives, and that progression in one area of behavior may *gratify* or be "motivated" by immature impulses.

Psychosexual fixations that survive into adulthood, and psycho-

---

[60] Freud, *A General Introduction* . . . , p. 319.
[61] Alexander, *op. cit.*, p. 69.

sexual regressions that occur in adults, may, if accompanied by the repression of superego motives, be manifested as perversions.

If the psychosexual impulses are repressed while the superego motives continue to operate consciously, perverted behavior will be inhibited, but the individual may suffer from a neurosis. This is implied in Freud's statement that "the neurosis is the negative of the perversion." [62]

ADJUSTIVE IMPLICATIONS

IN THE dynamics of fixation and regression there are positive and negative implications for adjustment.[63] Books on "mental hygiene" have tended to overemphasize the maladjustive implications of fixation and regression. Neither fixation nor regression can be said *necessarily* to interfere with the individual's happiness; on the contrary, there are occasions when *not* fixating or *not* regressing may interfere seriously with adequate adjustment.

Temporary and partial fixations and regressions occur in the everyday activities of every "normal" individual. Even fairly general and well-established fixations and regressions may function in the service of satisfactory adjustment.

But when a fixation or regression is permanent, general, established, and relatively infantile in its manifestations, maladjustive implications will necessarily be involved. In such cases, fixation or regression may function as a basis of neurosis, psychosis, or severe social maladjustment.

Some of the positive implications will be mentioned at the outset, since these are frequently overlooked.

Value of Temporary Regressions

Temporary regressions, which occur at intervals, may be necessary to adjustment. There must occur, it is believed, a proper balance between work and play, between sleep and activity, between attention to reality and attention to fantasy.

[62] Sigmund Freud, "Three Contributions to the Theory of Sex," in *The Basic Writings of Sigmund Freud*, A. A. Brill, ed. (New York, 1938), p. 625.

[63] It is assumed that the adjustive implications of progression are generally positive. When, however, the use of fixation or regression has positive implications, the use of progression should carry negative implications. Fixation, regression, and progression are, in this context, used in their historical and objective sense; from the individual's own point of view, every adjustment will probably involve progression in the dynamic sense.

Leisure activities, recreation, and rest will gratify motives that, during the individual's intense preoccupation with reality, must remain in a state of frustration. The gratification achieved by means of such temporary regressions will function to reorganize the motivational pattern, so that the individual can work efficiently when he redirects his attention to his mature responsibilities.

In other words, after a vacation, after recreation, after sleep, or after a temporary indulgence in fantasy, the previously frustrated motives will no longer function to distract the individual's attention from his work, since by means of temporary regression these motives will have been gratified sufficiently to lose their prepotence in the motivational pattern. The individual will become free to function in terms of his mature motives, which have attained, once again, a dominant status in his motivational pattern.

Value of Partial Fixations and Regressions

The maintenance of social approval is largely dependent on partial fixations and regressions. The person who is mature in every respect, the person who fails to demonstrate personal childishness in some aspects of his behavior, is frequently feared and hated as if he were inhuman or monstrous.

Since "being human" is a criterion in terms of which we are often judged by our fellow men, we cannot receive their full approval if we "take life too seriously." Moreover, since reality is not *inherently* funny, the sense of humor itself may depend upon the occurrence of regressive fantasies.

In our culture, then, we are expected to display some manifestations of fixation or of regression; our adequate adjustment will depend on our ability to demonstrate that we are not completely or permanently "grown up."

Value of General, Established Fixations or Regressions

Limitations of ability require that the individual adjust his level of aspiration (ego-ideal) to goals that he can realistically expect to attain. If an individual has already reached his maximum level, then to fixate at this level will be, for him, the most satisfactory adjustment.

Similarly, if an individual has attempted to achieve a goal above his level of ability, his best adjustment will involve regression to a lower level. In other words, there are occasions on which a relatively general and well-established fixation or regression will be the happiest ultimate solution.

Fixation or Regression as a Basis for Progression

It has already been pointed out that fantasy is a necessary basis for creative or constructive thinking. One must turn away, temporarily, from the frustrating features of reality in order to envisage the "shape of things to come"; whatever is constructed, in other words, must first have been perceived in fantasy. In this sense, fantasy—a regression—will function as the necessary basis for a progressive adjustment.

Continued fixation at a particular level of adjustment in some areas of behavior may provide the feeling of security that is required as a basis for the individual's progression to a higher level of adjustment in some other area of behavior. The individual may progress in certain respects while remaining fixated in other respects; after a particular progressive adjustment has been "consolidated," so that he feels secure in this adjustment, he may then progress in other respects. Bettelheim has cited the case of a little boy who, in learning to climb stairs, felt that he could manage the climbing only if he could hold his thumb in his mouth while doing so.[64]

In this connection, it should be pointed out, in agreement with Mowrer, that "behavioral changes are always *progressive* in the dynamic sense." [65] When the individual regresses, from the point of view of an external observer, or in the historical sense, he will be making what, for him, is the most adequate—the only possible—adjustment. "If such were not the case," according to Mowrer, "the regressive adjustment would be abandoned." [66]

Neurotic Fixation and Regression

Freud's theory of neurosis, stated succinctly, is that mature sexual expression is frustrated, that regression ensues, and that immature sexual impulses come into conflict with the more mature superego motives; the immature sexual impulses undergo repression, but thereafter express themselves in devious ways—that is, symbolically in the form of symptoms.[67] Fixation of a childhood neurosis may also, as we have seen, account for symptoms manifested at a later age.

[64] Bettelheim, *op. cit.*, pp. 221–4.
[65] Mowrer, *op. cit.*, p. 382.
[66] Mowrer, *op. cit.*, p. 380.
[67] Freud, *A General Introduction* . . . , pp. 301–15.

While fixation and regression, then, are by no means to be regarded as the sole basis of neurosis, it seems clear that either fixation or regression will function as one of the underlying factors.

Marital Maladjustments

Some instances of marital maladjustment have their basis in fixation. For example, Freud has made the following statement in regard to sexual impotence.

> . . . it may happen that the whole current of sensual feeling in a young man may remain attached in the unconscious to incestuous objects, or, to put it in another way, may be fixated to incestuous phantasies. The result of this is then total impotence. . . . Less severe conditions will suffice to bring about what is usually called psychical impotence. . . . The sensual feeling that has remained active seeks only objects evoking no reminder of the incestuous persons forbidden to it; the impression made by someone who seems deserving of high estimation leads, not to a sensual excitation, but to feelings of tenderness which remain erotically ineffectual. . . . Where such men love they have no desire and where they desire they cannot love. In order to keep their sensuality out of contact with the objects they love, they seek out objects whom they need not love. . . .[68]

If such a person were to marry, he could either love his wife for her personal qualities, or else he could have sexual relations with her while despising her as a person. To the extent that happy marital adjustment depends both upon love of the wife as a person and upon adequate sexual expression, the lack of either one of these features could be the basis of an unhappy marriage.

Integration of Heterosexual Object with Ego-Ideal

It has repeatedly been said that every man owes his success to a woman—to his mother, to his wife, or to both. In present-day American culture, as we know it, a man can hardly be happy without achieving success in two areas—in his family relations and in his chosen career. It is a rare man who can feel adequate unless his marriage is happy and unless he is, at the same time, economically successful.

Devotion to a wife (heterosexual object-choice) and devotion to an ego-ideal (narcissism) need not involve conflict; the man can inte-

[68] Freud, *Collected Papers*, IV, 207.

grate these objects of devotion, provided that the wife will encourage her husband in the pursuit of his ambition. With such encouragement and support, he will not feel that he is neglecting his wife when he devotes time to his career, nor that he is neglecting his career when he devotes time to his wife.

The wife likewise will have an ego-ideal that the husband can support through his respect for her interests. The happy marriage apparently depends upon the mutual integration of ego-ideals with the heterosexual object-choice—the wife and the husband supporting each other in the pursuit of ego-ideals, with a minimum of jealousy. The mature narcissism of each can be accepted by the other; to the extent that this occurs, their love for each other will be enhanced.

Social Support for Progression

The child can achieve progressive adjustments only if he receives adequate social support from adults. Parents, for example, can interfere seriously with the child's progressive adjustment by overprotection—that is, by guarding the child against the frustrating punishments he must inevitably face in making tentative efforts to "grow up."

A similar interference with progression may occur through parental neglect or through parental insistence that the child "grow up" too rapidly. The child's infantile fixations in some areas of behavior should be tolerated, so long as the child continues to demonstrate growth in other respects.

In other words, the child's progressive adjustment should neither be expected to occur without setbacks nor be expected to occur at a too rapid rate; the child should be permitted to risk the dangers he feels ready to face, but he should not be forced to meet dangers before he has decided that he is ready to meet them.

SUMMARY

THE CONCEPTS of fixation, regression, and progression refer to developmental aspects of behavior. Fixation involves *continuing* an immature behavior-pattern; regression involves *returning to* an immature behavior-pattern; and progression involves *developing* a new or qualitatively more mature behavior-pattern.

Regressions have been classified according to several criteria. *Object regression* involves a return to an object that was previously cathected; *need regression* involves a change in the need that is related to a given object; *instrumental act regression* involves a change in the quality of behavior employed to achieve a given kind of gratification in relation to a given object. Fixations, regressions, or progressions may be *temporary* or relatively *permanent;* they may be *situational* or *established;* they may be *partial* (involving small segments of motivation) or *general* (involving the total motivational pattern).

It is controversial whether regression involves the reinstatement of previously used behavior-patterns (historical conception), or whether it merely involves the adoption of behavior patterns that have immature characteristics (ahistorical conception); it is probable that most cases of regression are understandable in terms of both conceptions.

Fixation and regression may be manifested in a variety of behavior forms. Psychosexual fixations and regressions may involve sexual source (as in perversions and various oral and anal methods of pleasure-seeking) or sexual object (as in the practice of masturbation, in vanity, in inversion, etc.). General fixation or regression may be involved in sleep, in dreams, in fantasies, in recreation, in alcoholism, in enuresis, etc.

Anxiety functions as the basis of fixation and regression; whether a person will, at a given time, fixate, regress, or make a progressive adjustment will depend on the relative amounts of frustration involved in the different possibilities. Fixation or regression may function as a source of further anxiety through (1) the reactivation of early conflicts, (2) the frustration of immature impulses by social pressure, and (3) the conflict between immature motivation and mature superego motivation.

Fixation or regression may require repression of superego motivation, while progression may require repression of immature motivation. Psychosexual fixations or regressions may be expressed as perversions if psychogenic (superego) motives are repressed, or as neuroses if the immature sexual motives are repressed.

Neither fixation nor regression is necessarily maladjustive. Temporary regressions (sleep, rest, fantasy, recreation, etc.) will gratify motives that might otherwise continue to function as a distraction within the otherwise mature motivational pattern. Partial fixations or regressions will lend to the individual's behavior a quality of "being human," which may be necessary for the maintenance of gratifying social relations.

Fixation at an optimal level, or regression to this level after attempting too difficult a progression, may be necessary and desirable in order to achieve the highest degree of general gratification; in such a case, regression will function dynamically as a progressive adjustment.

Fantasy may be the indispensable basis for creative construction—that is, for progression; and continued fixation in some areas of behavior may provide the feeling of security necessary for progression in other areas of behavior.

Fixation or regression may have severe negative implications for adjustment, in that either may function in the development of a neurosis, and in that fixation may function to the detriment of marital adjustment.

Happy marriage probably requires, as a basis, the perceptual integration of the heterosexual object (husband or wife) with the ego-ideal (ambitions, aspirations, etc.). Such an integration will form the basis for expression of devotion to the husband or wife *through* devotion to ego-ideals, and vice versa.

Parents and other adults can support progressive adjustments in children by maintaining a middle position between overprotection and underprotection—that is, by permitting the child to encounter dangers when he feels ready, but not before he feels ready, to encounter them.

The following chapter will deal with the defensive functions of perceptual identification.

▶ Suggested Readings

Altus, W. D. "Constipation and Adjustment among Illiterate Males," *Journal of Consulting Psychology, 14* (1950), 25–31.

Axline, Virginia M. "Mental Deficiency—Symptom or Disease?" *Journal of Consulting Psychology, 13* (1949), 313–27.

Bach, G. R. "Young Children's Play Fantasies," *Psychological Monographs, 59*, No. 2 (1945).

Cameron, N. and Magaret, Ann. *Behavior Pathology*. Boston, 1951. Chaps. v, viii, pp. 130–53, 217–45.

Cattell, R. B. "The Riddle of Perseveration," *Journal of Personality, 14* (1946), 229–67.

Cattell, R. B. and Winder, A. E. "Structural Rigidity in Relation to Learning Theory and Clinical Psychology," *Psychological Review, 59* (1952), 23–39.

Cowen, E. L. and Thompson, G. G. "Problem Solving Rigidity and Personality Structure," *Journal of Abnormal and Social Psychology, 46* (1951), 165–76.

Eglash, A. "Perception, Association, and Reasoning in Animal Fixations," *Psychological Review, 58* (1951), 424–34.

Klee, J. B. "The Relation of Frustration and Motivation to the Production of Abnormal Fixations in the Rat," *Psychological Monographs, 56,* No. 4 (1944).

Kunst, M. S. "A Study of Thumb- and Finger-sucking in Infants," *Psychological Monographs, 62,* No. 3 (1948).

Luchins, A. S. "On Recent Usage of the Einstellung-Effect as a Test of Rigidity," *Journal of Consulting Psychology, 15* (1951), 89–94.

Luchins, A. S. "The Einstellung Test of Rigidity: Its Relation to Concreteness of Thinking," *Journal of Consulting Psychology, 15* (1951), 303–10.

Maier, N. R. F. *Frustration.* New York, 1949. Pp. 77–93.

Maier, N. R. F. and Ellen, P. "Can the Anxiety-Reduction Theory Explain Abnormal Fixations?" *Psychological Review, 58* (1951), 435–45.

Maier, N. R. F. and Ellen P. "Studies of Abnormal Behavior in the Rat: The Prophylactic Effects of 'Guidance' in Reducing Rigid Behavior," *Journal of Abnormal and Social Psychology, 47* (1952), 109–16.

McCann, W. H. "Nostalgia: a Review of the Literature," *Psychological Bulletin, 38* (1941), 165–82.

Mowrer, O. H. *Learning Theory and Personality Dynamics.* New York, 1950. Chap. xiii, pp. 361–83.

Rokeach, M. "Generalized Mental·Rigidity as a Factor in Ethnocentrism," *Journal of Abnormal and Social Psychology, 43* (1948), 259–78.

Ross, S. "Sucking Behavior in Neonate Dogs," *Journal of Abnormal and Social Psychology, 46* (1951), 142–9.

Seeman, W. "The Freudian Theory of Daydreams: An Operational Analysis," *Psychological Bulletin, 48* (1951), 369–82.

Symonds, P. M. *The Dynamics of Human Adjustment.* New York, 1946. Chaps. viii–ix, pp. 192–220.

Werner, H. "Abnormal and Subnormal Rigidity," *Journal of Abnormal and Social Psychology, 41* (1946), 15–24.

Werner, H. "The Concept of Rigidity: A Critical Evaluation," *Psychological Review, 53* (1946), 43–52.

Whiting, J. W. M. and Mowrer, O. H. "Habit Progression and Regression: a Laboratory Study of Some Factors Relevant to Human Socialization," in *Personality in Nature, Society, and Culture,* C. Kluckhohn and H. A. Murray, eds. New York, 1948. Pp. 315–24.

CHAPTER Ten

Perceptual Identification
(Symbolism)

. . . "identity," defined as "absolute sameness," necessitates "absolute sameness" in "all" aspects, never to be found in this world, nor in our heads.[1]

THE PROCESS of perceptual identification may function on the one hand to render adjustment possible, and on the other hand to render adjustment difficult for the individual. Like other defensive processes, this identification process is complexly interrelated with other personality functions.

DEFINITION

FREUD used the term *identification* to imply either of two clearly distinguishable processes. One of these processes involves the perception of identity among different (nonidentical) stimuli, and will hereafter be termed *perceptual identification*. The other process involves the development of characteristics similar to those of an admired

[1] Alfred Korzybski, *Science and Sanity* (Lakeville, Conn., 1948), p. 194. Reprinted by permission of The Alfred Korzybski Estate. Copyright, 1933, 1941, 1948, by Alfred Korzybski.

or respected model, and will hereafter be termed *developmental identification*.[2] The latter process will be discussed in Chap. XI.

The term *perceptual identification* refers to the process of interpreting two or more objects or events as if they were identical. Perceptual identification, in other words, involves imputing to different stimuli, which are in fact not identical, an equivalent (identical or nearly identical) meaning.[3] Whenever two processes, two objects, two symbols, a symbol and an object, etc., are interpreted as having identical value for the satisfaction or frustration of an active motivational pattern, perceptual identification may be said to occur.

This identification process may also be termed *symbolism*, since when it occurs a word, an object, a person, or a situation will be symbolic of—"stand for," or represent—another word, object, person, or situation.

OBJECTS INVOLVED IN PERCEPTUAL IDENTIFICATION

ANYTHING that resembles another object, or anything that has in experience been associated with another object, may be perceived as equivalent to this other object. Perceptual identification is not, of course, dependent on objective identities; if such were the case, perceptual identification could not occur, since no two objects or events can ever be truly said to be identical with each other.

The occurrence of perceptual identification is dependent on a failure to direct attention to differences between the objects that are perceived as equivalent to each other. Often perceptual identification will occur with respect to stimuli that exhibit very obvious differences.

The possibilities for perceptual identification include (1) identification of two external objects, (2) identification of the self with another person or object, and (3) identification of the self with a group.

Identification of Two External Objects

Any two things external to the self may be identified with each other. The individual may identify one word with another word, one

[2] Mowrer uses the term "developmental identification" with a less general meaning than this. The term "perceptual identification" has not previously been used in psychological discussions. (O. Hobart Mowrer, *Learning Theory and Personality Dynamics* [New York, 1950], pp. 590–6.)

[3] The use of the term "equivalent stimuli," as employed by investigators of animal behavior, implies that animals manifest perceptual identification when they fail to discriminate between nonidentical stimuli. The stimuli may be regarded as equivalent from the animal's point of view, since the animal's behavior in relation to them is approximately identical.

object with another object, one person with another person, one situation with another situation, a word with an object, person, or situation, an object with a person or situation, and so on. Almost anything may "stand for," represent, or symbolize almost anything else.

To one person, "woman" and "shrew" may have the same meaning; to another, any word that symbolizes a "dirty" object may itself be "dirty"; to still another, a statue may be the object of as much reverence as is the person it represents; to still another, the mother-in-law may be identified with the wife. Similar behavior will occur with reference to identified words, objects, persons, or situations.

Identification of Self with Another Person or Object

Anything the individual regards as "his own"—anything he protects from injury or toward which he expresses an attitude of loyalty—may be regarded as an object he has identified with himself. Allport has used the term "extension of the self" to refer to the perceptual identification of the self with an ever increasing number of persons and objects.[4]

The individual may identify himself with his material possessions, protecting them with the same devotion he would display in protecting himself against danger. Perhaps more frequently, the individual will identify himself with other persons—for example, members of his family—protecting them and looking after their welfare, remaining loyal to them in sickness and in health, and grieving at their disappointments and injuries.

Identification of Self with a Group

Just as the individual may identify himself with other persons, he may likewise identify himself with a group. This may be a group in which he already has membership or a group in which he aspires to attain membership status. When the individual identifies himself with a group, he will regard the successes and failures of the group as *his own* successes and failures.

Freud has distinguished between two types of emotional ties occurring among men—namely, between love and perceptual identification.[5] It is possible, however, that there is no clear dichotomy between love and perceptual identification: to the extent that one loves oneself

---

[4] Gordon W. Allport, *Personality: a Psychological Interpretation* (New York, 1937), pp. 217–20.
[5] Sigmund Freud, *Collected Papers* (London, 1950), V, 284.

(narcissism), one will love those persons and groups with whom one is perceptually identified.

FORMS OF EXPRESSION

THE VARIETY of perceptual identifications that may occur is almost as wide as the variety of stimuli that are involved in perception. As we have previously noted, any two objects may be identified with each other, provided that they exhibit some similarity, or provided that they have been associated in experience. The present treatment will be limited to a few of the common forms of behavior involving perceptual identification.

Language

It is, of course, common knowledge that words may "stand for" objects, processes, and relationships that occur in nature. Words are useful to adjustment, to the extent that they have ascertainable reference to processes observable in nature. But there are many words—such as "pixie," "brownie," "elf," "goblin"—that have no such natural reference. Whenever an individual behaves as if he believed in the occurrence of natural referents for these words, he will obviously be manifesting a maladjustive perceptual identification. Likewise, when the individual reacts strongly to the "four-letter words" that refer to sexual and excretory functions, he will be identifying symbols with the processes that are symbolized.[6]

Patriotic and Religious Symbols

There are a number of patriotic and religious symbols—the flag, the Bible, etc.—toward which everybody is expected to manifest an attitude of respect or devotion. These are symbols conventionally iden-

---

[6] Perceptual identification is involved in the confusion of different levels of abstraction—confusion of a word with the object it symbolizes, confusion of a description with an inference, etc. When a parent says, "You are naughty," on an occasion when one aspect of the child's behavior is troublesome, the parent identifies one instance of behavior with the child's whole personality. When an individual identifies the name "David Miller" with the word "Jew"—that is, when he identifies a unique personality with a stereotyped abstraction—he will behave toward the unique personality as he has been accustomed to behave toward the stereotyped abstraction. Evidently consciousness of abstraction, as this has been discussed by Korzybski, involves the avoidance of perceptual identification; it involves, in other words, the direction of attention to differences that occur among stimuli, in cases where such differences are relevant for adjustment.

tified with the institutions for which they stand. For many people it is unthinkable that one could show disrespect for one of the symbols and at the same time feel a sincere respect for the institution it represents.

This manifestation of perceptual identification is so ingrained in our culture that the individual's patriotism and his religious attitudes are often judged mainly in terms of his behavior toward the symbols; if he demonstrates respect for the flag and for the Bible, he may, without further evidence, be regarded as a loyal American who "lives up to" high ethical ideals.

Sympathy

Sympathy involves a perceptual identification of the self with another person. To be sympathetic with another person involves feeling as he feels: his happiness, his success, his misery, his melancholy will be experienced as if it were one's own.

Pity differs from sympathy in that pity involves the *avoidance* of perceptual identification; the pitied object is regarded as inferior to and different from oneself.

Production and Enjoyment of Literature

The writer often identifies with the characters he creates; his conscious or unconscious needs may gain symbolic fulfillment through their behavior. The reader's enjoyment of literature may be dependent on his identification with the author or with one or more of the characters. This principle is embodied in the use of the Thematic Apperception Test and similar projective tests of personality.

Freud has made the following statement regarding the perceptual identification of Dostoevsky with his characters:

> Dostoevsky's sympathy for the criminal is, in fact, boundless; it goes far beyond the pity which the unhappy wretch might claim. . . . A criminal is to him almost a Redeemer, who has taken on himself the guilt which must else have been borne by others. There is no longer any need for one to murder, since *he* has already murdered; and one must be grateful to him, for, except for him, one would have been obliged oneself to murder. That is not just kindly pity, it is identification on the basis of a similar murderous impulse. . . . There is no doubt that this sympathy by identification was a decisive factor in determining Dostoevsky's choice of material.[7]

[7] Freud, *Collected Papers*, V, 237.

Numerous psychological studies have been concerned with an attempt to discover the unconscious motivation of authors, on the basis of the hypothesis that authors identify (perceptually) with their characters.[8]

Dramatic Impersonation

Actors, like authors, often identify with the characters whom they portray. In order to act a role convincingly, the actor must "be" the character he impersonates; he must "live" his part. The following excerpt from a statement by Ethel Waters provides a clear illustration of this principle.

> *Mamba's Daughters* . . . was . . . a play ripped out of the life I'd always known and was still living. . . . I was Hagar that night. . . . And I had shown them all what it is to be a colored woman, dumb, ignorant, all boxed up and feeling everything with such intenseness that she is half crazy. . . . Playing in *Mamba's Daughters* enabled me to rid myself of the terrible inward pressure, the flood of tears I'd been storing up ever since my childhood.[9]

In the same book, Miss Waters has shown that women who saw *Mamba's Daughters* frequently identified with the main character in the play. "In their mind's eye I was transformed into Hagar." Women who saw the play would come backstage to tell Miss Waters about their troubles with men; but they would come to see Hagar rather than to see the actress who played the role. Miss Waters felt it necessary to remain in her stage clothes, so that these women would not be disillusioned.

Humor

Freud has suggested that the humorous attitude toward others and toward oneself may be accounted for in terms of perceptual identification: ". . . the humorist acquires his superiority by assuming the role of the grown-up, identifying himself to some extent with the father, while he reduces the other people to the position of children."[10]

When this humorous attitude is adopted in relation to the self, the

---

[8] Lawrence I. O'Kelly (*Introduction to Psychopathology* [New York, 1949], p. 512) has provided an excellent description of the role of perceptual identification from the point of view of the reader's enjoyment.

[9] Ethel Waters and Charles Samuels, *His Eye Is on the Sparrow* (Garden City, 1951), pp. 239–50. Reprinted by permission of Doubleday and Company, Inc. Copyright, 1950, 1951, by Ethel Waters and Charles Samuels.

[10] Freud, *Collected Papers*, V, 218.

individual's superego is identified with the father, while his ego is identified with the child. "To the super-ego, thus inflated, the ego can appear tiny and all its interests trivial. . . ." [11]

Dream Symbolism

The manifest content of dreams—what is actually experienced during dreams—was believed by Freud to consist of symbols representative of unconscious wishes. The function of the dream was believed to be that of providing symbolic gratification for otherwise frustrated wishes or motives. Such wish-fulfillment involves perceptual identification: the symbol of gratification is unconsciously perceived as identical with actual gratification.

While in any particular instance of dream interpretation the free associations of the dreamer should be relied on as much as possible for the interpretation of dream symbols, Freud believed that many symbols are quite generally used with similar meaning by different persons.[12]

The following excerpt provides an indication of what is meant by dream symbolism.

The number of things which are represented symbolically in dreams is not great. The human body as a whole, parents, children, brothers and sisters, birth, death, nakedness—and one thing more. The only typical . . . representation of the human form as a whole is that of a *house*. . . . People have dreams of climbing down the front of a house, with feelings sometimes of pleasure and sometimes of dread. When the walls are quite smooth, the house means a man; when there are ledges and balconies which can be caught hold of, a woman. Parents appear in dreams as *emperor* and *empress*, *king* and *queen* or other exalted personages. . . . Children and brothers and sisters are . . . symbolized by *little animals* or *vermin*. Birth is almost invariably represented by some reference to *water*. . . . For dying we have setting out upon a *journey* or *travelling* . . . *clothes* and *uniforms* stand for nakedness. . . . An overwhelming majority of symbols in dreams are sexual symbols. A curious disproportion arises thus, for the matters dealt with are few in number, whereas the symbols for them are extraordinarily numerous. . . . In the first place, the sacred number *three* is symbolic of the whole male genitalia. Its more conspicuous . . . part

[11] *Ibid.*, p. 219.
[12] Sigmund Freud, *A General Introduction to Psycho-Analysis* (New York, 1935), p. 135.

*. . . is symbolized . . . by objects . . . such as sticks, umbrellas,
poles, trees . . . knives, daggers, lances, sabres . . . guns, pistols*
and *revolvers . . . taps, watering cans,* or *springs . . . pulley
lamps, pencils which slide in and out of a sheath . . . pencils, pen-
holders, nail-files, hammers,* and other *implements.* . . . Male sexual symbols less easy to understand are certain *reptiles* and *fishes;*
above all, the famous symbol of the *serpent.* Why *hats* and *cloaks*
are used in the same way is certainly difficult to divine. . . . The
female genitalia are symbolically represented by all such objects as
share with them the property of enclosing a space or are capable
of acting as receptacles: such as *pits, hollows* and *caves,* and also
jars and *bottles,* and *boxes* of all sorts and sizes, *chests, coffers,
pockets,* and so forth. *Ships* too come into this category. . . .
Moreover, material of different kinds is a symbol of woman,—
wood, paper, and objects made of these, such as *tables* and *books.*
. . . The breasts . . . are represented by *apples, peaches,* and *fruit*
in general. . . . Many symbols stand for sexual organs in general,
whether male or female: for instance, a *little* child, or a *little* son
or daughter.[13]

The symbolism of dreams is complicated by the processes of *condensation* and *displacement.* Condensation involves the representation
of several different elements of "dream thoughts" by means of a single
symbol. Displacement involves a shift of emotional emphasis from an
element of the dream to which it appropriately belongs to some other
element of little importance. Thus, upon awaking, the dreamer will be
puzzled at his having experienced strong anxiety or great joy in relation
to something of little importance, or he will be bewildered at having
dreamed of some emotionally significant event without having experienced any feeling in relation to it.

Magic

Belief in the validity of magic procedures involves perceptual identification. Such procedures consist in doing something in relation to
symbols, with the belief that the processes or objects the symbols represent will undergo a similar fate. For example, an effigy may be
hanged, burned, or otherwise injured, with the faith that the person so
represented will suffer a similar injury.

[13] *Ibid.,* pp. 136–40.

Freud has described a number of different magic procedures, all of which involve identification of symbols with the things symbolized.[14] These include: committing an aggression against anything the enemy has discarded—for example, his hair or a part of his clothing—with the expectation that the enemy will suffer in a like manner; imitating clouds and rain in the hope that this activity will induce rain; showing the fields "the spectacle of human sexual intercourse" in order to increase the soil's fertility; avoiding the meat of certain animals in order to prevent an unborn child from developing the characteristics of such animals; "spitting on the hand which has caused an injury if one regrets having injured someone"; etc.

According to Erikson, the Yurok, who lives on the Klamath River and who is dependent on salmon fishing, "attempts to keep all tube-like things within and around him unobstructed and all fluid-ways uncontaminated," in order to insure that the river will continue to provide "an inviting waterway for the energetic salmon." [15]

Magic procedures are not, as is commonly believed, necessarily limited to the behavior of primitive peoples. There are, for example, people in our own culture who believe that one should plant potatoes on Good Friday if one wishes to make sure that they will "come up." In a similar connection, Freud has stated that

. . . our philosophy has preserved essential traits of animistic modes of thought such as the overestimation of the magic of words and the belief that real processes in the external world follow the lines laid down by our thoughts.[16]

The use of magical procedures, then, involves perceptual identification. Although these procedures are employed more widely among primitive peoples, they continue to influence the thinking processes of the most "enlightened." There are many among us who believe that "wishing will make it so."

[14] Sigmund Freud, "Totem and Taboo," in *The Basic Writings of Sigmund Freud*, A. A. Brill, ed. (New York, 1938), pp. 868–71.

[15] Erik H. Erikson, "Childhood and Tradition in two American Indian Tribes," in *Personality in Nature, Society, and Culture*, Clyde Kluckhohn and Henry A. Murray, eds. (New York, 1948), p. 185. (Reprinted from *The Psychoanalytic Study of the Child* [New York, 1945], Vol. I.) Reprinted by permission of International Universities Press, Inc., and Alfred A. Knopf, Inc. Copyright, 1945, by International Universities Press, Inc., 1948, by Alfred A. Knopf, Inc.

[16] Sigmund Freud, *New Introductory Lectures on Psycho-Analysis* (New York, 1933), p. 226.

Symptomatic Actions and Neurotic Symptoms

Symbolic acts that are carried out by "normal" people—acts representative of some unconscious or preconscious idea—are termed *symptomatic actions*. Freud has cited the following instructive example:

> I dined in a restaurant with my colleague . . . a doctor of philosophy. He spoke about the injustice done to probationary students, and added that even before he finished his studies, he was placed as secretary to the ambassador . . . to Chile. "But," he added, "the minister was afterwards transferred, and I did not make any effort to meet the newly appointed." While uttering the last sentence, he was lifting a piece of pie to his mouth, but he let it drop as if out of awkwardness. I immediately grasped the hidden sense of this symptomatic action, and remarked to my colleague, who was unacquainted with psychoanalysis, "You really allowed a very choice morsel to slip from you." He did not realize, however, that my words could equally refer to his symptomatic action, and he repeated the same words I uttered as if I had actually taken the words from his mouth: "It was really a very choice morsel that I allowed to get away from me." He then followed this remark with a detailed description of his clumsiness which had cost him this very remunerative position.[17]

Neurotic symptoms, like dreams, were believed by Freud to function as wish-fulfillments.[18] The patient is said to identify his symptoms with actions that would in reality provide gratification. In phobias, for example, fear may be manifested in relation to an animal symbolic of the dreaded father; in obsessions the patient may be preoccupied with something that actually is trivial, but that symbolizes something highly significant; compulsive ritualistic actions may represent the process of gratifying some repressed (often sexual) impulse. As Freud has expressed it, "the original (intolerable) idea has been replaced by another idea, the substituted idea." [19] Such substitution involves perceptual identification of the original idea with the substituted idea.

[17] Sigmund Freud, "Psychopathology of Everyday Life," in *The Basic Writings of Sigmund Freud*, A. A. Brill, ed. (New York, 1938), p. 137. Reprinted by permission of Ernest Benn, Ltd. and The Macmillan Company. Copyright, 1930, by The Macmillan Company, 1938, by Random House, Inc.

[18] Freud, *A General Introduction* . . . , p. 320.

[19] Sigmund Freud, *Collected Papers* (London, 1950), I, 132.

The following example provides an especially clear illustration of the symbolism that may be embodied in a symptom:

> For a long time she used to repeat a very curious and senseless obsessive act. She ran out of her room into the next, in the middle of which stood a table with a cloth upon it. This she pulled straight in a particular manner, rang for the housemaid, who had to approach the table, and then sent her off again on some indifferent errand. During her efforts to explain this compulsion it occurred to her that at one place on the tablecloth there was a stain and that she always arranged the cloth so that the housemaid was bound to see it. The whole scene proved to be a reproduction of an incident in her marriage. On the wedding-night her husband had met with a not unusual mishap. He found himself impotent, and "many times in the course of the night came hurrying from his room to hers" in order to try again. In the morning he said he would be shamed in the eyes of the hotel chambermaid who made the bed, so he took a bottle of red ink and poured its contents over the sheet; but he did it so clumsily that the stain came in a place most unsuitable for his purpose. With her obsessive act, therefore, she was reproducing the bridal night.[20]

In neurotic symptoms, then, the patient manifests actions symbolic of (perceptually identified with) actions that if actually carried out would function either to gratify or to frustrate the individual's impulses. Sometimes—perhaps usually—the symptom or symptoms will be representative of both the gratification and the frustration of such impulses; the symptoms, that is, will embody a compromise formation.

Delusions and Hallucinations

In so-called delusions of grandeur the patient may believe that he is Napoleon, or Jesus, or some other important personage. It is obvious that in such instances the patient has identified himself (perceptually) with the important personage he supposes himself to be.

Hallucinations involve the perceptual identification of images with sensory impressions, or the identification of "memory traces" with stimuli that arise from external sources. The person who "hears voices" or "sees visions" is perceiving internal stimuli as if they had originated outside himself.

[20] Sigmund Freud, *Collected Papers* (London, 1950), II, 29.

DYNAMIC RELATIONS WITH ANXIETY

PERCEPTUAL identification may be based on, and provide some relief of, pre-existing anxiety; and it may function as a basis for the development of subsequent anxiety.

Anxiety as a Basis of Perceptual Identification

Whenever an individual meets with frustration that he feels unable to overcome through his own efforts, he may resort to perceptual identification as a source of renewed strength and confidence. When, for example, the little boy finds himself in a fight with an adversary too powerful for him to master, he may boast: "My daddy can lick your daddy." Name-calling, which may also occur in such a situation, involves identifying the adversary with inferior classes of people, or with members of a subhuman species.

The chronically frustrated person may gain some relief by identifying himself with a group that successfully gratifies needs similar to his own; or he may gain relief by identifying with the characters of fiction, with historical figures, etc. By sharing vicariously in their successes, he may keep the intensity of his own frustrations within the limit of his tolerance.

HUMOR. The frustrated, the persecuted, and the chronically tormented may gain some relief through humor. The humorous story, as we have seen, involves identifying oneself with a person of superior status while identifying the "butt" of the story with a person of inferior status.

Through this medium, the individual can experience a temporary feeling of superiority in relation to his persecutors. Thus, students often enjoy stories that ridicule their professors; enlisted men appreciate stories relating to officers; employees like stories about their employers; members of minority groups are gratified by stories concerning the dominant regime; etc.

The humorous story, on the basis of the temporary feeling of superiority, provides a medium for the expression of aggression that cannot be expressed under ordinary circumstances. The following example will illustrate this function of humor among the oppressed:

In Prague they ask each other, "Did you hear about the two Communist officials . . . ?" It seems that two high Party executives were staring moodily across St. Wenceslaus Square at the end of a trying day of carrying out directives from Moscow.

"What do you think of the future of our beloved country under Communism?" one asked.

"The same as you do," replied the other.

"Oh, you do?" said the first. "In that case, Comrade, I shall have to report you immediately to the State Police!" [21]

IDENTIFICATION WITH AN AGGRESSOR. Individuals who cannot "fight back" in response to punishing social frustrations may identify (perceptually) with the aggressor. This process has been described at length by Anna Freud.[22] Identification with an aggressor is usually manifested as an impersonation: "By impersonating the aggressor, assuming his attributes or imitating his aggression, the child transforms himself from the person threatened into the person who makes the threat." [23]

Perceptual Identification as a Basis of Anxiety

While perceptual identification may have its origin in frustration and anxiety, and while it may bring about some relief of pre-existing anxiety, it may also function as a basis for subsequent anxiety.

PARENTAL IDENTIFICATION WITH CHILDREN. Parents frequently identify (perceptually) with their children: they "see" themselves in their children. This may be the basis of the anxiety parents experience when their children are unable or unwilling to "live up to" the parental standards. The parent is unable to tolerate in these little replicas of himself any behavior that conflicts with his (the parent's) ego-ideal or conscience motivation. "Having been taught to despise and abhor certain impulses in themselves, they will be angered or made anxious by manifestations of these impulses in the children for whom they are responsible." [24]

The occurrence of perceptual identification may be responsible for the fact that children's superego motives develop along the lines laid

[21] Richard Hanser, "Cracks Behind the Curtain," *The Reader's Digest* (December, 1950), pp. 130–1. Reprinted by permission of *The Freeman* and *The Reader's Digest.* Copyright, 1950, by The Freeman Magazine, Inc., and The Reader's Digest Association, Inc.

[22] Anna Freud, *The Ego and the Mechanisms of Defense* (New York, 1946), pp. 117–31.

[23] *Ibid.,* p. 121.

[24] O. Hobart Mowrer and Clyde Kluckhohn, "Dynamic Theory of Personality," in *Personality and the Behavior Disorders,* J. McV. Hunt, ed. (New York, 1944), p. 130.

down by the parents' own superego motives. The child's expression of impulses that conflict with the parents' standards can be the occasion of as much anxiety to the parents as if the parents' own behavior were involved. Since the child's "naughty" behavior and his "failures" will frustrate the parents' superego motives, the child will be punished on just those occasions when his behavior deviates from the parents' standards.

MARITAL FRUSTRATION ARISING FROM PERCEPTUAL IDENTIFICATION. It is a common observation that a marriage may become frustrating to the participants when their first child is born. One of the sources of this frustration may be that, now for the first time, the husband begins to identify his wife with his mother, and the wife begins to identify her husband with her father. "When this happens, the incest tabu of childhood is reactivated, with an ensuing inhibition of sexuality of more or less serious proportions." [25] Such inhibition of sexuality will function to disturb the harmony of the marital relationship.

IDENTIFICATION OF COMRADE WITH FATHER OR BROTHER. A source of severe conflict among combat personnel involves the identification of a comrade with the father or the brother. When a soldier's comrade is killed in battle, he may suffer from severe guilt or depression, and feel that he was responsible for his comrade's death. "Uncovering techniques quickly expose the fact that Joe, who was killed in battle, was only a current edition of a competitive brother, toward whom the patient had much unconscious hostility." [26]

In terms of an unconscious identification, the soldier who has lost his comrade in battle may feel guilty and depressed, just as he would feel if he had lost his brother or his father, toward whom he had directed ambivalent attitudes of love and hostility.

How the loss of a loved (and hated) person may be the source of guilt and depression will become clear in the following section.

IDENTIFICATION OF SELF WITH A LOST LOVE-OBJECT. When the individual must renounce a love-object, through the latter's death or through the latter's failure to reciprocate the love directed onto him, the individual who suffers such a loss will often identify himself with the renounced love-object.

But love-objects are usually the objects of *ambivalent* attitudes—the objects of hostility as well as of love—since they usually serve as

[25] *Ibid.*, p. 130.
[26] Roy R. Grinker and John P. Spiegel, *Men under Stress* (Philadelphia, 1945), p. 361.

frustrating agents in some respects and as the agents of gratification in other respects. When the individual identifies himself with a lost love-object, he himself becomes the object of his own hostility as well as the object of his own love. "The ego itself is . . . treated as though it were the abandoned object; it suffers all the revengeful and aggressive treatment which is designed for the object." [27] The individual, that is to say, *displaces* his ambivalent attitude from the love-object onto himself.

In the case of "normal" grief, the individual will usually reproach himself partly on the basis of his identification with the lost love-object, and partly on the basis of a magical belief that his hostile wishes have been responsible for the loved one's death. Such a magical belief, as we have seen, also involves perceptual identification: the thought is identified with the deed.

INTERRELATIONS WITH OTHER DEFENSES

PERCEPTUAL identification may function as a necessary basis for displacement and projection, which are to be discussed in subsequent chapters. The present section will deal with some of the interrelations between perceptual identification and the processes of suppression, repression, denial, fixation, and regression.

Suppression, Repression, and Denial

Suppression, repression, and denial are processes through which data are temporarily or permanently excluded from consciousness. The process of perceptual identification becomes possible by virtue of the perceptual neglect of differences between the self and another person, between the self and a group, or between two or more external symbols, objects, or processes. This neglect of differences involves the momentary suppression of knowledge regarding characteristics of the self, the repression of motives, or the denial of characteristics occurring in other persons, groups, or external situations.

The individual who can identify with the suffering religious martyr must suppress or repress the "wicked" impulses that function in himself but are not so apparent in the martyr; the adolescent girl who identifies with a movie actress must be forgetful of the fact that she lacks the beauty, the maturity, or the charm of the actress; the reader or playgoer who identifies with Hamlet must, at least temporarily, be

[27] Freud, *A General Introduction* . . . , p. 370.

unaware of his own lack of princely status and of the fact that nobody has recently killed his own father and married his own mother.

The operation of repressed motives may in many cases be at the basis of perceptual identification. The individual may be able to perceive his identity with another person, or with a group, by virtue of the fact that he (unconsciously) perceives the other person or group in the process of gratifying motives that he has repressed. He may identify with the aggressive soldier on the basis of his repressed hostility, or with some notorious reprobate on the basis of his repressed sexuality.

Fixation and Regression

A clear instance of the manifestation of fixation or regression in combination with perceptual identification is afforded by the hallucinatory dream experience. The dream involves regression to visual representation—a representation that the dreamer interprets as objectively real; and the symbolism of the dream involves a perceptual identification of the symbol with the object or process that is symbolized. Hallucinations, delusions, and neurotic symptoms likewise involve regression in combination with perceptual identification.

The worshipful attitude in relation to a religious symbol and the patriotic attitude in relation to the flag of one's country are attitudes of a regressive nature, in that they involve a childlike humility, resembling the attitude of a child in relation to his parent; at the same time, of course, these attitudes involve identifying the symbols with the concepts they symbolize.

ADJUSTIVE IMPLICATIONS

PERCEPTUAL identification is equivalent to a process of unconscious abstraction. That is to say, when perceptual identification occurs, two stimuli or two situations are perceived identically on the basis of some similar characteristic, while differences between the stimuli or between the situations are perceptually neglected.

Adjustment to the world would not be possible without the operation of this process of abstraction (this perceptual identification), since without its occurrence every new situation, being actually different from every previous one, would require a creative readjustment on the part of the individual. Every new situation would be perceived as a difficult problem.[28]

[28] For an excellent description of the adjustment difficulties that can occur on the basis of an *inability* to employ the process of abstraction, see Eugenia

With the occurrence of perceptual identification, the individual can adjust adequately to the routine circumstances of life through the economical procedure of selecting reactions that have proved adequate in previous situations that are similar in relevant respects. He can sit on chairs, write with pencils, read books, eat at tables, etc., that he has never previously seen, on the basis of his recognition that these are similar to (not *really* identical with) the chairs, the pencils, the books, and the tables he has used on previous occasions. Similarly, he can smile back at a stranger who smiles at him, even though the stranger's smile is different from every other smile he has previously seen. Were it not for this unconscious recognition of similarities—were it not for this process of abstraction or perceptual identification—every new smile would function as a difficult enigma, rather than as a stimulus for the ready establishment of a friendly human relationship.

On the other hand, Korzybski has pointed out that there are dangers to adjustment which follow from perceptual identification.[29] The chief danger, perhaps, lies in the possibility that identification may occur on the basis of irrelevant similarities. If, for example, an individual should try, as small children do, to eat the picture of a cake, he will not be able, in this manner, to achieve any relief of hunger. Although the picture may "look like" a cake, it cannot in fact *be* a cake. The identification can only be made on the basis of a similarity that is irrelevant from the standpoint of eating.

Since identifications can be, and often are, made on the basis of irrelevant similarities, Korzybski[30] has stressed the value of becoming conscious of abstracting—just as Freud has stressed the value of conscious functioning in general. When the individual abstracts *consciously*—when his conscious ego-functions operate effectively—the danger of his identifying on the basis of irrelevant similarities (and of his neglecting relevant differences) will be minimized.

Identification of the self with another person, or with a group, may likewise be considered essential to adequate adjustment; and it may also involve dangers to adjustment. The perception of the identity of one's needs and interests, or of the identity of one's goals, with those of another person or with those of a group will provide the necessary basis for co-operative social efforts. But if one identifies with the wrong per-

---

Hanfmann, Maria Rickers-Ovsiankina, and Kurt Goldstein, "Case Lanuti: Extreme Concretization of Behavior Due to Damage of the Brain Cortex," *Psychological Monographs*, 57, No. 4. (1944).

[29] Korzybski, *op. cit.*, pp. 412–25.

[30] *Ibid.*, pp. 412–25.

son or with the wrong group, the identification may function as a basis for co-operative efforts of a criminal or disreputable nature.

The recognition of relevant similarities between oneself and another person may be necessary, also, as a basis for developmental identification—that is, as a basis for becoming even more like the other person than one already is. In the interest of effective adjustment, however, perceptual identification should be discriminating; the perception of complete identity with another person, on the basis of some trivial similarity, may function as a deterrent to further development.

The man who is sure that he *is* Napoleon can recognize no need to improve himself; the women who cries in a movie on the basis of a feeling that she *is* the pathetic heroine has lost the desirable consciousness of abstraction which the literary critics refer to as "psychic distance"; the modern American who cannot look an Indian in the face, on the basis of a feeling that he *is* one of the white pioneers who displaced the Indians from their land, is, again, failing to discriminate in terms of relevant differences between himself and members of past generations; the parasitic scion of a hard-working father may feel that he *is* his father, and that the money he spends is an evidence of *his own* social value.

Perceptual identification, then, may be considered essential to adjustment when it is accompanied by sufficient consciousness of abstraction; but it must be considered detrimental to adjustment when it is based on attention to trivial similarities and on a failure to take account of relevant differences.

SUMMARY

THE PROCESSES of identification may be clarified by distinguishing between perceptual identification (interpreting objects, events, persons, etc., as if they were identical) and developmental identification (the development of behavior similar to that of another person or group of persons).

Perceptual identification (symbolism) is involved in language, in patriotic and religious symbols, in sympathy, in the production and enjoyment of literature, in dramatic impersonation, in humor, in dream symbolism, in magic, in symptomatic actions and neurotic symptoms, and in delusions and hallucinations. Any two stimuli that are in any detail similar to each other or that have been associated together in experience may become the objects of perceptual identification.

Anxiety may function as the basis of perceptual identification. When the individual is frustrated, he may gain vicarious gratification through identification with successful persons. He may also gain relief from anxiety through humor, and through perceptual identification with an aggressor.

Perceptual identification may, in turn, function as a source of anxiety. Parents may be frustrated by the behavior of a child with whom they identify. Each parent may, on the arrival of a child, identify the other with his own parent of opposite sex, thus reactivating the incest taboo in relation to his marriage partner. The identification of a comrade with a father or a brother may reactivate ambivalent attitudes that were originally directed to the father or to the brother. Grief and depression may arise through identification of the self with a lost love-object.

Perceptual identification manifests interrelations with other defensive processes. Identification is facilitated by repression, suppression, and denial; and many forms of behavior combine aspects of fixation and regression with aspects of perceptual identification.

Perceptual identification may be regarded as essential to adjustment, but it involves danger to adjustment in that identification may be based on irrelevant similarities between the processes, objects, or persons that are identified. This danger may be reduced through becoming conscious of abstraction.

The following chapter will deal with the defensive functions of developmental identification.

▶ Suggested Readings

Allport, G. W. *Personality: a Psychological Interpretation.* New York, 1937. Chap. x, pp. 259–85.

Allport, G. W. "The Psychology of Participation," *Psychological Review,* *52* (1945), 117–32.

Ammons, R. B. and Ammons, H. S. "Parent Preferences in Young Children's Doll-Play Interviews," *Journal of Abnormal and Social Psychology, 44* (1949), 490–505.

Blum, G. S. and Hunt, H. F. "The Validity of the Blacky Pictures," *Psychological Bulletin, 49* (1952), 238–50.

Cantril, H. "Identification with Social and Economic Class," *Journal of Abnormal and Social Psychology, 38* (1943), 74–80.

Cattell, R. B. "Principles of Design in 'Projective' or Misperception Tests of

Personality," in *An Introduction to Projective Techniques*, H. H. Anderson and Gladys L. Anderson, eds. (New York, 1951) Chap. iii, pp. 55–98.

Centers, R. "Nominal Variation and Class Identification: The Working and the Laboring Classes," *Journal of Abnormal and Social Psychology, 45* (1950), 195–215.

Dymond, Rosalind F. "A Scale for the Measurement of Emphatic Ability," *Journal of Consulting Psychology, 13* (1949), 127–33.

Dymond, Rosalind F. "Personality and Empathy," *Journal of Consulting Psychology, 14* (1950), 343–50.

Freud, Anna. *The Ego and the Mechanisms of Defense*. New York, 1946. Chap. ix, pp. 117–31.

Freud, S. "The Interpretation of Dreams," in *The Basic Writings of Sigmund Freud*, A. A. Brill, ed. New York, 1938. Chap. vi, 319–467.

Freud, S. "Psychopathology of Everyday Life," in *The Basic Writings of Sigmund Freud*, A. A. Brill, ed. New York, 1938. Chap. ix, pp. 129–40.

Freud, S. "Analysis of a Phobia in a Five-Year-Old Boy," *Collected Papers*. London, 1950. III, 149–289.

Freud, S. "The Occurrence in Dreams of Material from Fairy-Tales," *Collected Papers*. London, 1950. IV, 236–43.

Freud, S. "The Theme of the Three Caskets," *Collected Papers*. London, 1950. IV, 244–56.

Freud, S. *A General Introduction to Psycho-Analysis*. New York, 1935. Chaps. 10, 17, pp. 133–50, 228–41.

Freud, S. "Metapsychological Supplement to the Theory of Dreams," *Collected Papers*. London, 1950. IV, 137–51.

Freud, S. *Group Psychology and the Analysis of the Ego*. London, 1949. Chap. vii, pp. 60–70.

Freud, S. *New Introductory Lectures on Psycho-Analysis*. New York, 1933. Chap. i, pp. 15–46.

Fromm, E. *The Forgotten Language*. New York, 1951. Chaps. i–iii, pp. 3–46.

Greene, J. E. "Motivations of a Murderer," *Journal of Abnormal and Social Psychology, 43* (1948), 526–31.

Herma, H., Kris, E., and Shor, J. "Freud's Theory of the Dream in American Textbooks," *Journal of Abnormal and Social Psychology, 38* (1943), 319–34.

Johnson, W. *People in Quandaries*. New York, 1946. Chaps. v–vii, pp. 91–168.

Jones, E. "The Symbolic Significance of Salt in Folklore and Superstition," *Essays in Applied Psycho-Analysis*. London, 1951. II, 22–109.

Korzybski, A. *Science and Sanity*. Lakeville, Conn., 1948. Chap. vi, pp. 76–84.

Korzybski, A. "The Role of Language in the Perceptual Processes," in *Per-*

ception: an Approach to Personality, R. R. Blake and G. V. Ramsey, eds. New York, 1951. Chap. vii, 170–205.

Lassner, R. "Playwriting and Acting as Diagnostic-Therapeutic Techniques with Delinquents," *Journal of Clinical Psychology, 3* (1947), 349–56.

Lewin, K. *A Dynamic Theory of Personality.* New York, 1935. Chap. vi, pp. 180–93.

Meer, B. and Singer, J. L. "A Note on the 'Father' and 'Mother' Cards in the Rorschach Inkblots," *Journal of Consulting Psychology, 14* (1950), 482–84.

Mowrer, O. H. and Lamoreaux, R. R. "Conditioning and Conditionality (Discrimination)," *Psychological Review, 58* (1951), 196–212.

Murphy, G. *Personality: a Biosocial Approach to Origins and Structure.* New York, 1947. Chaps. xi, xvi, xvii, pp. 247–69, 391–432.

Pascal, G. R., Ruesch, H. A., Devine, C. A., and Suttell, B. J. "A Study of Genital Symbols on the Rorschach Test: Presentation of a Method and Results," *Journal of Abnormal and Social Psychology, 45* (1950), 286–95.

Rapoport, A. *Science and the Goals of Man.* New York, 1950. Chap. viii, pp. 62–9.

Rosen, E. "Symbolic Meanings in the Rorschach Cards: a Statistical Study," *Journal of Clinical Psychology, 7* (1951), 239–44.

Sanford, R. N. "Identification with the Enemy: a Case Study of an American Quisling," *Journal of Personality, 15* (1946), 53–8.

Sechehaye, M. A. *Symbolic Realization.* New York, 1951. Pp.17–143.

Sherif, M. *An Outline of Social Psychology.* New York, 1948. Chap. xii, pp. 282–313.

Stekel, W. *How to Understand Your Dreams.* New York, 1951. Pp. 1–298.

White, R. W. "Interpretation of Imaginative Productions," in *Personality and the Behavior Disorders*, J. McV. Hunt, ed. New York, 1944. Chap. vi, pp. 214–51.

CHAPTER Eleven

Developmental Identification (Introjection)

. . . when a boy identifies himself with his father, he wants to be like his father . . . his ego is altered on the model of his father. . . .[1]

THE PROCESS of developmental identification accounts, in large part, for the humanization of the individual; it accounts for the development of superego motivation, for the development of many human skills, and for the enrichment of personality. But this humanization is not without its heavy cost to the individual; it complicates his life by laying the foundation for many conflicts that could not occur in the presocialized, id-dominated child.

DEFINITION AND DIFFERENTIATION

DEVELOPMENTAL identification implies a process of personality growth—a process of socialization and humanization; as such, it must be differentiated from perceptual identification, which was treated in the preceding chapter.

Development Identification

The term *developmental identification* implies the development of behavior—especially the development of motivation—similar to that of

[1] Sigmund Freud, *New Introductory Lectures on Psycho-Analysis* (New York, 1933), pp. 90–1.

another person or group of persons. This identification process, in other words, involves a genuine tendency to become, in major or minor respects, like some other person or group of persons.

The terms *introjection* and *introception* may be regarded as synonymous with the term developmental identification. The term *imitation* should probably be reserved to imply *conscious* attempts to become like another person, while the term developmental identification may imply either conscious or unconscious tendencies to become like an admired or respected model. Indeed many of the significant aspects of an individual's adult personality must be accounted for in terms of the *unconscious* operation of developmental identification (introjection or introception).

Objects Involved in Developmental Identification

Any person or group, whether real or fictitious, may function as a model for developmental identification. This identification may be based on admiration, on love, or on the ambivalent attitude of respect (love and fear). The individual will emulate a person or group whom he perceives to be successful in gratifying needs that are similar to his own; he will try to become like those whom he loves but cannot have, in order that his narcissism may function in terms of their lovable qualities; and he will adopt the motivation of respected individuals— for example, parents—and groups in order to avoid their displeasure, or in order to avoid punishment.

IDENTIFICATION WITH ANOTHER PERSON. The development of psychogenic motivation (superego motivation) involves the process of introjection or developmental identification. It seems probable that *negative* psychogenic motives (conscience motives) must develop on the basis of the ambivalent attitude of respect for the model; once developed, these negative motives will function to protect the individual from punishment and disapproval. It seems probable, on the other hand, that *positive* psychogenic motives (ego-ideals) must develop on the basis of admiration or love for the model; once developed, these positive motives will render possible the perceptual identification of the self with the model, so that the individual may perceive in himself some of the qualities of the admired model or love-object.[2]

[2] O. Hobart Mowrer, *Learning Theory and Personality Dynamics: Selected Papers* (New York, 1950), pp. 590–6, has called the former process (identification on the basis of respect) "defensive identification" and has called the latter process (identification on the basis of admiration or love) "developmental identification." In the present treatment, developmental identification is employed as a general term to imply both of these processes.

IDENTIFICATION WITH A GROUP. The individual may identify developmentally with a group in which he has membership or in which he aspires to attain membership. The development of group standards, group attitudes, group values, group ideals, etc., will help the individual to participate in the group's activities and to maintain the group's approval. If the individual belongs to a church, for example, he may develop its special standards—possibly avoid card-playing, smoking, drinking, or dancing, even though parental discipline may never have been concerned with these particular aspects of his behavior.

To the extent that the individual identifies developmentally with the group, he may come to identify with it *perceptually;* he may acquire a "sense of belonging," or begin to perceive himself as a genuine member of the group, feeling that he can share in its special privileges and responsibilities.

Developmental Identification as Distinguished from Perceptual Identification

It should be apparent that perceptual identification and developmental identification are distinctly different concepts, referring to distinctly different processes.

Perceptual identification involves identity among perceptions; two or more objects are interpreted as equivalent in meaning. On the basis of perceptual equivalence, equivalent behavior will occur. For example, if the word "spit" is perceived as equivalent to actual spit, the word will seem as abhorrent as the spit itself.

Developmental identification may be dependent on the initial perception of a *difference* between the self and the model; then, as the individual becomes more and more like the model, the process may terminate in perceptual identification of the self and the model. If, for example, a boy perceives a difference between himself and his father, a process of developmental identification may be initiated, so that the boy will become more and more like his father; this process may continue until another model is substituted for the father or until perceptual identification occurs.

The two identification processes may be distinguished in terms of the fact that perceptual identification primarily involves *perception* (interpretation), while developmental identification primarily involves *learning;* however, just as perception and learning are invariably interrelated, so also are the two processes of identification.

FORMS OF EXPRESSION

THROUGH developmental identification, the individual becomes socialized; he develops skills that will be useful to him in a variety of situations; and he develops a complex personality, derived from many sources.

Socialization

Socialization refers to the development of values that are maintained in a given society.

> . . . it is chiefly the traditional patterns which parents and educators, policemen and judges, and, indeed, all socially responsible adults, as carriers of the culture, are *expected* to uphold and to teach, by example, by persuasion, and by an accepted, culturally defined system of rewards and punishments. The process of inculcating and learning these patterns, until they become "second nature," is termed "socialization." [3]

The development of superego functions (psychogenic motives) is implied by the term socialization; and ". . . the establishment of the super-ego can be described as a successful instance of identification with the parental function." [4] To the extent, then, that the individual develops functions (especially motives) like those of the parents, he may be said to become socialized—provided, of course, that the parents are themselves typical representatives of their culture.

If the individual conforms only on the basis of fear, without having developed motives that are consistent with the behavior demanded of him, he may resent the necessity of conforming. "A high degree of repressed resentment is," according to Kluckhohn and Murray, "indicative of a fundamental emotional maladjustment, and, hence, of the partial failure of the socialization process, regardless of how successful the individual may be in 'winning friends and influencing people.' " [5]

Development of Skills

The development of skills involves identification; the individual aims at becoming as able as his model to deal with features of reality.

[3] Clyde Kluckhohn and Henry A. Murray, eds., *Personality in Nature, Society, and Culture* (New York, 1948), p. 23.
[4] Freud, *New Introductory Lectures* . . . , p. 91.
[5] Kluckhohn and Murray, *op. cit.*, p. 25.

Social skills are especially dependent on developmental identification; the individual learns how to smile, how to give an impression of personal warmth, how to speak with tact and courtesy, how to walk, how to dress, etc., through his observation of the manner in which admired persons perform these actions.

The children of happily married parents, for instance, are more likely than the children of unhappily married parents to become themselves happily married, since they will have developed, through identification, some of the attitudes, skills, and personal qualities of the parents. Learning how to "get along with people" is largely based on the presence of models who are themselves able to demonstrate this skill.

The educative process, both in its formal and in its informal aspects, can be seen to depend upon identification with persons who already have the kind of knowledge and skills the individual desires to attain. Or, more correctly, both the individual's desire for, and his procedure of attaining, knowledge and skills will depend upon such identification.

The parent in whose footsteps the child follows, and the teacher who has the most enduring influence upon the pupil or student, must be one whom the child, the pupil, or the student can admire and respect; he must be one whom the young person, of his own accord, can choose as a worthy model for emulation.

Enrichment of Personality

The development of a richly unique personality is a function of the fact that many different models are alternately, and successively, involved in identification. If only one model—for example, one parent—were involved, personalities would "run in families" to a much greater extent than they are known to do; in other words, the world would become populated with monotonous "chips off the old block." The concept of "like father, like son" would become a source of ennui, rather than continuing to be a rare source of pride to the narcissistic parent.

To be sure, the parents are usually the *first* models for developmental identification. But there characteristically occurs some disillusionment, which motivates the child to identify with other persons.

> For a small child his parents are at first the only authority and the source of all belief. The child's most intense and most momentous wish during these early years is to be like his parents (that is, the parent of his own sex) and to be big like his father and mother.

But as intellectual growth increases, the child cannot help discovering by degrees the category to which his parents belong. He gets to know other parents and compares them with his own, and so comes to doubt the incomparable and unique quality which he has attributed to them. Small events in the child's life which make him feel dissatisfied afford him provocation for beginning to criticize his parents, and for using, in order to support his critical attitude, the knowledge . . . that other parents are in some respects preferable to them.[6]

We may suppose that, just as the child becomes disillusioned with respect to his parents, he will become disillusioned with respect to his successive models of the future. Thus his personality, in the end, will be built upon the basis of a long series of identifications; in some respects he will be like his parents, in some respects like each of several admired or respected teachers, in some respects like the different heroes he has encountered in fiction, biography, the movies, etc., in some respects like ministers, doctors, or other respected people in his community, and so forth. Since his personality has been derived from so many different sources, it will be a complex and unique organization, both interesting to other people and difficult for him to integrate.

DYNAMIC INTERRELATIONS WITH ANXIETY

DEVELOPMENTAL identification occurs on the basis of anxiety, and it may become the source of subsequent anxiety.

Anxiety as a Basis of Developmental Identification

Either the positive attitude of love (admiration, affection) or the ambivalent attitude of respect (love and fear) may function as a basis of developmental identification. In either case, identification may be said to be based upon anxiety, and to function, at least temporarily, in the interest of relieving anxiety.

LOVE AS A BASIS OF DEVELOPMENTAL IDENTIFICATION. Two dynamic interrelations have been described to account for developmental identification on the basis of love, admiration, or affection: (1) the frustrated individual may admire and emulate persons who appear to be successful in gratifying motives similar to his own; and (2) the individual who has lost, or who fears the possible loss of, a love-object

[6] Sigmund Freud, *Collected Papers* (London, 1950), V, 74.

may develop characteristics of the love-object in order that he may "keep" a part of the love-object within himself.

Masserman has described the first of these interrelations, as follows:

> . . . person A will emulate (*i.e.*, "identify" with) the behavior of person B if that behavior seems to gain advantages and attain goals that A longs to secure for himself. . . . Early identifications . . . tend to be fantastic and exaggerated. Thus, when fantasies of emancipation and self-sufficiency are stirred in a normal boy he will dress and play the part of the over-masculine cowboy, the brave fireman, or the aggressive soldier; later still, in response to his adolescent erotic strivings he will slick his hair and adopt the mannerisms of dress and speech of the romantic screen actor who is the current idol of his girl acquaintances. Similarly, in adult life, he will continue to "idealize" and attempt to imitate those who, to his thinking, have achieved satisfactions in the particular fields of endeavor that primarily concern him.[7]

Here it is possible to see a close relationship between perceptual and developmental identification. The individual perceives that a model has motivation like his own: he impersonates the model in terms of the latter's gratifying behavior; this brings the temporary gratification that is afforded by fantasy. But the individual then perceives that his identity with the model is defective and temporary—and on the basis of this frustrating perception he may make *genuine efforts to become more like the model.*

The second of the interrelations between love and developmental identification has been described by Mowrer.[8] Insight into this interrelation is afforded by Mowrer's experience with the conditions under which several species of birds can learn to "talk."

> . . . the indispensable precondition for a bird's learning to talk is that you must make him *like* you; you must, in other words, make a "pet" of the bird, which implies in more than a . . . figurative sense that you *adopt* him. You, personally, must feed, water, and otherwise care for the bird and spend a good deal of time in its presence; and as you thus attend to its wants and interests, you utter the words or phrases which you want the bird to learn to say.

[7] Jules H. Masserman, *Principles of Dynamic Psychiatry* (Philadelphia, 1946), pp. 140–1.
[8] Mowrer, *op. cit.*, pp. 578–616.

. . . Soon the bird reaches the point at which it is obviously "glad to see" and equally "glad to *hear*" the trainer. Said otherwise, the trainer's sights and sounds take on secondary-reward value for the bird. . . . The bird, provided it belongs to one of the "talking" species, can make a great range and variety of sounds; and if one of these happens to resemble, even slightly, one of the trainer's sounds, that sound will, by the principle of generalization, have some secondary-reward value.[9]

In brief, then, the bird's motivation to learn to talk arises from the fact that his own words become a perceptual substitute for the beloved trainer. This *perceptual* identification of the trainer with the sound of his words (even when the sound is made by the bird itself) will provide the basis for *developmental* identification: the self-articulated words will gratify needs that would be gratified by the trainer's presence. Thus, accórding to Mowrer, "the bird (or baby) utters its first words as a means of reproducing a bit of the beloved and longed-for trainer."[10]

The basis for this identification is, of course, frustration, which arises, according to Mowrer, "from a sense of helplessness and loneliness: the parent or parent-person is *absent*, and the infant wishes he were *present*."[11] The only utility of the new behavior, at first, will be its autistic value—its value for retaining in fantasy whatever, owing to its absence, cannot be had in fact. Later, however, this behavior may become useful for gratifying other needs, since it will be a kind of behavior that the model himself (for example, the parent) has found useful for gratifying his own needs.

RESPECT AS A BASIS OF DEVELOPMENTAL IDENTIFICATION. Mowrer has applied the term "defensive identification" to cases of (developmental) identification which are based upon respect.[12] The parent, for example, may become an object of fear and hostility in terms of his power to punish the child, as well as an object of love in terms of his function as a gratifying agent. According to Mowrer, "the parent or parent-person is *present*, and the infant wishes he were *absent*."[13] But this hostile wish in relation to the parent comes into conflict with the child's love for the parent, so that the child experiences "acute anxiety at the prospect of his really being separated, physically or emotionally"

[9] Mowrer, *op. cit.*, pp. 579–81.
[10] Mowrer, *op. cit.*, p. 590.
[11] Mowrer, *op. cit.*, p. 592.
[12] Mowrer, *op. cit.*, pp. 590–6.
[13] Mowrer, *op. cit.*, p. 592.

from the father or mother.[14] This conflict is solved through identification with the parent—first, perceptually ("identifying with the aggressor") and later, developmentally (becoming motivationally more and more like the parent).

When the child's own psychogenic motivation has become like that of the parent, the child's autonomous behavior will conform to the parent's expectations, so that punishment (and fear of punishment) will be avoided. Not only will punishment be to a large extent avoided but the child will also achieve gratification of a positive nature through the parent's demonstration of love and approval.

Moreover, as Mowrer and Kluckhohn have stated, "by emulating, or *identifying* with the parents, the child achieves a kind of short-cut solution to many dilemmas which might otherwise be . . . difficult of solution." [15] Behavior that the parent has developed for the solution of his own problems will, when taken over by the child, have value for the solution of the child's (similar) problems.

Developmental Identification as a Source of Anxiety

Developmental identification may function as a source of anxiety in at least three ways: (1) through the development of superego motives that conflict with id motives; (2) through the development of mutually inconsistent (conflicting) superego motives; and (3) through the development of parentally (or socially) disapproved motives.

ID-SUPEREGO CONFLICTS. As previously indicated in Chap. IV, biogenic id-motivation will frequently conflict with conscience motivation, or with ego-ideal motivation, with accompanying guilt or inferiority feelings. The impulses that the individual comes to regard as evil will arouse guilt; the impulses that conflict with the attainment of ambitions, ideals, or aspirations will arouse feelings of inferiority.

MUTUALLY INCONSISTENT SUPEREGO MOTIVES. The individual may identify developmentally with different models, taking from each a part of his total pattern of psychogenic motivation. The individual will then be likely to manifest different ambitions, moral standards, aspirations, values, etc., which are in conflict with one another: to satisfy his ambition, he must compromise his ethical standards; to fulfill his personal duties to his family, he must frustrate his ambition; etc.

As we have seen earlier, the individual may develop incompatible

[14] Mowrer, *op. cit.*, p. 592.
[15] O. Hobart Mowrer and Clyde Kluckhohn, "Dynamic Theory of Personality," in *Personality and the Behavior Disorders*, J. McV. Hunt, ed. (New York, 1944), p. 125.

psychogenic motives even though he identifies with only one cultural representative (e.g., a parent), since the culture itself may harbor inconsistent values. One of the dangers to the adequate adjustment of children lies in the fact that the two parents may themselves express incompatible standards; partial identification with each parent may thus become the basis of incompatible psychogenic motives in the child.

DEVELOPMENT OF SOCIALLY DISAPPROVED MOTIVES. Complete identification with a parent cannot be accomplished by the child, since sexual behavior and aggression, especially, may be acceptable in the parent but not in the child. Thus the child who is being punished by a parent may not with impunity strike the parent in retaliation. The child may not identify developmentally in the areas of sexual and aggressive behavior without incurring punishment.

The child, moreover, is likely to identify with persons in the community or with heroes of fiction (e.g., in comic books) who are regarded by adults generally as reprehensible characters. On the basis of some admirable characteristic—which even criminals, prostitutes, etc., may manifest—the child may possibly emulate the reprehensible as well as the admirable characteristics. To the extent that the individual develops such objectionable motivation, he will, in the presence of parents, teachers, or other cultural representatives, become the object of criticism and punishment.

INTERRELATIONS WITH OTHER DEFENSES

DEVELOPMENTAL identification manifests functional interrelations with other defensive processes. Some of these interrelations will be described below.

Repression

Developmental identification, like other defensive functions, operates at a relatively unconscious level. The individual does not consciously decide to become like some admired or respected model; he develops similar motivation and similar behavior without consciously intending to do so.

This means, of course, that repressed motivation will be gratified by means of developmental identification. For example, according to Freud's view, the "superego is . . . the heir to the Oedipus complex and only arises after that complex has been disposed of" through repression.[16] In other words, the motivation for the development of superego motives consists in the repressed (unconscious) ambivalent attitude toward the parent.[17]

Fixation and Regression

The duration of an individual's fixation of love (affection, admiration) on a particular object (e.g., the parent) may be an important factor in determining the degree of resemblance between the individual and his model. If a fixation is relatively permanent, the child may become a replica of the parent; if a fixation is highly transitory, the child may show little resemblance to the parent.

Probably for the optimum socialization of the child, the parental fixation should continue until the child has established a reasonably stable pattern of superego motivation—assuming, of course, that the parent himself functions as an authentic representative of the fundamental values of his culture.

Freud has taken the position that identification represents a regression from the level of object-love.

> Identification is a very important kind of relationship with another person, probably the most primitive, and is not to be confused with object-choice. . . . If one has lost a love-object or has had to give it up, one often compensates oneself by identifying oneself with it; one sets it up . . . inside one's ego, so that in this case object-choice regresses, as it were, to identification.[18]

From this point of view, identification involves the choice of one's ego as an object of love; that is, identification involves narcissism. But this is a *secondary* narcissism: the superego, once developed, becomes, through *perceptual* identification with the parent, the new object of love (and fear). In other words, the occurrence of developmental identification—actually coming to resemble the parent—facilitates perceiving the self (ego) as a reasonable substitute for the parent.

[16] Sigmund Freud, *An Outline of Psychoanalysis* (New York, 1949), p. 121.

[17] The boy's Oedipus complex, for example, will involve much hostility and fear and some love in relation to the father, and it will involve much love and some hostility and fear in relation to the mother. In other words, the boy will fear and hate his father too much and will love his mother too much. After repression, the excessive fear, hostility, and love will function unconsciously. Becoming *like* the parents in certain respects will make it possible for the boy to express his fear, hostility, and love in relation to certain aspects of his own personality.

[18] Freud, *New Introductory Lectures* . . . , pp. 90–1.

Perceptual Identification

Developmental identification, as previous discussions have indicated, is related to perceptual identification. Each process may reinforce the other. Playing a role, through perceptual identification with the father, for example, will elicit gratifying responses from the parent; this may motivate efforts to become more genuinely like the parent; these efforts, in turn, will yield gratification, not only in terms of the parental responses but also in terms of the child's increasingly realistic perception of identity with the beloved parent. Like Mowrer's talking birds, he can see characteristics of the beloved object in his own behavior. What began as a perceptual identification in fantasy will become, through developmental identification, a rewardingly realistic perception of resemblance.

Likewise, to the extent that the individual identifies perceptually with a group, he will participate in its activities and so develop its standards; and, as such standards are developed, his perceptual identification will be reinforced. In other words, group loyalty and group morale are dependent upon these interrelations between perceptual identification and developmental identification.

ADJUSTIVE IMPLICATIONS

DEVELOPMENTAL identification functions significantly in the general adjustment of the individual. It accounts for his humanization—his socialization—as well as for the sources of much conflict and anxiety. Some of the adjustive implications may be described as follows.

Punishment as Related to Developmental Identification

As we have seen, developmental identification (introjection) is based upon frustration. When it derives from an attitude of love, it is based on the perception of loss or absence of the loved object; when it derives from an attitude of respect, it is based not only on fear of loss of the loved object but also on fear of other frustrations and punishments. Obviously, conditions of complete and continual gratification cannot give rise to the development of new motivation or to the development of new behavior-patterns.

In order to insure the development of adequate superego motivation, punishment in some form is probably necessary. This, of course, does not imply that punishment should be severe. All that is required is that the child perceive frustration in association with disapproved forms of behavior—and, of course, reward in association with approved forms of behavior.

Punishment of disapproved behavior should occur in the context of a secure parent-child relationship. Punishment or harsh treatment should be avoided except on occasions that involve misbehavior; and the child should not be pampered to the extent that he can "get away with murder." In either case, the introjection process will lack adequate motivation: if the child is frequently punished without regard to the nature of his behavior, he will anticipate harsh treatment regardless of how "good" he tries to be; and if he is pampered and loved without regard to his behavior, he will anticipate love regardless of how "bad" his behavior happens to be. Indeed, under such conditions the child will have no basis at all for learning what will ultimately be expected of him, since he can perceive no differential treatment in relation to his behavior.

On the other hand, if the child consistently experiences frustration or punishment in relation to behavior that is disapproved by society, and if he perceives rewarding social relations in connection with approved behavior, he should be expected to develop psychogenic motivation in conformity with the social norms.

Punishment should be relatively mild in terms of the child's interpretation of it; if punishment is too severe, the child may develop superego motives that are too exacting, so that his every minor departure from social standards will be accompanied by severe guilt feelings.

Basis of Self-Control

Developmental identification (introjection) underlies the development of psychogenic motives—the superego motives: moral standards, values, ideals, aspirations, etc.—that function to guide the individual's behavior along socially approved lines. Such superego motives, once they become operative, will form the basis of self-control: the individual will become "free" to behave in ways that are, at once, consistent with his own personality and consistent with the values of his culture. The individual will become able, on the basis of his own motivation, to avoid punishment and social frustration, and to gain social rewards. Superego motives have survival value within the society of their origin, and they provide the individual with positive goals for growth and self-actualization.

If the individual's superego motives are to have survival value in the society at large, however, they must be in conformity with the values of the general society. In order to insure that the developing child will introject standards that conform to the expectations of his society, the parents themselves must be individuals who have become adequately socialized. This follows from the fact that a child's superego motivation is patterned, in fundamental respects, after that of the parents.

Importance of Parental Compatibility

Mowrer has emphasized that normal personality development depends significantly on the marital compatibility of parents.

> In the ideal family constellation, a little boy finds it very natural and highly rewarding to model himself in his father's image. The father is gratified to see this re-creation of his own qualities, attitudes, and masculinity; and the mother, loving the father, finds such a course of development acceptable in her son. . . . But where there is parental disharmony, all this is changed. If there is chronic antagonism between husband and wife, the boy discovers that if he identifies with his father it is at the price of losing his mother's love and approval; if she is antagonistic toward and disapproving of the husband, she will feel scant enthusiasm for seeing her son become "just like *him*." If, on the other hand, the boy tries to take his mother as a personal model, he will almost certainly incur his father's displeasure and also risk the general opprobrium connected with being a "sissy.". . .[19]

When the parents are incompatible and mutually hostile, they will probably be committing a serious error by remaining married to each other "for the sake of the children."

Choice of Appropriate Models for Identification

In order that the child may develop psychogenic motives with maximum survival value for him in his particular society, his identifications must be based on models who are themselves adequately socialized. "Without a background of critical experience, positive identification may be made with people or with character traits that are

[19] Mowrer, *op. cit.*, pp. 596-7.

maladjustive. The child can as easily assume the bad as the good traits of a parent or companion." [20] Hardly a person lives who does not have some behavior characteristic that a child can perceive as lovable. On the basis of the one lovable characteristic, the child may emulate other characteristics that are socially disapproved.

Indulgence Before Discipline

Mowrer has stressed, as has Ribble,[21] the desirability of "loving care and indulgence" in the earliest phase of infant care.

> It is probably only by allowing early experience to be divided into two stages—loving care and indulgence, which leads to developmental identification and skills; and discipline, which leads to defensive identification and character—that the basis is laid for normal personality and effective and satisfying participation in the adult life of one's society. . . .[22]

In other words, during the first few weeks after birth the infant's needs should be gratified almost as soon as they are felt; this should serve to develop unmixed love for the parent. Later, and gradually, discipline should be imposed (frustrations that are within the child's frustration tolerance), for the development of socialized self-control on the basis of negative psychogenic motivation (superego motivation).

SUMMARY

DEVELOPMENTAL identification (introjection; introception) involves the development of behavior similar to that of another person or group of persons. When the process operates consciously, it may be termed *imitation*.

[20] Lawrence I. O'Kelly, *Introduction to Psychopathology* (New York, 1949), p. 513. Reprinted by permission of Prentice-Hall, Inc. Copyright, 1949, by Prentice-Hall, Inc.

[21] Margaret A. Ribble, "Infantile Experience in Relation to Personality Development," in *Personality and the Behavior Disorders*, J. McV. Hunt, ed. (New York, 1944), pp. 621–51. (This contradicts the Watsonian view that infants should be allowed to cry alone and be forced, from the first, to adhere to rigid feeding-schedules, etc. The danger of "spoiling" very young infants has been much overemphasized.)

[22] Mowrer, *op. cit.*, p. 596. (According to Mowrer's usage, "developmental identification" is based on love, while "defensive identification" is based on respect. Both of these terms are included in the term developmental identification, as it is used in the present treatment.)

Developmental identification may occur in relation to another person who is loved or respected, or in relation to a group. Developmental identification differs from perceptual identification in that the former involves primarily a learning process, while the latter mainly involves perception.

Developmental identification is involved in the socialization of the individual (the introjection of superego motives), in the development of skills, and in the enrichment of personality.

Anxiety may function as a basis of developmental identification. The frustration that is at the basis of developmental identification may have its origin in the positive attitude of love, or in the ambivalent attitude of respect, for the model. Developmental identification may, in turn, function as a source of anxiety (1) through the development of superego motives that conflict with id motives, (2) through the development of mutually inconsistent superego motives, and (3) through the development of socially disapproved motives.

Developmental identification manifests interrelations with other defensive processes. Repression of certain attitudes and impulses underlies this process of identification. The duration of fixation is related to the ultimate degree of similarity between the individual and any given model. And developmental identification may be based on an initial perceptual identification of the self with a model.

The introjection of superego motivation probably requires punishment as a basis. Such superego motivation will be most adequately developed when the parent consistently punishes disapproved behavior and maintains a social relationship that promises the child love and security as a reward for approved behavior. Punishment should be relatively mild, from the child's point of view, in order that superego motives may not become too severe and exacting.

Superego motives, once they become operative, will form the basis of self-control. On the basis of the individual's own psychogenic motivation, the individual will behave in ways that are at once consistent with his own personality and consistent with the expectations of other people.

Normal development of the child will depend on the compatibility of his parents, on the choice of appropriate models for identification, and on the occurrence of indulgent (gratifying) parental treatment prior to the imposition of disciplinary measures.

The following chapter will deal with displacement as a defensive process.

▶ **Suggested Readings**

Bateson, G. "Cultural Determinants of Personality," in *Personality and the Behavior Disorders*, J. McV. Hunt, ed. New York, 1944. Chap. xxiii, II, 714–35.

Davis, A. "Socialization and Adolescent Personality," in *Readings in Social Psychology*, Revised Edition, G. E. Swanson, T. M. Newcomb, and E. L. Hartley, eds. New York, 1952. Pp. 520–31.

Freud, S. *Group Psychology and the Analysis of the Ego*. London, 1949. Chap. vii, pp. 60–70.

Freud, S. *The Ego and the Id*. London, 1950. Chap. iii, pp. 34–53.

Hutt, M. L. and Miller, D. R. "Value Interiorization and Democratic Education," *Journal of Social Issues*, 5 (1949), 31–43.

Kluckhohn, C. and Murray, H. A. *Personality in Nature, Society, and Culture*. New York, 1948. Pp. 21–9.

Mead, Margaret. "Social Change and Cultural Surrogates," in *Personality in Nature, Society, and Culture*, Clyde Kluckhohn and Henry A. Murray, eds. New York, 1948. Chap. xxxvi, pp. 511–22.

Miller, D. R. and Hutt, M. L. "Value Interiorization and Personality Development," *Journal of Social Issues*, 5 (1949), 2–30.

Mowrer, O. H. *Learning Theory and Personality Dynamics*. New York, 1950. Chaps. xxi, xxiv, pp. 573–616, 688–726.

Murphy, G. *Personality*. New York, 1947. Pp. 491–5.

Sherif, M. *An Outline of Social Psychology*. New York, 1948. Chaps. xi-xiii, pp. 248–338.

Symonds, P. M. *The Dynamics of Human Adjustment*. New York, 1946. Chap. xiv, pp. 318–335.

White, R. W. *The Abnormal Personality*. New York, 1948. Pp. 156–67.

CHAPTER Twelve

Displacement

That the lonely spinster transfers her affection to animals, that the bachelor becomes a passionate collector, that the soldier defends a scrap of colored cloth—his flag—with his life-blood, that in a love-affair a clasp of the hands a moment longer than usual evokes a sensation of bliss, or that in Othello a lost handkerchief causes an outburst of rage—all these are examples of psychic displacements which to us seem incontestable.[1]

PROGRESSIVE adjustment, from infancy to maturity, depends on a sequence of displacements. But many displacements are maladjustive, in that they will function to develop frustrating human relationships.

DEFINITION

DISPLACEMENT involves the transfer of a motivational cathexis from one object to another. When a motive cannot be gratified in relation to a particular object, or when gratification is difficult, the motive may be gratified in relation to a substitute object (which is perceptually identified with the original object).

[1] Sigmund Freud, "The Interpretation of Dreams," in *The Basic Writings of Sigmund Freud*, A. A. Brill, ed. (New York, 1938), p. 246. Reprinted by permission of George Allen & Unwin, Ltd. and The Macmillan Company. Copyright, 1923, by The Macmillan Company, 1938, by Random House, Inc.

When displacement occurs, the individual will remain aware of the nature of his original motivation, but he will be unaware of the identity of the original object in relation to which gratification was anticipated—that is, the original object-cathexis will have been repressed. Although the individual will continue to be aware, for example, that his motivation is sexual or aggressive in nature, he will have "forgotten," through repression, the nature and identity of the original object. In terms of the total need integrate, only the object will have undergone repression.

Displacement may occur when the general nature of a motive is acceptable to the individual—that is, when it is consistent with his dominant motivation—and when it is acceptable to persons who are in a position to punish him, but when its gratification *in relation to a particular object* is unacceptable to himself or to others.

Aggressive and sexual motives are frequently gratified in relation to substitute objects: one may not "strike one's grandmother" or attack a superior, but one may punish a child or "take one's aggression out" on an inanimate object or on a recognized enemy; one may not give physical or verbal expression to sexual desires in relation to just any member of the opposite sex, but one may have sexual relations with a marriage partner.

In brief, then, it may be said that displacement involves the substitution of an acceptable object for motivation that has been aroused in relation to some other object. This other object, in relation to which a motive has been aroused, will be regarded, for some reason, as an unsuitable object for providing gratification of the individual's need.

FORMS OF EXPRESSION

THE EXPRESSIONS of displacement may be considered from two points of view: (1) from the point of view of the motives and attitudes commonly displaced, and (2) from the point of view of the objects commonly cathected through the process of displacement.

Motives and Attitudes Commonly Displaced

Since sexuality, hostility, and fear are frequently unacceptable or intolerable in their original forms—that is, in relation to their original objects—these motives are frequently involved in displacement.

LOVE AND SEXUALITY. Love and sexuality, as we have previously seen, involve essentially the positive cathexis of objects, with the aim of deriving pleasure. In this sense, whatever is sought as an object of pleasure may be regarded as a sexual object or as an object of love.

According to Freud, ". . . the sexual instincts . . . have in a high degree the capacity to act vicariously for one another and . . . they can readily change their objects." [2]

> The sexual instincts are remarkable for their plasticity, for the facility with which they can change their aims, for their inter-changeability—for the ease with which they can substitute one form of gratification for another, and for the way in which they can be held in suspense. [3]

In view of the "plasticity" of sexual impulses, they can be re-garded as particularly amenable to displacement—and particularly amenable to sublimation, reaction formation, and other defensive modi-fications.

The previous discussion of psychosexual development (Chap. VIII) has dealt with some of the displacements that normally occur in relation to sexual objects—from the mother or the nurse to the ego functions, to other members of the same or the opposite sex, to the ego-ideal, etc.

The history of any person's love relationships will provide ample exemplification of the possibilities for displacement of love from one object to another. Beginning, for example, with the normal girl's Oedipal attachment to her father, it is possible to trace all of her subse-quent love affairs back to this original source. The girl's first "boy friend" may resemble her father in physical appearance or in some other important characteristic; indeed, the breaking off of this first heterosexual object-cathexis may occur on the basis of a too-conscious recognition of this similarity, since guilt will arise from the sense of risking an incestuous relationship. [4] Successive "boy friends" may, in their turn, manifest more and more remote (less and less consciously perceptible) similarities to the father and to previous "boy friends," until ultimately the "one and only" person—a man who is in essential respects irresistible—arrives in the girl's perception.

This man of her final choice is likely to be one who is *uncon-*

---

[2] Sigmund Freud, *Collected Papers* (London, 1950), IV, 69.
[3] Sigmund Freud, *New Introductory Lectures on Psycho-Analysis* (New York, 1933), p. 134.
[4] This is really the second heterosexual object-attachment, since, of course, the girl's Oedipal attitude toward her father will have been the first.

sciously, rather than consciously, identified with her father; she can regard him as a fitting object for conjugal love, since, to her unconscious perception, he *is* her father, but since, from the point of view of her conscious perception, he is somebody very different from her father. Thus, the girl's heterosexual love must go through a number of successive displacements before she can eventually find a suitable object for marriage.

With regard to pregenital and aim-inhibited sexual tendencies, which are frequently treated as sexual abnormalities, a number of displacements have been noted to occur.[5] Some of these will be described.

Voyeurism, or *scoptophilia*—the tendency to look at the genitals of another person—may undergo a slight displacement, so that the objects of visual interest will become the secondary sexual characteristics (e.g., the breasts and the general figure); or it may undergo an extreme displacement, so that the objects of interest will become beautiful clothes or beautiful objects in general. "Direct voyeurism," as Masserman has stated, "is frowned upon, except, of course, at art galleries, burlesque shows, and Danse Moderne recitals." [6]

Exhibitionism—the tendency to display one's own genitals—may undergo displacement so that it will be manifested as a tendency to display one's athletic prowess or to display one's special skills and accomplishments.

Fetishism involves displacement in that the original sexual object has been replaced by "some partial sex object, such as a particular portion of the body, or even more remotely, a lock of hair or an article of clothing." [7]

Coprophilia—an interest in one's own excrement—may undergo displacement so that the new objects of love or interest will become money and property ("filthy lucre"). "The interest which has hitherto been attached to excrement is carried over on to other objects—for instance, from faeces on to money." [8]

If we agree with Freud's interpretation of love and sexuality— that is, if we regard love and sexuality as comprising any and all instances of positive cathexis—then it becomes possible for us to agree

---

[5] Aim-inhibited sexual tendencies are manifestations of love that has been "desexualized," in the sense that direct organ-pleasure is no longer the primary sexual intention. Aim-inhibited tendencies will be described in more detail in Chap. XIV.

[6] Jules H. Masserman, *Principles of Dynamic Psychiatry* (Philadelphia, 1946), p. 36.

[7] *Ibid.*, p. 44.

[8] Sigmund Freud, *Collected Papers* (London, 1950), V, 90.

that anything the individual "likes" or "loves" has become, *through displacement*, an object of love or sexuality.

AGGRESSION AND HOSTILITY. Since hostility, like love, is subjected to strict social regulation, the individual will learn early in life that there are in his social world many "unsuitable" objects of aggression. When such objects are perceived as the sources of frustration, the individual must displace his aggressive motivation onto other (more "suitable," safer) objects. Some of the displacements that occur in relation to aggressive motivation have previously been described in Chap. V.

FEAR AND ANXIETY. Fear, as we have seen (Chap. VI), may be regarded as objectified anxiety—that is, as anxiety in relation to a negatively cathected object; fear motivates the individual to escape from or to avoid the object. It seems reasonable to regard many objects of fear as objects onto which anxiety has been displaced.

The phobic reaction provides an example of displaced anxiety. "The content of the phobia," according to Freud, "has an importance comparable to that of the manifest dream—it is a façade. . . . It is . . . in agreement with this that many of these dreaded things have no connection with danger, except through a *symbolic* relation to it." [9] The object of a phobia symbolizes—is perceptually identified with—the original object of anxiety, while the original object has, as a function of repression, lost its conscious connections with anxiety. An excellent example of this is to be found in Freud's description of the phobia of a five-year-old boy, Little Hans.[10] In this case, the little boy feared horses, which turned out, upon analysis, to function as symbolic substitutes for the boy's father.

Worry may be regarded as involving the indiscriminate displacement of anxiety onto whatever objects seem momentarily to warrant (provide rationalizations for) the anxiety. The chronic worrier, the victim of free-floating anxiety, may be thought of as one who has repressed the object of some fundamental anxiety and who continually displaces the anxiety onto objects that, in themselves, involve little realistic danger.

Guilt and inferiority feelings, like other forms of anxiety, may undergo displacement: the act or the motive that was the original occasion of guilt becomes lost to perception through denial or repres-

[9] Sigmund Freud, *A General Introduction to Psycho-Analysis* (New York, 1935), p. 356.
[10] Sigmund Freud, *Collected Papers* (London, 1950), III, 149–289.

sion, while the guilt or inferiority feelings become displaced onto something of trivial significance. What the individual feels guilty or inferior *about*, then, becomes something he can tolerate in conscious perception. For example, the original basis of guilt may have been an awareness of homosexual motivation, but through displacement, the individual may feel guilty about having mistreated his wife.

Many neurotic symptoms involve the displacement of anxiety onto objects that are perceptually identified with the unconscious source of anxiety, but that to the outsider appear trivial and meaningless. For example, according to Freud, ". . . the mechanism of . . . displacement . . . dominates the mental processes in the obsessional neurosis." [11] The patient is deeply concerned with carrying out seemingly foolish ceremonials, since there has occurred ". . . a displacement from the actual important thing on to an insignificant one which replaces it." [12] The neurotic, by displacing his anxiety onto trivial objects, is able to defend his ego from the perception of the original source of anxiety.

> The modern compulsive hand-washer must, like Lady Macbeth, rout the "damned spot" by real or symbolic movements that remove the pollution. In Lady Macbeth's case the thought that she is a murderess cannot directly force its way to her attention, but the associated thought of bloodstained hands can do so; it is obviously not a stain or spot, but the guilt it stands for, that is compulsively rubbed off. . . . [13]

Objects Cathected through Displacement

It has been noted that love and sexuality (positive cathecting tendencies), hostility (negative destructive tendencies), and fear (negative avoiding tendencies) are amenable to displacement. This is probably tantamount to stating that all forms of motivation may undergo displacement.

We have now to consider the kinds of objects that may be cathected through displacement. It is likely that any object, whatever its nature, may be cathected to almost any motive. What the individual loves, what the individual is hostile toward, and what the individual

[11] Sigmund Freud, *Collected Papers* (London, 1950), II, 33.
[12] *Ibid.*, p. 34.
[13] Gardner Murphy, *Personality: a Biosocial Approach to Origins and Structure* (New York, 1947), pp. 550–1. Reprinted by permission of Harper & Brothers. Copyright, 1947, by Harper & Brothers.

fears may change from time to time: his motives will be displaced from one object to another, and the characteristics of the objects that are cathected through displacement may be as various as the characteristics of human experience itself.

OTHER PERSONS. Since other people—the major objects in the social environment—are the most potent sources of human frustration and gratification, it is obvious that love, hostility, and fear, as they are expressed in the life of a given individual, will frequently be displaced from one person to another.

The individual's life, as he develops and interacts with other persons, may be characterized as a continual process of "falling in love" and "falling out of love," making friends of enemies and enemies of friends, overcoming fears and developing newer and subtler fears.

The love, the hostility, or the fear that was originally directed toward the parent becomes displaced onto siblings, onto neighborhood contemporaries, onto teachers, onto lovers and sweethearts, onto competitors and employers and employees, onto colleagues and friends, onto strangers and enemies and the often unseen members of other nations, religions, or races of men. Since other people function as the main sources of frustration and gratification, other people will become the most frequent objects for the displacement of motives.

Transference is a term often used to describe these person-to-person displacements. The understanding and management of the transference process was regarded by Freud as a fundamental requirement for successful psychotherapy.

> . . . the patient sees in his analyst the return—the reincarnation— of some important figure out of his childhood or past, and consequently transfers on to him feelings and reactions that undoubtedly applied to this model. . . . This transference is *ambivalent:* it comprises positive and affectionate as well as negative and hostile attitudes toward the analyst, who, as a rule, is put in the place of one or other of the patient's parents, his father or his mother. . . . [In the transference] the patient produces before us with plastic clarity an important part of his life history. . . . It is as though he were acting it in front of us instead of reporting it to us. . . . The danger of these states of transference evidently consists in the possibility of the patient misunderstanding their nature and taking them for fresh real experiences instead of reflections of the past.

. . . It is the analyst's task to tear the patient away each time from the menacing illusion, to show him again and again that what he takes to be new real life is a reflection of the past. . . .[14]

Although transference was first conceptualized in a therapeutic setting, it should be clear that this process will occur in all of the individual's personal relationships. Through perceptual identification of one person with another, the individual will displace his attitudes from one to the other; in each of his personal relationships, he will be reacting to people he has previously known perhaps to a greater extent than he will be reacting to the person who is momentarily present in an objective sense.

In this process, of course, there are dangers to adjustment, just as there are dangers to therapy: to a great extent, the individual's displacements will involve reactions to illusions. Any interaction between two individuals, both of whom will inevitably be displacing attitudes from previously known persons onto each other, can become a vicious circle of misunderstanding from which the participants cannot readily extricate themselves.

THE SELF. When love, fear, or hostility cannot be gratified adequately in relation to external objects, these attitudes may be displaced onto the self as an object. Narcissism, as we have seen, involves such a displacement of love onto the self. When the negative superego motives are personified as "conscience," they may, as part of the self, become the objects of fear and hostility, through displacement of these attitudes from the parent or from some parent substitute.

ANIMALS. Attitudes that were previously cathected to persons may be displaced onto animals. In the life of an individual who has been frustrated in his human relationships, a pet such as a dog or a cat may take the place of human objects of love or affection. "A dog is man's best friend" implies the occurrence of such a displacement. Animal phobias, such as that in the case of Little Hans, usually involve the displacement of fear from a person onto an animal. And, of course, animals frequently become objects of aggression through its displacement from human agents of frustration.

INANIMATE OBJECTS. Inanimate objects may become cathected by an individual's love, as when a woman loves her clothes and her jewelry, as when a man loves his car and his matched golf-clubs, as when a scholar loves the books in his library. Since such inanimate ob-

[14] Sigmund Freud, *An Outline of Psychoanalysis* (New York, 1949), pp. 66–9.

jects cannot have been the original objects of love, they must have been cathected through the process of displacement. Again, the individual may "take out his aggression" on inanimate objects—by chopping wood, by kicking a ball, by wrecking manmade or natural "obstructions to progress," and so on. Many phobias represent the outcome of a displacement of fear onto inanimate objects.

ABSTRACT IDEALS. When the individual professes to love democracy and to hate Communism, he gives expression to love and hostility that have been displaced onto abstract ideals. The love of truth, the love of beauty, the love of nature, the love of good, the love of "learning," etc., represent displacements of love onto abstract ideals. Hatred of evil, ugliness, hypocrisy, intolerance, bigotry, or dishonesty may represent the displacement of hostility from human frustrating agents onto abstract ideals. Fear of God, fear of the Devil, fear of fate, etc., illustrate displacements of fear onto abstract ideals.

SYMBOLS. From a strict point of view, it may be considered that every instance of displacement involves displacement onto a symbol— for another person, the self, an animal, an inanimate object, or an abstract ideal may become cathected through displacement only by virtue of its being symbolic of the original object from which the motive has been displaced. For example, many of the symbols of sexual organs and of the sexual act occur in the form of inanimate objects (Cf. Chap. X).

Abstract ideas are especially difficult to represent without symbols —words, emblems, flags, crosses, etc. Words, of course, function to provide a highly flexible system of symbolic representation. The attitude toward one's country and its government may be displaced onto such words as "democracy," "Americanism," "freedom," and "free enterprise." The religious attitude of worshipful reverence may be displaced onto a cross, onto a six-pointed star, or onto the Bible. In brief, whatever is symbolic of an abstract ideal may be cathected through displacement; whatever is perceptually identified with an original object may itself become the substitute object of a particular motive.

DYNAMIC RELATIONS WITH ANXIETY

DISPLACEMENT, like other defensive measures, may be said to have its origin in anxiety; and it may, in turn, become the basis of further anxiety.

Anxiety as a Basis of Displacement

The preceding discussion has indicated that displacement may occur when the original object of a motive becomes unacceptable to the individual. The basis of its unacceptability lies in the fact that gratification of the motive in relation to its original object will involve the frustraton of some other motive or motives; such a conflict, of course, will involve anxiety. Displacement will function, then, to relieve anxiety.

If, on account of a personal deficiency or on account of the competitive activity of other persons, the individual is *unable* to gratify a motive in relation to a particular object, then in order to attain gratification at all he must displace the motive onto some substitute object. If he cannot have the woman of his first choice, he must displace his love onto a second choice; if he is weak in comparison with a frustrating agent, he must displace his hostility onto an object he does not fear; if he does not have enough money to buy an expensive automobile then perhaps he can displace his love onto a less pretentious vehicle. Frustration will be relieved through the acceptance of a substitute, though there may remain some conscious regret that the first choice was not available.

If the gratification of a motive in relation to the original object involves conflict with superego motives, displacement may occur without conscious regret, since *repression* of the original motivational cathexis will usually occur. Thus, in the case of a phobia involving displacement of fear from the father onto an animal, the individual will have repressed his original fear toward his father; and in the case of the dissolution of the Oedipus complex, the child will displace love from the parent of opposite sex, and hostility from the parent of the same sex, onto other objects.

An ambivalent attitude (love and hostility, love and fear, or fear and hostility) that is directed toward the same person will frequently function as the occasion for displacement. Such a conflict in relation to the same object will make it impossible to behave "wholeheartedly" toward the object in question. The presence of the object (usually a person) or the very thought of the object may arouse severe anxiety.

Either aspect of the ambivalent attitude may then be displaced onto some other object, with accompanying relief of anxiety. The child who loves and fears a strict parent may continue to love his parent but come to fear certain forms of conduct; or he may continue to fear the parent, while displacing his love onto somebody else. The wife who loves and hates her husband may displace her hostility onto the husband's mother; or she may displace her love onto another man and resolve her conflict by divorce. The child who fears and hates a parent may continue to fear the parent (and other authorities) and displace his hostility onto members of another race; or he may continue to hate the parent, while displacing his fear onto strangers. The individual may originally love, hate, and fear the same person, and later resolve his conflict by displacing two components of the attitude onto other objects, while maintaining a conscious attitude of love, hate, or fear toward the original object.

Displacement as a Basis of Anxiety

While displacement may function to relieve pre-existing anxiety, it may lead to further anxiety, through the development of frustrating human relationships, or through restriction of the ego.

FRUSTRATING HUMAN RELATIONSHIPS. Whoever becomes, through no fault of his own, the object of another's displaced motivation may have great difficulty in understanding the other's behavior in relation to him. Though the individual who displaces may, by so doing, improve some of his human relationships, he may establish other relationships of a frustrating character. His occupational environment will become less frustrating if he displaces hostility from his employer or from his competitors onto his wife and children; but the improvement in his occupational relationships will occur at the cost of an equal or greater deterioration in his family relationships. The individual who has displaced fear from a parent onto strangers may thereby improve his social relationship with the parent, but on future occasions his need to establish co-operative and amicable relations with persons outside the family may be continually frustrated by his timid and fearful social approach —whose origin he may long since have forgotten.

RESTRICTION OF THE EGO. The displacement of fear or hostility may seriously restrict the ego functions of the individual. In the case of a phobia, to take an extreme example, the individual will become limited by his fear: he will avoid, at any cost, those objects or situations onto which he has displaced his fear. "Little Hans . . . imposes a restriction upon his ego; he evolves the inhibition against going out in order not to encounter horses." [15] Again, the displacement of fear onto strangers may function to limit the individual's social relationships. And

[15] Sigmund Freud, *The Problem of Anxiety* (New York, 1936), p. 62.

the displacement of hostility may function to bring about a limitation of social outlook: the individual's hatred of minorities, for example, will seriously curtail his democratic sympathies.

DYNAMIC INTERRELATIONS WITH OTHER DEFENSES

DISPLACEMENT, like any other defense, will seldom function in isolation: it may function in combination with other defenses; it may be dependent on the operation of other defenses; it may aid in maintaining other defenses; and so forth. Displacement manifests interrelations with repression, with fixation and regression, with perceptual identification, with developmental identification, and with other defenses that will be treated in subsequent chapters.

Repression

In our definition of displacement, is was pointed out that displacement may involve repression; though the motive itself does not undergo repression, but continues to function consciously, its original object-cathexis will be repressed if that cathexis happens to conflict with stronger superego motives.[16]

If superego motivation is not involved—that is, if the frustration of the motive in relation to its original object does not involve a conflict with conscience or ego-ideal motivation—repression need not occur. One will remain conscious of the desire for a steak, even though hamburger has been accepted as a substitute; but one will likely repress incestuous wishes when the Oedipal cathexis has been displaced by normal heterosexual interests.

Since displacement involves gratification of a motive in relation to a new and more acceptable object, the occurrence of displacement will render unnecessary the repression of the motive itself, which in relation to its original object was highly unacceptable to the individual. Thus one may, after a successful displacement, maintain awareness of one's sexual motivation without suffering anxiety; but if displacement had not occurred—if the sexual motivation had maintained its in-

---

[16] In this discussion, of course, it should be understood that conscious representations of appropriate instrumental acts will remain relatively unchanged when displacement occurs. Since the nature of the gratifying instrumental act will continue to be represented in consciousness, the individual will remain aware of the general nature or intent of his motives.

cestuous object-cathexis—intense anxiety would be experienced in relation to sexuality itself, because it would conflict with one's conscience.

Since it is possible to discover acceptable objects for all human motives, the occurrence of a successful displacement should render unnecessary the complete repression of any motive.

Fixation and Regression

Fixation and displacement may be regarded as occurring in response to opposite tendencies: the more rigid are the individual's fixations, the less possible will it become for him to displace attitudes from one object to another.

Object regression and progression, on the other hand, are functionally equivalent to displacement: regression involves displacement onto objects that previously were appropriate, while progression involves displacement onto objects that successively become appropriate with the increasing age of the individual.

The *object* of an instinct . . . may be changed any number of times in the course of the vicissitudes the instinct undergoes during life; a highly important part is played by this capacity for displacement in the instinct. . . . A particularly close attachment of the instinct to its object is distinguishable by the term *fixation*. . . .[17]

There are marked individual differences with regard to the rigidity-flexibility continuum as it is expressed in human behavior. The difference between the two extremes is said to be ". . . comparable to that experienced by a sculptor according as he works in hard stone or soft clay." [18]

Perceptual Identification

In order that a motive may be displaced from one object onto another, it is necessary that the two objects be perceptually identified with each other. The perceptual similarity—the identical interpretation —of the two objects will render probable the occurrence of identical (highly similar) behavior in relation to them. It is more nearly correct to say that behavior in relation to them will be similar rather than identical, since only a part of the individual's total motivation will be dis-

[17] Freud, *Collected Papers*, IV, 65.
[18] Freud, *Collected Papers*, V, 344.

placed from one object to some specific other object. Displacement, in any case, may be considered to be dependent upon the perceptual identification of the original object with the object onto which a part of the individual's motivation is displaced.

Transference—which, as we have seen, is an instance of displacement—may involve the transfer of a friendly, a hostile, or a fearful attitude from the father onto the analyst, who is at least temporarily identified with the father. To repeat a quotation from Freud: ". . . the patient sees in his analyst the return—the reincarnation—of some important figure out of his childhood or past, and consequently transfers on to him feelings and reactions that undoubtedly applied to this model." [19]

In the case of the animal phobia of Little Hans, the child was able to identify the father with horses, since for children, as Freud has stated,

> . . . the gulf between man and animal is not yet recognized, certainly not so overemphasized as later. The adult male, admired but also feared, still belongs in the same category with large animals, which one envies for many things but against which one has also been warned because they can be dangerous.[20]

Developmental Identification

Superego motives are acquired, as we have seen, through the process of developmental identification. When Freud stated that the superego is the "heir" of the Oedipus complex, he implied that the attitudes previously directed toward the father and the mother are *displaced* onto the personified superego motives.[21] Fear of the parents becomes fear of conscience; love of the parents becomes love of the ego-ideal.

The superego, which was formed by a process of developmental identification, becomes identified perceptually with the parents, so that it becomes the new object of attitudes previously directed toward the father and the mother. It can be seen, then, that the transformation of the Oedipus complex into the superego involves the interplay of perceptual identification, developmental identification, and displacement.

[19] Freud, *An Outline of Psychoanalysis*, p. 66.
[20] Freud, *The Problem of Anxiety*, p. 32.
[21] Freud, *New Introductory Lectures* . . . , p. 91.

ADJUSTIVE IMPLICATIONS

THE QUESTION whether the net influence of displacement is favorable or unfavorable to human adjustment cannot, of course, be answered in a simple fashion. On the one hand, it would be impossible for an individual to reach maturity without employing displacement; but on the other hand, the use of displacement will involve certain dangers to adjustment.

Development as a Sequence of Displacements

The development of personality from its infantile state to maturity involves, as we have seen, a sequence of motivational displacements. Displacement is antithetical to fixation: the occurrence of one is inversely related to the occurrence of the other. The maturation of interests and of social relations will depend, then, upon the occurrence of displacements in an orderly sequence: what the child loves, fears, and hates must give way to relatively more mature objects of love, fear, and hate. The attitude of dependence the child expresses in relation to his parents, for example, may become, with maturity, an attitude of loyal dependence in relation to God and country.

Were it not for the possibility of displacement, it seems likely that nobody could develop loyalty to the highest values of the culture, such as religion, patriotism, science, art.

Human Relations as Related to Displacement

Characteristically, the outcome of displacement is that the individual's relations with some persons will be improved, while his relations with other persons will be rendered more difficult. In the solution of ambivalence (e.g., love and hostility) toward a parent, the child's relationship with the parent will be improved through displacement of hostility; however, his relationship with the new object of hostility will thereby become disturbed.

To the extent that negative attitudes are characteristically displaced onto persons with whom the individual need not associate in everyday life, while his positive attitudes are maintained in relation to his closest associates, the net influence of displacement will be to improve the individual's human relations.

But this will not necessarily be the case; for, in view of economic necessity, the individual may displace the hostility that has developed from occupational frustrations onto his wife and children, so that his relations with them may become embittered; or the teacher may "bear up" under the frustrations in her home, only to become a severe disciplinarian in relation to the pupils entrusted to her.

Anti-Minority Prejudice as a Function of Displacement

Members of minority groups are common objects of displaced hostility. To the extent that the individual is willing to limit his human relationships to association with members of his own race, nationality, or class, he may displace hostility onto minority groups with a minimum of anxiety. But for the person who evaluates highly the ideal of democracy, such displacement will entail conflict and anxiety.

Socially Constructive Displacements

Displacement need not incur distressing social friction, since negative attitudes may be displaced onto nonhuman objects. One may displace any excessive unrequited libido (positive cathexis) onto abstract ideals, such as democracy, truth, beauty, science, or humanity. One may displace hostility onto the "stubborn" aspects of nature in order to bend them to human uses, or onto intolerance, Communism, fascism, unlawfulness, or "sin." One may displace fear or respect onto God, onto authority, or onto law.

The mature individual may be characterized as one who has developed motivational cathexes (through displacement) that are in accord with the higher values of his society.

SUMMARY

DISPLACEMENT involves the transfer of motivational cathexis from one object to another. When, owing to either an internal or an external frustration, a motive cannot be gratified in relation to the object to which it was originally cathected, some new object may be substituted in its place.

Motives that are commonly displaced include love and sexuality, aggression and hostility, and fear and anxiety. Objects that may be newly cathected through the displacement process include other persons, the self, animals, inanimate objects, abstract ideals, and symbols.

Displacement may relieve the anxiety that underlies it, but it may, in turn, function as a source of subsequent anxiety. If the gratification of a motive in relation to a particular object cannot be achieved, displacement onto another object may provide the motive with substitute gratification. When displacement occurs, it may lead to the development of frustrating human relations or to ego restriction.

Displacement involves repression of motivational cathexes. It does not involve repression of the conscious representation of appropriate instrumental acts; when displacement occurs, in other words, the individual remains aware of the nature of his motivation.

Displacement may be regarded as the antithesis of object fixation; regression involves displacement onto objects that were suitable to an earlier adjustment; and progression involves displacement onto objects that become appropriate with increasing age.

The choice of an object for displacement depends on its perceptual identification with the original object. Superego motives, which are dependent on developmental identification, become the objects of attitudes previously directed toward the parents.

The development of personality, from infancy to maturity, may be regarded as a progressive sequence of displacements. When displacement occurs, the individual's relations with some persons will be improved while his relations with other persons may be rendered more frustrating. Anti-minority-group prejudice is partly to be explained in terms of the displacement of hostility.

Disturbed human relations are not a necessary outcome of displacement, since unrequited love, as well as fear and hostility, may be displaced onto aspects of nature which function to gratify or to frustrate human needs, or onto abstract ideals and reprehensible practices.

The following chapter will deal with the process of projection.

▶ Suggested Readings

Alexander, F. and French, T. M. *Psychoanalytic Therapy*. New York, 1946. Chap. v, pp. 71–95.

Brush, F. R., Bush, R. R., Jenkins, W. O., John, W. F., and Whiting, J. W. M. "Stimulus Generalization after Extinction and Punishment: An Experimental Study of Displacement," *Journal of Abnormal and Social Psychology*, 47 (1952), 633–40.

Cass, Loretta K. "Parent-Child Relationships and Delinquency," *Journal of Abnormal and Social Psychology*, 47 (1952), 101–4.

Dollard, J., Doob, L. W., Miller, N. E., Mowrer, O. H., and Sears, R. R. *Frustration and Aggression*. New Haven, 1939. Pp. 41–4, 105–7.

Dollard, J. and Miller, N. E. *Personality and Psychotherapy*. New York, 1950. Chap. xvii, pp. 260–80.

Freud, S. "Wit and Its Relation to the Unconscious," in *The Basic Writings of Sigmund Freud*, A. A. Brill, ed. New York, 1938. Pp. 656–63.

Freud, S. "A Special Type of Choice of Object Made by Men," *Collected Papers*. London, 1950. IV, 192–202.

Freud, S. "On Narcissism: an Introduction," *Collected Papers*. London, 1950. IV, 30–59.

Freud, S. "The Dynamics of the Transference," *Collected Papers*. London, 1950. II, 312–22.

Freud, S. "Fetishism," *Collected Papers*. London, 1950. V, 198–204.

Freud, S. *A General Introduction to Psycho-Analysis*. New York, 1935. Lect. xxvii, pp. 374–89.

Hartley, E. L. "The Generalized Nature of Prejudice," in *Outside Readings in Psychology*, E. L. Hartley, H. G. Birch, and Ruth E. Hartley, eds. New York, 1950. Pp. 670–5.

Himelhoch, J. "Is There a Bigot Personality?" in *Outside Readings in Psychology*, E. L. Hartley, H. G. Birch, and Ruth E. Hartley, eds. New York, 1950. Pp. 676–88.

Kuhlen, R. G. and Johnson, G. H. "Changes in Goals with Adult Increasing Age," *Journal of Consulting Psychology, 16* (1952), 1–4.

Lindzey, G. "An Experimental Examination of the Scapegoat Theory of Prejudice," *Journal of Abnormal and Social Psychology, 45* (1950) 296–309.

Miller, N. E. "Theory and Experiment Relating Psychoanalytic Displacement to Stimulus-Response Generalization," *Journal of Abnormal and Social Psychology, 43* (1948), 155–78.

Murphy, G. *Personality*. New York, 1947. Chap. viii, pp. 161–91.

Symonds, P. M. *The Dynamics of Human Adjustment*. New York, 1946. Chap. xi, pp. 252–69.

Tolman, E. C. "Identification and the Post-War World," *Journal of Abnormal and Social Psychology, 38* (1943), 141–8.

Veltfort, Helene R. and Lee, G. E. "The Cocoanut Grove Fire: A Study in Scapegoating," *Journal of Abnormal and Social Psychology, 38* (1943), No. 2, Supplement, 138–54.

Wood, A. B. "Transference in Client Centered Therapy and in Psychoanalysis," *Journal of Consulting Psychology, 15* (1951), 72–5.

Wyatt, F. "The Self-Experience of the Psychotherapist," *Journal of Consulting Psychology, 12* (1948), 82–7.

Yarrow, L. J. "The Effect of Antecedent Frustration on Projective Play," *Psychological Monographs, 62*, No. 6 (1948).

Zawadzki, B. "Limitations of the Scapegoat Theory of Prejudice," *Journal of Abnormal and Social Psychology, 43* (1948), 127–41.

CHAPTER Thirteen

Projection

And the demons came out from the man, and entered into the swine: and the herd rushed down the steep into the lake, and they were drowned.[1]

WHEN the individual cannot accept "the demons within himself," he may become sensitized to their operation in other persons. He may thereby gain some vicarious gratification—and some relief from his anxiety—by observing, in other persons, the fulfillment of his repudiated (repressed) motives. But though the individual may gain relief from some of his anxiety by this means, it is probable that his projections will "create" more anxiety than they can relieve.

DEFINITION AND DIFFERENTIATION

PROJECTION, like displacement, will function to maintain the repression of unacceptable motivation. But projection involves a more thoroughgoing repression than that which underlies displacement.

Projection

Projection involves the repression of an unacceptable or an externally frustrated motive, and the development of hypersensitivity to its

[1] Luke viii–33.

operation in other persons or things. When the individual employs projection, his attention will be focused on the operation of the repudiated motive in other personalities, so that he will be shielded from the necessity of observing its operation in himself.[2]

Moreover, through an unconscious (perceptual) identification with other persons, the individual will achieve vicarious gratification of the motive that has undergone repression; thus he will be able to keep the intensity of the repressed motive below the intensity of the "repressing forces," and will be able to maintain the repression.

Through projection the motivation of other persons will be falsified in two respects: (1) in that projection will involve perceiving the repudiated motive as operating *consciously* in others, whereas in fact it will likely be operating *unconsciously* in others, as well as in the personality of the projecting individual; and (2) in that projection will involve the exaggeration of a particular motive in others, so that their motivational patterns will seem to be dominated by the repudiated motive of the projecting individual.

The projecting individual will frequently tend to magnify his own role as a cathected object of other persons' motives: they will not only seem hostile, for example, but they will seem hostile toward him.

Projection as Differentiated from Displacement

Repression is more thoroughgoing in the case of projection than in the case of displacement. The projecting individual loses awareness that a particular motive functions within his personality; he repudiates it completely as a function of his own, and allows himself consciously to perceive it only as a function of other personalities.

The displacing individual, on the other hand, maintains awareness of a particular motive and recognizes it as his own; he represses only the fact of its cathexis to an original object, and allows himself consciously to perceive its relation to some new, more acceptable object.[3]

----

[2] Projection involves perceptual selectivity in terms of the individual's motivation; it is more consistent with his motivation to see a particular motive functioning in others than to see it functioning in himself.

[3] In terms of the components of a need integrate, it may be said that displacement will occur when the conscious representation of the *object* has undergone repression, but projection will occur when the conscious representations of both the *object* and the *instrumental act* have undergone repression. As long as the individual remains aware of the nature of the appropriate instrumental act, he can recognize the nature of his motivation, and he can employ displacement; but when the individual has lost awareness of the nature of the appropriate instrumental act, he will experience anxiety, which he cannot relieve by displacement alone, since he will not know what to do even in relation to a substitute object.

Originally, for example, the individual may hate his father: if he were to employ projection, he might perceive his father as hating him; if he were to employ displacement, he might perceive himself as hating his boss; if he were to employ projection and displacement in combination, he might perceive his boss as hating him.

FORMS OF EXPRESSION

THE NATURE of the projection process may further be clarified in terms of some of its forms of expression. The forms of expression may be considered in terms of (1) the motives that are frequently projected, (2) the objects onto which motives are frequently projected, and (3) some of the psychotic manifestations of projection.

Motives Frequently Projected

Motives that are commonly projected include love and sexuality, aggression, jealousy, fear and anxiety, and guilt and inferiority feelings.

LOVE AND SEXUALITY. Socialized adults usually find their pregenital sexual impulses to be unacceptable—that is, to be inconsistent with their superego motives. Some adults, on the basis of their unusual experiences, will find their heterosexual (mature genital) impulses to be unacceptable. And there are even persons who, on the basis of their frustrating experiences with human relations, will find their aim-inhibited sexual impulses (affectionate and friendly impulses) to be unacceptable. In such persons, on the basis of such development, sexual impulses may be repressed and their repression maintained by the auxiliary process of projection. What they dare not perceive consciously in themselves they can perceive in others.

We have previously described some of the modifications in behavior which occur with the displacement of such pregenital impulses as voyeurism, exhibitionism, fetishism, and coprophilia. More radical modifications will occur when these impulses are projected.

Projected *voyeurism* will be manifested as an interpretation that others are inordinately curious about sexual matters. The individual who has projected his voyeuristic tendencies may be especially careful to prevent others from seeing him in a nude or partly undressed condition. If projected voyeurism occurs in combination with displacement, the individual will be secretive about various other aspects of his life, such as his ambitions and special projects he is working upon.

Projected *exhibitionism* may be expressed as an interpretation that others are careless about exhibiting themselves. The individual may look the other way when there seems to be the slightest possibility that he will see anything he doesn't wish to see (if he also manifests a reaction formation against voyeuristic tendencies), or (if such a reaction formation has not occurred) he may "take in the show" that everybody appears to be providing for his free enjoyment. Or he may have contempt for people, which is rationalized on the basis of his belief that they are incurably addicted to exhibiting themselves.

Fetishism, which involves a prior displacement, may manifest itself as the (projected) perception of fetishism in others.

Coprophilia may be projected in the form of contempt for people who are "filthy" or "unclean." [4]

The individual who has repressed his "normal" heterosexual impulses may project them onto others. He may perceive friendly overtures on the part of others as a manifestation of their trying to be "fresh"—as an indication that there is ulterior sexual motivation at the basis of their friendly behavior. He may perceive the younger generation as "sexually loose"—interpreting their normal heterosexual social relations as a manifestation of impending evil. He may want to ban books or movies or dancing on the basis that they may overstimulate the sexuality of the young or of the young in heart.

The individual who projects his aim-inhibited affectionate impulses will perceive other persons as "too friendly" or as too demanding of affection. Since he cannot consciously perceive his own need for affection he may regard most people as immature or inefficient, since they "waste so much time" in social activities. He may be greatly inclined, through projection also of his own repressed homosexual tendencies, to think of intimate friendships as manifestations of overt homosexuality.

AGGRESSION AND HOSTILITY. The projection of aggressive impulses involves a too-ready perception of aggressive motivation or hostile attitudes in other persons or things. Hostility toward another person may be turned into fear of him by means of a process in which the other person is perceived as one who harbors hostility; he is therefore an object of fear.

Logically the person on whom his own hostile impulses will be projected is the person against whom they are directed. The result

---

[4] In many of these examples, of course, other defensive mechanisms may be operative in combination with projection. Projective characteristics are exemplified only to the extent that the projecting individual fails to recognize that his repressed motives are operative in himself, while he gives undue conscious emphasis to their operation in others.

is that this person now assumes formidable proportions in his mind. . . . A wife who is ignorant of her own impulses to ruin her husband and subjectively convinced that she is most devoted may, because of this mechanism, consider her husband to be a brute wanting to harm her.[5]

The "Oedipus complex," according to Freud, gives way to "castration fear." Such a transformation of attitude—from hatred of the father to fear of the father—may be accounted for in terms of the child's projection of hostility; after such a projection the child will perceive the father as an object of fear—as a person who is hostile toward him.

Freud has interpreted fear of the dead as an instance of projected hostility.

The survivor thus denies that he has ever harboured any hostile feelings against the dead loved one; the soul of the dead harbours them instead and seeks to put them into action during the whole period of mourning. In spite of the successful defense which the survivor achieves by means of projection, his emotional reaction shows the characteristics of punishment and remorse, for he is the subject of fears and submits to renunciations and restrictions, though these are in part disguised as measures of protection against the hostile demon. Once again, therefore, we find that the taboo has grown up on the basis of an ambivalent emotional attitude.[6]

JEALOUSY. According to Freud, jealousy "is compounded of grief, the pain caused by the thought of losing the loved object, and of the narcissistic wound, in so far as this is distinguishable from the other wound; further, of feelings of enmity against the successful rival, and of a greater or lesser amount of self-criticism which tries to hold the person himself accountable for his loss." [7] In other words, jealousy consists of a complex of attitudes, some of which are directed toward others and some of which are directed toward the self.

Jealousy may be further analyzed if we recall that grief involves displacement onto the self of ambivalent attitudes (love and hostility) that were previously directed toward a love-object, with which the

[5] Karen Horney, *The Neurotic Personality of Our Time* (New York, 1937), p. 70.

[6] Sigmund Freud, *Totem and Taboo*, translated by James Strachey (New York, 1952), p. 61. Reprinted by permission of Routledge and Kegan Paul, Ltd. Copyright, 1950, by Routledge and Kegan Paul, Ltd.

[7] Sigmund Freud, *Collected Papers* (London, 1950), II, 232.

self is perceptually identified. Thus, jealousy may be thought of as consisting of an ambivalent attitude (love and hostility) directed toward the self, together with a hostile attitude directed toward a successful rival. (The love-object, if not perceived as irretrievably lost, may be the partial recipient of the ambivalent attitude, consisting of love and hostility.)

If an individual represses and projects his jealousy, he may perceive his rival as hostile toward him and regard the rival with fear; he may perceive the love-object as having ambivalent attitudes toward him, and interpret the conscious expressions of her love as disguises for her hostility. This may become the basis of a mild (or severe) persecutory delusion, manifesting itself as fear that the sweetheart and rival are plotting to damage or destroy him.

Jealousy itself may have its origin in the projection of unfaithful impulses onto the love-object.

> It is a matter of everyday experience that fidelity, especially that degree of it required in marriage, is only maintained in the face of continual temptation. Anyone who denies this in himself will nevertheless be impelled so strongly in the direction of infidelity that he will be glad enough to make use of an unconscious mechanism as an alleviation. This relief—more, absolution by his conscience—he achieves when he projects his own impulses to infidelity on to the partner to whom he owes faith.[8]

Delusional jealousy, according to Freud, operates as a defense against homosexual impulses. The patient projects his love of another man onto the woman; that is, he sees the woman as being in love with another man, rather than perceiving his own homosexual impulses in relation to the other man. The patient then expresses jealousy toward the persons in question, even though there may have been little basis in fact for his perception of the woman's infidelity.

FEAR AND ANXIETY. Since, for many persons in our society, fear and anxiety are unacceptable motives, these may frequently be projected onto other persons and things. The repression of fear and anxiety may be maintained through exaggerated attention to the anxiety of others.

The husband may maintain his courage in the face of difficulties by keeping his attention focused on the anxieties of his wife; the soldier may project his fears onto the enemy, thus becoming in his own per-

[8] *Ibid.*, p. 233.

ception fear-inspiring rather than fearful; the mother may lose awareness of her own anxiety through attention to the anxieties of her child; and all of us may lose the perception of our own anxiety by focusing our attention upon the anxieties of persons who are "less fortunate" than ourselves.

GUILT AND INFERIORITY FEELINGS. Guilt may be regarded as another name for fear of conscience; the ego perceives that the conscience (which is usually *personified* in perception) is directing hostility toward it. When guilt is projected, the individual will perceive fear in others rather than fear in himself.

It is probable also that hostility will be projected from conscience onto the ego, and displaced from the ego onto other persons, so that instead of perceiving guilt the individual will perceive only that he is hostile toward other persons or things. The expression of this hostility against other persons or things will transform the self-punishment of guilt into punishment of others. Thus, guilt may be kept from the individual's conscious perception through the expression of hostility.

And it is probable that it will be just those persons with the most occasion for guilt who will be most hostile in their reactions toward others. Blaming others for one's frustrations may, in this sense, be regarded as a projection of guilt; it also involves displacement of hostility from the self onto others.

Feelings of inferiority involve an unfavorable comparison of the self with the ego-ideal. When feelings of inferiority are projected, the individual will perceive others, rather than himself, as inferior to the ego-ideal. The self-criticism involved in feelings of inferiority will then become criticism of others. This perception of inferiority in others will defend the ego against the wounding self-perception of inferiority.

The hostility involved in inferiority feelings will be *displaced* from the ego onto others; while the motives that are at the basis of failure to live up to the ego-ideal will be *projected* onto others.

Since both guilt and inferiority feelings involve complex motivation, it is probable that on most occasions a part of the motivation will be *projected* while another part will be *displaced*. If projection alone occurred, the projecting individual would perceive others as *feeling* guilty or as *feeling* inferior; but such "pure" projection hardly ever occurs.[9]

---

[9] The possibilities are probably all accounted for when we have considered the projection of love, of hostility, and of fear. Jealousy, guilt, inferiority feelings,

Objects of Projection

Unacceptable motives may be projected onto other persons, onto animals, onto natural events, onto supernatural concepts, or onto artistic creations.

OTHER PERSONS.   Other persons become most frequently the objects of projected motives, since they are of course similar in many respects to the projecting individual and can therefore reasonably be regarded as having motives of the kind that are being projected.

In the everyday life of most individuals, in the presence of friends, associates, and acquaintances, projection in some degree probably occurs continually. The individual will be more sensitive to the unconscious motives of others than he can be to his own. This makes for at least some degree of a "holier than thou" attitude in one's everyday relationships—an attitude that, if carried to the extreme, can be highly disruptive of human relations.

Possibly much of the difficulty involved in international diplomacy may come from the mutual projection of unworthy motives from one national leader to another. Each will likely regard himself and his motives as being without stain, while attributing to the other motives of the basest sort. Thus each will see in the other much reprehensible motivation and will regard the other with extreme caution, interpreting his peaceful overtures as a disguise for some dirty work that is being carried on in secret. Thus, no national spokesman will be willing to admit that his own nation has been an aggressor, but will insist, on the contrary, that his nation has been the victim of aggression.

The objects of prejudice are frequently the objects of projected motivation. Motivation that the prejudiced person cannot allow himself to perceive in his own personality will be seen with utmost clarity in the personalities of "inferior" groups.

> . . . ethnic hostility is a projection of unacceptable inner strivings onto a minority group. . . . We project our hatred into the other person so that it appears to us not as if we hate him, but that he hates us. Thus in a devious way we not only try to get rid of an emotion which is not acceptable to our conscience (superego), we are also now justified in hating the other person if we so desire,

and the like may be considered to involve complex combinations of love, fear, and hostility. It becomes possible to understand the operation of projection, or of any other mechanism, with regard to any of these complex combinations only by considering what transformations occur in the expression of each of the separate components.

because we think he is hating us. . . . The outgroup provides subjects onto which [members of the ingroup] can project the rejected part of those tendencies which created an inner conflict. . . . That this is so can be seen from the fact that the outgroup is always accused of satisfying needs which are common to all men. No child wants to be and remain clean; everybody would like to live at a leisurely pace, to have money, and to enjoy sexual gratification. . . .[10]

In general, it may be said that the individual who is most disturbed by the operation of unworthy motives in other persons is likely to be one who has had great difficulty in keeping the same motives repressed in himself.

ANIMALS. Animals, like other persons, may become the objects of projected motivation. "Biblical literature," comments O'Kelly, "gives us the unforgettable picture of the Hebrew tribal rite of periodically casting the sins of the people into a goat and then chasing the goat into the wilderness." [11] Children's comic books perform a useful function in providing for the projection of unworthy human impulses onto animal characters. Fairy tales also contain many animal characters onto which unacceptable human motives may be projected.

NATURAL EVENTS. Human motives are frequently projected onto natural events. Hostility is often attributed to storms, to the sea, to the cold winter winds, etc. On the other hand, beneficence and affection are sometimes attributed to sunshine, to rain, or to the welcome shade of a spreading tree. In literature, for example, the motives of the characters are commonly reflected in the description of such things as weather or landscapes. Some of the stories of Edgar Allan Poe are especially noteworthy for their projection of human motives and human actions onto the background of natural events.

SUPERNATURAL CONCEPTS. Various unacceptable impulses may be projected onto such concepts as fate, destiny, the Devil or demons, and the gods (or God). Fate may be regarded as hostile, and the Devil may be regarded as the focal point of all evil impulses.

A progressive renunciation of inherent instincts . . . appears to be one of the foundations of human civilization. Some part of this

[10] Bruno Bettelheim and Morris Janowitz, *Dynamics of Prejudice: a Psychological and Sociological Study of Veterans* (New York, 1950), pp. 42–3. Reprinted by permission of Harper & Brothers. Copyright, 1950, by Harper & Brothers.

[11] Lawrence I. O'Kelly, *Introduction to Psychopathology* (New York, 1949), p. 516.

repression is effected by means of the various religions, in that they require individuals to sacrifice the satisfaction of their instincts to the divinity. "Vengeance is mine, saith the Lord." In the development of the ancient religions one seems to find that many things which mankind had renounced as wicked were surrendered in favor of the god, and were still permitted in his name; so that a yielding up of evil and asocial impulses to the divinity was the means by which man freed himself from them. For this reason it is surely no accident that all human characteristics—along with the crimes they prompt—were freely attributed to the ancient gods. . . .[12]

ARTISTIC CREATIONS. The artist may project his own motives onto the characters or onto the characteristics of his art. As Freud has maintained, the psychological novel probably involves projection of certain motives onto one character and projection of other motives onto other characters.

The psychological novel in general probably owes its peculiarities to the tendency of modern writers to split up their ego by self-observation into many component-egos, and in this way to personify the conflicting trends in their own mental life in many heroes.[13]

Probably in this instance, as in the case of other artistic creations (music, drama, painting, sculpture, etc.), the author projects his unacceptable motives onto one or more characters (or characteristics), while he projects his acceptable motives onto other characters (or characteristics).

The appreciation of literature and art also probably involves both the projection of unacceptable motivation and the projection of acceptable motivation onto different characters or characteristics of the artistic production. On the basis of such projections, perceptual identification and vicarious gratification will be facilitated.

Psychotic Manifestations

Delusions and hallucinations, which are characteristic symptoms in many of the severe psychoses, involve projection.

[12] Freud, *Collected Papers* (London, 1950), II, 34-5.
[13] Sigmund Freud, *Collected Papers* (London, 1950), IV, 180.

DELUSIONS. Delusions involve beliefs that are "widely deviant from the cultural norm, and impervious to persuasion or reason." [14]

. . . the conviction may appear that something is wrong in the atmosphere, that hypnotism is being practiced or their minds being read, that they are being compelled to do things and think things, that machines are being used on them or that parts of their body are undergoing some kind of a structural change.[15]

Delusions of self-observation, in Freud's interpretation, involve projection of superego motives.

The institution of conscience was at bottom an embodiment, first of parental criticism, and subsequently of that of society. . . . The voices, as well as the indefinite number of speakers, are brought into the foreground again by the disease, and so the evolution of conscience is regressively reproduced. . . . His conscience then encounters him in a regressive form as a hostile influence from without.[16]

Delusions, in "pure" form, involve extreme sensitivity to the scrutiny of the patient by living individuals in his environment. The people are really there, but they are perceived as if they were continually watching him and criticizing him (even though, in fact, they may be paying little or no attention to him).

HALLUCINATIONS. Hallucinations frequently involve peopling the environment with persons (and things) that are really not there; the personified superego is projected into the environment, where it is seen or heard to carry out observations and criticisms of the individual. The "voice" of conscience is perceived to emanate from a "real" external person, who is visible or audible only to the hallucinating individual.

DYNAMIC RELATIONS WITH ANXIETY

PROJECTION has its basis in conflict and anxiety, and it will function to relieve anxiety; but it will also function as the basis of much subsequent frustration.

[14] Jules H. Masserman, *Principles of Dynamic Psychiatry* (Philadelphia, 1946), p. 271.

[15] Norman Cameron, "The Functional Psychoses," in *Personality and the Behavior Disorders*, J. McV. Hunt, ed. (New York, 1944), II, 890.

[16] Freud, *Collected Papers* (London, 1950), IV, 53.

Anxiety as a Basis of Projection

When superego motives are frustrated by the actual or the antici-pated gratification of some motive—that is, when this latter motive is unacceptable to the individual—the conscious conflict may be reduced by means of projection. When the individual projects, it is as if he has said: "*I* am not immoral. *I* am not inferior. It is *he* who is immoral and inferior."

This process will function to gratify the individual's superego motivation. Moreover, he can then avoid the "immoral" or "inferior" person, refusing to associate with him, whereas there was previously no way by which he could successfully avoid perceiving the *motive* as long as he regarded it as a part of himself.

> . . . the still helpless organism had the capacity for making a first orientation in the world by means of its perceptions, distinguish-ing both "outer" and "inner" according to their relation to actions of the muscles. A perception which is made to disappear by motor activity is recognized as external, as reality; where such activity makes no difference, the perception originates within the subject's own body—it is not real. To be thus able not only to recognize, but at the same time to rid himself of, reality is of great value to the individual. . . . That is why he takes such pains to *project, i.e.,* to transfer outwards, all that becomes troublesome to him from within.[17]

It is believable that on certain occasions the superego motives, rather than the id motives that conflict with them, will be projected. This may be one of the mechanisms by which the psychopath can rid himself of conflict—by which he can blithely gratify his biogenic mo-tives without regard for law or for moral restrictions. If his superego motives have been projected onto the representatives of law and order, he can avoid them and maintain an attitude of sublime contempt in re-lation to them.

Thus far, then, it is clear that the normal individual can gratify his superego motives, and that the psychopath can gratify his biogenic motives, by means of projection. But repression and projection cannot *really* "get rid of" the projected components of a conflict; the repressed and projected motives will continue to function unconsciously.

The anxiety that is consciously experienced after the repression

[17] Freud, *Collected Papers* (London, 1950), IV, 148.

and projection of these motives will, however, be reduced to the extent that the projecting individual identifies himself (unconsciously) with the objects of projection. By means of this perceptual identification, the individual can achieve vicarious gratification as he observes the operation of his own repudiated motives in the behavior of other people.

Projection as a Basis of Anxiety

While projection may rid the individual of anxiety that was based on his original conflict, it may become the source of further anxiety through the disturbance it creates in his human relationships.

While the objects of projection may indeed harbor *unconsciously* the motives attributed to them through projection, it will be, for them, a severe frustration to have a projecting individual behave as if these motives were in *conscious* operation.

Nobody likes to be "misunderstood"; every self-respecting person likes to regard himself as a person of dignity and purity of intention. Individuals will be insulted or shocked when the projecting individual attributes to them any form of reprehensible motivation.

The projecting individual will, therefore, frequently "put his foot in his mouth" when he associates with other people; his human relations will become frustrating to the extent that his social behavior is initiated in terms of his projections. Projecting his love, he may expect more wholehearted responsiveness than others are willing to show; projecting his hostility, he may be unduly fearful; projecting his fear, he may be frustrated by the fact that other persons appear to fear him and to avoid him.

DYNAMIC INTERRELATIONS WITH OTHER DEFENSES

PROJECTION manifests interrelations with repression, with fixation and regression, with perceptual identification, with developmental identification, with displacement, and with other defenses that will be treated in subsequent chapters.

Repression

It has previously been indicated that projection involves repression of motives that are unacceptable to the individual. Rather than consciously perceive the operation of such unacceptable motives in his own personality, the individual will perceive their operation in other personalities. His sensitivity to the functioning of such motives in others will aid the individual in maintaining their repression: since they are so obvious in others, the individual will not need to see them in himself.

Fixation and Regression

The individual can avoid the perception of his own childish motivation by projecting immature motivation onto other persons. He can continue his fixation, or remain regressed, without experiencing anxiety in this regard so long as he can compare himself favorably with other people; and his projection of immature motivation onto others will help to make possible such a favorable comparison. "These others," he can say, "are childish, while I am mature."

Perceptual Identification

The objects of projection are frequently—perhaps usually—perceptually identified with the self.

> . . . persons upon whom we project tend to be like ourselves. . . .
> Hospitalized patients with delusions of persecution were found to cast in the role of *persecutors* the members of their families who were psychologically most like themselves. . . . Not recognizing their own hostile wishes, they unconsciously followed the line of least resistance in "finding" a person who harbored hostile wishes. . . .[18]

As we have previously noted, the projected motivation of the individual can gain some degree of gratification when the objects of projection are identified with the self; unconscious gratification will occur when the projected motives are observed to be gratified by other persons.

Not only the "evil" impulses that are in conflict with conscience, but also the frustrated ego-ideals of the individual may be projected onto objects that the projecting individual identifies himself with. The projection of ego-ideals is exemplified in the case of the parent who projects his frustrated ambitions onto his child. The parent who, on account of disappointment in his own achievements, has partially or completely repressed his ambitions may perceive these ambitions in his child. The child's success, then, will become the parent's own success,

---

[18] Gardner Murphy, *Personality: a Biosocial Approach to Origins and Structure* (New York, 1947), p. 546.

to the extent that perceptual identification with the child has occurred.

Anna Freud has employed the term "altruistic surrender" to imply the projection of ego-ideals onto another person with whom the projecting individual has identified himself.

> Any number of cases . . . can be observed in everyday life, when once our attention has been called to this combination of projection and identification. . . . For instance, a young girl, who had scruples . . . about marrying . . . did all she could to encourage her sister's engagement. A patient, who suffered from obsessional inhibitions in spending any money on herself, had no hesitation in spending lavishly on presents. Another patient, who was prevented by anxiety from carrying out her plans for travel, was quite unexpectedly pressing in her advice to her friends to do so. . . . The most familiar representative of this type of person is the public benefactor, who with the utmost aggressiveness . . . demands money from one set of people in order to give it to another.[19]

Developmental Identification

Projection may, in one sense, be regarded as the antithesis of developmental identification or introjection. Through projection, the individual will "lose" some of his motivation, since he can perceive it as belonging only to other personalities; through developmental identification, on the other hand, the individual will gain new forms of motivation.

From another point of view, however, it must be considered that projection is dependent on the prior occurrence of developmental identification. Projection cannot operate except on the basis of repression; and it may be correct to say that repression itself will depend upon the prior development of superego motivation (by means of developmental identification).

Displacement

Anna Freud has described a case in which displacement and projection were employed successively as defenses against anxiety.

> In order to solve the problem of ambivalence she displaced outwards one side of her ambivalent feeling. Her mother continued to

[19] Anna Freud, *The Ego and the Mechanisms of Defense* (New York, 1946), pp. 139–41.

be a love-object, but, from that time on, there was always in the girl's life a second important person of the female sex, whom she hated violently. . . . But even the displaced hatred was a source of much suffering. . . . The little girl's ego now resorted to a second mechanism. It turned inwards the hatred, which . . . had related exclusively to other people.[20] The child tortured herself with self-accusations and feelings of inferiority. . . . But this measure, too, proved inadequate as a means of mastering the situation. The patient then entered on a process of projection. The hatred which she had felt for female love-objects or their substitutes was transformed into the conviction that she herself was hated, slighted or persecuted by them. Her ego thus found relief from the sense of guilt.[21]

It is likely that in this case the displacement of hostility onto the self functioned *in combination with* the projection of hostility—that is, the girl's hostility against herself (first occurring through displacement) was projected onto other persons.

Possibly the general tendency for the individual to regard himself as the object of his own projected motives must involve such a combination of projection and displacement: through displacement, the self will become the object; and through projection, the motive will seem to become a process that is operative only in somebody else.

ADJUSTIVE IMPLICATIONS

AS COMPARED with displacement, for example, projection has little to recommend itself. Most of its implications are unfavorable to the individual's adjustment. When carried to an extreme, projection may manifest itself as paranoia, a psychotic disorder that is characterized by delusions. Even in its less extreme manifestations, projection may be regarded as delusional, since it involves seeing others as they are unable to see themselves. The objects of projection will regard themselves as the victims of misinterpretation—that is, as the objects of a false belief.

[20] [*This "turning inwards" may be regarded as a special instance of displacement; the attitude is displaced from an external object onto the self. This need not, therefore, be referred to as a second mechanism.*]

[21] *Ibid.*, pp. 48-9.

Ego Restriction Occasioned by Projection

The ego functions of the individual will be restricted to the extent that insight into his own motivation becomes deficient. Projection involves, as we have seen, the maintenance of such a deficient insight; the individual cannot become aware of his own frustrated motives, since his attention is so exclusively directed upon the expression of these motives by other people.

The individual who cannot know that he has sexual impulses, who cannot know that he feels hostile toward frustrating agents, or who cannot know that he fears anything, will be at a disadvantage in his attempts to achieve a rational adjustment to the various features of reality.

Projection as a Basis of Disturbed Human Relations

One of the most frustrating human experiences involves having others see us in a different light than that in which we see ourselves. We prefer to have others take for granted that our conscious motives are genuine—that we are, in a word, sincere. We have our own repressions, which we would like to maintain without disturbance. When the projecting individual attributes to us motives that we feel (consciously) we do not have, our own defensive processes will be endangered. The "shoe that fits" will often hurt us most.

Thus, the use of projection as a defense, while it may help the projecting individual to defend himself against anxiety, will threaten the integrity of the defenses others have adopted. This will constitute a severe frustration, so that the one who employs projection will be likely to become an object of intense hostility; his human relations will inevitably become frustrating.

Projection of Ego-Ideals

When the parent or the teacher projects his own frustrated ego-ideals onto the child, this may on occasion be advantageous to the child himself, since the parent or teacher will function as a source of aid and encouragement. Such a mutually advantageous relationship can be expected to occur when the child himself happens to accept the ego-ideal in question.

But innumerable cases occur in which the child finds that a parent's projected ego-ideal is in conflict with an ego-ideal of his own; he may wish to become a writer, for example, while his father wants him to become a lawyer.

If, in the latter example, the boy should choose to work toward his own ideal, the parent will be frustrated; if the boy should follow his father's dictates, he may suffer years of frustrating monotony while in training as a lawyer, only to become a mediocre success, or indeed eventually to toss aside his previous training and follow his own original desire in the matter. Thus both the child and the parent will have suffered losses, which need not have occurred but for the parent's unfortunate projection.

SUMMARY

PROJECTION involves the repression of an unacceptable motive and the development of hypersensitivity to its operation in other persons or things. While displacement requires repression of only the conscious representation of an original object-cathexis, projection requires repression also of the conscious representation of an instrumental act by means of which gratification has been anticipated. Thus the individual who employs displacement will remain aware of the nature of his motivation, while the individual who employs projection will not be able to recognize his repudiated motivation as his own, but will be able only to recognize its operation in other people.

Motives that are commonly projected include love and sexuality, aggression and hostility, jealousy, fear and anxiety, and guilt and inferiority feelings. The objects of projected motivation include other persons, animals, natural events, supernatural concepts, the self, and artistic creations. The psychotic manifestations of projection include delusions and hallucinations.

Projection has its source in anxiety, but it will lead to further frustration and anxiety. The projection of unacceptable motives will aid in maintaining the repression of such unacceptable motives— thereby gratifying the opposing components of the conflict. Projection, in combination with perceptual identification, will provide vicarious gratification of the repressed and projected motivation. But the use of projection will ordinarily lead to disturbances of human relations, and therefore to further anxiety.

Projection will aid in maintaining the repression of unacceptable motives. Fixations or regressions may be maintained without conscious anxiety, through the projection of immature motives onto other persons. The objects of projection are frequently perceptually identified with the self.

Projection depends upon repression, which in turn depends on the operation of superego motivation, which in turn depends upon the process of developmental identification. Displaced motivation may subsequently be projected; and projected motivation may frequently be displaced from one object to another.

Projection functions principally as a hindrance to human adjustment. Through the use of projection the ego functions will be restricted and human relations will become frustrating. Even the projection of ego-ideals may lead to frustration both in the projecting individual and in the object of projection.

The following chapter will be concerned with the mechanism of sublimation.

▶ **Suggested Readings**

Cameron, N. "The Development of Paranoic Thinking," *Psychological Review*, *50* (1943), 219–33.

Freud, Anna. *The Ego and the Mechanisms of Defense*. New York, 1946. Chap. x, pp. 132–46.

Freud, S. "Psycho-analytic Notes upon an Autobiographical Account of a Case of Paranoia (Dementia Paranoides)," *Collected Papers*. London, 1950. III, 387–470.

Freud, S. "Certain Neurotic Mechanisms in Jealousy, Paranoia, and Homosexuality," *Collected Papers*. London, 1950. II, 232–43.

Holt, R. R. "The Accuracy of Self-Evaluations: Its Measurement and Some of its Personological Correlates," *Journal of Consulting Psychology*, *15* (1951), 95–101.

Sears, R. R. "Experimental Studies of Projection: I. Attribution of Traits," *Journal of Social Psychology*, 7 (1936), 151–63.

Sheerer, Elizabeth T. "An Analysis of the Relationship between Acceptance of and Respect for Self and Acceptance of and Respect for Others in Ten Counseling Cases," *Journal of Consulting Psychology*, *13* (1949), 169–75.

Symonds, P. M. *The Dynamics of Human Adjustment*. New York, 1946. Chap. xiii, pp. 296–317.

Webb, W. B. "Self-Evaluation compared with Group Evaluations," *Journal of Consulting Psychology*, *16* (1952), 305–7.

CHAPTER Fourteen

Sublimation

The suggestion that art, religion and social order originated in part in a contribution from the sexual instincts was represented by the opponents of analysis as a humiliation of the highest possessions of civilization.[1]

WHEN a frustrated motive undergoes sublimation, the consciously represented motivation of the individual becomes highly acceptable, and the expression of this motivation involves behavior that is accorded general social approval. For this reason, sublimation is regarded as one of the most adaptive of the defenses.

DEFINITION OF SUBLIMATION

ACCORDING to Murray, the term *sublimation* "should be applied to a form of substitution in which a primitive act or cathection is replaced by an act or cathection that is less crude and less objectionable." [2] Freud, in discussing *sexual* sublimations, stated similarly that in sublimation "both object and aim are changed, so that what was originally a sexual instinct finds satisfaction in some achievement which is no longer sexual but has a higher social or ethical evaluation." [3]

Sublimation, then, may involve a change in the aim of a motive

[1] Sigmund Freud, *Collected Papers* (London, 1950), V, 169.
[2] Henry A. Murray, *Explorations in Personality* (New York, 1938), p. 394.
[3] Freud, *Collected Papers* (London, 1950), V, 132–3.

(the kind of action to be employed for gratification) or a change in object cathexis (displacement).

The term *sublimation* may be defined as *any transformation of a need integrate such that its expression will conform more adequately to the social values of the society*. This transformation may involve a change in the aim or mode of action (instrumental act) that is employed for gratification, or it may involve a change in the object. Thus, the aim of sexual intercourse may be changed to the aim of social conversation, or the object of voyeurism may be changed from the female genitals to the beauty of nature.

The term sublimation, as here defined and as currently employed, embraces many instances of displacement. It is probable, also, that instances of sublimation which involve changes in motivational aim may be subsumed under other defense mechanisms.[4]

FORMS OF EXPRESSION

AS PREVIOUSLY noted, sublimation may involve either a transformation of aim or a transformation of object cathexis. Freud has used the term *aim-inhibited impulses* to refer to motives in which a transformation of aim—that is, a transformation of instrumental act—has occurred.[5] The sexual impulse, for example, was said to achieve partial gratification through preliminary activities, such as approaching and engaging another person in conversation. Sublimations that involve changes in object cathexis are, of course, special instances of displacement.

The subsequent treatment will distinguish between these two classes of sublimations by referring to the former as *aim-sublimations* and to the latter as *object-sublimations*.

In describing forms of sublimated expression, we shall consider particularly the psychosexual sublimations and the aggressive sublimations.

Psychosexual Sublimations

Freud has stated that sexual impulses are especially susceptible to sublimation and to various other defensive modifications.[6] This perhaps

---

[4] It is probable, indeed, that sublimation should be considered strictly an evaluative concept. This point will be discussed in subsequent sections of the present chapter and in the following chapter.

[5] Sigmund Freud, *The Ego and the Id* (London, 1950), p. 55; *New Introductory Lectures on Psycho-Analysis* (New York, 1933), p. 133.

[6] Freud, *New Introductory Lectures . . .* , p. 134.

can be accounted for in terms of the fact that sexual expression in its direct form is nonessential for the organic survival of the individual.

The expression of warm, positive feelings toward other people may be regarded as having an erotic basis.

> . . . we have to conclude that all the feelings of sympathy, friendship, trust and so forth which we expend in life are genetically connected with sexuality and have developed out of purely sexual desires by an enfeebling of their sexual aim, however pure and non-sensual they may appear in the forms they take on to our conscious self-perception. To begin with we knew none but sexual objects; psycho-analysis shows us that those persons whom in real life we merely respect or are fond of may be sexual objects to us in our unconscious minds still.[7]

In other words, friendship and positive social feelings may be regarded as aim-sublimations of sexuality. If such positive feelings are directed toward persons of the opposite sex, they may be considered sublimations of heterosexual impulses; if directed toward persons of the same sex, they may be regarded as sublimations of homosexuality.

Secondary narcissism (positive cathexis of ego-ideals) may be considered an object-sublimation;[8] the ego as a love-object is replaced by values, ideals, ambitions, etc. "That which he projects ahead of him as his ideal is merely his substitute for the lost narcissism of his childhood—the time when he was his own ideal."[9]

Oral impulses may be sublimated in a number of ways. Smoking cigarettes and chewing gum, for example, have been considered to be sublimations of oral erotism.

> I was once called in to see an old man of about ninety. I found him sitting in his chair, sucking his thumb. His son said to me: "You see, doctor, he sits there just like a child, sucking his thumb." Upon investigation, I found that this habit was revived when the family physician ordered the old man's pipe to be taken away. . . . We know of course that smoking . . . is a substitute for the erstwhile nipple. . . . In any case, this senile man who had been deprived

---

[7] Sigmund Freud, *Collected Papers* (London, 1950), II, 319.

[8] Of course, in this instance, as in many others, aim-sublimation is also involved.

[9] Sigmund Freud, *Collected Papers* (London, 1950), IV, 51.

by the doctor of the only pleasure left in his life regressed to the earliest autoerotic outlet and sucked his thumb.[10]

Kissing, like smoking and chewing, may involve object-sublimation; kissing is, however, so recognizably erotic that it has been regarded in some societies with abhorrence (through reaction formation).

Aim-sublimations of oral sexuality may take such forms as sarcasm, oratory, or poetry.[11] In these activities the original act of sucking is no longer apparent. Acquisitiveness and greediness may also be included among the oral sublimations.[12]

Among the sublimated expressions of *anal erotism* may be mentioned the activities of the collector of stamps, of art objects, of matchbooks.[13] The collector is said to have sublimated his coprophilic or anal-retentive impulses. Painting and sculpture have also been interpreted in this manner; these activities are said to be substitutes for the individual's childhood desire to play with his own excretions.[14]

The preceding instances involve object-sublimations in particular; the most frequently mentioned aim-sublimations constitute the so-called *anal character*.

The persons whom I am about to describe are remarkable for a regular combination of the three following peculiarities: they are exceptionally *orderly, parsimonious*, and *obstinate*. . . . "Orderly" comprises both bodily cleanliness and reliability and conscientiousness in the performance of petty duties: the opposite of it would be "untidy" and "negligent." "Parsimony" may be exaggerated up to the point of avarice; and obstinacy may amount to defiance, with which irascibility and vindictiveness may easily be associated. . . . Now anal erotism is one of those components of the instinct which in the course of evolution and in accordance with our present civilizing education has become useless for sexual aims; it would therefore be no very surprising result if these traits of orderliness, parsimony, and obstinacy, which are so prominent in per-

[10] A. A. Brill, *Lectures on Psychoanalytic Psychiatry* (New York, 1946), pp. 172–3. Reprinted by permission of Alfred A. Knopf, Inc. Copyright, 1946, by Alfred A. Knopf, Inc.

[11] *Ibid.*, p. 173.

[12] Karen Horney, *New Ways in Psychoanalysis* (New York, 1939), p. 54.

[13] Franz Alexander, *Fundamentals of Psychoanalysis* (New York, 1948), p. 111.

[14] Horney, *op. cit.*, p. 54.

sons who were formerly anal erotics, turned out to be the first and most constant results of the sublimation of anal erotism.[15]

The trait of orderliness will, of course, involve, in combination with sublimation, a reaction formation against the original pleasurable cathexis of excrement.

Genital sexuality, especially as regards the reproductive function, may be sublimated in the form of creative activities (art, literature, music, etc.) as well as in the form of gardening, agriculture, animal husbandry, and similar occupational activities.[16] "In sexual propagation a new organism is created; in artistic, literary, and scientific work some new object of art or scientific knowledge emerges." [17] The creative and productive activities of art, of agriculture, of science, and of technology may be regarded as sublimated expressions of genital sexuality, since they eventuate in something new and since the newly created objects and ideas are "loved" by their creators, as a father might love his child. The practice of referring to such products of one's creative activity as "brain children" lends credence to this interpretation.

Sublimated *voyeurism*, or sublimated sexual curiosity, may be manifested in the research activities of the scientist, in the news-gathering activities of the reporter, in the personality investigations of the clinical psychologist or the psychiatrist, and in the medical practice of the gynecologist.

> Specially combined unconscious drives may . . . be sublimated in more specific directions: anatomic inquisitiveness and a desire for quasi-thaumaturgic powers to heal by the effective laying on of hands may combine in the unconscious motivations of a surgeon, just as, perhaps, a somewhat different type of curiosity and quest for omnipotence may actuate a psychiatrist. . . .[18]

Sublimated *exhibitionism* may be expressed in tendencies of the individual to "show off" his achievements, to make impressive personal appearances, or to reach a position of fame or notoriety in the public eye. Such bids for attention may be interpreted as sublimated sexual exhibitionism.

Sexual *masochism* may be sublimated in the form of the need to be humiliated—to assume the role of a "henpecked" husband or a down-

---

[15] Freud, *Collected Papers*, II, 45–7.

[16] Alexander, *op. cit.*, pp. 111, 113.

[17] Alexander, *op. cit.*, p. 111.

[18] Jules H. Masserman, *Principles of Dynamic Psychiatry* (Philadelphia, 1946), p. 37.

trodden "Sad Sack" or "Caspar Milquetoast." *Sadism* may be expressed
in sublimated form as strong self-assertive or aggressive-dominative
tendencies; it may be expressed occupationally in the practice of medicine or dentistry, in the work of the business executive, or in the function of a military officer or prison guard.[19]

The incestuous sexual attachment that is said to occur during the
Oedipal phase may be manifested, in one of its sublimated forms, as
reverence for motherhood or respect for authority.

The desire for children, which Freud has interpreted as an object-
sublimation of "penis-envy," [20] may undergo further sublimation, so
that it will be perceived as a need to minister to the wants of dependent
individuals. This sublimated motivation may then be expressed in the
activities of the teacher, the nurse, the social worker, or the humanitarian.

Sublimated male *homosexuality*, according to Richards, may be
expressed in "activities that are essentially feminine, such as in art, in
nursing, in hairdressing, in dancing, or in interior decorating. In the
same way the truly homosexual woman may sublimate her basic impulses in activities that are essentially masculine." [21]

Aggressive Sublimations

The sublimation of aggressive motivation may take the form of
any occupational or nonoccupational activity that expresses aggression
against acceptable objects or that expresses aggression in a subtle or
indirect manner. In other words, aggressive motivation, like sexual
motivation, may undergo either object-sublimation or aim-sublimation.

Object-sublimations of aggression have already been treated in the
discussion of displacement (Chap. XII). These may include such activities as social reform, aggressive sports, and occupational functions that
express aggression against acceptable objects—fighting against crime
and evil, conquering natural elements, etc.

Aggressive sports are sublimations of destructive, competitive, and
even homicidal impulses. . . . In sports like boxing and wrestling
the original desire to injure one's opponent is more obvious than
in tennis, golf, or chess.[22]

[19] Horney, *op. cit.*, pp. 53–4.
[20] Freud, *New Introductory Lectures* . . . , pp. 170–5.
[21] T. W. Richards, *Modern Clinical Psychology* (New York, 1946), p. 108.
Reprinted by permission of McGraw-Hill Book Company, Inc. Copyright, 1946,
by McGraw-Hill Book Company, Inc.
[22] Alexander, *op. cit.*, pp. 110–11.

Aggressive sports, to some extent, and fighting against social evils, to an even greater extent, involve aim-sublimation as well as object-sublimation: the kind of activity that is expressed in relation to the new object is different from the kind that was originally intended for the frustrating agent from which aggression has been displaced.[23]

There are certain occupations, however, that involve little aim-sublimation—little change in the kind of activity aimed at the objects of aggression. For example, the butcher or the slaughterhouse worker may do to animals what he unconsciously might wish to do to frustrating people. Perhaps the same might be said of the professional soldier, who is engaged to kill the enemy (rather than to kill the people who actually frustrate him).

Aim-sublimations of aggression (with or without concurrent object-sublimation) will include all of the subtle or indirect methods of injuring other people or things. Our discussion of aggression (Chap. V) has already treated some of the forms of aggressive sublimation, such as the use of verbal (instead of physical) attacks and the use of aggressive fantasies.

DYNAMIC INTERRELATIONS WITH ANXIETY

PREVIOUS discussions have indicated that defensive mechanisms are based on anxiety, and that the defensive mechanisms themselves will, in turn, function as sources of further anxiety. This generalization holds for sublimation as well as for the other defenses.

Anxiety as a Basis of Sublimation

The sublimative transformation of motives would serve no adjustive purpose, were it not that the motives in their original form have functioned as sources of anxiety. Sexuality, aggression, and other unacceptable motives are unacceptable to the individual for the very reason that they meet with frustration. They are frustrated, at first, primarily by social agents—specifically, by the parents and by subsequent parent-substitutes—and later by the operation of the individual's own superego motives. When sublimation occurs, the previously frustrated motives will gain some degree of gratification; with the reduction of frustration will occur a comparable reduction in anxiety.

[23] After one has come to hate certain kinds of "evils," the evils themselves may, of course, be interpreted as the agents of frustration.

Sublimation as a Basis of Anxiety

While it is clear that sublimation has its source in anxiety and that sublimation will function for the relief of anxiety, the case is not so clear for the conception of sublimation as a basis of anxiety. It follows from the definition of sublimation that it may be expected to be one of the most adequate and stable of the defenses: by definition, sublimation is an evaluational concept that implies the modification of motives to bring them into accord with the moral values of society. It would appear, then, that the use of sublimation should not lead to social frustrations or to disturbances in the individual's relations with other people.

Probably, however, sublimation will lead to frustration and anxiety when this process is carried to too great an extreme. Murray, for example, has pointed out that the sexual sublimations occurring during adolescence should change from "ethereal romanticism to physical objectification." [24] In other words, sublimations of sexuality (especially of mature genital sexuality), and perhaps also of aggression, may be carried so far and become so firmly entrenched that they will later function as fixations, to the detriment of progressive adjustment. The individual whose sublimations have been carried to their extreme may, therefore, be looked upon as impractical—as a dreamer or an eccentric. To this extent, then, sublimation may function as a source of anxiety.

RELATIONS WITH OTHER DEFENSES

THE DISCUSSION of sublimation has already indicated some of the interrelations that occur between this mechanism and other mechanisms of defense. Sublimation is dynamically interrelated with repression, with fixation and regression, with perceptual identification, with developmental identification, with displacement, and with projection, as well as with other defenses that have not yet been described.

Repression

When a motive undergoes sublimative transformation, either its original aim or its original object-cathexis must undergo repression. That is, sublimation involves the repression of certain aspects of unacceptable motivation, and the substitution in consciousness of a modification acceptable socially and personally.

[24] Murray, *op. cit.*, p. 394.

Fixation and Regression

At the time when a motive first undergoes sublimation, the sublimation may be regarded as a socialized progression; the motive has been modified to conform with social expectations. In this sense, at least, sublimation involves the antithesis of fixation or regression. But a sublimation may become fixated, so that in time it will come to be regarded as a manifestation of immaturity; and, according to Murray, "sublimation may be an escape and, in that sense, a regression." [25]

It is questionable whether sublimation, as an evaluative concept, should be applied to instances that involve fixation or regression, except perhaps in the case of a *temporary* regression (e.g., the sublimative expression of aggression through sports or hobbies).

Fixation may be at the basis of certain sublimations. For example, psychosexual fixations at pregenital levels of development may undergo sublimation, and thus become unobjectionable in the mature personality.[26]

Perceptual Identification

Object-sublimations involve perceptual identification of the originally cathected object with an acceptable substitute object. For example, the man who vents his aggression onto a golf ball may (unconsciously) identify the ball with the boss who has recently humiliated him, or with a competitor who has just gained an important contract he had hoped to get for himself.

Aim-sublimations involve the perceptual identification of an original gratifying activity with a substitute activity; the substitute activity becomes gratifying by virtue of such an identification. Thus, social conversation (as a sublimation of sexual motivation) may be pleasurable to the extent that it can be identified (unconsciously) with sexual activity.

Developmental Identification

It is likely that sublimation involves nothing more than the substitution of ego-ideal motivation for sexual, aggressive, and other forms of id motivation. And, as we have seen, it is by means of developmental identification that ego-ideals (positive psychogenic motives) become functional in the personality. In one of his discussions of the dissolution

[25] Murray, *op. cit.*, p. 394.
[26] Sigmund Freud, *An Outline of Psychoanalysis* (New York, 1949), pp. 30–1.

of the Oedipus complex, for example, Freud has suggested such an interpretation.

> The object cathexes [of the Oedipus complex] are given up and replaced by identification. The authority of the father or the parents is introjected into the ego and there forms the kernel of the super-ego, which takes its severity from the father, perpetuates his prohibition against incest, and so insures the ego against a recurrence of the libidinal object-cathexis. *The libidinal trends belonging to the Oedipus-complex are in part desexualized and sublimated, which probably happens with every transformation into identification; in part they are inhibited in their aim and changed into affectionate feelings. . . .*[27]

This excerpt suggests strongly that Freud believed the process of developmental identification to involve the substitution of ego-ideals in place of personal sexual objects (in this case, the parents) who have become unacceptable objects for sexual cathexis—though remaining suitable objects for aim-inhibited sexual cathexis (that is, for affectionate feelings). It is even possible to interpret the aim-inhibited impulses (affectionate feelings, etc.) as ego-ideals (positive psychogenic motives).

Displacement

The previous discussion has distinguished between aim-sublimations and object-sublimations; as we have seen, the latter are instances of displacement. Such displacements are termed sublimations in view of their social acceptance; sublimation becomes merely an *evaluative concept*. In other words, socially acceptable displacements are termed object-sublimations.

Projection

Sublimation may, in certain instances, function in combination with projection. The reformer may be one who has sublimated his aggression (having displaced it onto "evil") and who has projected some of his own "evil" impulses onto mankind in general or onto special groups of mankind. Religious leaders of the humanitarian stamp may have sublimated their affectionate impulses (having displaced them onto "humanity") and, at the same time, may have projected their "evil" impulses onto mankind; thus, out of love for humanity, they strive to rid the people of their "evil" impulses.

[27] Freud, *Collected Papers*, II, 273. (Italics mine.)

SUBLIMATION AND FUNCTIONAL AUTONOMY

SUBLIMATION has been defined in the early part of this chapter as a concept implying that some degree of gratification of the original motive will continue to be achieved in terms of its sublimative transformation. Some degree of sexual gratification, for example, is expected to occur as a function of such aim-inhibited expressions as social conversation and affectionate feelings.

The concept of functional autonomy, on the other hand, implies that psychogenic motives will function independently of the biogenic motives associated with their original development—that psychogenic gratification will occur without any accompanying gratification of a more fundamental need.

Thus we have in the concepts of sublimation and of functional autonomy what seem to be mutually exclusive contradictions. It appears that if the sublimation concept possesses validity, then the concept of functional autonomy must be invalid; and it appears that if the concept of functional autonomy is valid, then the concept of sublimation must be invalid.

Masserman, in support of the sublimation concept, has implied that psychogenic motives will continue throughout life to function, instrumentally, for the satisfaction of more basic needs.

> For instance, the student may have begun to wonder whether any of his "physiologic needs" were really being satisfied by reading this book, yet a little reflection will, perhaps, dispel some of his justifiable misgivings. Thus: why *is* he reading this book? To gain, or at any rate seek, knowledge. To what end? To be a more capable—or at least a more widely read—psychologist, physician, social worker or whatever. But why be one? Here the replies may consist of protestations, more or less vehement or sincere, that the reader wants to prepare himself for future research, enlighten the current darkness of his chosen field, serve suffering humanity, and so on. But further and franker introspection will reveal that beneath such rationalizations lie somewhat more mundane, though still quite complex strivings. These may be actuated by desires for prestige, financial gain, opportunities for marriage, a favorable environment for a future family and other quite realistic—and withal quite human—motivations. Finally, even these "social" strivings,

however displaced, rationalized or sublimated, can be traced to more nearly elemental sexual or parental drives, and lastly, needs for sustenance, shelter, protection from injury and other such physiologic determinants as emerge when the core of our living is stripped of its multiple-faceted social adaptations and verbal embellishments. True, what civilization we have is comprised of these cultural deviations and elaborations of our basic needs, and studies of such processes are rightly of paramount concern to the social sciences. . . .[28]

Allport, however, who was the author of the concept of functional autonomy, regards sublimation as a concept of doubtful validity.

. . . (1) As applied to highly specific organic tensions (hunger, need for oxygen, or physiological sex processes) the concept has absolutely no applicability. . . . Local segmental tensions can only be relieved in ways specifically suited to them. (2) As applied to the distraction of attention from an unwelcome interest—by keeping otherwise occupied—the concept is really a misnomer. One reduces anger by leaving the scene of provocation and taking up some absorbing occupation; not by sublimation, but through a redirection of attention and interest. (3) As applied to the fatiguing out of generalized concurrent tensions accompanying a specific state of unrest, the doctrine has more merit. The diffuse somatic restlessness induced by thirst, sexual desire, and the like can often be reduced by irrelevant activity that fatigues the organism as a whole. (The *specific* segmental tension however is not directly relieved by such activity.) (4) As a still more complex concept, implying that an individual may without serious conflict forego some specific gratification, provided that he finds other sources of equal satisfaction, sublimation is a useful doctrine. In such instances, the individual simply disregards his unfulfilled desires, letting them atrophy, or repressing them without disaster, in the interest of an alternative plan of life that satisfies not these desires but satisfies *him* as a whole man. But in such a case the original psychoanalytic definition of the term is violated, for the individual is *not sublimating the original energy* at all. He is busy doing something quite different, namely, leading a satisfying life in spite of the lack of fulfillment of a certain desire.[29]

[28] Masserman, *op. cit.*, p. 106.
[29] Gordon W. Allport, *Personality: a Psychological Interpretation* (New York, 1937), p. 185 n.

Mowrer has likewise expressed dissatisfaction with the concept of sublimation, and has replaced it with the concept of substitution.

> . . . Freud wrote voluminously about a highly questionable process which he termed *sublimation.* . . . A more felicitous conception is that of *substitution*, the process of replacing immediate, infantile, organic pleasures by the more enduring satisfactions which come from a sense of full and responsible observation of the rules and principles governing the activities of family, community, state, nation, and of the human enterprise generally. In so accepting these rules and principles, one wins back to a fuller and more assured satisfaction of even the instinctual needs than seems possible in any other pattern of existence. . . .[30]

The views of Allport and of Mowrer will be seen to be consistent with our present interpretation of sublimation as the substitution of ego-ideals for id motivation. In a general way, as suggested by Mowrer in the preceding excerpt, such a substitution may serve as a basis for the achievement of living conditions in which the biogenic motives will be assured satisfaction; and this point of view is not appreciably different from that which was expressed by Masserman, as quoted above. This indirect form of gratification, however, seems not to be what Freud had in mind when he used the term sublimation, since the term implied *repression* of the motive as it functioned prior to its sublimative transformation.

The contradiction that is seemingly implicit in the terms sublimation and functional autonomy can probably be resolved in terms of Allport's fourth application—that sublimation involves repression of id motives and the substitution of psychogenic motives whose gratification serves to *satisfy the whole person.*

This interpretation seems to be consistent with Freud's usage of the term *sexual* to imply any instance of positive cathexis: the over-all intention of the organism will be the same, whether it be carried out by sexual union of the genitals or by verbal and other indirect modes of communion with persons and things. Similarly, the total intention of the organism will be the same, whether it be expressed through physical assault on a person or through verbal assault against "sin" or "evil."

[30] O. Hobart Mowrer, "Learning Theory and the Neurotic Paradox," in *Learning Theory and Personality Dynamics*, O. Hobart Mowrer (New York, 1950), pp. 528–9. (Reprinted from *American Journal of Orthopsychiatry, 18* [1948], 571–610.) Reprinted by permission of *American Journal of Orthopsychiatry* and The Ronald Press Company. Copyright, 1948, by American Orthopsychiatric Association, 1950, by The Ronald Press Company.

This total intention—the satisfaction of the whole person—seems to be all that is implied by the conception that sublimation involves substitute gratification of motives.

No contradiction, then, need be implied between the concepts of sublimation and functional autonomy, if *sexuality* is understood to imply all instances of positive cathexis, if *aggression* is understood to imply all instances of negative-destructive cathexis, and if *fear* is understood to imply all instances of negative-escape cathexis.[31]

If the concepts of functional autonomy and sublimation cannot adequately be reconciled, even in terms of the conception just mentioned, then it appears that, of the two concepts, functional autonomy, rather than sublimation, should be rejected. If we analyze the need integrate (or the motive) into its components—that is, into a need, an instrumental act, and an object—it appears that the *need* aspect of a motive cannot be learned. In other words, the need must be a fundamental *biogenic* aspect of all motives.

When only the need (without an instrumental act or an object) is represented in consciousness, *anxiety* will be experienced; but, on the basis of learning, this anxiety may acquire substitute instrumental acts and substitute objects for its relief or gratification. Psychogenic motives will, then, always consist of a basic core of biogenic need-tension (anxiety) which has been psychogenically connected with conscious representations (anticipations) of a gratifying instrumental act and a gratifying object.

In terms of this conception, sublimation, rather than functional autonomy, can be regarded as the more adequate concept relating to psychogenic motivation.[32] Whenever a psychogenic motive is gratified, it will necessarily relieve an underlying biogenic need-tension in relation to an instrumental act and an object that have been acquired (cathected) on the basis of learning.[33]

[31] This controversy between adherents of sublimation and adherents of functional autonomy may be seen as an instance of failure to note that different levels of abstraction are taken for granted by the adherents of the two points of view. Certainly sublimation of sexuality does not frequently yield genital, oral, or anal satisfaction of a direct kind, but it yields *sexual* satisfaction on the higher level of abstraction, in the sense of establishing pleasurable relations with a positively cathected object. One doesn't kill one's father by writing a book espousing atheism, but one destroys or nullifies, for some at least, the "faith of our fathers."

[32] Not only sublimation, however, but also the other defensive modifications of a motive will always involve psychogenic transformations of instrumental acts and objects in order to achieve gratification of the biogenic need-tension.

[33] The principle of regression to biogenic motivation seems, in terms of this analysis, either to be invalid or to be improperly named. When "regression to biogenic motivation" occurs, it occurs through the fact that many psychogenic

ADJUSTIVE IMPLICATIONS

SUBLIMATION, especially of sexual motivation, was said by Freud to function as an important basis of human achievement.

> This very incapacity in the sexual instinct to yield full satisfaction as soon as it submits to the first demands of culture becomes the source . . . of the grandest cultural achievements, which are brought to birth by ever greater sublimation of the components of the sexual instinct. For what motive would induce man to put his sexual energy to other uses if by any disposal of it he could obtain fully satisfying pleasure? He would never let go of this pleasure and would make no further progress.[34]

It is probable that a similar statement could be made concerning the sublimation of aggression and fear.

Sublimation may be regarded as a frequent outcome of plus-plus conflicts; such being the case, sublimation should be expected to bring satisfaction to the individual who employs this method of defense: for, whichever choice occurs in a plus-plus conflict situation, the outcome will be gratifying.

Specifically, the conflict that underlies sublimation requires a choice between biogenic gratification and gratification of an ego-ideal. Sublimation, as we have seen, involves acting in conformity with the ego-ideal, while repudiating the biogenic motive. This may account for the high social evaluation that is accorded sublimation as a defensive process.

If sublimation commonly depends upon a plus-plus conflict, this implies that sublimation will be fostered when maximum emphasis is placed upon providing the child with desirable alternatives for his disapproved behavior. Rather than shouting "Don't" and administering severe punishment, the parent should help the child to discover socially approved ways of attaining satisfaction.

---

instrumental acts have become, on the basis of changed circumstances, extremely inappropriate as indirect means of insuring gratification of organic needs. Under normal conditions, being a "moral" individual with high ideals of achievement will insure satisfaction of the basic needs; but, under conditions of social and economic distress, these psychogenic values will become maladaptive or relatively useless. "Regression to biogenic motivation," then, will actually amount to a substitution of relatively crude and direct instrumental acts for relatively sophisticated and refined instrumental acts. In other words, it will involve regression to more primitive *psychogenic* motivation.

[34] Freud, *Collected Papers*, IV, 216.

SUMMARY

SUBLIMATION involves a transformation in the aim (instrumental act) or in the object of a motive, so that its expression will conform to the dominant values of society.

Motives that are commonly sublimated include the sexual impulses and the aggressive impulses. Warm feelings of friendship and affection may be regarded as aim-sublimations of sexuality.

Secondary narcissism, expressed as devotion to ego-ideals, may involve object-sublimations of primary narcissism. Oral impulses may gain sublimative expression through smoking, chewing gum, kissing, sarcasm, oratory, poetry, etc. Anal impulses may be expressed in sublimated form as the "anal character," or as collecting, painting and sculpture, etc.

Genital sexuality may gain sublimative gratification through such activities as art, literature, music, gardening, agriculture, animal husbandry, science, and technology.

Sublimated voyeurism may take the form of scientific research, news-gathering, or the investigations of clinical psychologists and psychiatrists. Exhibitionism may take the form of displaying one's achievements or seeking fame.

Sexual masochism may be sublimated in the form of a need to be humiliated; while sadism may take the form of aggressive-dominative activities, or of such occupations as medicine and dentistry.

Incestuous erotism may be sublimated to become reverence for motherhood or respect for authority. Sublimated homosexuality may be manifested in activities that belong, by custom, to the sex role of the opposite sex.

Aggressive sublimations involve the expression of aggressive motivation in subtle or indirect ways. Object-sublimations may include such activities as social reform, aggressive sports, conquering natural elements, and working as a butcher or professional soldier. Aim-sublimations may involve verbal attack or aggressive fantasies.

Anxiety functions as the basis of sublimative transformations; were it not for the occurrence of anxiety, the original motive would achieve expression without undergoing any transformation. If sublimation is carried to the extreme of "impracticality," or if it becomes too firmly fixated, sublimation may become a basis of anxiety—though, by definition, sublimation can be expected to become the source of only a *minimum* of anxiety.

Sublimation may occur in combination with any or all of the other defensive mechanisms.

There seems to be no necessary contradiction between the concepts of sublimation and of functional autonomy. If sexuality is interpreted as equivalent to positive cathexis, if hostility is interpreted as equivalent to negative-destructive cathexis, and if fear is interpreted as equivalent to negative-escape cathexis, then the concepts of sublimation and functional autonomy may, at a high level of abstraction, be regarded as equivalent concepts. If, however, a choice need be made between the two concepts, there is reason to regard sublimation as the more useful.

Sublimation has been regarded as an important basis of civilized human achievements. The parent may foster sublimation by providing the child with sympathetic guidance in the choice of acceptable, to replace unacceptable, forms of gratification.

The mechanism of reaction formation will be discussed in the following chapter.

▶ Suggested Readings

Chassell, J. "Vicissitudes of Sublimation," *Psychiatry, 1* (1938), 221–32.

Freud, S. *Civilization and Its Discontents.* London, 1951. Pp. 7–144.

Glover, E. "Sublimation, Substitution, and Social Anxiety," *International Journal of Psychoanalysis, 12* (1931), 263–97.

Hart, H. H. "Sublimation and Aggression," *Psychiatric Quarterly, 22* (1948), 389–412.

Lewin, K. *A Dynamic Theory of Personality.* New York, 1935. Chap. vi, pp. 180–93.

Symonds, P. M. *The Dynamics of Human Adjustment.* New York, 1946. Chap. xvii, pp. 405–23.

Taylor, W. S. "Alternative Response as a form of 'Sublimation,' " *Psychological Review, 39* (1932), 165–73.

Wallin, J. E. W. *Personality Maladjustments and Mental Hygiene.* New York, 1949. Pp. 497–502.

CHAPTER Fifteen

Reaction Formation

. . . whosoever smiteth thee on thy right cheek, turn to him the other also.[1]

W HEN reaction formation occurs, the individual's conscious motivation will undergo a marked degree of defensive modification. A motive that is unacceptable to the individual will be replaced by its conscious opposite. By means of reaction formation, then, the individual can deny the nature of his fundamental motivation, so that the demands of his conscience will seem to him to be the main determinants of his behavior. In a very real sense, as we shall see, reaction formation involves the substitution of conscience (negative superego-motivation) for positive id-motivation.

DEFINITION AND DIFFERENTIATION

WHILE both sublimation and reaction formation involve modifications in conscious motivation—while both involve the substitution of superego motivation for id motivation—they may be clearly differentiated on the basis of the kinds of superego motivation they in-

[1] Matthew v–39.

volve. *Undoing* and *compromise formation*, which resemble these processes in certain respects, will also be defined in this section.

Reaction Formation

Reaction formation involves the defensive transformation (in consciousness) of a motive into its opposite. "When a repressed impulse is
replaced by another impulse of character opposite or antagonistic to it,
we speak of reaction formation." [2]

In other words, when reaction formation occurs, an unacceptable
need-integrate, as it is represented in consciousness, will be transformed
into a need integrate of opposite intention; the original impulse in relation to a particular object (or in relation to all objects in a general category) will undergo repression, and this will be replaced in consciousness by an *opposite* impulse in relation to the object (or in relation to
all objects in a general category). [3]

Thus, a sexual impulse in relation to homosexual objects may be
replaced by conscious disgust in relation to homosexual objects; aggressive impulses toward animals may be replaced by excessive kindness
toward animals; or sexual impulses that are directed toward the mother-
in-law may be transformed into conscious antagonism.

Reaction Formation as Differentiated from Sublimation

Both sublimation and reaction formation involve modifications of
conscious motivation. In the case of sublimation, the modification in the
aim or in the object of a motive will be just sufficient to permit gratification with a minimum of anxiety; that is, some degree of gratification
of the original motive will be achieved through gratification of its substitute. Thus sexual gratification in some degree may be achieved
through the social interactions of friendship.

In the case of reaction formation, however, there occurs a firm,
conscious denial of the motive itself, as well as of any motivation that
the individual can consciously interpret as a remote substitute for the
original. For example, a reaction formation against sexual impulses may

---

[2] Thomas M. French, "Clinical Approach to the Dynamics of Behavior," in
Personality and the Behavior Disorders, J. McV. Hunt, ed. (New York, 1944),
p. 263.

[3] Reaction formation, like aim-sublimation, involves a transformation in the
instrumental act, while the need and the object remain relatively unchanged. When
reaction formation occurs, the original instrumental act is replaced in consciousness
by an instrumental act of opposite intention; a negative instrumental act is substituted for a positive one, or a positive instrumental act is substituted for a negative one.

be manifested as a frigid aloofness in regard to other people, whereas a sublimation of sexual impulses may be manifested as pleasurable warmth toward other people.

Perhaps the clearest differentiation between sublimation and reaction formation may be made in terms of the kind of motivation that is substituted for the original conscious motivation.

Sublimation involves the substitution of *positive* motivation for *positive* motivation, or of *negative* motivation for *negative* motivation; but reaction formation involves the substitution of *negative* motivation for *positive* motivation, or of *positive* motivation for *negative* motivation.

When sexuality undergoes sublimation, for example, the individual will remain aware of positive motivation in some form; but when reaction formation occurs in relation to sexuality, the individual will become conscious of negative motivation (hostility, fear, or a combination of hostility and fear) in relation to sexual acts or sexual objects.

Undoing

Undoing was described by Freud in his book, *The Problem of Anxiety*. Freud discussed this process in connection with *isolation*, which represents a sort of halfway point between suppression and repression. Freud regarded undoing and reaction formation as the defensive processes most characteristic of the obsessive or compulsive neurosis.

Undoing, like reaction formation, involves replacing a behavior tendency by its opposite. But whereas reaction formation refers to a modification in conscious motivation, undoing refers to *a motor act*, an act that cancels or nullifies the significance of a preceding act. Reaction formation involves a relatively *continuous perception* of motivation opposite in tendency to the motivation that has been repressed; but undoing involves a *succession of acts* that are of opposite significance.

> [Undoing] . . . is a kind of negative magic which by means of a motor symbolism would "blow away," as it were, not the consequences of an event (an impression, an experience), but the event itself. . . . In compulsion neurosis . . . the individual's second act abrogates or nullifies the first, in such manner that it is as though neither had taken place, whereas in reality both have done so. . . . The effort at "undoing" finds its reflection in the normal sphere in the resolve to treat an occurrence as *non arrivé*. . . .[4]

[4] Sigmund Freud, *The Problem of Anxiety* (New York, 1936), pp. 53–4.

Thus, in normal life, *undoing* may be said to occur when the individual, after having been overtly aggressive toward another person, behaves on the next occasion with excessive kindness and courtesy, without bothering to apologize for his previous behavior.

Compromise Formation

Compromise formation is manifested by neurotic symptoms that represent simultaneously, or successively, the gratification of opposite or incompatible motives.

> [The symptoms] . . . are in fact . . . the effects of *compromises* between two opposed tendencies, acting on one another; they represent both that which is repressed, and also that which has effected the repression and has co-operated in bringing them about. The representation of either one or another of these two factors may predominate in the symptom, but it happens very rarely that one of them is absent altogether. In hysteria a collaboration of the two tendencies in one symptom is usually achieved. In the obsessional neurosis the two parts are often distinct: the symptom is then a double one and consists of two successive actions which cancel each other.[5]

The concept of compromise formation, then, seems to include the concept of undoing: while undoing refers to the *successive* gratification of opposed tendencies, compromise formation may refer either to the *successive* or to the *simultaneous* gratification of opposed (conflicting) tendencies.

Both compromise formation and undoing involve symptoms or symptomatic acts that symbolize the gratification of opposing motives. Compromise formation and undoing may be regarded as simultaneous or successive expressions of both sublimation and reaction formation; they symbolize gratification and renunciation of unacceptable motivation.[6]

---

[5] Sigmund Freud, *A General Introduction to Psycho-Analysis* (New York, 1935), p. 265.

[6] From the point of view of the individual's unacceptable motivation, sublimation involves a disguised form of gratification, while reaction formation involves a renunciation. From the point of view of the substituted conscious motivation, both sublimation and reaction formation involve gratification. All behavior may be regarded as involving compromise formation, since any instance of behavior must gratify a combination of different motives, some of which are contradictory to other motives in the total pattern.

FORMS OF EXPRESSION

BRILL has referred to reaction formation—the expression of a tendency that is the opposite of an original impulse—as a "dam of civilization," since it functions to prevent an unacceptable impulse from breaking through to overt expression.[7] Sexuality and aggression are most commonly involved in reaction formation.

Reaction Formations against Psychosexual Impulses

Reaction formation is one of the principal defensive measures employed against anxiety stemming from sexual conflicts. It represents the conquest of pleasurable anticipation by the moral forces of the culture. The sexual impulses become associated with attitudes of disgust, shame, etc.

Pregenital impulses, especially, lose their pleasurable qualities through reaction formation.

> The sexual feelings of these infantile years would on the one hand be unusable, since the procreating functions are postponed—this is the chief character of the latency period; on the other hand, they would as such be perverse, as they would emanate from erogenous zones and from impulses which in the individual's course of development could only evoke a feeling of displeasure. They, therefore, awaken psychic counter-forces (feelings of reaction), which build up the . . . psychical dams of disgust, shame, and morality.[8]

Reaction formation against pleasures connected with the *oral* zone may be expressed as a loss of appetite, as verbal taciturnity (reaction formation against an oral sublimation), or as a feeling of disgust in relation to kissing, smoking, or chewing gum. Brill has pointed out, for example, that the Japanese, unlike modern Americans, abhor kissing; Rodin's famous statue, titled "The Kiss," was said to have caused a riot when it was put on display in Tokyo.[9]

The oral-incorporative attitude of dependence—which is manifested in infancy as dependence on an adult for the satisfaction of all needs, especially of the need for milk—is in conflict with the ego-ideals

[7] A. A. Brill, *Lectures on Psychoanalytic Psychiatry* (New York, 1946), p. 217.

[8] Sigmund Freud, "Three Contributions to the Theory of Sex," in *The Basic Writings of Sigmund Freud*, A. A. Brill, ed. (New York, 1938), p. 584.

[9] Brill, *op. cit.*, p. 174.

of most adults; the reaction formation against it may take the form of exaggerated self-sufficiency, social aloofness, or independence of attitude.[10] The reaction formation against greediness, which is a sublimative manifestation of oral erotism, may take the form of excessive generosity.[11]

Reaction formations against *anal erotism*—against coprophilia, or the delight in one's own excrement or in dirtiness—will be manifested in the form of excessive orderliness, excessive cleanliness, and excessive neatness, along with disgust at the sight or thought of anything unclean.[12] Such a reaction formation is usually implied when a person is said to be "nasty nice."

> Feelings of revulsion and shame may have been instilled in [the infant] by repeated severe reproofs for his dirty habits. As a result of excessive discipline, he may eventually become overfastidious, and his exaggerated nicety may extend to many things. It may show itself, for example, in excessively precise speech or in absurd fussiness about trivial matters, such as a speck on the garment or on the skin (misophobia). Later in life, his reaction formation might extend to disgusting sights and show itself in tendencies to vomit or in feelings of nausea. . . .[13]

Reaction formations against mature *genital sexuality* may be expressed in the form of exaggerated disgust or loathing at the mention or the thought of sexual expression; or they may take the form of militant opposition to "vice" in any of its various categories.

> These are the persons who frequently hold high moral standards and preach them in and out of season, are militant in opposing public dance halls, houses of prostitution, abortion, and birth-control measures. They censor the overt expression of sex in movies, books and plays, regarding such expression as unmoral and filthy.[14]

Among adolescents, reaction formation against sex may be mani-

[10] Karen Horney, *New Ways in Psychoanalysis* (New York, 1939), p. 26; Percival M. Symonds, *The Dynamics of Human Adjustment* (New York, 1946), p. 427.

[11] Horney, *op. cit.*, p. 66.

[12] Franz Alexander, *Fundamentals of Psychoanalysis* (New York, 1948), pp. 98, 105; Sigmund Freud, *New Introductory Lectures on Psycho-Analysis* (New York, 1933), p. 140.

[13] J. E. Wallace Wallin, *Personality Maladjustments and Mental Hygiene* (New York, 1949), p. 294. Reprinted by permission of McGraw-Hill Book Company, Inc. Copyright, 1935, 1949, by McGraw-Hill Book Company, Inc.

[14] Symonds, *op. cit.*, p. 432.

fested as "touchiness" in regard to "necking" or in regard to the verbal discussion of sex; it may even extend to the avoidance of social contact with persons of the opposite sex.

Reaction formation against *homosexuality* may be expressed as a certain degree of misanthropy, with the avoidance, as much as possible, of companionable relations with members of one's own sex. The individual who feels uncomfortable when in the presence of persons of his own sex may be so on the basis of such a reaction formation.

Freud believed that delusions of persecution, which occur as a major symptom of paranoia, are based on a reaction formation against homosexual impulses, with the subsequent *projection* of the transformed impulses onto another person.

> We consider . . . that what lies at the core of the conflict in cases of paranoia among males is a homosexual wish-phantasy of *loving a man.* . . .
>
> The proposition "I (a man) love him" is contradicted by:
>
> (a) Delusions of persecution; for it loudly asserts: "I do not *love* him—I *hate* him."
>
> This contradiction . . . cannot, however, become conscious to a paranoiac in this form. . . . Consequently the proposition "I hate him" becomes transformed by *projection* into another one: "*He hates* (persecutes) *me*, which will justify me in hating him." And thus the unconscious feeling . . . makes its appearance as though it were the consequence of an external perception:
>
> "I do not *love* him—I *hate* him, because HE PERSECUTES ME."
>
> Observation leaves room for no doubt that the persecutor is some one who was once loved. . . .[15]

Against *sadistic* tendencies, the reaction formation may be expressed as excessive kindliness.[16] Against *masochistic* tendencies, which ordinarily involve enjoyment of suffering, the reaction formation may assert itself as conscious resentment that one is required to suffer so much indignity and humiliation.

Modesty, shyness, or shame may be the expression of a reaction formation against *exhibitionistic* tendencies;[17] while against *voyeurism* the reaction formation may be manifested as disgust or lack of curiosity concerning sexual matters.[18]

[15] Sigmund Freud, *Collected Papers,* translated by Alix and James Strachey (London, 1950), III, 448–9. Reprinted by permission of The Hogarth Press, Ltd.

[16] Horney, *op. cit.,* p. 56.

[17] Alexander, *op. cit.,* p. 105.

[18] Symonds, *op. cit.,* p. 432.

Puritanism or asceticism may be regarded as a reaction formation against the desire to experience any form of pleasure (which, in Freud's view, is the equivalent of sexuality). Anna Freud has emphasized that ascetic reactions often function as a major defense against the powerful sexual impulses of adolescence.[19]

Freud has taken the position that superego motives arise as reaction formations against the Oedipus complex.

> The significance of the Oedipus complex began to grow to gigantic proportions and it looked as though social order, morals, justice and religion had arisen together in the primaeval ages of mankind as reaction-formations against the Oedipus complex.[20]

This is a significant point which will be discussed in a subsequent section.

Reaction Formations against Aggressive Impulses

Aggressive impulses cannot, in view of societal prohibitions, be expressed in their crude forms. One means of keeping them under control is provided by reaction formation. After a reaction formation against aggressive impulses has occurred, the individual will behave toward frustrating agents as if their behavior were gratifying. Instead of hostility, he will express tenderness; instead of hate, he will express love; instead of irritability, he will express patience and politeness; instead of belligerence, he will express submissiveness and humility.[21]

> The camp counselor . . . is afraid of his impulse to beat up the unbearably cocky ten-year-old; hence he maintains before his own eyes the self-picture of a benign, ever-patient father. If holding up this picture is not sufficient to quell the opposing images, he overtly enacts the role of the patient, loving observer, lives as an impossibly patient and forgiving person; the other boys and visitors at the camp wonder how he can ever maintain his equanimity in the face of such irritations. . . .[22]

Reaction formations against hostility remind us of "passive resistance," as it was practiced by Gandhi, and indeed of the Christian doc-

[19] Anna Freud, *The Ego and the Mechanisms of Defense* (New York, 1946), pp. 167–9.

[20] Sigmund Freud, *Collected Papers* (London, 1950), V, 129.

[21] Anna Freud, *op. cit.*, p. 51; Alexander, *op. cit.*, p. 105.

[22] Gardner Murphy, *Personality: a Biosocial Approach to Origins and Structure* (New York, 1947), p. 551.

trine that, instead of striking back, one should turn the other cheek in invitation to an aggressor.

Neurotic Symptoms as Compromise Formations

Neurotic symptoms, especially the symptoms of obsessional neurosis, have been interpreted as symbolic representations of reaction formation against unacceptable impulses.[23]

> The content of her obsessional neurosis consisted in a tormenting obsession about washing and cleanliness and in exceedingly vigorous protective measures against wicked injuries which others might have to fear from her; that is to say, it consisted of reaction-formations against anal-erotic and sadistic impulses. . . .[24]

Since obsessive and compulsive symptoms frequently represent reaction formations against impulses, their true motivational sources may be sought in tendencies that are opposite in character to the symptoms themselves.

But since neurotic symptoms can best be understood as *compromise formations*, the symptoms can be expected also to represent gratification of the original tendencies. Some of the characteristics of the symptoms will thus symbolize gratification of repressed impulses, while other symptomatic characteristics will symbolize reaction formations against such gratification.

DYNAMIC INTERRELATIONS WITH ANXIETY

REACTION formation, like all other defensive mechanisms, has its basis in anxiety; and it will function as the source of subsequent anxiety.

Anxiety as a Basis of Reaction Formation

Reaction formation involves the conscious expression of one aspect of a plus-minus conflict, while the other aspect is kept under repression; reaction formation, that is, has its basis in ambivalence. Since reaction formation involves the compulsive expression of one aspect of a conflict, it will function as a solution—however precarious the solution may be—of the conflict; and it therefore will function as a defense

---

[23] Freud, *A General Introduction* . . . , pp. 327, 332.
[24] Sigmund Freud, *Collected Papers* (London, 1950), II, 126.

against anxiety. Mowrer has further clarified the defensive value of reaction formation:

> The element of conflict in such a situation emerges, not only from
> the love-hate ambivalence per se, but also from the knowledge
> (often unverbalized) that overt expression of hostility would result
> in "loss of love" (punishment, deprivation, isolation, etc.). Antici-
> pation of such a loss arouses anxiety, and in the attempt at "de-
> fense" against the latter the most elaborate efforts may be made to
> conceal and deny the component of hostility. How can the defense
> be managed better than by continual testimony, in word and act,
> of affection and solicitude? . . .[25]

Guilt and inferiority feelings may also be reduced as a function of
reaction formation, since through this mechanism the individual may
gain a feeling of self-righteousness.[26]

While reaction formation will relieve one aspect of conflicting
motivation in terms of its direct compulsive expression, it becomes necessary to account for the relief of the *repressed* aspect of the conflicting
motivation. Unless some form of gratification is insured, the repressed
motivation will be experienced in the form of conscious anxiety or in
the form of some "anxiety equivalent."

It appears reasonable to interpret the individual's compulsive emphasis on an opposite kind of expression as functioning in the interest of
gratifying his repressed motivation. Excessive expressions of love, affection, or solicitude may serve an aggressive aim; the recipient of excessive solicitude may find it a source of extreme frustration. Excessive
aggressiveness may serve a sexual aim; this is quite apparent, for example, in the behavior of the sadistic lover. Excessive fear may serve
the positive aim of love or sexuality; for the individual who is terror-
ized in the presence of a love-object will make his love apparent in
terms of his extreme reaction.

Another possibility that should not be overlooked is that behavior
which expresses an opposite intention on the conscious level may be
identified unconsciously with the instrumental acts that have undergone
repression, so that the expression of a reaction formation may bring
about *symbolic* gratification of the repressed motive. Thus, sadistic

[25] O. Hobart Mowrer, *Learning Theory and Personality Dynamics: Selected
Papers* (New York, 1950), p. 385.
[26] Abraham H. Maslow and Bela Mittelmann, *Principles of Abnormal Psychology: the Dynamics of Psychic Illness* (New York, 1941), pp. 161–2.

cruelty may be symbolic of sexual expression; fear of women may be symbolic of expressing love for women; kindness toward a person may be symbolic of an aggressive assault.

In actuality, then, although on the basis of his reaction formation the individual will consciously perceive only one aspect of his conflicting motivation, and although he will be aware only of his intention to behave in conformity with his conscious motivation, his behavior will function to gratify both aspects of his conflict. He will either perceive outcomes that satisfy his repressed motivation, as when he observes the frustration of a person in relation to whom he is oversolicitous; or he will unconsciously perceive his own actions as symbolic of instrumental acts he has consciously renounced, as when he identifies an aggressive action with the sexual act.

Reaction Formation as a Basis of Anxiety

Reaction formation may become a source of anxiety through the fact that it provides only a precarious defense against the original anxiety, through the fact that it may prevent the gratification of normal motives, and through the fact that the overemphasis of particular behavior-tendencies that it involves may lead to social frustrations.

Much energy is spent in the "leaning over backwards" that reaction formations involve. It is only by compulsive emphasis on antithetical ideas and opposite behavior that the individual can maintain repression of the other aspect of his conflict. The "solution," in other words, will be an unstable one, in danger of being replaced by its opposite at any moment. Such a "breakthrough" of the repressed motivation may then be followed by guilt and by the reinstatement of reaction formation. Thus there may occur a sequence of contradictory behavior-manifestations accompanied by periodic surges of anxiety.

On the other hand, reaction formations that have been useful to adjustment at a certain period in life may become strongly fixated, so that they will continue to maintain the repression of motives that at a later period should, in the interests of mature adjustment, become available for expression. Reaction formations, in other words, may become "obsolete." This is especially true in the case of the sexual motive and, perhaps to a lesser extent, in the case of the aggressive motive.

Social frustrations will arise when the individual is regarded by others as one who is lacking in warmth or in spontaneous human qualities—when he seems to be aloof or cold, overly conscientious, excessively kind to the point of "making it hurt," etc. Not only will he lack acceptability as a social companion, but he may become an easy victim of persons who wish to exploit him for their own private purposes.

RELATIONS WITH OTHER DEFENSES

REACTION formation is dynamically interrelated with repression, with fixation and regression, with perceptual identification, with developmental identification, with displacement, with projection, and with sublimation.

Repression

As previously mentioned, reaction formation involves the repression of unacceptable impulses and their replacement in consciousness by impulses of a directly antithetical character. The conscious emphasis on the opposite of an original tendency will aid in maintaining repression of the original tendency.[27]

Fixation and Regression

Fixation at a pregenital level of sexual development will frequently be overcome by means of a reaction formation; the child will make a progressive adjustment when he begins to experience disgust in relation to thumb-sucking or in relation to the sight of excrement. Later in his socialization, the child may manifest disgust in relation to words that refer to anal or genital functions. Still later, in response to frustration, he may regress to the point of using these "obscene" words; or, in the case of a psychotic breakdown, he may even regress to the point of soiling himself without compunction. Thus, the nullification of reaction formation may represent a regressive adjustment. On the other hand, the physician or the physiologist, or for that matter the parent of an infant, may manifest progression when his disgust in relation to physiological functions is replaced by a matter-of-fact attitude.

Perceptual Identification

If an object or activity against which a reaction formation has developed is identified with some second object, the second object may likewise become the object of reaction formation. If, for example, a certain kind of food is identified (on the basis of visual similarity) with

[27] Freud, *The Problem of Anxiety*, p. 30.

excrement, the food may itself be regarded with disgust. Or, if one identifies oneself with a downtrodden group that is the object of pity, one may become the object of self-pity.

Developmental Identification

Just as sublimation may be regarded as consisting of the substitution of ego-ideals for unacceptable id-motivation, reaction formation may be regarded as the substitution of conscience (negative psychogenic motivation) for id motivation. And, of course, conscience motives become functional through the process of developmental identification. The internalized "thou shalt not" will be maintained in consciousness, while the object of the prohibition—that is, the positive cathexis—will remain repressed. The pleasure in excremental functions will be replaced by disgust; the pleasure in exhibitionism will be replaced by modesty; the pleasure in aggression will be replaced by patient tolerance. In other words, conscience motives may be interpreted as reaction formations against the opposite aspects of plus-minus conflicts.

Displacement

Since displacement involves the transfer of an attitude from one object to another object with which it is perceptually identified, it will be seen that reaction formation is interrelated with displacement through the process of identification. If an individual has developed a reaction formation against a certain object, this reaction formation will probably be displaced onto any other object with which it is perceptually identified. Thus, if the individual has developed modesty with respect to exhibiting his body, he may displace this attitude onto other aspects of his personality which he unconsciously wishes to display.

The behavior of the antivivisectionist can probably be accounted for in terms of displacement in combination with reaction formation. Hostility toward people remains conscious and active, while the reaction formation against this hostility is displaced onto animals. Masserman has quoted from a letter which he received from such an antivivisectionist, an excerpt from which is given here:

"... My greatest wish is that you have brought home to you a torture that will be a thousand fold greater than what you ... are doing to little animals. ... If you are an example of what a noted psychiatrist should be I'm glad I am just an ordinary human being without letters after my name. I'd rather be just myself with a clear conscience, *knowing I have not hurt any living creature*, and can sleep without seeing frightened, terrified dying cats—because I know they must die after you have finished with them. No punishment is too great for you and I hope I live to read about your mangled body and long suffering before you finally die—and I'll laugh long and loud." [28]

There are many such "animal-lovers," who believe that no kindness can be too great to be bestowed on animals, and that no cruelty can be great enough to punish those who "mistreat" animals.

Projection

Reaction formation against "evil" motives may function in combination with projection of these impulses onto other persons. The reaction formation may then be generalized, or displaced onto the objects of projection. Thus, the individual who hates "sin" most strongly, and who cannot endure the thought of committing a "sinful" act, will be likely to see sinfulness manifested in the people around him, and to feel disgusted by the actions of these other people.

In other words, having developed a reaction formation against his own unacceptable motives, the individual will project these motives onto others; he will then find their expression in other people as disgusting as if they were expressed by himself. For example, the individual who is overly "nice" in speech will be disgusted by the "nasty" language other people employ.

Sublimation

Reaction formations may be sublimated, and sublimated motivation may subsequently become the object of reaction formation. Previous mention has been made of the "anal character," which involves the sublimation of reaction formations against anal erotism.[29] Masserman has given a further example, as follows:

> . . . A man who had made millions by exploiting the demociliary or occupational needs of Negroes in a large city endowed a foundation dedicated to research on the supposedly obscure causes of inter-racial tensions and unrest.[30]

[28] Jules H. Masserman, *Principles of Dynamic Psychiatry* (Philadelphia, 1946), p. 35 n.
[29] Freud, *Collected Papers*, II, 45–50.
[30] Masserman, *op. cit.*, p. 36.

Thus, the reaction formation against aggressive exploitation took a sublimated form.

On the other hand, sublimation *may be followed by* reaction formation. An individual may, for example, sublimate his exhibitionism, so that he will enjoy displaying his skills and personal accomplishments; the reaction formation against this sublimation may then take the form of modest retirement, with the deliberate avoidance of public display.

ADJUSTIVE IMPLICATIONS

AS WE have seen, reaction formation will develop most frequently in a plus-minus conflict situation—in a conflict involving ambivalence. This being the case, we should expect that punishment as a method of discipline (instead of pointing out desirable alternatives) will be an important factor in the development of reaction formations. Whatever the child is consistently punished for should become the object of a reaction formation.

Reaction formation will function to limit the individual's spontaneity, since his basic impulses will be "throttled" at their inception. He can only behave in a way that restrains direct gratification, rather than enjoy a form of substitute gratification, as he might in terms of a sublimation.

. . . The wish must be handled, managed, kept under control. The usual result is reaction formation in the form of a drive to limit all his primitive, impulsive, pleasure-seeking activities; he gives up to the environment. *In extreme cases*, being organized around a tabu, one becomes parsimonious, stingy, meticulous, punctual, tied down with petty self-restraints. Everything that is free, uncontrolled, spontaneous is dangerous. Papa will spank. Play safe; put the books back in the right place; rule the note paper neatly; pay your bills on the first of the month; be good. But be sure to take no pleasure in your goodness; be harsh with yourself, with all sinners.[31]

In general, all of the adjustive implications that follow from the principles of *developmental identification on the basis of respect* (Chap. XI) may be regarded as adjustive implications in relation to reaction formation.

[31] Murphy, *op. cit.*, p. 747.

SUMMARY

REACTION formation involves the transformation of a motive into its conscious antithesis. Undoing involves the alternate occurrence of motor activities that function to cancel each other. Compromise formation involves the simultaneous gratification, through a symptom, of incompatible motives.

While sublimation permits substitute gratification for the original motive, reaction formation involves a firm denial of gratification. Such symptomatic manifestations as compromise formation and undoing may be regarded as the simultaneous or the successive expressions of sublimation and reaction formation.

Reaction formations against sexual impulses may take the form of disgust, shame, or abhorrence in relation to sexual objects and acts.

Reaction formations against oral erotism include loss of appetite, verbal taciturnity, disgust in relation to kissing, chewing, or smoking, exaggerated self-sufficiency, social aloofness, and independence of attitude. Reaction formation against anal erotism may involve disgust at the sight or the thought of anything unclean, with a tendency toward exaggerated orderliness, neatness, and cleanliness.

Reaction formation against genital sexuality may involve disgust in relation to the thought of sexual expression; combined with aggressive sublimation, it may involve militant opposition to "vice."

Reaction formation against homosexuality may involve misanthropy, with avoidance of companionable relationships with persons of the same sex. Excessive kindliness may be a reaction formation against sadism; resentment of hardship may be a reaction formation against masochism. Modesty may be a reaction formation against exhibitionism, while lack of curiosity may be a reaction formation against voyeurism.

Puritanism or asceticism may be a reaction formation against pleasure-seeking (sexual) tendencies in general. The superego may represent a reaction formation against the Oedipus complex.

Reaction formations against aggressive impulses may take the form of excessive tenderness, love, patience, politeness, submissiveness, or humility.

Anxiety functions as a basis of reaction formation; in the absence of anxiety, the original motives would find expression without undergoing a transformation. Conscience motivation is directly gratified through reaction formation; the other (unacceptable) aspects of conflicting motivation will be gratified either through the fact that com-pulsive emphasis on its opposite will achieve the original aim, or through the fact that the substituted (opposite) behavior will be (un-consciously) identified with the original (repudiated) instrumental act.

Reaction formation may function as a basis of anxiety through the fact that it requires much energy and is therefore an unstable defense, and through the fact that social frustrations may occur on the basis of the individual's deficiency in warmth or spontaneity.

Reaction formation may be interrelated with any or all of the other defensive mechanisms. Especially noteworthy is the probable re-lation between reaction formation and developmental identification; it appears likely that reaction formation involves the substitution of con-science for id motivation.

Reaction formation functions to limit the individual's spontaneity. Reaction formations against normal biogenic impulses will be fostered through severe or consistent punishment, with a minimum of guidance in relation to acceptable alternatives for disapproved behavior.

The following chapter will deal with the generalized defenses, in-cluding rationalization, compensation, and withdrawal.

► **Suggested Readings**

Fenichel, O. "The Counter-Phobic Attitude," *International Journal of Psy-choanalysis, 20* (1939), 263–77.

Freud, S. "Obsessive Acts and Religious Practices," *Collected Papers*. Lon-don, 1950. II, 25–35.

Freud, S. "Character and Anal Erotism," *Collected Papers*. London, 1950. II, 45–50.

Freud, S. "The Predisposition to Obsessional Neurosis," *Collected Papers*. London, 1950. II, 122–32.

Freud, S. *The Problem of Anxiety*. New York, 1936. Chap. vi, pp. 53–8.

Mowrer, O. H. *Learning Theory and Personality Dynamics*. New York, 1950. Pp. 384–9.

Symonds, P. M. *The Dynamics of Human Adjustment*. New York, 1946. Chap. xviii, pp. 424–39.

CHAPTER Sixteen

Generalized Defenses: Rationalization, Compensation, and Withdrawal

What's in a name? that which we call a rose
By any other name would smell as sweet.[1]

RATIONALIZATION, compensation, and withdrawal have frequently been treated as if they were concepts on the same level of generality as repression, fixation, identification, displacement, etc.[2] It seems justifiable, however, to regard them as generalized concepts that may include any or all of the other defense-concepts treated in previous chapters. In the same sense that our concept of "animal" includes the concepts "dog," "cat," "camel," "horse," "ostrich," etc., our concepts of "rationalization," "compensation," and "withdrawal" should each include the concepts of "fixation," "displacement," "projection," "sublimation," etc.

Any of the specialized defensive processes—fixation, perceptual

[1] Shakespeare, *Romeo and Juliet*, Act II, Scene ii.
[2] Textbooks in general psychology make minimal distinctions among defense concepts in terms of their relative generality. This practice is analogous to treating "trees," "maples," "spruce," "deciduous trees," "oaks," etc., as co-ordinate terms.

identification, projection, sublimation, etc.—may function as a rationalization, as a compensation, or as a method of avoiding reality (withdrawal), just as any of the specific fruits—an apple, a peach, a plum, a grape—may function as a fruit, as an item of commerce, or as an object of beauty.

It will be the purpose of the present chapter to define the generalized defenses—rationalization, compensation, and withdrawal—and to illustrate the fact that each of the generalized defenses involves activities that, with equal justification, may be termed projection, repression, sublimation, etc., instead of rationalization, compensation, or withdrawal.

RATIONALIZATION

BY MEANS of rationalization, the individual can maintain a self-concept that conforms with his "higher" values. He can regard himself as a person of integrity to the extent that he can understand his behavior in terms of his rationalizations.

Definition

Rationalization implies the justification of one's behavior in terms of acceptable motivation. When the individual rationalizes, he will regard his own behavior as the outcome of "good intentions" in combination with events over which he has no control.

Rationalization has frequently been treated as if it were employed only when the individual's behavior suggests the operation of unacceptable motivation, or when his behavior fails to comply with social demands. But from an appropriately general point of view rationalization may imply any and all instances of self-justification, whether in excuse of seemingly reprehensible behavior, in depreciation of publicly proclaimed heroism, or in exultation over some remarkable success or demonstration of "goodness."

In other words, the term rationalization may correctly be applied to any and all cases in which the individual consciously "understands" or consciously "explains" the basis of his behavior to himself or to others.[3]

[3] Though rationalization involves conscious "understanding" or conscious "explanation," it should not be understood to involve a conscious attempt to give *misleading* explanations. Conscious attempts to give misleading explanations should be termed lying or hypocrisy rather than rationalization.

Rationalization as a Function of Specific Defenses

It can be demonstrated that any of the specific defenses may function as a rationalization or as a basis of rationalization. The operation of specific defenses, in other words, will make it possible for the individual to justify his behavior *in terms of acceptable motivation*. The individual will, in any case, seek consciously to understand his behavior; and, through the operation of specific defenses, the individual's self-justification *will become acceptable* to himself and to other people whose approval he values.[4]

REPRESSION AND RELATED PROCESSES.   Rationalization involves justifying one's behavior in terms of motivation that is consistent with one's ego-ideals, with one's conscience, and with the behavior standards current in one's society. The individual can justify his behavior only in terms of motivation he "knows" about—that is, in terms of *conscious* motivation. Since much of his total motivation has undergone repression, his "explanations" will be incomplete, distorted, or false. In other words, his rationalizations will be a function of his insight; and to the extent that his insight is deficient, his rationalizations will deviate from a true description of his motivation.

Since the repressed motivation of the individual will consist largely of *unacceptable* motivation, the individual will consciously "know" about motivation that is of an acceptable nature. Thus, when he "explains" his behavior, his "explanations" will be largely in terms of acceptable motivation.

FIXATION, REGRESSION, AND PROGRESSION.   The nature of the individual's self-justification may be correlated with the maturity of his conscious motivation. The child who has not learned to control his aggression may "explain" it by saying: "He hit me first." The adolescent may justify his attack against a contemporary by saying: "He used a dirty word in front of my girl." The young adult may justify a similar attack by saying: "He needed a lesson in manners." And a more mature

---

[4] When Percival M. Symonds, *Dynamics of Human Adjustment* (New York, 1946), p. 454, defines rationalization as "faulty thinking which serves to disguise or hide the unconscious motives of behavior and feeling," he implies that rationalization is an independent defensive process rather than the outcome of other defensive processes. It seems likely that such an implication is incorrect—in other words, that rationalization becomes possible only on the basis of other defensive processes that function to "disguise or hide the unconscious motives of behavior." It is probably also misleading to imply that rationalization is distinguishable from other instances of thinking on the basis of its faulty characteristics; it seems justifiable to generalize that *all* thinking is faulty, since we can assume that all thinking must be carried out on the basis of insufficient data.

adult, in similar circumstances, may say: "I couldn't stand by and let him corrupt the morals of young people."

With increasing maturity, in other words, the individual's conscious motivation will become less and less egocentric, and his rationalizations will reflect his increasing conscious concern with the broader implications of his behavior.

A fixation, a regression, or a progression may itself function as a rationalization. When the individual's love is fixated on a person or on a place, the individual's conscious motivation may be expressed by: "There's nobody like that little mother of mine," or by: "Be it ever so humble, there's no place like home." When the individual's love regresses to narcissism, his conscious motivation will be expressed in the form of statements that compare him favorably with others. And when the individual makes a progressive adjustment, he will feel fortunate in having escaped from an anxiety-ridden situation into one that promises greater satisfaction. In brief, then, a fixation, a regression, or a progression will usually be accompanied by conscious motivation supporting the particular adjustment that has occurred.

On the other hand, the individual will often rationalize a fixation or a regression in terms of factors that are irrelevant to his immature motivation. He may blame external circumstances; he may re-evaluate his goals; or he may interpret his behavior in terms of the subtle operation of some high purpose. He may blame external resources or the social order for his failure to achieve desirable progressive adjustments. He may use the "sour grapes" rationalization—that is, he may discount the value of some goal he previously sought to attain—in order to justify a fixation. He may explain smoking or drinking (oral fixations or regressions) in terms of his belief that his efficiency or his social compatibility is thereby improved.

PERCEPTUAL IDENTIFICATION. The individual will frequently justify his behavior in terms of his identification of different objects, situations, or persons. He may justify his hatred of the current enemy by saying: "They are nothing but fanatical beasts." He may explain his treatment of a minority-group member by saying: "He is only a dirty foreigner." He may account for his fear of a strange dog by saying: "Dogs are vicious." Or he may justify his courteous treatment of an elderly woman by saying: "After all, she's somebody's mother."

In each of these instances, the rationalization involves stating that since two or more persons or objects are identical they deserve similar treatment.

DEVELOPMENTAL IDENTIFICATION.   On the basis of developmental identification, the individual will acquire psychogenic motives that possess high survival value in his society. Such motives—the conscience motives and the ego-ideals—will, in the normal individual, become highly acceptable and will function as the motives in terms of which he will most frequently justify his behavior.

To the extent that developmental identification occurs, the individual will acquire acceptable motives on the basis of which to rationalize his behavior.

It often occurs that behavior actually based on fundamental values —acquired through developmental identification—may be rationalized in terms of more recently acquired values.

> Every person grows up a citizen of a country, a member of a church, and a member of a political party with certain basic personal values and philosophy. Later he finds it necessary to justify his membership in his political party, his adherence to a certain church, his loyalty to a club or state, and searches for reasons and arguments which will justify his choice.[5]

Since his most fundamental values were developed through a more or less unconscious process of identification, the individual cannot know the true basis of much of his behavior. His problems would be greatly simplified if he could admit frankly—or if he really could know —that much of what he does is simply a function of the fact that his parents provided a pattern for him to emulate.

DISPLACEMENT.   Displacement involves the transfer of motivational cathexis onto an acceptable object. In this sense, displacement functions as a rationalization: the individual's self-justification will, to a certain extent, become acceptable in terms of his conscious attitude in relation to the object.

If love has been displaced onto an acceptable object, the individual can understand his behavior in relation to the object in terms of his love for it. If fear has been displaced onto an animal, for example, the individual can justify his avoidant behavior in terms of his fear. In other words the individual can rationalize his behavior, at least initially, in relation to the objects of displacement in terms of his conscious (acceptable) attitude toward the objects.

But in time the individual—and others—will begin to question the basis of the attitude itself. And, since the individual will ordinarily have

[5] Symonds, *op. cit.*, p. 458.

no understanding of the displacement process, and since he would not be able to accept its implications if he did understand it, he will have to look for reasons to justify his attitude. He will then perceive actual or projected characteristics in the object which will "explain" the origin of his attitude in relation to it.

If he has displaced his hostility onto a minority group, he will be likely to justify his attitude on the basis of his perception of reprehensible characteristics in members of the minority group; he will note that they are "stupid," "dishonest," "unclean," "mercenary," etc. If he has displaced his love from his mother onto his sweetheart, and if he—and the sweetheart—cannot remain contented with the fact of being in love, but begin to require further "explanations," then he will have to find and verbalize her lovable characteristics.

PROJECTION. When projection occurs, the individual can justify his behavior in terms of the unacceptable motivation that appears to underlie the behavior of other people. If, for example, the individual has repressed and projected his hostility, he cannot be expected to understand that any of his own behavior has been motivated by unconscious hostility; he will justify his mistrust and fear of others in terms of his overemphasis on their hostile motivation. If he has projected his homosexual motivation onto other men, he will consciously justify his avoidance of other men in terms of his belief that they have homosexual intentions in relation to him. Or if he has projected his narcissism onto other men, he will explain his contempt for them in terms of his conscious belief that they are too ambitious, too haughty, too vain, etc.

SUBLIMATION. When a motive undergoes sublimation, the individual will become conscious of the motive only in its acceptable form. Thus he will be able to understand his behavior in terms of motivation that is acceptable to him and to others. In other words, an individual who has successfully sublimated his unacceptable motives will be able to justify all of his behavior in terms of his sublimations.

The scout leader who has sublimated his homosexual motivation can justify the amount of time he spends with boys in terms of his civic and humanitarian interests. The scientist who has sublimated his voyeuristic tendencies can explain his activities as the outcome of a consuming passion to understand nature. And the surgeon who has sublimated his aggression can account for his professional zeal in terms of his humanitarian aim to diminish human suffering.

REACTION FORMATION. Since on the basis of reaction formation the individual becomes conscious of motives that are antithetical to his unconscious (unacceptable) motives, he will be likely to see his behavior as justifiable in terms of acceptable motivation. He can justify his excessive emphasis on cleanliness by his conscious disgust in relation to anything unclean. He can justify his aloofness on the basis of his conscious reaction against the thought of being dependent on others. He can explain his avoidance of sexual relations and sexual conversation by his conception that sex is evil or immoral. And he can explain his kindness, politeness, or courtesy in terms of his conscious attitude that it is wrong to frustrate or to hurt other people.

Integrative Summary

Rationalization involves justifying one's own behavior in terms of acceptable motivation. The individual seeks, more or less continuously, to understand his own behavior. Since the operation of any specific defense or combination of defenses will render the individual's *conscious* motivation acceptable to himself and to others, it becomes possible for the individual to understand his behavior in terms of acceptable motivation.

It may appropriately be concluded, then, that rationalization will be an outcome of the operation of any specific defense—that the individual's ability to perceive his behavior in terms of acceptable motivation will be increased whenever any specific defensive process occurs.

COMPENSATION

TO THE extent that the individual is able to compensate for feelings of inferiority, he will be able to maintain a relatively optimistic self-concept.

Definition

Compensation implies any and all activities that function to reduce feelings of inferiority or feelings of inadequacy. When the individual perceives that his behavior fails to conform to the demands of his ego-ideal—when he perceives any defect or inadequacy in his capacity or in his motivation—he will be likely to develop feelings of inferiority. Compensation is said to occur when the individual's activities lead to a reduction of such feelings of inferiority. Any favorable change in the individual's conscious perception of himself will function as a compensation for inferiority feelings.

Compensation as a Function of Specific Defenses

The operation of any of the specific defenses can be shown to eventuate in a changed self-perception. The operation of any one, or a combination of several, of the specific defenses will function to bring about a favorable change in the individual's conscious perception of himself as compared with his ideal of himself. In other words, any of the specific defenses will function as a compensation for feelings of inferiority—as a method of reducing feelings of inadequacy.

REPRESSION AND RELATED PROCESSES. When the individual can perceive within himself the operation of "unworthy" or "immoral" impulses, he will perceive these as imperfections or inadequacies. In other words, the conscious perception of id impulses will function to frustrate the individual's ego-ideals, and thus will become the occasion for feelings of inferiority.

To the extent that such "unworthy" impulses undergo repression, the individual's conscious perception will be relieved of them, so that they will no longer function to disturb the individual's self-esteem. In this manner repression will operate as a compensation for feelings of inferiority.

If, on the other hand, the individual's "nobler" positive psychogenic motives undergo repression, a similar increase in self-esteem will occur, since the individual's behavior will not have to conform to high standards in order to be perceived as a source of pride.

FIXATION, REGRESSION, AND PROGRESSION. Whenever the individual is confronted with problems he cannot solve—whenever he is faced with frustrations he cannot overcome—he will be likely to feel inferior or inadequate.

If a progressive adjustment involves the anticipation of such difficulties, the individual may remain fixated at his present level of adjustment; if his present adjustment involves such difficulties, he may regress to an earlier adjustment or progress to a new adjustment that promises a higher level of success.

In any of these cases, his fixation, his regression, or his progression will, at least temporarily, function as a compensation for feelings of inferiority aroused by his inability to cope with more difficult problems.

PERCEPTUAL IDENTIFICATION. Perceptual identification of the self with another more successful person, or with a successful group, will function as a compensation for personal inadequacy or feelings of inferiority. The small boy who is about to be beaten into submission by an older boy can regain his self-esteem by saying: "My dad can lick your dad," or: "My dad makes more money than yours." The brow-beaten adult can assuage his feelings of inadequacy by contemplating the greatness and the invincibility of his nation. The disappointed adolescent lover can maintain his self-esteem by identifying with the "great lovers" of fiction or with the "glamor boys" of stage and screen.

DEVELOPMENTAL IDENTIFICATION. The child who, prior to his developmental identification with a respected or admired adult, may have had feelings of inferiority or inadequacy will achieve compensation and relief from such feelings after he can begin to see in himself the strengths that were perceptible only in the model. Through the development of superego motives, the individual will become more nearly independent and self-sufficient in the guidance of his own behavior; he therefore can experience a higher degree of self-esteem.

DISPLACEMENT. When an individual is frustrated by persons against whom he cannot retaliate or by situations he cannot hope to change, he will be likely to feel helpless and inferior. He can compensate for such inferiority feelings by displacing his hostility onto objects that are, for him, acceptable substitutes—that is, onto objects that "deserve" aggressive treatment, onto objects he is able to injure, or onto objects that will not be able to retaliate.

PROJECTION. When the individual projects his unacceptable motivation onto other people, he will be able to perceive that he is "better" than others; by this means he will be able to avoid feelings of inferiority. Likewise, when the parent projects his ambitions onto his son, and through identification perceives the son's success as his own success, the parent will thereby compensate for feelings of inferiority and a sense of failure.

SUBLIMATION. On the basis of sublimation, the individual will be able to see himself as a person motivated by high ideals; he will therefore, in this sense, be able to avoid feelings of inferiority. So long as the individual can regard himself as a person who works toward the achievement of high ideals, and so long as he can see himself as one whose motivation is "clean" and "wholesome," he can avoid feelings of unworthiness.

REACTION FORMATION. Since reaction formation aids in preventing the individual from perceiving his "crude" and "inferior" motivation, it will function as a defense against inferiority feelings. The individual, on the basis of his reaction formations, may regard himself as a paragon of virtue, and so will have little occasion to feel inferior.[6]

Integrative Summary

Compensation implies any and all activities that function to reduce feelings of inferiority or feelings of inadequacy. All of the specific defenses can be shown to function as compensations, in the sense that they will bring about favorable changes in the individual's self-perception.

WITHDRAWAL

IT IS probably true that all animals with the power of motility will make efforts to avoid nonoptimal living conditions. "*Protection* against stimuli," as Freud has maintained, "is an almost more important function for the living organism than *reception* of stimuli." [7] The "lower" organisms—the organisms that have relatively simple structures—will make random avoidance reactions whenever nonoptimal environmental conditions occur; thus, if they are "lucky," they will escape into an area where optimum conditions prevail.[8]

The human organism can escape from anxiety-arousing aspects of reality not only by means of physical withdrawal but also by means of defensive mechanisms that will remove such aspects of reality from conscious perception.

Definition

Withdrawal implies the avoidance of any aspect of external or internal reality. It implies any "escape reaction" that will eventuate in the individual's failure to perceive any "dangerous" characteristic of the external or internal environment.[9]

Some aspects of reality—the external aspects—can be avoided by means of a *physical* withdrawal; the individual can avoid perceiving many aspects of external reality by going away from certain situations

[6] Franz Alexander, *Fundamentals of Psychoanalysis* (New York, 1948), pp. 104–8, has treated reaction formation and overcompensation as equivalent concepts.

[7] Sigmund Freud, *Beyond the Pleasure Principle* (London, 1950), p. 32.

[8] See, for example, John F. Dashiell, *Fundamentals of General Psychology* (Boston, 1937), pp. 28–37.

[9] It is relevant to note that defenses against anxiety have frequently been referred to as "escape mechanisms."

when they have been approached, or by failing to enter or to approach such situations. One can avoid perceiving an enemy's hostility or his aggression by staying away from vicinities in which the enemy might make an appearance. One who fears high places may remain on the ground level rather than climb mountains or stand on the roofs of high buildings. One who is anxious in social situations may keep away from social gatherings.

But *internal* aspects of reality cannot be avoided by means of a physical withdrawal. The individual cannot escape from disturbing aspects of his own personality except by means of some process that will protect his conscious perception against "seeing" what he cannot accept in himself. Any process that will achieve this goal—to prevent the individual from perceiving (consciously) the disturbing aspects of internal reality—may be said to function as a withdrawal mechanism.

Withdrawal as a Function of Specific Defenses

Each of the specific defenses against anxiety can be shown to function as an "escape mechanism," as a method of withdrawal, as a method of avoiding the anxiety-arousing aspects of reality. Each will modify the individual's *perceptual* environment through the exclusion of disturbing aspects of the *objective* environment.

REPRESSION AND RELATED PROCESSES. Whenever any aspect of the individual's motivation undergoes repression, the individual will be able to avoid the conscious perception of an important aspect of reality. Ego functions will be restricted, to the extent that they are deprived of data concerning the individual's motivation.

Again, whenever the process of denial operates with respect to characteristics of external reality, the individual will be able thereby to avoid important aspects of the environment. The individual's mental withdrawal will be as effective as if it were a withdrawal in the physical sense.

Even the processes of suppression and restraint will operate temporarily to prevent active participation with reality. As long as the individual suppresses or restrains his impulses in relation to a particular object, he will of course be avoiding the full implications of these impulses in relation to the object.

FIXATION, REGRESSION, AND PROGRESSION. Any fixation, regression, or progression will operate as a withdrawal mechanism, in the sense that it will function as an escape from some other actual or anticipated adjustment. Fixation will operate as an avoidance of aspects of reality which would be involved in an anticipated regression or progression. Regression or progression will operate as an avoidance of the aspects of reality which have been associated with a previous adjustment.

In other words, a fixation, a regression, or a progression will occur at just those times when some other adjustment would involve aspects of reality which the individual cannot face. Regressive adjustments such as recreation, daytime fantasies, sleep, and the wish-fulfilling hallucinations of the dream quite clearly involve temporary withdrawals from the frustrating features of reality; but fixations and progressions will likewise involve withdrawal.

PERCEPTUAL IDENTIFICATION. Perceptual identification involves avoiding differences that distinguish the self from others, symbols from the objects or processes they symbolize, different persons from one another, and so on. No two objects or processes can be objectively identical.

When perceptual identification occurs, the differences among objects and processes will not be perceived. The awareness of such differences can function as a source of anxiety.

If the child remains aware that he is weak and helpless when compared with his father, he will experience anxiety; by "identifying with the aggressor"—that is, by neglecting to perceive the difference between himself and the more powerful father—he can reduce his anxiety.

Or, when the (fixated) lover identifies his sweetheart (unconsciously) with his mother, he can feel dependent on his sweetheart for affectionate protection against the anxiety-inducing difficulties of the adult world; he can be "her child," so to speak, if she happens to be willing to let him play that role.

DEVELOPMENTAL IDENTIFICATION. Through the development of superego motivation, the individual can avoid some of the features of objective reality which he previously had to face—especially the objective danger of punishment by external authorities.

But on the basis of developmental identification the individual must face a new kind of reality—the reality of motivation that conflicts with the expression of his fundamental impulses. If the ensuing conflict eventuates in repression of id impulses, then the reality of these will be avoided by conscious perception.

DISPLACEMENT. Since every person with whom the individual associates will, on a particular occasion or on different occasions, frustrate some of the individual's motives and gratify others, ambivalence toward other persons will be unavoidable unless some procedure is employed to avoid either the reality of the frustration or the reality of the gratification. The reality of frustration may be avoided by the displacement of fear or hostility; the reality of gratification may be avoided by the displacement of love.

Displacement not only will aid the individual in avoiding the reality of his ambivalent attitudes but also will help him to withdraw from the reality of *any* unacceptable object-cathexis he may happen to establish. Thus, the displacement of love from an incestuous object will function as an escape from the dangers of an incestuous relationship. Or the displacement of hostility onto abstract ideals will function as a withdrawal from the reality of disturbing human relationships.

PROJECTION. It is obvious that certain aspects of internal reality can be avoided by the individual through the projection of his motives onto others. He will no longer "see" in himself the operation of motives that have been projected. Moreover, since projection functions to overemphasize the reality of *projected* motives in other persons, the reality of their other motives will probably be overlooked by the projecting individual.

SUBLIMATION. Sublimation, like all of the other defensive measures that involve repression, will aid in the avoidance of certain aspects of internal reality. After the sublimative transformation of his motives, the individual will see himself as a "higher type of being"—as a person who lacks the crasser forms of motivation which are attributed to "lower forms of life." He will, in other words, lose sight of the crude biogenic motivation that determined his behavior at an earlier time (and of course continues to determine his behavior).

REACTION FORMATION. Reaction formation will help to maintain the repression of unacceptable impulses. As long as the individual can be aware only of the opposite tendencies, he can avoid the reality of his own "baser" motivation. If he is modest, if he is disgusted by excremental and genital functions, if he is patient and kindly in his conscious attitudes toward others—then he can avoid realizing that he would like to display himself and his attainments, that he would enjoy pregenital and genital stimulation, and that he would like to be irritable, hostile, or sadistic.

Integrative Summary

The operation of any specific defense will help the individual to escape from frustrating features of reality. From this point of view, all of the specific defenses may be regarded as protective mechanisms; they will function to protect the individual against frustrating perceptions. And, to the extent that specific defenses operate to remove aspects of reality from the individual's conscious perception, the individual can, on the basis of his defenses, be said to withdraw from frustrating situations—to avoid aspects of reality—just as effectively as if he were to depart physically from regions of danger.

SUMMARY

RATIONALIZATION, compensation, and withdrawal should be regarded as generalized defenses, since they will include any of the specific defensive functions treated in previous chapters. That is, any specialized defense or combination of specialized defenses will function as a rationalization, as a compensation, or as a method of withdrawing from frustrating aspects of reality.

Rationalization—the justification of one's behavior on the basis of acceptable motivation—will occur in terms of the fact that whenever any defensive process is employed the individual's conscious motivation will be modified in the direction of acceptability.

Compensation—the reduction of feelings of inferiority or feelings of inadequacy—will occur whenever any specific defensive process brings about a favorable change in the individual's conscious perception of himself.

Withdrawal from frustrating aspects of reality will be achieved whenever a defensive process functions to remove such aspects of reality from the individual's conscious perception.

► Suggested Readings

Barbash, J. T. "Compensation and the Crime of Pigeon Dropping," *Journal of Clinical Psychology*, 8 (1952), pp. 92–4.

Fisher, V. E. *An Introduction to Abnormal Psychology*. New York, 1937. Rev. ed. Chap. vi, pp. 85–105.

Freud, Anna. *The Ego and the Mechanisms of Defense*. New York, 1946. Chaps. vi–vii, pp. 73–99.

Murphy, G. *Personality*. New York, 1947. Chap. xxiv, pp. 564–93.

O'Kelly, L. I. *Introduction to Psychopathology*. New York, 1949. Pp. 488–503.

Shaffer, L. F. *The Psychology of Adjustment*. Boston, 1936. Pp. 168–72, 156–63, 173–83.
Symonds, P. M. *The Dynamics of Human Adjustment*. New York, 1946. Chaps. xx, xxii, xix, pp. 440–53, 454–68, 487–519.
Wallin, J. E. W. *Personality Maladjustments and Mental Hygiene*. New York, 1949. 2d ed. Pp. 338–46, 378–97, 358–77.

Glossary

THE FOLLOWING TERMS have been defined according to the usage of this book. Certain terms within the definitions are printed in *italic* type: the glossary carries full definitions of these terms in the proper alphabetical places. The reader who desires a more adequate understanding of the concepts defined in this glossary should consult the SUBJECT INDEX in order to locate more extended discussions in the text.

adjustive implications.   The significance of any group of adjustive principles for the solution of the problems of everyday living. The applied psychology of adjustment; traditionally termed "mental hygiene."

adjustment.   The process of avoiding frustration and achieving gratification. The process of establishing optimal relationships between the individual's motivational pattern and the conditions of external reality.

adjustment mechanism.   See *defense.*

affective.   See *emotional.*

aggression.   An act whose intention is to frustrate, injure, or destroy an individual or object.

aggressive catharsis.   The relief or reduction of aggressive motivation through any act of aggression.

ahistorical regression.   The primitivation of behavior patterns. (Synonym: *regression* [Lewin].)

aim.   See *instrumental act.*

aim-inhibited impulse.   An impulse (motive) that has undergone a transformation of aim (instrumental act) in the direction of increased social acceptability. (Synonym: *aim-sublimation.*)

aim-sublimation.   A sublimative transformation in the instrumental act (aim) by means of which gratification of a particular need is anticipated. See *aim-inhibited impulse.*

altruistic surrender.   A term used by Anna Freud to denote the projection of ego-ideals onto another person with whom the projecting individual perceptually identifies himself.

ambiguity.   The condition or state of being *ambiguous*.

ambiguous.   Subject to relatively great individual differences in interpretation.

ambivalence.   An attitude that involves a combination of positive and negative *cathexis* or valence in relation to a particular *object*. See *plus-minus conflict*.

ambivalent.   Characterized by a combination of positive and negative *cathexis* or valence in relation to a particular *object*.

anal character.   A sublimative transformation of anal-erotic impulses, involving the personality traits of orderliness, parsimony, and obstinacy.

anal phase.   According to Freud's theory of psychosexual development, the second autoerotic phase, during which the anal region is said to be the primary source of sexual excitation.

analysis.   See *psychoanalysis*.

analyst.   See *psychoanalyst*.

anger.   An emotional process that is aroused during *frustration*. Anger involves a need in combination with imagined aggression against objects in general (with no recognized specific object). Sometimes termed "free-floating aggression."

anxiety.   Any motivational excitation or tension that occurs without conscious representation of a gratifying instrumental act and without conscious cathexis of a gratifying object. (Synonyms: *need; id functions*.)

anxiety equivalent.   Conscious awareness of the "physiological" manifestations of anxiety without any accompanying awareness of apprehension.

anxiety tolerance.   See *frustration tolerance*.

appetite.   Positive motivation. See *love; sexuality; libido*.

asceticism.   A way of life involving extreme repressive or inhibitory control of pleasurable impulses.

attitude.   Any complete need-integrate, motive, or impulse. See *need integrate*.

autoerotic.   See *narcissistic*.

autoerotism.   See *narcissism*.

aversion.   Negative motivation. See *hostility; fear*.

behavioral immaturity [Lewin].   A state characterized by (1) a narrow range of activities and interests; (2) relative inconsistency and high susceptibility to disorganization and disruption; (3) organization in terms of restricted areas of the temporal and spatial environment; (4) direct interdependence; and (5) a low degree of perceptual realism. See *behavioral maturity* [Lewin].

behavioral maturity [Lewin].   A state characterized by (1) a wide variety of behavior patterns; (2) complex, hierarchical, and complicated organization of behavior; (3) extensive life space and space of free movement; (4) organizational interdependence of behavior; and (5) a high degree of perceptual realism.

biogenic.   Originating in the biological nature of the organism. Dependent upon hereditary and maturational factors rather than upon learning. (Synonyms: basic; physiological; viscerogenic; primary; unlearned; organic.)

castration fear.   Fear of castration. Responsible, according to Freud, for the repression of the *Oedipus complex.* Castration fear is said to be induced on the basis of threatened castration as punishment for masturbating and for sexually cathecting the mother.

catharsis.   Relief of any form of motivation. In psychotherapy, catharsis refers to the relief of previously repressed or long-frustrated motivation.

cathect.   To form a motivational relationship with an object. To establish or maintain cathexis in relation to an object.

cathection.   See *cathexis.*

cathexis.   The motivational relationship between a need and an object, or between a person and an object. Cathexis may be positive (goal-seeking), negative (goal-avoiding; goal-destructive), or ambivalent. (Synonym: valence.)

client-centered therapy.   A method of psychotherapy which provides a permissive therapist-patient or counselor-client relationship in which the patient or client is free to explore and to communicate his motivation without fear of humiliation or depreciation, and in which the therapist or counselor limits his activities to that of communicating his understanding of the patient's or client's motivation ("reflection of feeling"). (Synonym: nondirective therapy.)

cognitive functions.   Intellectual processes, such as perception, learning, thinking, and voluntary action. See *ego functions.*

compensation.   Any activity that functions to reduce feelings of inferiority or feelings of inadequacy.

complicated organization.   Organization of behavior which involves: (1) the continuation of a behavior sequence following its interruption; or (2) the simultaneous operation of different behavior-units that are organized on the basis of unrelated motives; or (3) the occurrence of behavior representing two or more levels of meaning.

compromise formation.   The successive or the simultaneous gratification of opposed (conflicting) motives, usually by means of a neurotic symptom (a symbolic gratification). Compromise formation may be regarded as involving both *sublimations* of, and *reaction formations* against, the more basic (less sophisticated) of the conflicting motives.

conative perseveration.   The tendency to continue to completion any particular sequence of *instrumental acts* once such a sequence has begun to occur.

conflict.   The simultaneous operation of incompatible motives. (Synonym: *internal obstruction.*)

conscience.   The negative psychogenic aspects of motivation, including moral prohibitions and psychogenic aversions.

conscience motives.   See *conscience.*

coprophilia.   Interest in (positive cathexis of) excrement, particularly one's own.

danger.   The quality attributed to any frustrating object or situation that induces fear. The individual regards himself as helpless to commit successful counter-aggression against such an object or situation.

defense.   Any technique by means of which *anxiety* may be reduced or relieved. A defense involves modification of one or more aspects of the consciously functioning *need-integrate* or motive. (Synonyms: defense mechanism; adjustment mechanism; defense dynamism.)

defense dynamism.   See *defense.*

defense mechanism.   See *defense.*

delusion.   A belief that differs markedly from the prevailing beliefs in a given society. Psychopathological delusions usually refer to the status of the patient in relation to other people or to some internal condition of the patient.

denial.   A repression-like process by means of which knowledge concerning features of external reality becomes relatively inaccessible to conscious perception.

developmental identification.   The development of motivation or behavior similar to that of a loved or respected model. (Synonyms: introjection; introception.)

direct interdependence.   Interrelations among different functions of the organism which occur prior to functional differentiation.

displacement.   A defense mechanism that involves the transfer of motivational *cathexis* from one object to another (substitute) object. The substitute object is perceptually identified with the object from which the motivational cathexis has been displaced. See *transference.*

displeasure.   The conscious experience that occurs during frustration— that is, during relatively strong motivational excitation in the absence of anticipated tension-reduction.

dissociation.   The separation of previously associated conscious functions through the process of repression or through some repression-like process. Some of the dissociated functions remain conscious, while others become *unconscious* or *preconscious*.

double approach-avoidant conflict.   A conflict that is perceived to require a choice between alternatives in relation to both of which the individual manifests *ambivalence*. Either alternative is perceived to involve both frustration and gratification.

dynamic.   Characterized by the occurrence of equilibrium-seeking tendencies within a system of events (within an organism). See *dynamic psychology*.

dynamic psychology.   Any system of psychological interpretation which emphasizes the significance of motivational principles in the determination of behavior.

dynamic regression.   See *ahistorical regression*.

ego functions.   Relatively conscious cognitive or intellectual processes— including perception, learning, thinking, and voluntary action.

ego-ideals.   The positive psychogenic aspects of motivation, including ideals, values, ambitions, and other psychogenic appetites.

ego regression.   The adoption of immature modes of perceiving, thinking, and acting. See *regression*.

ego restriction.   Any reduction in the adequacy of ego functions which occurs on the basis of *repression, inhibition, denial*, or *withdrawal* from external situations.

ego strength.   The degree of integrative adequacy with which the ego functions are able to operate. See *intelligence*.

emotion.   A complex process involving a state of disequilibrium among the psychosomatic processes. All objectless aspects of motivation. Motivation occurring in the absence of conscious object-cathexis.

emotional.   Referring to emotions.

energy level.   The amount of utilizable energy that develops on the basis of the normal metabolic functions of a given organism. This varies from individual to individual and probably owes its origin to hereditary or constitutional factors.

enuresis.   Uncontrolled or difficultly controlled tendency to urinate. Frequently involves bed-wetting.

environment.   See *perceptual environment*.

erogenous zone.   See *erotogenic zone*.

erotic.   Referring to love or sexuality.

erotogenic zone.   Any zone or region of the body in which sexual excitation is perceptually localized. See *source*.

established regression.   Regression that continues to be maintained regardless of changes in the situation. Opposite of *situational regression*.

exhibitionism.　　The impulse that is gratified through displaying one's own genitals, or through displaying oneself in a nude or semi-nude condition.

external deprivation.　　The loss of some external resource by means of which gratification has previously been achieved.

external obstruction.　　The interposition of a barrier between the person and a cathected object, or an external interference with the use of a particular instrumental act for achieving gratification.

external privation.　　The long-term lack or nonpossession of external resources that are perceived as necessary for gratifying a need.

failure of repression.　　The reinstatement in consciousness of a previously repressed (unconscious) function. This is likely to occur on the basis of inadequate gratification of needs, through failure to adopt a defense mechanism that will provide adequate substitute methods of relieving anxiety.

fear.　　An attitude that is aroused in relation to a frustrating agent against which the individual is, for some reason, relatively powerless to commit successful aggressive action. Fear involves the motivation to escape from a dangerous object or situation. Fear may be regarded as a biogenic reaction to *frustration.*

fetishism.　　Sexual motivation or sexual behavior that involves the *cathexis* of some nonliving object, such as a shoe, a garment, or some other symbol.

fixation.　　A cessation in the normal development of any form of behavior. The failure to develop a new pattern of behavior in response to changed conditions. The persistence of a form of behavior or motivation beyond the age at which it is considered appropriate.

fixation, psychosexual.　　The arrest of certain components of the sexual impulse at an early stage of development. A cessation with respect to some aspect of psychosexual development.

formal regression.　　See *regression* [Lewin]; *ahistorical regression.*

free association.　　In *psychoanalysis,* the process of giving free rein to thoughts, ideas, impulses, images, fantasies, etc., without critical or conscious direction. Ideas that have previously been related in experience will, by this means, tend to occur in relation to one another.

free-floating aggression.　　See *anger.*

free-floating anxiety.　　General apprehensiveness that is indiscriminately experienced in relation to various objects and situations rather than in relation to some particular object. (Synonyms: anxious expectation; expectant dread.)

frustrating agent.　　The person or object that an individual perceives to be directly responsible for his frustration on any particular occasion.

frustration. The perception of an actual (immediate) or potential (delayed) interference with the gratification of a motive.

frustration-aggression hypothesis. The hypothesis that aggression is based on frustration and that frustration always leads to some form of aggression.

frustration tolerance. The capacity of the individual to endure frustration without resorting to maladaptive *defenses.* (Synonyms: need tolerance; anxiety tolerance.)

functional autonomy. The conception that psychogenic motives will gain functional independence from, or will continue to function in the absence of, the antecedent motives from which they originally developed.

fundamental rule. In psychoanalytic therapy, the requirement that the patient give verbal expression to any and all material that enters his conscious perception, regardless of its nature—even though it appear trivial, illogical, immoral, obscene, or otherwise objectionable in terms of the patient's customary standards of evaluation.

general regression. A regression that involves a relatively large proportion of the individual's total behavior. Opposite of *partial regression.*

genital phase. According to Freud's theory of psychosexual development, the fourth and final phase, which begins at puberty, and during which the genitals of the respective sexes are said to be the primary sources of sexual excitation.

genitalia. See *genitals.*

genitals. The sexual organs of either sex. (Synonym: *genitalia.*)

goal object. See *object.*

gratification. The relief of any form of motivational excitation. Tension reduction.

grief. Ambivalence (love and hostility) that has been displaced onto the self, following the loss of a loved (and hated) object.

guilt. An anxiety-like process that arises on the basis of the self-frustration of conscience (negative psychogenic) motivation. Guilt involves a need for punishment in combination with a fear of punishment.

habit. An instrumental-act fixation. A relatively fixated mode of response that occurs in relation to a particular object during the functioning of a particular need.

habit regression. See *regression; retrogression.*

hallucination. A perception that occurs in the absence of any external referent.

hatred. An established attitude of hostility in relation to a particular object.

heterosexual.   Referring to the opposite sex. Relating to preference for members of the opposite sex as potential love-objects.

hierarchical organization.   The organization of molar behavior-units in terms of more inclusive molar behavior-units.

hierarchy.   Any system or organization in which the parts are ordered according to some criterion of evaluation. A hierarchy may be ordered in terms of a continuum extending from highest to lowest, from best to worst, from largest to smallest, etc.

hierarchy of values.   An organization of motives or values ordered in terms of their relative importance as evaluated by the individual. (Synonym: philosophy of life.)

historical regression.   The reinstatement of any formerly manifested behavior pattern or of any previously functional form of motivation.

homeostasis.   The tendency of the organism to maintain dynamic equilibrium. Specifically, the tendency to maintain equilibrium among physiological processes.

homosexual.   Referring to the same sex. Relating to preference for members of the same sex as potential sexual objects. An individual who manifests inversion or homosexuality.

homosexuality.   See *inversion.*

hostility.   The total need-integrate that is aroused during frustration. Hostility involves a need in combination with imagined instrumental acts (injurious modes of action) in relation to a definite person or object. Hostility may be regarded as a biogenic reaction to *frustration.* (Synonym: aggressive motivation.)

id functions.   Biogenic needs, tensions, or excitations that occur without conscious representation of gratifying instrumental acts or objects. (Synonym: *anxiety.*)

id-id conflict.   A conflict between or among incompatible biogenic needs.

id-superego conflict.   A conflict between a biogenic need and a psychogenic motive.

idealization.   The exaggerated estimation of any love-object. The process of overestimating or aggrandizing a sexual (positively cathected) object.

identification.   See *developmental identification; perceptual identification.*

imitation.   A conscious process of developmental identification.

immaturity.   See *behavioral immaturity* [Lewin].

impulse.   See *need integrate.*

incest.   Sexual motivation or sexual practices in relation to a sexual object who is closely related by heredity. Specifically, sexual motivation or sexual practices in relation to a member of the immediate family. See *Oedipus complex.*

incestuous. Referring to sexual objects who are closely related by heredity. Specifically, relating to sexual objects who are members of the immediate family.

inferiority feelings. An anxiety-like process that occurs on the basis of the frustration of ego-ideals (positive psychogenic motivation).

inhibition. An automatic (unconscious) process by means of which motor functions become inaccessible to conscious (voluntary) control.

insight. In psychotherapy, the reinstatement in consciousness of previously repressed material and its perceptual integration with other conscious material.

instinct. A complete *need integrate*. (Synonyms: *motive;* impulse; *attitude.*)

instrumental act. The behavior tendency that is aroused when a particular need arises. The behavior pattern in terms of which gratification of a particular need is anticipated. An aspect of the *need integrate*. (Synonyms: mode; aim.)

instrumental act frustration. The perception of interference with gratification of a need by means of some specific instrumental act.

instrumental-act regression. The reinstatement of a former pattern of behavior in order to gratify a given need in relation to a given object. The primitivation of the behavior pattern employed to gratify a given need in relation to a given object.

intelligence. The relative degree of competence with which the individual is able to gratify his total pattern of motives. The degree of competence with which the individual is able to select and employ procedures that integrate the demands of all of his important motives. See *ego strength.*

internal deprivation. The loss of a function, or the reduction in the adequacy of a function, by means of which gratification has previously been achieved.

internal obstruction. The simultaneous operation of incompatible motives. When incompatible motives function simultaneously, the gratification of either one is perceived to exclude, at least temporarily, the possibility of gratifying the other. (Synonym: *conflict.*)

internal privation. A long-standing defect or deficiency in some function that is perceived to be necessary for achieving gratification.

introjection. See *developmental identification.*

inversion. The *cathexis* of a love-object of the same sex. (Synonym: homosexuality.)

isolation. A relatively automatic process by means of which conscious functions become *preconscious.*

jealousy. A complex of attitudes, involving ambivalence (love and hostility) in relation to the self and the love-object, and hostility in relation to a successful rival.

latency period.   According to Freud's theory of psychosexual development, a period extending from the *phallic phase* until puberty during which the child's sexual attitudes (autoerotic and *Oedipal*) are maintained under *repression.*

level of aspiration.   The standards of self-achievement which the individual has adopted. See *ego-ideals.*

libertinism.   A way of life involving unrestrained expression of impulses without regard to the established moral values of the society.

libidinal.   Referring to libido, love, or sexuality.

libido.   Sexual excitation or sexual need. This term is frequently generalized to imply any form of positive motivation in relation to any potentially gratifying object. (Synonym: *love.*)

life space.   See *perceptual environment.*

love.   Any form of positive motivation in relation to a gratifying or potentially gratifying object. Love may be regarded as a biogenic reaction to gratification. See *libido; sexuality.*

magic.   Action in relation to a symbol, taken in the belief that the person or thing represented by the symbol will undergo a similar fate.

manifest content.   The content (of dreams or of symptoms) as it is consciously experienced.

masochism.   A sexual perversion that involves suffering and humiliation as a necessary condition for achieving sexual gratification. More generally, a relatively permanent tendency to enjoy frustration, pain, injury, suffering, humiliation, etc.

maturity.   See *behavioral maturity* [Lewin].

minus-minus conflict.   The simultaneous occurrence of two or more incompatible negative motives. The minus-minus conflict is perceived to require choice between equally frustrating alternatives. (Synonyms: abient-abient conflict; double-abient conflict; avoidant-avoidant conflict; negative-negative conflict.)

mode.   See *instrumental act.*

model.   A loved or respected person whose characteristics are adopted by means of developmental identification.

molar behavior-unit.   An inclusive unit that involves all of the behavior of the individual from the moment when he begins to seek a particular goal until the moment when the original goal is attained or when some other goal is substituted for it. Different molar units differ in duration and complexity and are often organized in terms of some hierarchical principle.

moral anxiety.   See *guilt.*

motivation.   1. The organization of principles relating to the operation of motives. 2. The organized pattern of motives that at any particular time co-operate in determing behavior. (Synonym: *motivational pattern.*)

motivational pattern.   The organization among all of the motives that are operative in a given individual at a given moment.

motive.   1. A generic term used to imply needs, drives, desires, wishes, wants, urges, impulses, instincts, purposes, ideals, values, etc. 2. A need integrate.

narcissism.   Any manifestation of sexuality in relation to the self or in relation to the self-concept. Positive cathexis in relation to the self-concept or in relation to ego-ideals. See *primary narcissism; secondary narcissism.*

narcissistic.   Referring to *narcissism* or positive cathexis of the self.

need.   A motivational stimulus, an unpleasant excitation, a tension state, or a disturbance in the organism's equilibrium. An aspect of the *need integrate.* See *source.*

need frustration.   The perception of complete interference with gratification of a need by any conceivable method in relation to any conceivable object.

need integrate.   An integration consisting of a tension (need; excitation) in combination with the conscious representation (anticipation) of a gratifying instrumental act and the conscious representation of a gratifying object. (Synonyms: *motive;* impulse.)

need for punishment.   A motive whose relief depends upon the perception of frustration or punishment. See *masochism.*

need regression.   The reinstatement of a former source of motivational excitation, usually occurring on the basis of a failure of repression. For example, regression from genital to anal or to oral sexuality.

neurosis.   A personality disorder involving symptoms that are usually not so severe as to render the patient unable to support himself, nor so severe as to endanger the safety of others. (Examples: hysteria, hypochondria, obsessive or compulsive neurosis, neurasthenia.)

neurotic anxiety.   See *anxiety.*

nondirective therapy.   See *client-centered therapy.*

object.   Anything in relation to which the gratification (relief) of a need is anticipated. Anything that may become an object of perception may function as an object in relation to which a particular need may be gratified. (Synonyms: goal; goal object.)

object frustration.   The perception of interference with the gratification of a need in relation to some specific object.

object regression.   The reinstatement of a former object-cathexis.

object sublimation.   A displacement that involves the substitution of a relatively acceptable object-cathexis for a relatively unacceptable object-cathexis.

objective anxiety.   See *fear*.

obsession.   A neurotic symptom involving conscious preoccupation with some relatively trivial matter, which symbolizes gratification or frustration of a repressed impulse.

Oedipal.   Characterized by the attitudes peculiar to the *Oedipus complex*.

Oedipus complex.   A complex of attitudes said to occur during the *phallic phase.* The boy is said to be in love with the mother and to be jealous and hostile toward the father. The girl is said to be in love with the father and to be jealous and hostile toward the mother.

oral incorporation stage.   A postulated stage in the *oral phase* of psychosexual development, during which sexuality is said to be concerned mainly with the oral reception of food (milk) and other objects.

oral phase.   According to Freud's theory of psychosexual development, the earliest *autoerotic* phase, during which the mouth is said to be the primary source of sexual excitation.

oral sadistic stage.   A postulated stage in the *oral phase* of psychosexual development, during which sexuality is said to be centered in a tendency to bite the mother's breast and other objects.

organism.   Any dynamic system of events that are interrelated in such a manner that a change introduced anywhere in the system will be followed by compensatory changes in other parts of the system. Such compensatory changes operate toward a re-establishment of equilibrium.

organismic.   Referring to the characteristics that are common to organisms. Referring to dynamic interrelatedness, which involves tendencies to maintain or to re-establish equilibrium among the different processes of a system.

organizational interdependence.   Interrelations among different functions of the organism which occur on the basis of learned co-ordination of previously differentiated functions.

paranoia.   A *psychotic* condition that is chiefly characterized by the occurrence of *delusions*.

parapraxis.   Unconsciously motivated symptomatic actions, such as slips in speech or writing, inability to recall another person's name, the forgetting of one's promises and resolutions, mistakes in one's actions.

partial regression.   A regression that involves only a minor proportion of the individual's total behavior. Opposite of *general regression*.

penis envy.   According to Freud, an attitude occurring in girls during the *phallic phase.* The girl is said to be envious of the boy for his possession of a penis, and to be hostile toward the mother for having brought her into the world "so insufficiently equipped."

perception. The process of organizing into a meaningful pattern external and internal stimuli. The meaningful pattern that occurs through the dynamic organization of external and internal stimuli.

perceptual environment. The momentary perception of a pattern of stimulation, consisting of components from internal and external sources. See *perception.*

perceptual identification. A process that involves interpreting two or more objects or events as if they were identical. (Synonym: symbolism.)

perceptual realism. Ability to discriminate clearly between reality and fantasy.

permanent regression. A regression that is of relatively long duration. Opposite of *temporary regression.*

perversion. Sexual motivation and sexual behavior involving seeking and obtaining pleasurable stimulation in nongenital *erotogenic zones.*

phallic phase. According to Freud's theory of psychosexual development, the third *autoerotic* phase, during which the penis (in boys) or the clitoris (in girls) is said to be the primary source of sexual excitation.

phobic reaction. Fear (usually intense) in relation to some specific object or situation that is merely symbolic of some actual danger situation.

pleasure. The conscious experience that occurs during relatively rapid tension-reduction.

pleasure principle. The principle that, according to Freud, fundamentally governs behavior—namely, the tendency to avoid discomfort, pain, or unpleasantness and to seek pleasurable relief. According to this principle, behavior is instigated by unpleasant excitation, and it functions to reduce excitation or tension. See *reality principle.*

plus-minus conflict. The simultaneous occurrence of both negative and positive motivation in relation to a given *instrumental act* or in relation to a given *object* or combination of objects. Plus-minus conflicts are perceived to require the acceptance of frustration along with gratification. (Synonyms: *ambivalence;* adient-abient conflict; approach-avoidant conflict; positive-negative conflict.)

plus-plus conflict. The simultaneous operation of two or more positive, but incompatible, motives. This may involve the desire to achieve goals that are incompatible, the desire to achieve the same goal by means of two or more incompatible methods, or the desire to gratify different needs that cannot be relieved by the same method or in relation to the same object. (Synonyms: adient-adient conflict; double-adient conflict; approach-approach conflict; positive-positive conflict.)

preconscious.   Any function is said to be preconscious, or to operate preconsciously, if it can become an object of the individual's conscious perception through normal attentive effort.

pregenital impulses.   Sexual motivation arising from excitation in the oral or anal regions.

prepotent.   Characterized by great relative strength. A motive is said to be prepotent when it is one of the strongest motives in the *motivational pattern.*

primary anxiety.   The operation of a need that has never yet been integrated with any *instrumental act* or any *object* in terms of which to achieve gratification. (Synonym: basic anxiety.)

primary frustration.   The perception of motivational excitation. The mere functioning of an active need. See *need; id functions; primary anxiety.*

primary narcissism.   Positive cathexis of *ego functions.* Pleasurable gratification of sexual excitations through self-stimulation.

progression.   The development of a new behavior-pattern in response to changed conditions, or the adoption of a behavior pattern having more mature characteristics than the behavior pattern it replaces. The opposite of *regression.*

progressive.   Referring to *progression.*

progressive adjustment.   See *progression.*

projection.   Hypersensitivity to the operation of one's own repudiated (repressed) motives in other persons or things. Projection involves a tendency to perceive others as being consciously motivated by impulses that are unacceptable in the self, and a tendency to overemphasize the significance of such motives in the determination of other people's behavior.

projective test.   Any standard stimulus situation having relatively high *ambiguity* which is designed for personality diagnosis. Interpretation of responses to such a test is based on the principle that *perception* and action in response to an *ambiguous* situation is determined primarily by factors within the personality, which are subject to wide individual variation.

psychoanalysis.   1. The theoretical interpretation of personality dynamics which was formulated by Freud. 2. A method of *psychotherapy* in which the patient engages in *free association* under the guidance of an analyst, whose function is to aid the patient in conforming to the *fundamental rule,* to interpret the patient's *resistances,* and to interpret the patient's *transferences.*

psychoanalyst.   A psychotherapist who employs the techniques of *psychoanalysis.*

psychogenic.   Originating on the basis of learning. (Synonyms: derived; social; sociogenic; secondary; learned; functional.)

psychological environment.   See *perceptual environment.*

psychological field.   See *perceptual environment.*

psychoneurosis.   See *neurosis.*

psychosis.   A personality disorder involving symptoms that are so severe as both to render the patient unable to support himself, and to endanger the safety of others. (Synonym: insanity.)

psychosomatic.   Referring to the interrelations that occur among all of the functions of the organism. The term implies that no valid distinction, other than an arbitrary one, can be made between "psychic" or "mental" and "somatic" or "physiological" functions.

psychosomatic defense.   An "organic" symptom that functions to reduce *frustration, conflict,* and *anxiety.*

psychotherapy.   Any therapeutic technique that depends solely upon the use of communicative procedures (often verbal) in the patient-therapist relationship.

psychotic.   Pertaining to a *psychosis.* Any person who manifests a psychosis.

punishment.   The use of *aggression* in order to control another person's behavior.

rationalization.   The justification of one's behavior in terms of acceptable *motivation.*

reaction formation.   The transformation of a *need integrate* into one of opposite intention. The transformation of a negative *instrumental act* into a positive instrumental act, or of a positive instrumental act into a negative instrumental act.

realism of perception.   See *perceptual realism.*

realistic perception.   See *perceptual realism.*

reality principle.   The behavioral principle that, according to Freud, supersedes the *pleasure principle.* The tendency to recognize that pleasure can be achieved only in limited degree and only in accordance with the requirements of reality, by the use of techniques that conform with social prescriptions and with limiting material conditions. See *pleasure principle.*

reality testing.   The act of frustrating another person in order to determine the limits of his *frustration tolerance.* Usually refers to a child's indulging in "bad" behavior to determine "how much he can get away with" before receiving punishment.

regression.   The reinstatement of any behavior pattern that the individual has previously manifested, or the adoption of a behavior pattern having less mature characteristics than the one it replaces. See *retrogression* [Lewin]; *regression* [Lewin].

regression [Lewin].   The adoption of any behavior pattern that has more primitive (less mature) characteristics than the behavior pattern it replaces. The primitivation of behavior. See *regression.*

regression, psychosexual.   The reinstatement of former sexual attitudes. The recurrence of immature sexual impulses or the reinstatement of a former ("outgrown") object-cathexis.

regressive.   Referring to, or having the characteristics of, *regression.*

repression.   A relatively automatic (relatively unconscious) process by means of which conscious or *preconscious* functions become, and continue to remain, *unconscious.*

resistance.   Any manifestation, during *psychotherapy,* of the patient's inability to recall events that he has experienced in the past. See *repression.*

respect.   An *ambivalent* attitude that involves both *love* and *fear* in relation to the same *object.*

restraint.   A conscious process by means of which impulses are prevented from being carried into action, or prevented from being expressed.

retrogression [Lewin].   The reinstatement of a previously employed mode of behavior or form of motivation. See *regression.*

Rorschach Test.   A *projective test* consisting of ink-blots, to which the subject responds by telling what the blots (or parts of the blots) remind him of. Subsequent personality diagnosis is based on the principle that the structure of the subject's personality determines the nature of his *perceptions.*

sadism.   A sexual perversion that involves committing *aggression* against the sexual object as a necessary means of achieving sexual gratification. More generally, a relatively permanent tendency to enjoy committing aggression against other persons or objects.

scoptophilia.   See *voyeurism.*

secondary anxiety.   Anxiety that occurs through the *repression* of consciously represented instrumental acts and objects in terms of which gratification has previously been anticipated. Secondary anxiety may be based on the repression of love, of fear, or of hostility. See *anxiety.*

secondary frustration.   See *frustration.*

secondary narcissism.   Positive cathexis of *ego-ideals.* Secondary narcissism is said to occur during the *latency period* and to be manifested in varying degrees throughout adolescence and maturity.

self-actualization.   The development of the individual's potentialities. Achievement of the highest possible degree of *ego-ideal* gratification.

self-punishment. Any self-imposed *frustration*. Usually motivated by the unconscious need for punishment. See *need for punishment; masochism.*

sexuality. Sexual motivation. In its most general sense, as employed by Freud, sexuality involves any and all impulses to achieve pleasurable stimulation through relating oneself to a positively cathected object. See *libido; love.*

situational regression. Regression that occurs only in specific situations or in specific kinds of situations. Opposite of *established regression.*

socialization. The development of motives and corresponding behavior-patterns that are similar to those manifested by the authentic representatives of one's culture, or that are similar to those prevailing in one's society.

source. The region of the body in which excitation is perceptually localized and in which pleasurable (relieving) stimulation is sought. An aspect of the *need integrate.* See *need.*

space of free movement. All of the activities that are possible for the individual at any given time.

sublimation. Any motivational transformation or modification that eventuates in a *need integrate* manifesting a higher degree of conformity with the prevailing social values. The substitution of relatively sophisticated and relatively acceptable *instrumental acts* and object cathexes for relatively primitive and relatively unacceptable ones.

sublimative. Referring to a motivational transformation in the direction of higher sophistication or higher social acceptability.

superego functions. The positive and negative psychogenic aspects of motivation. See *conscience; ego-ideals.*

superego motives. See *superego functions.*

superego-superego conflict. A conflict between or among incompatible psychogenic *motives.*

suppression. A conscious process by means of which conscious functions become *preconscious.*

symbolism. See *perceptual identification.*

sympathy. A response that depends upon the *perceptual identification* of the self with another person or object. The process of "feeling with" another person—enjoying his pleasure, suffering from his misery, etc.

symptomatic action. Any action that is representative (symbolic) of the gratification of some *unconscious* or *preconscious* motive. Symptomatic actions occur in the everyday life of normal individuals. (Synonym: *parapraxis.*)

temporal regression. See *retrogression* [Lewin]; *historical regression.*

temporary regression. A regression that is of short duration. Opposite of *permanent regression.*

testing reality.   See *reality testing.*

Thematic Apperception Test (TAT). A *projective test* consisting of pictures, to which the subject responds by telling stories. Subsequent personality diagnosis is based on the principle that the subject's *motivational pattern* determines the *motivation* attributed to characters in the stories, and that the nature of his life situation determines the type of frustrations attributed to them.

topical regression.   See *ego-regression.*

topographical regression.   See *ego-regression.*

transference.   The displacement of motivational *cathexis* from one person onto another person. In *psychotherapy,* the displacement of cathexis from previously known persons onto the psychoanalyst or psychotherapist.

traumatic situation.   A frustrating situation that arouses in the individual a feeling of helplessness. A danger situation in which the individual feels unable to commit a successful aggression and unable to make a successful escape.

unconscious.   Any function is said to be unconscious, or to operate unconsciously, if it cannot, through normal attentive efforts, become an object of the individual's conscious perception.

undoing.   A succession of motor acts that are of opposite significance. Each action functions to cancel or nullify the preceding action.

valence.   See *cathexis.*

voyeur.   An individual who manifests *voyeurism.* A "peeping Tom."

voyeurism.   The impulse that is gratified through looking at the genitals of another person, or, more generally, through looking at another nude or semi-nude person.

voyeuristic.   Pertaining to *voyeurism.*

withdrawal.   The avoidance of any aspect of external or internal reality.

Name Index

Subject Index

Italicized TERMS APPEARING IN THIS INDEX ARE DEFINED IN
THE Glossary.

A NOTE ON THE TYPE

This book was set on the Linotype in Janson, a recutting made direct from the type cast from matrices (now in possession of the Stempel foundry, Frankfurt am Main) made by Anton Janson some time between 1660 and 1687.

Of Janson's origin nothing is known. He may have been a relative of Justus Janson, a printer of Danish birth who practiced in Leipzig from 1614 to 1635. Some time between 1657 and 1668 Anton Janson, a punch-cutter and type-founder, bought from the Leipzig printer Johann Erich Hahn the type-foundry that had formerly been a part of the printing house of M. Friedrich Lankisch. Janson's types were first shown in a specimen sheet issued at Leipzig about 1675. Janson's successor, and perhaps his son-in-law, Johann Karl Edling, issued a specimen sheet of Janson types in 1689. His heirs sold the Janson matrices in Holland to Wolffgang Dietrich Erhardt of Leipzig.

Composed, printed, and bound by KINGSPORT PRESS, INC., *Kingsport, Tennessee. Designed by* HARRY FORD.